CHARTING THE SHAPE
OF EARLY MODERN
SOUTHEAST ASIA

ANTHONY REID

SILKWORM BOOKS

ISBN 974-7551-06-3

This edition is published in 1999 by
Silkworm Books
104/5 Chiang Mai–Hot Road, Suthep, Chiang Mai 50200, Thailand
E-mail: silkworm@loxinfo.co.th
http://www.silkwormbooks.info

Set in 10 pt. Garamond by Silk Type

Printed in Thailand by O.S. Printing House, Bangkok

3 5 4 2

CONTENTS

PREFACE

The essays in this volume represent the evolution of my thinking on early modern Southeast Asia over a long period, from 1975 to 1996. Of the twelve chapters, nine have appeared already in some form, though in most cases in places not readily accessible to the broader community of Southeast Asia scholars.

Chapters 3, 5 and 11 were presented at conferences in 1994–6, the first two in Bangkok and the last in Canberra, but have not been previously published.

The chapters have been arranged in roughly chronological order of their themes, not the order in which they were conceived. In fact the last chapter was the first to be conceived and delivered, at a time when I was just beginning to contemplate serious writing about the early modern period. Now that that chapter of my life is concluding, it seems timely to bring some of the different writings together.

I am particularly grateful to Clare Guenther for having systematized the references, compiled a single bibliography, and established some consistency of format. Through her efforts this has become a book rather than a set of papers.

With gratitude I acknowledge the publishers of the original papers, for permission to reprint here: chapter 1, adapted from "Introduction: A Time and A Place," in *Southeast Asia in the Early Modern Era*, ed. A. Reid, Cornell University Press, 1993; chapter 2, "The Islamization of Southeast Asia," in *Historia: Essays in Commemoration of the 25th Anniversary of the Department of History*, University of Malaya, eds. Muhammad Abu Bakar et al., Malaysian Historical Society, 1984; chapter 4, "The Rise and Fall of Sino-Javanese Shipping," in *Looking in Odd Mirrors: The Java Sea*, eds. V. J. H. Houben, H. M. J. Maier and W. van der Molen, Vakgroep Zuidoost Azië en Oceanië, Rijksuniversiteit te Leiden, 1992; chapter 6, "The Rise of Makassar," in *Review of Indonesian and Malaysian Affairs* 17, Winter/Summer 1983, Sydney University; chapter 7, "A Great Seventeenth Century Indonesian Family: Matoaya and Pattingalloang of Makassar," in *Masyarakat Indonesia* VIII (1), 1987, LIPI, Jakarta; chapter 8, "Early Southeast Asian

Categorizations of Europeans," in *Implicit Ethnographies: Encounters between European and Other Peoples in the Wake of Columbus*, ed. Stuart Schwartz, Cambridge University Press, 1994; chapter 9, "Slavery and Bondage in Southeast Asian History," in *Slavery, Bondage and Dependency in Southeast Asia*, ed. A. Reid, St Lucia: University of Queensland Press, 1983; chapter 10, "The Origins of Poverty," in *Scholarship and Society in Southeast Asia*, ed. W. E. Willmot, NZASIA Occasional Paper 2, 1979; chapter 12, "Heaven's Will and Man's Fault," Flinders Asian Studies Lecture 6, Adelaide: Flinders University, 1975.

Anthony Reid

MAPS, TABLES, ILLUSTRATIONS

MAPS

TABLES

ILLUSTRATIONS

GLOSSARY

Arya (J)	Aristocratic title
Ata (Mak)	Slave, subject
Babad (J)	Chronicle
Bakufu (Jp)	Tokugawa administration
Berkat (A/M)	Spiritual blessing
Bupati (J)	Royal representative, local governor
Cakravartin (S)	World-ruler
Cash (A-I)	Copper or lead-tin alloy coin
Cultuurstelsel (D)	[Forced] cultivation system
Hikayat (M)	Story, chronicle
Idulfitri (A)	Feast to mark the end of the fasting month
Jong (J/M)	Junk; large trading vessel
Kadi (A/M)	Judge in Islamic law
Kafir (A/M)	Infidel; unbeliever
Katipunan (Tag)	Abbreviation for *Kataastaasan Kagalanggalang na Katipunan ng mga Anak ng Bayan*, Highest and Most Respectable Sons of the People; revolutionary secret society
Kiwi (M, from Ch)	Travelling merchant
Khalif (A)	Representative (of the Prophet); head of the Muslim community
Korakora (Maluku)	Sailing galley with outriggers
Kramat (A/M)	Holy grave
Kris (M/J)	Dagger
Mandala (S)	Concentric diagram, Buddhist microcosm of the universe
Naga (S)	Mythological snake
Nakhoda (M)	Shipowner or owner's representative on the ship; super-cargo.
Orangkaya (M)	Aristocrat, generally with wealth from trade
Orang asli (M)	Indigenous population of Malayan peninsula
Petak (M)	Partition of cargo space on ship

Pasisir (J)	Coastal lowlands (specifically northern coast of Java)
Patih (J)	Title of governors, aristocrats
Peranakan (M)	Local-born
Perang sabil (M)	Holy war
Priyayi (J)	Aristocrat
Puputan (B)	Mass suicide
Ratu adil (J/M)	[Messianic] righteous king
Sakdina (T)	Merit points; system of social rank
Sakti (S)	Power, especially spiritual
Sangha (P)	The brotherhood of monks in Hinayana Buddhism
Sejarah (M)	History
Syahbandar (M)	Harbour-master
Totok (Ch)	Newcomer, China-born Chinese
Ulama (A/M)	Islamic scholars (plural in Arabic, but here used also for singular)

A=Arabic, A-I=Anglo-Indian, B=Balinese, Ch=Chinese, J=Javanese, Jp=Japanese, M=Malay, Mak=Makasarese, P=Pali, S=Sanskrit, Tag=Tagalog, T=Thai

CHAPTER ONE

INTRODUCTION:
EARLY MODERN SOUTHEAST ASIA

The early modern period is increasingly recognized as a watershed in human history. For the first time the world was physically united by the opening of direct trade routes between Europe and every other corner of the globe. Yet at least by the second half of the seventeenth century, it is now clear, northwestern Europe and Japan parted company from the other Eurasian civilizations to pursue their capitalist transformations. The relations between the countries of Europe's Atlantic seaboard and the rest of the world became ever more weighted with inequality, not only in military effectiveness (the first sign to appear), but in productivity, technology, scientific method and eventually self-esteem.

While Europe's "miracle" is difficult to disentangle from its military and economic domination of more populous quarters of the world, Japan followed a very different route. Isolating itself from all foreign contact save that provided by tightly-controlled Dutch and Chinese trade at Nagasaki, the Tokugawa shogunate unified the country, banned the use of firearms, and developed a flourishing urban economy which laid the basis for Japan's twentieth-century rise. By holding its population constant while substantially increasing productivity and welfare, Japan achieved economic advances in the seventeenth and eighteenth centuries which matched those of the most advanced European countries (Smith 1988, 15–49).

The Japanese case in particular, and the globalization of the issues in general by many of the most influential modern historians (Braudel, Wallerstein, Barrington Moore, Cipolla, Parker), have made it clear that the early modern period is critical for every part of the world. If the capitalist "miracle" was not limited to Europe, then each case needs to be studied with care to examine what happened and why. We can no longer think in simplistic terms of winners and losers, of capitalist Europe and a third world

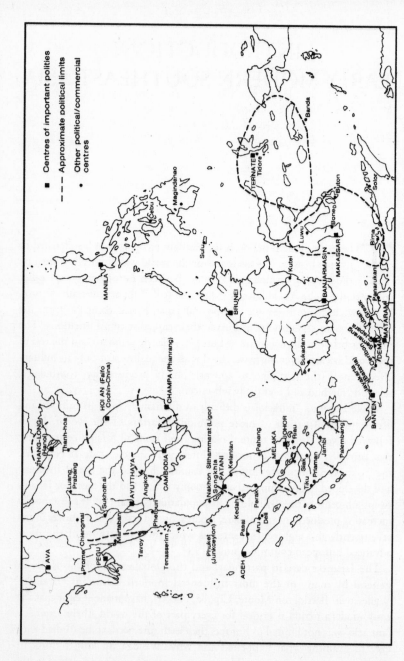

MAP 1 POLITICAL CENTRES OF EARLY MODERN SOUTHEAST ASIA

doomed to stagnation and poverty, but rather of a variety of ways of coping with the explosive forces at work in the period.

Japan belatedly forced itself upon the attention of economic historians by its spectacular twentieth century performance, which undermined attempts to identify unique socio-cultural features of Europe which made capitalism possible. Although Japan was the first Asian country to complete the transition to industrial capitalism, it is certainly not the last. Southeast Asian economies too, led by Singapore, Malaysia and Thailand, have recently grown as rapidly as any known to history. There too economic confidence gives rise to intellectual confidence. Instead of the question what was "wrong" with Asian cultures, as was frequently asked only a few decades ago, attention begins to be paid to what is "right" about them. Neither question is helpful, but it is no longer possible to assume that the place of Asia in the static or declining "third world" was ordained by environment or culture.

In the extraordinary period between the fifteenth and the seventeenth centuries, Southeast Asia played a critical role. The global commercial expansion of the "long sixteenth century" necessarily affected it immediately and profoundly, as the source of many of the spices in international demand and as a maritime region athwart vital trade routes. It was the region most affected by the explosion of Chinese maritime activity at the beginning of the fifteenth century, and the source of the spices and much of the pepper that drew the Spanish to America and eventually the Philippines, and the Portuguese to India and Southeast Asia. The quickening of commerce, the monetization of transactions, the growth of cities, the accumulation of capital and the specialization of function which formed part of a capitalist transition elsewhere, undoubtedly occurred rapidly also in Southeast Asia during this period. The changes wrought in belief and cultural systems were even more profound. Islam and Christianity became the dominant religions of the Archipelago and pockets of the Mainland, while Buddhism was transformed by its alliance with centralizing states in Burma, Siam, Laos and Cambodia.

On the other hand no part of Asia suffered more quickly or profoundly the effects of European intrusion. Through warfare, impregnable fortifications and monopoly commerce, Europeans had by 1650 gained control of the vital ports and products which had previously linked the region to the expanding world economy. Although they remained minor, peripheral players in the ongoing life of the region, they had changed the delicate balance between commerce and kingship. Like Japan, yet even more abruptly, Southeast Asian countries all discovered the negative side of the expansion of global commerce and the rapid advance of military technology. Unlike Japan, they were unable to insulate themselves from it without fundamental change to their political systems.

A PLACE

For these reasons Southeast Asia is a region which has a vital place in resolving the crucial dilemmas of early modern history. But is it a region at all? Unlike western Europe, India, the Arab World, China or even "Sinicized" east Asia as a whole, it has no common high religion, language or classical culture (except those it loosely shares with India), and has never been part of a single polity. Its very name is an externally-imposed geographical convenience, which has only recently replaced even less satisfactory terms such as Further India or Indo-China.

Yet those who travel to Southeast Asia from China, India, or anywhere else, know at once that they are in a different place. In part this is a question of environment. Physically marked by its warm climate, high and dependable rainfall, and ubiquitous waterways, Southeast Asia developed lifestyles dominated by the forest, the rice-growing river-valleys, and fishing. Its people grew the same crops by the same methods, ate the same food in the same manner, and lived in similar houses elevated on poles against the perils of flood or forest animals. Its geography militated against the unified empires arising from great rivers or vast plains. It generated instead a multiplicity of political forms interlinked by the ease of waterborne transport.

Paradoxically, it is the diversity of Southeast Asia and its openness to outside influences which is its pre-eminent defining characteristic. Every state of the region was built on cultural trade-offs both internal and external. Overall population density was low, probably averaging no more than six per square kilometre in this period. Pockets of dense settlement around trading cities and permanent rice-fields were surrounded by forests thinly peopled by shifting cultivators. This created a fundamental dualism of hill and valley, upstream and downstream, interior and coast. In coastal waters boat-dwelling "sea nomads" had similar relations with rulers ashore. No state incorporated these peoples fully. They remained an "uncivilized", stateless, or "free" penumbra of the state, often indispensable providers of forest or sea products, messengers, warriors and slaves—tributary but distinct.

Despite their dependence on such hinterland peoples, rulers were more preoccupied by their relations with rival powers controlling other rivers and ports. Even if the stronger rulers claimed through their titles and the architecture of their capitals to be *cakravartin* world-rulers embodying on earth the Indic gods in heaven, they were all intensely conscious that they inhabited a pluralistic world. Political life was an endless struggle for people, for trade and for status between rival centres. The exchanging of envoys and letters was one of the finer political arts, and words and gestures were studied for the slightest hint of superiority or inferiority. Success in this competitive world was measured by the number of ships in the harbour, of men, boats and elephants in royal processions, of tributaries from nearby and equals from afar who paid their respects to the king.

Between about 1400 and 1700, universalist faiths based on sacred scripture took hold throughout the region. Eventually they created profound divisions between an Islamic arc in the south, a Confucian political orthodoxy in Vietnam, a Theravada Buddhist bastion in the rest of the Mainland and a Christian outrider in the Philippines. Yet even in the process of religious change there was a common openness to outside ideas, a common need for allies from further afield in order to subordinate rivals closer to hand.

Perhaps the key fact that made Southeast Asia a region was that the barriers which separated it from China and India were more significant than any internal boundaries. The majority of outsiders who came to the region did so by means of long sea voyages. Malay-speakers (who in this period included maritime traders of every ethno-linguistic group) identified their region as "below the winds", in distinction to the world of outsiders (especially Indians, Arabs and Europeans) who came from "above the winds" by taking advantage of the prevailing Indian Ocean monsoon. For Chinese and Japanese, Southeast Asia was the "south seas", also reached by sea. Even adoption of outside faiths did not eliminate the distinctiveness of a region uniquely defined by nature. The mountain barriers across the north of the region, and the sea elsewhere, ensured that while Southeast Asians were endlessly involved in exchanges of territory, people, and ideas with each other, invasions from the rest of the Asian land mass were few and migrations gradual.

Vietnam's relation with China might appear to give the lie to the above. Ruled by the Middle Kingdom for most of the first Christian millennium, Vietnam acquired its writing system and consequently much of its literary culture from China. Yet alone of the southern regions conquered by the Han and Tang Dynasties, the people of the Red River delta retained sufficient of their identity to claim their independence in 939, and reclaim it on each subsequent occasion Chinese armies invaded. The last serious invasion was that of the Ming, who reoccupied Vietnam from 1407 to 1428 but were driven out by the Vietnamese hero Le Loi, founder of the most brilliant of Vietnamese dynasties. Under the Le rulers Vietnamese political institutions were rebuilt in a more Confucian mould than ever, but the centralized mandarinate which resulted was used to ensure that Vietnam remained permanently independent of China.

Vietnam thus became a barrier to any further Chinese southward expansion by land. Although the hills which formed its northern border were by no means impassable, they were sufficient to serve as a stable frontier for a thousand years. By contrast Vietnam's southern border was constantly changing, as Vietnamese armies had the better of their ceaseless wars first with Champa and later with Cambodia. It is therefore impossible to draw a line round early modern Southeast Asia which excludes Vietnam. Despite its cultural and commercial links with China, Vietnam was Southeast Asian. Particularly so was the southern Vietnamese kingdom established by Nguyen Hoang on former Cham territory. Not only through its intermingling of Vietnamese and Austronesian (Chamic) peoples, but also through its physical environment, its place in Asian trade, and the timing of its rise to prominence, this kingdom was characteristic of early modern Southeast Asia.

A TIME

As historiography has begun to break out of a European mould and consider comparative questions on a broader basis, the category Early Modern has gained currency. As against such older terms as Renaissance, Reformation, or Age of Discovery, it has the advantage of being less culture-bound to a European schema, less laden with triumphalist values.[1] Nevertheless it has its own burden of associations, implying that it is in this period that we see the emergence of the forces which would shape the modern industrial world. That implication seems acceptable at the global level, provided there is no suggestion that all its constituents were somehow locked into the same path.

Definitions vary, but all those who use the term early modern include in it the sixteenth and seventeenth centuries, with more or less extension backward into the fifteenth[2] and forward into the eighteenth. Southeast Asianists are only now beginning to apply the term to their region,[3] however, and some justification is required as to how we propose to apply it. In the past historians of Mainland Southeast Asia (and to a lesser extent Java) have typically periodized in terms of dynasties (e.g. "Late Ayudhya", "First Toungoo", "Le"), while the rise of Islam and the coming of Europeans have been seen as the major turning points in the islands. Despite the desire of a post-colonial generation to escape from Eurocentric assumptions, those who have generalized about the whole region have found it difficult to avoid the Portuguese arrival at Melaka (Malacca) in 1509 as a turning point.

Only in one respect can this be accepted without qualification. The sources available to the historian change in nature and increase greatly in quantity with the opening of the sixteenth century. The Portuguese, and still more their successors the Spanish and Dutch, chronicled and described Southeast Asia in far greater detail than the Arabs and Chinese before them. The bronze-plate inscriptions which had been the major indigenous sources were already becoming scarce in the fourteenth century. They are replaced by royal and religious chronicles, poetry, and edifying texts written on ephemeral materials, increasingly paper. Virtually no such texts have survived from before 1500. The earliest substantial works surviving are copies from the eighteenth and nineteenth centuries, with only a handful of sixteenth and seventeenth century texts preserved by chance in European libraries.

When we look with care at the factors critical to the early modern era in Southeast Asia, however, most of them begin before the arrival of European fleets. These are examined below under four heads: a commercial upturn; new military technology; the growth of new, more centralized states; and the spread of externally-validated scriptural orthodoxies in religion. While the sixteenth century materials can be read to reconstruct the fifteenth, it must be admitted that the evidence available to document these trends before 1500 remains unsatisfactory. I have argued elsewhere (Reid 1990a, 5-6) that 1400 is a more satisfactory beginning for this critical period of change than 1500, but the fragmentary nature of the evidence makes any such precision highly problematic.

COMMERCIAL UPTURN

The determination of the Portuguese and Spanish to find the sources of pepper, clove and nutmeg was a consequence of their growing importance in European life. In the 1390s about six metric tons of cloves and one and a half of nutmeg reached Europe each year from Maluku in eastern Indonesia. A century later this had risen to fifty-two tons of cloves and twenty-six of nutmeg. The spices were carried across the Indian Ocean by Muslim traders of various nationalities to markets in Egypt and Beirut where they were purchased by Italian merchants, predominately Venetians. This was of course only a small branch of Southeast Asia's trade, but its rapid expansion in the fifteenth century was probably replicated elsewhere. The fifteenth century was a time of expansion in population and international commerce not only in the Mediterranean but also in Southeast Asia's largest external market, China. The reign of the second Ming Emperor Yongle (1403–22) was a period of completely exceptional Chinese involvement with the region, which appears to have stimulated the pepper and clove trade, increased the circulation of silver and other metals, and given rise to a number of new port-cities.

While the economic history of the fifteenth century must remain speculative, a peak in Southeast Asian commercial activity in the early seventeenth century is clearer. England and Holland joined the Chinese, Japanese, Spanish, Portuguese and Indians in competing to buy the products of the region—pepper, cloves, nutmeg, cinnamon, sandalwood, lacquer, silk and deer-hides. Prices were kept high by a massive inflow of silver from Japan and the New World. Indian cloth of all kinds was imported to the region in exchange for these exports. The data suggest that in 1600–40 both the silver influx and imports of Indian cloth were at a peak which was not again reached until the eighteenth century (Reid 1990a, 4–21).

This international competition narrowed to a few players in the second half of the seventeenth century. The Japanese stopped coming by Tokugawa decree in 1635; the Gujeratis, Arabs and Persians found the European pressure too great; the Portuguese lost their stronghold of Melaka to the Dutch in 1641. The Dutch East India Company (VOC) established a monopoly of nutmeg in 1621, and of cloves during the 1650s. Some degree of competition remained in other products, but the VOC's ability to dominate Southeast Asian supplies made these exports less attractive in world markets.

New products were exported from Southeast Asia in the eighteenth century on a larger scale than ever before—notably sugar, coffee and tobacco. These however were plantation crops largely managed by Europeans and Chinese. The now-dominant Dutch and English Companies found opium more suitable than Indian cloth as an import to Southeast Asia, since they could monopolize supply and reap enormous profits.

NEW MILITARY TECHNIQUES

Advances in technology are most quickly borrowed in the military sphere. It is a question of survival. Firearms are a case in point. Their use is documented in India and China in the fourteenth century, almost simultaneously with their first impact on European battles. Naturally cannons and bombards also came to Southeast Asia, well ahead of Vasco da Gama. U Kala's usually reliable chronicle of Burma mentions the use of firearms by Indian soldiers in Burma from the end of the fourteenth century (Lieberman 1980, 211). The presence of firearms is much better documented a century later, when the Portuguese describe, perhaps with some exaggeration, the guns they encountered in the region. In Melaka in 1511, they claimed to have captured three thousand pieces of artillery, mostly of bronze, including a huge bombard sent as a present to the Sultan from the ruler of Calicut in South India. Many cannons were imported by Muslim traders from India, the Middle East and even Europe, while others of an ornate dragon type were brought in by the Chinese. Nevertheless there were also gun-founders in the city, allegedly "as good as those in Germany" (Albuquerque 1557, II: 127–8).

Although in this respect also the beginnings of change predated 1500, the remark made by an Italian historian in the 1520s about Europe would have applied equally to Southeast Asia: "Before the year 1494, wars were protracted, battles bloodless . . . and although artillery was already in use, it was managed with such lack of skill that it caused little hurt". (Guicciardine, cited in Parker 1988, 10).[4] Hence the initial impact of the far more rapid fire the Portuguese were able to deliver in their attack on Melaka or later in Maluku was profound (*Sejarah Melayu* 167; Galvão 1544, 171; Reid 1993a, 219–33, 270-81; Lieberman 1980, 215).

The advantage of surprise was short-lived. Southeast Asian states quickly devoted themselves to acquiring Portuguese-style arquebusses and cannon and the means to manufacture them. Foreign traders appeared the most adept at the new technology—notably Portuguese, Turks, Gujeratis, Japanese and local Muslim minorities such as Chams, Malays and "Luzons" (Muslim Tagalogs). These were bribed or forced to become artillerymen in the campaigns for the more ambitious kings of the sixteenth century, and eventually formed the first professional armies of the region. Two successive Toungoo kings who unified Burma in the period 1531–81, Tabinshweihti and Bayinnaung, made most effective use of both foreign mercenaries and firearms. An Italian visitor claimed Bayinnaung had accumulated eighty thousand arquebusses and adapted them effectively for firing from elephants (Fredericke 1581, 248).

These military achievements undoubtedly helped create an unprecedented accumulation of power, which at its height ruled most of present-day Burma and Thailand. To a lesser degree the same methods helped Demak to become the strongest power in Java during the reign of Sultan Trenggana (1520–51) and mad Aceh, Makasar and Ayudhya (Siam) relatively strong and centralized powers in the early seventeenth century. Nguyen Hoang's creation of a state in central Vietnam also owed much to his mobilization of the new weapons.

The Archipelago states were particularly attracted to the largest possible cannons. In the late sixteenth century Aceh was manufacturing bigger cannon than European visitors had seen, as a result of instruction in the 1560s by Turkish craftsmen. Very large cannons were also being made in Manila when the Spanish took it in 1570, while Mataram and Makasar in the seventeenth century each cast a cannon more than five metres long (Reid 1982, 4; Lombard 1990, II: 179). Poorly mounted and virtually immobile, these monsters were appreciated not so much for the targets they hit as for the awe their semi-magical powers inspired.

New naval technologies were also introduced in the sixteenth century. Chief among them were the fast war galleys which were adopted from the Mediterranean model, with both Turks and Europeans playing a role in their spread. Scores of large galleys were built for sixteenth century rulers of Aceh (Manguin 1993), but this type of vessel had an even longer history in

Maluku, where the *korakora* dominated naval warfare from the sixteenth century to the nineteenth. There appears to have been little use of firearms on shipboard prior to the European intrusion. Asian vessels adopted small cannon quickly thereafter, but naval firepower and mobility remained one area in which the Europeans retained a decisive edge.

The other such area was fortification. By introducing to Southeast Asia the new European ideas of defence behind low but thick walls surmounted by batteries of guns, with bastions projecting to provide a field of fire along the walls, the Portuguese made themselves impregnable in Melaka, Ternate and elsewhere, the Spanish in Manila and Zamboanga, and the Dutch in Batavia, Makasar and Maluku. During the early modern period these remained enclaves with little direct influence on their hinterlands, but they provided a permanence which few indigenous dynasties could match. Local rulers responded by building forts more substantial than any traditional defence works, but these proved ultimately incapable of defending their major ports against sustained Dutch offensives.

NEW STATES

Southeast Asia was a place of fluid pluralisms, where states rose and fell relatively frequently. The early modern period witnessed the rise of many of the states which have defined Southeast Asia's modern identities, both national and ethnic. In each case the new military techniques played a part in enabling dynamic rulers to come to the top. The expansion of commerce was also a factor in every case, but in different degrees. Fifteenth century Melaka was one of the new states created by commerce, its capital not on a river but directly on the sea (like its contemporary Grisek in Java, and later Ternate, Makasar and Banten), its import tariffs low, its population inherently urban and pluralistic. Such other states as Aceh, Banten, Makasar and Nguyen Vietnam became important during the most intense period of commercial competition and expansion (c.1560–1630), and could not have done so without the spices and pepper of the Archipelago, and the Sino-Japanese trade of Faifo in the Nguyen dominions.

Other factors aided these unprecedented concentrations of power—Islamic and European models in the Archipelago, and the personal character and relationships of Nguyen Hoang in Vietnam (Taylor 1993). In Sumatra, Mindanao and Burma the critical intersection was between the upstream and downstream foci of power. The new factors sketched above gave downstream commerce the upper hand in the late sixteenth and early seventeenth century, but the agricultural areas upstream eventually escaped from that attempt to construct a centralized state.

Even in the older-established states of the Mainland, the early modern period saw a significant shift. The revisionist scholarship of Nidhi Aewsrivongse has advanced the effective centralization of the Thai polity from the fifteenth century to the reign of Naresuan (1590–1605), when it was stimulated by the commercial and military factors already discussed (Ishii 1993). The Burma depicted by Lieberman undergoes the same move towards "political centralization and cultural homogenization" in the sixteenth century, even if for him that process continued largely uninterrupted in the seventeenth and eighteenth centuries, although the proportion of revenue the state derived from trade declined after 1630 (Lieberman 1993).

SCRIPTURAL ORTHODOXIES

The strong kings of the early modern period favoured, as Lieberman (1993) puts it, "textually-based, externally-validated . . . sources of authority over local traditions". Whether they always succeeded in moving popular belief in that direction is less clear. Taylor (1993) protests that in Vietnam "the Neo-Confucian ideology adopted by fifteenth century kings actually retreated before a resurgence of Buddhism and animism" in the subsequent two centuries.

The conversion of the lowland Philippines to Catholicism in the period roughly 1580–1650 is the best documented case of dramatic religious change, though the conversion of much of eastern Indonesia to Islam in the same period is hardly less spectacular. I have argued that the advances of scriptural Islam and Christianity form part of a pattern related to the peak of the commercial upswing. The causes in this case are not simply a more commercial mentality, but direct contacts with the sources of the scriptural traditions, the interests of centralizing rulers in legitimation by some external point of reference, and a militant polarization between the two faiths which drew sharp religio-political boundaries (Reid 1993a, 140–92; Reid 1993c, 151–79).

The tendency towards unification of the Theravada Buddhist *sangha*, through state patronage of reforms and reordinations on the Sri Lanka model, has some analogies with the mass religious change in the Islands (Swearer and Premchit 1978, 20–33; Than Tun 1985, x–xii). Clearly the process was less sudden and dramatic in most cases, however, particularly because the confrontation between Theravada orthodoxy and animist sacrifices lacked the urgency of that between Islam and Christianity. My argument that there was a retreat of this scriptural trend in the Archipelago in the late seventeenth century is rejected by Lieberman (1993) for the Buddhist societies. He argues rather a continuing trend towards cultural uniformity and royal control into the eighteenth century and beyond. Nevertheless, the secular advances he identifies in the late seventeenth and eighteenth centuries (through royal examination of monks, and a tendency toward lay writing in the vernacular rather than monastic writing in Pali) may have parallels in contemporary trends in Southeast Asian Islam and Christianity.[5]

CAPITALISM AND THE END OF A PERIOD

While we should not expect every part of a highly complex region to march in step, Southeast Asia as a whole offers a fine laboratory to look at some of the crucial global questions of the early modern period. Do the tendencies we have remarked above continue until they were overtaken by the rise of industrialization and modern imperialism (affecting Southeast Asia chiefly after 1800), or do they reach some kind of crisis or resolution which we might take as the end of the early modern period? There is an important debate about whether the seventeenth century should be regarded as a watershed for the region or should not (Reid 1993c). Alternative turning points have already been identified by historians—the European intrusion around 1500 and the impact of an industrializing Europe around 1800. The candidates for major turning points are thus not different from those argued by European and comparative historians, and the choice, as Wallerstein (1980, 7) points out, has much to do with our "presuppositions about the modern world".

From a Southeast Asian standpoint, the argument for a turning point around 1650 rests on the region's relations with other peoples (primarily Europeans, but also Chinese), and on the place of international commerce in the life of states. In 1600 Southeast Asians interacted as equals with Europeans; in 1700 the inequalities were already manifest. This change in the balance of power became apparent sooner "below the winds" than elsewhere in Asia because of its maritime character and its reliance on the world market for spices and aromatics, but it was essentially a change in the relations between northwestern Europe and the rest of the world. The debate continues as to the causes of this shift. Was it the rise of capitalism in Europe, a decline or critical failure in Asia, or some combination of the two? Were military, economic, technical or cultural factors more central to the way it turned out?

Most historians would accept that the monopoly the Dutch established over supplies of nutmeg (in 1621) and clove (by the 1650s), their conquest of such key commercial centres as Makasar (1669) and Banten (1682), and their strong-armed quasi-monopoly over most of the other export centres of the Indonesian archipelago, constituted a major setback to indigenous commerce in the islands, and weakened the control of maritime states over their hinterlands. The Spanish conquest of the Philippine archipelago was still more profound an eclipse of indigenous polities and their commercial involvement. The open question is whether these losses were part of a more general "crisis" for Southeast Asia (and perhaps some other parts of Asia), of which military defeat was only one aspect (see Reid 1990b, 639–59).

Lieberman has examined this possibility and rejected it for Burma and to some extent for Southeast Asia as a whole (Lieberman 1993, 1997). He concludes that there was some discontinuity in the seventeenth century, through the removal of the capital far inland and the reduced role which seaborne commerce played thereafter in the revenues and the calculations of the Burmese state. In his view the continuities were still more striking, however. The integration of Shans and Mons into a Burman-dominated polity, begun by the First Toungoo kings in the sixteenth century, was continued in the seventeenth and eighteenth with a steadily increased degree of cultural homogeneity. Despite reduced interest in maritime trade, the monetization of the economy continued to increase throughout the eighteenth century.

Dhiravat na Pombejra (1993) has also shown for Siam that older western strictures about a retreat into isolation and stagnation are wide of the mark. European trade with Siam certainly languished after the 1688 revolution, but Chinese and Muslim trade continued and may even have grown to fill the gap. While there was an "administrative decline" after 1688 in terms of the crown's ability to control its subjects, the mid-eighteenth century was a period of great cultural flowering.

Any conclusion must re-emphasize that Southeast Asia was a region united by environment, commerce, diplomacy and war, but diverse in its fragmented polities and cultures. In this it had more in common with Europe than with the great land masses of Asia. Part of its fascination is the diversity of its reactions to the pressures of the period. Generalizations are always suspect.

The balance of evidence seems nevertheless to be that the seventeenth century, particularly its middle decades, was critical for Southeast Asia's reactions to increased military and economic pressure from the new Dutch-dominated world-system. These reactions necessarily involved some degree of retreat from what came to appear an excessive reliance on international commerce. In global terms the share of Southeast Asians in that commerce was undoubtedly reduced. When the region is seen in its own terms, however, words such as decline and stagnation are entirely inappropriate. There was constant change and adaptation to difficult circumstances. The cultural and political achievements of the eighteenth century were at least as remarkable as those of the seventeenth or the sixteenth. Many of the trends set in motion during the early modern era were developed into the foundations of modern Southeast Asia.

NOTES

1. The Center for Early Modern History at the University of Minnesota makes the point that comparative study is particularly fruitful in this period, and that "early modern History requires equal attention to very different cultures as they come into contact with each other".

2. The University of Minnesota is more expansive, taking in 1350 to 1750.

3. The first use of which I am aware is a Michigan dissertation by James Pfister (1972) referring to 1500–39. More recently Victor Lieberman (1990, 70–90) has taken it up.

4. Cf. Reid (1988, 121–8).

5. There is not only a shift in Islamic writing from Arabic to Malay and Javanese in the seventeenth century, but a further shift from Malay into local vernaculars in the eighteenth—notably Achehnese and Bugis.

CHAPTER TWO

THE ISLAMIZATION OF SOUTHEAST ASIA

L ike any other religious tradition, Islam in Southeast Asia presents us with both inside and outside evidence about its history. The inside evidence is pious nature, as is, for example, the internal evidence about the conversion of Britain to Christianity. No historical event could more obviously be a part of God's purpose for man, and therefore the aspects of the story recalled by Muslim writers are naturally those which show the divine purpose at work. While almost all the Southeast Asian chronicles describe supernatural events which accompany the conversion of a state to Islam, the differences between the type of divine intervention are certainly instructive. Malay chronicles like those of Pasai, Melaka, and Patani do not differ markedly from accounts from other parts of the world. They emphasize divine revelation through dreams, such as those of the rulers of Pasai and Melaka in turn; or the miraculous powers of a holy man of God, such as Shaikh Sa'id of Pasai in his healing of the ruler of Patani (Brown 1953, 41–2, 52–4; "Hikayat Raja-Raja Pasai", 116–20; *Hikayat Patani*, I: 71–5; see also the discussion of these texts in Drewes 1968, 436-8). Although these chronicles are not averse to describing the powers of rulers and the origins of states in older pre-Islamic terms of magical potency *(sakti)* they keep their description of the Islamization process within bounds which would probably have been acceptable to Muslims in most parts of the world. In the Javanese Islamic tradition and its Banjar offshoot, however, one finds more frankly pre-Islamic religious elements. The clearest religious motive for conversion offered in the *Hikayat Bandjar* is that the chief of Jipang in East Java "was very astonished when he saw the radiance *(cahaya)* of Raja Bungsu [i.e. Raden Rahmat]". He knelt at Raja Bungsu's feet and requested to be converted to Islam (*Hikayat Bandjar*, 420). From the *babads* emanating from what Ricklefs

MAP 2 INDIAN OCEAN PORTS

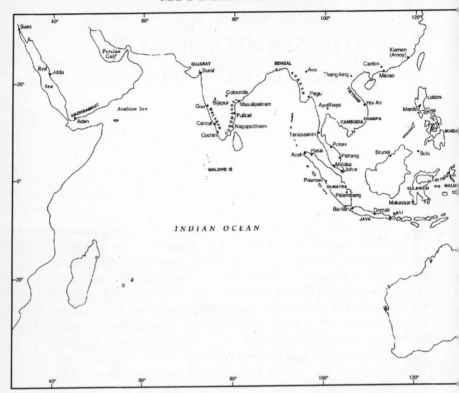

(1978, 2) calls the "quasi-Islamic tradition" of Java, come stories still more frankly heterodox in the type of powers which they attribute particularly to such great mystics as Sunan Kali Jaga and Sheikh Siti Jenar.

In comparison with most great religious changes in world history, we are comparatively well endowed also with outside sources basically unsympathetic or hostile to the Islamization process. Ever since Marco Polo (1298, 225) reported that "the people of Perlak (Nth Sumatra) used all to be idolaters, but owing to contact with Saracen merchants, who continually resort here in their ships, they have all been converted to the law of Mahomet", there have been Christian observers committed to excluding any religious explanation of the change. Tomé Pires and the other sixteenth century Iberians who took a great interest in this subject tended to follow Marco Polo in emphasizing that contact with Muslim merchants from the west was a sufficient explanation of Islamization.

It is tempting to the polemicist to raise one or the other of these two points of view into an adequate explanation for Islamization, so that a somewhat false debate has emerged. On the one hand we have van Leur and Schrieke stressing the alteration in trading patterns and the dominance of Muslims in Indian Ocean trade of the twelfth to sixteenth centuries; and going on to make political factors even more crucial than commercial ones. Van Leur, who rather absurdly refuses to allow that Islam offered any "higher civilization" to Southeast Asia, insists that the struggle between Portuguese and Muslims confirmed an already established pattern whereby Islam was hardly more than a symbol of political alliance with one side against the other (Leur 1955, 110–14; Schrieke 1955–7, I: 1–82; II: 230–67). On the other side of the debate, A.H. Johns and Fatimi take more seriously the evidence of the "inside" sources, and develop a rival explanation of the Islamization process centred on mystical Sufi preachers who "were proficient in magic and possessed powers of healing; and not least . . . were prepared to use the terms and elements of pre-Islamic culture in an Islamic spirit" (Johns 1961, 15; see also Fatimi 1963, esp. 92–9).

This antithesis stands in need of a rigorous synthesis. The rival explanations both contain much truth, but they are talking about different phenomena. The Islamic presence was of course brought by trade, and often consolidated by political and military power. Without the mercantile success of Muslims, Southeast Asians could never have been confronted with the option of Islam at all, and without the backing of state power the option would not have reached those outside the trading centres. Yet every Southeast Asian who embraced Islam had to undergo his own process of inner conversion, his own reconciliation between long-held assumptions about the shape of the world and the central features of the new doctrine. Given the paucity of autobiographical evidence on this personal dimension we would be wise at the outset to acknowledge the limitations of any discussion of motivations. Nevertheless, by combining the evidence of history on the period in question with the insights of anthropologists on the nature of Southeast Asian religious experience and conversion, the debate can be advanced in a number of key areas.

DEALING WITH THE DEAD

The ethnographic works of the last hundred years on the remaining "animist" traditions of Southeast Asia have made certain consistencies of religious belief very clear. The most striking common feature of these religious systems is the continuing involvement of the dead in the affairs of the living. Disease, misfortune and crop failure are held to be caused by the displeasure of ancestral spirits who have not been honoured with the appropriate rituals, or by the malevolence of restless or unhappy spirits of the dead which may be counteracted by the protection of the "good" or happy ancestors. The ritual expression of this belief is the centrality in all such religious systems of elaborate feasting for the dead, and of the subsequent invocation of ancestral spirits at every important *rite de passage* or agricultural ritual of the calendar. Not unnaturally, when names were required to distinguish this traditional religion from Islam or Christianity, it was frequently designated the "Way of the Ancestors" (Sa'dan Toraja *Aluk to Dolo;* East Sumba *Marapu*).[1]

We have sixteenth and seventeenth century evidence from Spanish and Portuguese sources on the religious beliefs of the people of Luzon, the Visayas, and South Sulawesi (Bugis and Makasarese) before their conversion to Christianity and Islam respectively. This confirms that death-rituals and propitiation of the ancestral dead were remarkably similar to the pattern we know among non-Muslim peoples of Borneo and Sulawesi in modern times (on the pre-Hispanic Philippines see Morga 1971, 278–81; Chirino 1969, 327–9; Pigafetta in Nowell 1962, 163–7; Phelan 1959, 23–4; on pre-Islamic South Sulawesi, see Pelras 1989, 153-84). The Hinduism of Bali appears to have demanded little alteration to the ways in which the dead were regarded there, with offerings and death-rituals even today as central as in the "animist" little traditions (Gerdin 1981, 17–34; Hooykaas 1976, 39–50). In a less overt manner, the popular religious practice of even the people of the Archipelago who have been Muslim or Christian for centuries reveals the continuing importance of the dead in the ritual preoccupations of the living. In short, it is possible to conclude that the dominant religious belief-system of the Southeast Asia to which Islam came in the fourteenth to seventeenth centuries was one of deep ritual concern for the propitiation of the dead. In comparison with this popular pattern, the Brahmanic influence at many of the royal courts was very much more limited in scope, save perhaps in parts of Java.

Such concern for the ritual well-being of the dead would appear to be incompatible with Islam, with its intolerance of idolatry and polytheism, and its consequent insistence that burials should be simple and immediate, the dead returning to God as unadorned as they came from him at birth. Indeed the abrupt change of burial practice with the acceptance of Islam appears to be one of the most striking successes of the new religion. In those parts of Sulawesi which accepted Islam in the seventeenth century, valuable ceramics were buried with the dead to accompany them in their journey to the hereafter, and these can be dated to various periods in the tenth to sixteenth centuries, but appear to cease abruptly with Islam. The extravagant feasting which non-Muslim parts of the Archipelago associate pre-eminently with death-rituals, was transferred among Muslims to weddings, and to a lesser extent to circumcisions. With some notable exceptions, such as the rulers of Melaka, early Aceh and Mataram, the graves of Muslims even in the earliest period of Islam were relatively modest (for the rich tombs of the Melaka kings see Albuquerque 1557, III: 136; and for those of Aceh, Davis 1905, II: 321–2).

Nevertheless Islam demonstrated to Southeast Asians that it had its own ways of ensuring that the spirits of the dead were at peace, and even of invoking those spirits for the well-being of the living. It is now well-known that it was in the mystical form brought by initiates of the Sufi orders (Arabic *tariqa*, Malay *tarekat*) that Islam primarily recommended itself to Southeast Asians of the fourteenth to seventeenth centuries. We will be mistaken, however, if we think of this Sufism only in terms of the path to direct or ecstatic union with God taught in many of the early Malay and Javanese Islamic texts (edited examples include Nieuwenhuijze 1945; Drewes 1969; Johns 1965; Naguib al-Attas 1970). During the period of most rapid conversions to Islam in Southeast Asia, Sufism at the popular level had become a means of linking the individual believer with the spiritual power (Arabic *baraka*, Malay *berkat*) of holy men, apostles, rulers, founders of orders, and others whose *baraka* was manifested in numerous miracle stories. From this period, as Trimingham (1971, 26) puts it, "No clear distinction can henceforth be made between the orders and saint-veneration, since God's protégés *(awliya'li'llah)* are within the orders." The spiritual power of these dead saints was invoked to help the living partly through the chain *(silsila)* of spiritual genealogy which linked each Sufi teacher ultimately to the venerated founder of his order, but also through visitations *(ziyara)* to the tombs of holy men, where offerings were frequently made.

> The mystic carries out a *ziyara* for the purposes of *muraqaba* (spirit communion) with the saint, finding in the material symbol an aid to meditation. But the popular belief is that the saint's soul lingers about his tomb and places *(maqam)* specially associated with him whilst he was on earth or at which he had manifested himself. At such places his intercession can be sought. (Trimingham 1971, 26)

These features of Sufism were to be found throughout the Muslim world, but were especially marked in India and Southeast Asia, where the expanding faith tended to take the form of "a holy-man Islam" (Trimingham 1971, 22). The seeking of the *berkat* of holy men at their tombs has of course been a very marked feature of Southeast Asian Islam in modern times, wherever a stricter spirit of modernism has not taken root. Many of the tombs now most widely venerated are those of the apostles thought to have introduced Islam to each area, such as those of the nine walis of Java, or of Dato ri Bandang in Makasar. Still more honoured are the graves of those who popularized a particular Sufi order, such as Abdar-Rauf of Singkil, the "Shaikh Kuala" beloved of the Acehnese, who introduced the Shattariyya *tariqa* to Indonesia in the seventeenth century, or Shaikh Yusuf, the great teacher of the Khalwatiyya order, who even in his lifetime was held by the people of Makasar "in such great love and awe as though he was a second Muhammad" (Governor Hartsik of Makasar 1689 cited in Andaya 1981, 277).[2] Although the earliest Sufi orders in Southeast Asia appear not to have been as highly structured as in other parts of the Muslim world, the extreme reverence for such figures and their graves confirms that it was indeed Sufi masters and practices which made the greatest impact in the region. An orthodox Muslim code of ethics from sixteenth century Java warns its readers against the most popular of all the orders, the *Kadiriyya,* and goes on proclaim, "It is unbelief to say that the great imams are superior to the prophets, or to put the saints (*wali*) above the prophets, and even above our lord Muhammad" (Drewes 1978, 38–9). Whether living or dead, the holy men of early Islam in Southeast Asia were accepted as having supernatural power similar to that of the ancestors. Their graves replaced the resting places of the spirits of the dead as centres of pilgrimage, meditation, and petition (for a nineteenth century missionary view of the process of Islamization in an animist Indonesian culture, see Simon 1912; more modern anthropological accounts are Miles 1966, 1976).

The words of prayer were changed into an Islamic form much more quickly than the purposes to which prayer was put. To exorcize a malevolent spirit or to invoke a protective ancestral one, an Arabic prayer was at least as powerful as the mantra it replaced. For the most part Arabic terminology was quickly introduced in the religious area—*baca do'a* (to read an [Arabic] prayer) becoming the standard term for an invocation or blessing; *roh* (plural *arwah)* becoming accepted as the Islamic equivalent of the key Austronesian concept of *semangat* (soul-substance or spirit); and such words as *berkat* and *kramat* describing the power that emanated from the graves of the saints. There are however some interesting indigenous survivals. The word *ngaji (kaji, mengaji)* normally used for recitation of the Koran, for the souls of the departed as well as for other purposes, is an Austronesian word probably from the same root as the *ngaji* still used by animists in Flores in recent times to describe the ritual prayers addressed to the ancestors (Novena 1982, 13–24; for a review of the literature on *semangat* and its relationship with Sufi concepts of *roh* see Endicott 1970, esp. 28–51). Similarly, Southeast Asian Islam took over an older indigenous word *sembahyang* (*sembah*=veneration, *hyang*=god(s), lord) as the most usual term for personal prayer, including the daily *salat*.[3]

Also worthy of further study is the role of the prayer litany known in Indonesia as the *Tahlil* (the first words of the confession of faith, *La ilaha illa Allah*), because that phrase is repeated many times in its opening chant. The form of this prayer is popularly attributed to Abd al-Kadir Jilani, the most widely venerated of all the Sufi masters, which leads us to suspect that it may have been spread through Indonesia by the earliest adherents of Kadiriyya mysticism in the sixteenth and seventeenth centuries. In Maluku (the Moluccas), where this is the litany normally used for the dead, it takes the form of a prayer for the spirit of the Prophet, then for the spirits of the ancestors of the host family, especially the recently deceased, then for the ancestors of all present, and finally for all those who have died in the faith. It is recited not only at funerals, but at the specified intervals after death (three, seven, forty, hundred days) when ritual meals are held, at visits to graves, and at the annual commemoration of the dead.[4] Whether or not in the same form, a *Tahlil* chant for the dead was also practised widely in Malaya, Sulu, Java and Sumatra (for Malaya, Skeat 1900, 406–8; for Java, Kumar 1985, 21, 25, 177n28; for Sumatra, Pijper 1934, 178–81; for Sulu, Kiefer 1972, 132).

The way in which the elaborate pre-Islamic feasting of the dead on their way to the land of the spirits gradually gave way to Islamic practice is easier to observe in a relatively recently Islamized area such as South Sulawesi. When James Brooke was in the Bugis area in 1840, he noted that there was still a forty-day period of public feasting at the death of important people, with relatives of the deceased slaughtering buffaloes, goats, and chickens to feed all who attended (Brooke 1848, I: 87–8; for similar extravagant feasting in Bengkulen in the 1920s see Pijper 1934, 179–81). Even today many Bugis continue to distinguish a proportion of their property under the name of *ampikale*, the original purpose of which was to cover the substantial costs of this forty-day feasting after death. Today this portion goes to reward the member of the family who has borne most of the burden of caring for the deceased in old age (Maruzi 1981, 74).

As Snouck Hurgronje saw it, after the ritual meals for the dead on the third, seventh, hundredth (or in Java up to thousandth) day after their death, the spirit of the dead was no longer individually remembered and propitiated, but rather merged into the collective "spirits of the departed". These are especially remembered throughout Islamic Southeast Asia on the eighth month of the lunar calendar (*Sha'ban*) known in Java as *Bulan Arwah* (the month of the spirits), and in Aceh and elsewhere as "the month of the rice feasts", since every family must hold a feast in honour of its ancestors during that month. "According to the official or learned conception this is done in order to bestow on the deceased the recompense earned by his good work; according to the popular notion it is to let them enjoy the actual savour of the good things of the feast." (Snouck Hurgronje 1906, I: 221)

In the Arab world the month regarded as most appropriate for honouring the dead is the seventh, though the practice is by no means on the Southeast Asian scale. Snouck Hurgronje, noting that South India shared the Southeast Asian preference for the eighth month, saw this as further evidence for the Indian origin of Indonesian Islam. Equally significant, however, is the popular association between the honouring of the ancestors and the rituals associated with the fasting month (the ninth) and the feasts which end it at *Idulfitri*. Southeast Asian Muslims in general (though this is nowhere so marked as in Sulawesi and Maluku) concentrate their visits to the family graves in the last few days of the eighth month, and the first days of the tenth, the latter being part of an Indonesian tradition at *Idulfitri* of asking forgiveness of one's elders, living and dead, for the misdeeds of the past year. It may therefore be that the preference of the eighth month for honouring the ancestors derives from an earlier transitional phase in which the feasting of *Idulfitri*, and the ritual of fasting and of breaking the fast, was replacing the feasts which traditionally had accompanied death rituals and offerings to the ancestors.

URBANIZATION AND LOCIAL CHANGE

If we have learned anything from the debate sparked by Weber's *The Protestant Ethic and the Spirit of Capitalism*, it is that profound religious change in a society is accompanied by major changes in the social and economic order. The causal relationship between the two is highly complex, so that we must be on guard against simplistic explanations which either see religious change as purely a consequence or rationalization of economic change, or which by contrast see actions in the economic area flowing solely from the ideal types presented by religion and ideology. We are on safer ground in understanding changes in the social area as mutually reinforcing, with an infinite variety possible in the mix. At least for the relatively self-contained world of the animist, however, this process of mutually reinforcing change seems often to have been initiated by the invasion of economic and political forces from outside. The last century witnessed a period of such inescapable change for many interior or upland peoples of Southeast Asia (see Simon 1912, esp. 46–7, 70–1; Coté 1979; Miles 1976). I suggest that the period when many of the major Southeast Asian states accepted Islam was

[margin note, handwritten]: profound religious change ⊕ social + econ. order ≠ in a mutually reinforcing + complex fashion // in terms of SEA animism, however, the change often seems to be initiated by the invasion of econ + poli forces from outside

similarly one of inescapable change, to which the growth of trade and of trading cities was the initial spur.

Although our knowledge of the earlier period is still very sparse, there can be no doubt that the scale of Southeast Asian trade began to expand very rapidly in the late fourteenth century, and continued to do so into the seventeenth century. The reasons were in part the "spice-orgy" which began to affect Europe after the Crusades, and the organization of the Red Sea-Suez route to the Mediterranean for spices and Chinese goods by the Mamelukes about 1345; in part the great increase of Chinese activity in Southeast Asia in connection with the early Ming dynasty. As a result of this trade, cities developed with astonishing rapidity. Melaka, Grisek, and Makasar we know to have developed from little more than villages to cosmopolitan cities with populations of fifty thousand or more within a century. Aceh, Banten, Patani and Ayudhya also grew to great conurbations (Reid 1980; this argument is treated more extensively in chapters 2 and 3 of Reid 1993a). Like any great cities, they were markets for ideas as well as merchandise. The Chinese brought much new knowledge of material culture, bronze-casting, gunpowder, scales, shipbuilding, and also some new tastes in food and drink; Indian merchants brought methods as developed as any in the world; "the Arab arithmatic" was being studied in Aceh in 1620 (Beaulieu 1666, 99); the Makasarese prince Pattingalloang a little later insisted on obtaining from the Europeans at his court the latest in scientific knowledge from Europe, including an expensive new telescope with which Galileo had begun to revolutionize the view of the cosmos (see chapter 7). Although Arabic, Italian, and Portuguese were spoken in many of the bigger cities, it was Malay above all which made it possible for Southeast Asians to learn of each other's cultures and of the visitors from outside the region. Magellan could make good friends in the Visayas because the Malay-speaking Sumatran slave he had brought around the world was well understood there (Pigafetta in Nowell 1962, esp. 136–7). His colleague Pigafetta appeared to think that "these Moors" had only one language, whether it was in the Philippines, Borneo, Maluku or Timor, and that of course was Malay (Nowell 1962, 227–36).

We know much less about the hinterlands behind these interconnected urban cities of Southeast Asia, but enough to see that the gulf from town to country was an immense one. The Melaka case is the most extreme, with little but forest once away from the urban and coastal area. Before the rise of Aceh the commercial cities of northern Sumatra are always described as enclaves surrounded by tattooed cannibals. Since Sultan Iskandar Muda is described as meeting a crafty bow-legged Batak when he was out hunting, even Aceh in his days cannot have extended far into the interior (Iskandar 1958, 146-8). In South Celebes, despite its apparent homogeneity of culture, the picture is the same. "The nearer we drew to Makassar . . . the more civilized we found the people", remarked Navarrette (1962, I: 111) as he followed the coast down from the north in 1657. To the English in Makasar, the Bugis who periodically disturbed the peace of the city appeared like wild men who "amaze and terrify" the city (IOL, G/10/1, ff. 82, 117, 202). Even in Java, where the modern convention is the reverse one of contrasting the refined kraton culture of inner Java with the more gauche and materialistic *pasisir*, there is much evidence to suggest that Demak, Cirebon, Tuban, Grisek and Surabaya were the real centres of Javanese civilization at least until they fell before the arms of Sultan Agung in the seventeenth century (Graaf and Pigeaud 1974, 165–6).

The gulf between civilized city and primitive countryside can partly be explained by the strong foreign element in the early growth of these cities. Chinese are now admitted to have had a major part in the founding of Grisek, Japara, Ayudhya, and Nakhon Srithammarat (Ligor) in the late fourteenth and early fifteenth centuries. They had much to do with the growth of Melaka and Patani in the same period, though Javanese and Gujeratis soon became even more numerous. Malays and Javanese in Ternate, Malays and Portuguese in Makasar, Malays, Chinese and Gujeratis in Banten all contributed much to the urban population and the emerging urban culture. Yet it would be a great mistake to minimize the importance of that new culture by seeing the new cities as some sort of disaggregated pastiche of foreign elements. All of these cities shared a culture which was Malayo-Muslim and an urban settlement pattern which was very distinctively Southeast Asian.

The pressures of rapid urbanization and social change can be viewed from the perspective of the villager drawn into the rapidly growing trade centres, or from the point of view of whole societies exposed to rapid social change as their role in world trade grew. The latter is perhaps best seen in Makasar, where we are particularly well provided with internal and external sources covering its rise from a local animist village at war with all its neighbours in the early sixteenth century, to the great metropolis and trading centre of eastern Indonesia by the early seventeenth. The city must have had a population approaching fifty thousand by 1615, when 1,260 houses were burned down without disrupting the city as a whole, and when the English saw the king review thirty-six thousand fighting men called up at only twenty-four hours notice (IOL, G/10/1, ff. 5 and 9). The Makasarese may have been an extreme case of openness to change and to new ideas because of the very speed of their urbanization pattern. The Gowa chronicle reads like a series of "firsts", as it notes which king was the first to erect brick walls, which the first to cast guns, to organize a new aspect of government, and of course to conquer and make tributary each surrounding state. Despite this rapid change, when the first substantial Dutch description of the city gives us a glimpse in 1607, just after the formal acceptance of Islam, it was still a largely animist culture:

> The various fruits of India abound there, also goats, buffaloes, and pigs, though these are now difficult to obtain, because the King accepted the Mohammedan Law four years ago . . . The men carry usually one, two, or more balls in their penis, of the same size as those of Siam, but not hollow or clinking, rather of ivory or solid fishbone, which is now also declining among them because of the change of sect; while they were heathen the women cut off their hair with a comb, but they now have it washed long, and bind it in the manner of the Malay women; the female slaves whom one sees carrying water in the back streets have their upper body with the breasts completely naked, and wear trousers which come up to the navel. When they wash they stand mother-naked, the men as well as women, which I have seen in no other place in the Indies as I have here. (*Begin ende Voortgang*, III: 82)

Just forty years after this report, another visitor to Makasar noted that "there are . . . no hogs at all because the natives, who are Mohammedans, have exterminated them entirely from the country", while "the women are entirely covered from head to foot, in such fashion that not even their faces can be seen" (Hertz 1966, 206–7). The change in every aspect of life was profound and rapid. Despite the seemingly very short history of urban civilization in South Sulawesi, European accounts agree that the seventeenth century Makasarese were "a very good people to deal with and to live by; and which hold good right and justice, and order after their manner" (Hugh Frayne to Downtown 1610, in *Letters Received*, II: 71).

If the Islamization of Makasar was exceptional, it was less because of the speed of the social change which accompanied it, than because there was a real choice for Makasar between Christianity and Islam. This is the point of the widespread European accounts, current as early as the 1640s, about a decision by the Makasar elite to let God decide for them between Islam and Christianity by means of a contest, to see whether Muslim Aceh or Christian Melaka would be the first to respond to a request for missionaries (Hertz 1966, 207; Boxer 1967, 3n; Navarrette 1962, I: 113). The "race" as such may be a legend, as Noorduyn (1956, 247–67) has convincingly argued, but the Portuguese were correct in lamenting that they had had a chance to Christianize Makasar and had lost it largely by default. The Makasarese profited from both Portuguese and Malay trade and had some knowledge of the doctrines upheld by each. At least in the case of the great Arung Matoaya, who guided Makasar into a wider world through Islam, there is no doubt that there was a conscious weighing of two rival worldviews, and an intellectual decision between them (Noorduyn 1956, 247–67; and see chapter 7).

For most Southeast Asians there was no such conscious decision between rival systems of equal relevance. Rather was it a question of a new *ilmu*, a new system of controlling the supernatural forces around them, to be judged primarily in terms of its results and its consonance with the new and desired lifestyle. An anthropologist has recently described the constant religious experimentation on the part of Ngaju Dayaks in Borneo, deserting one shaman or one set of spirits for another in accordance with the perceived results. A Dayak Christian missionary described their approach as follows to this field-worker:

> Dayaks play politics with supernatural beings. No one could deny that they are religious. But their interest in religion is a matter of tactics. The more a man knows about ritual, the more he can do for his own and his family's welfare. A person's wealth is proof of his theological knowledge. They are continually changing their adherence from one set of spirits to another. If they make the right moves they will die rich and buy their way into Heaven with huge animal sacrifices. If they die in poverty they may remain in eternal Purgatory. (Miles 1976, 5; see also Volkman 1979, 4 for wealth as a sign and product of spiritual power.)

Islam is perhaps of all great world religions the most congenial to trade, and both the Quran and the Hadith heap praise upon the "trustworthy merchant" who trades profitably for the benefit of himself, his family, and worthy causes (see most recently Rodinson 1977, 16–19). In Southeast Asia Islam was brought by traders, and quickly associated itself with the relatively opulent and sophisticated lifestyle of the mercantile cities. In Luzon, when Islamization was still at an early stage, it was reported that,

> some are Moros, and they obtain much gold, which they worship as a God. All their possessions are gold and a few slaves . . . They believe that paradise and successful enterprises are reserved for those who submit to the religion of the Moros of Borney [Brunei], of which they make much account . . . These are a richer people, because they are merchants, and with their slaves, cultivate the land (de Sande in Blair and Robertson 1903–9, IV: 67–8).

Islam, in other words, was identified with wealth, success, and power for many Filipinos. It is scarcely surprising that those who were ambitious, particularly in the area of trade, began to assimilate towards Islam even before they understood anything about its central doctrines. The early Spanish chroniclers often spoke as though all of the lowland people of Luzon were "Moros", although this can only have been in terms of the most superficial cultural borrowing. "In the villages nearest the sea" many did not eat pork, although they could not explain why to the Spanish and appeared not even to know the name of Mohammad ("Relation of the Conquest of the Island of Luzon," 20 April 1572, in Blair and Robertson III: 165; see also III: 74, 297, 300; V: 83).

For other reasons too the more commercially inclined must quickly have been attracted towards the new faith. The spirits of the ancestors, the trees and the mountains did not travel easily. The trader who moved from place to place needed a faith of broader application. If he moved beyond his own island he needed the Malay language and he needed acceptance and contacts in the trading cities. Islam provided both a faith and a social system for such traders. Few Visayans, for example, entered the markets of Melaka, Brunei or Banten clad only in a loin-cloth of tree-fibre cloth, tattooed and long-haired like their countrymen at home. Modification of dress towards the Malay pattern probably preceded formal acceptance of Islam by such traders.

Wherever an earlier Brahmanic influence had not reached, with its exalted sense of kingship sanctioned by religious ritual, there was little to oppose the steady assimilation towards the faith of the traders who brought new wealth and power. This was the case in the Philippines in the sixteenth century, and presumably also in Maluku in the fifteenth. Some Ternate traditions as later recorded make no distinction between the coming of the Muslim traders and the formal acceptance of Islam:

They say that they took these [royal] titles from the Javanese who made them Muslims and introduced coinage into their country, as well as the gong, the *serunai*, ivory, the *kris* (dagger), and the law, and all the other good things they have.[5]

THE MAJOR STATES

Elsewhere, in the major city-states, a situation quickly developed where "the king is a pagan; the merchants are moors". This is how Rui de Brito described Brunei in 1514 (de Sá 1954, I: 68), and the same must have applied to Samudra in 1282 (when a non-Muslim king sent Muslim envoys to China), to Patani in the fourteenth century (*Hikayat Patani*, II: 222), Melaka in the early fifteenth, Banjarmasin in the early and Makasar in the late sixteenth century (*Hikayat Bandjar* 262, 370, 430; and see chapter 6). Even in

MAP 3 SPREAD OF ISLAM IN SOUTHEAST ASIA

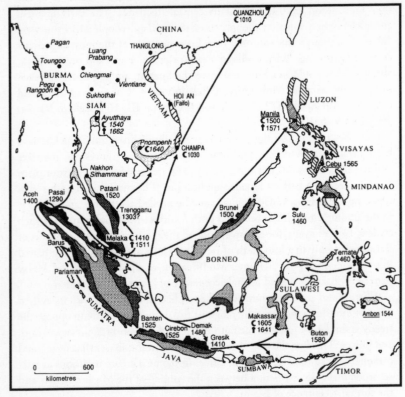

Christain by 1600	Muslim by 1500	Muslim centres	: Pasai 1290
Christain by 1700	Muslim by 1600	Christain centres	: Manila 1571
Christain minorities	Muslim by 1700	Theravada Buddhist centres: *Pegu*	
	Muslim minorities	Dates indicate earliest substantial Muslim (**c**) or Christian (**†**) presence	

→ 14ᵗʰ C. Majapahit 15ᵗʰ–17ᵗʰ C. Ayudhya
[great centres of Buddhist civilization) Muslim
traders were firmly est. @ the capital +
appeared to have better links w/ the court than any

other
commercial
element
although
the court
possessed
sacral
traditions
incompatible
w/ Islam +
disapproving
of the
commercial
community

fourteenth century Majapahit and fifteenth to seventeenth century Ayudhya, great centres of Buddhist civilization, Muslim traders were firmly established at the capital, and appeared to have better links with the court than any other commercial element, including non-Muslim Chinese. Nevertheless, such courts possessed sacral traditions of kingship which were clearly incompatible with Islam, and typically they looked down on the whole commercial community as of relatively low status. How then did the conversion of such courts come about?

Intermarriage between wealthy traders or *shahbandars* and the court circle has been frequently mentioned in this connection. In a sense this is to beg the question however. Brahmano-Buddhist rulers might readily take girls of low estate into their palace as concubines or lesser wives, but to accept a marriage partner as of equal status was to set the seal on Islamization, rather than to bring it about. There had usually to be either a conscious decision to accept the new faith and social system, or else an element of force.

An important factor here was that each of these proud states which declined to accept Islam was in danger of being outflanked by rival states. Samudra-Pasai was not the first state in North Sumatra to adopt Islam. All sources agree that at least Perlak and Aru preceded it by a few years. Similarly Patani was preceded by Terengganu and Melaka by its neighbour Pahang not to mention its more distant rival Pasai (*Hikayat Patani* I: 3–4). In South Sulawesi it is Luwu, surprisingly not a particular centre of trade at all, which is acknowledged as the first Muslim state, a few years ahead of Makasar. On the one hand these pioneer Muslim states must have helped to make Islam respectable in the eyes of the more stubbornly Brahmanic courts, in some cases even apparently attracting rival members of the ruling dynasty to their side. On the other they posed the danger of a wholesale desertion by Muslim traders to the alternative centre.

In Java and in Javanized Banjarmasin, this sort of pressure and example was clearly insufficient. In some cases the Muslim *kauman*, as it would now be called, ceased to give allegiance to the ruling dynasty and entered a state of civil war from a rival capital. Grisek was apparently in such a state in the early sixteenth century when it was described by Tomé Pires (1515, 193). The ruler of one side of the river, Pate Cucuf (Patih Yusuf), was born in the trading community of Melaka of mixed Javanese-Malay parentage, and had command of much more wealth and men. His antagonist on the other side of the river, who must have been defeated soon after these words were written, "sets himself up as a knight" (*presume de cavaleiro*)—obviously having a better claim to *priyayi* status. In Banjarmasin the great length of the Barito river gave better opportunities for the rival elements to keep out of each other's way. Raden Samudra, claimed by the *Hikayat Bandjar* to be a nephew of the ruler, set up his rival capital much lower down the river near the site of the present Banjarmasin, and quickly attracted or forced (the *Hikayat* mentions only force) the traders to join him there. After this it was only a short step for him to make an alliance with the crusading centre of Demak, accept Islam, and make war against his more stubborn rival with the help of all these Islamic elements (*Hikayat Bandjar*, 45–9, 398–439).

Almost all the indigenous chronicles are at pains to establish continuity between the new Islamic rulers and the earlier dynasties—sometimes through

rather transparent devices. The Portuguese on the other hand are inclined to
stress the lowly origin of the Muslim rulers, particularly in Java. The truth
may be closer to the former than the latter. Tomé Pires' informants on Java
were presumably Javanese, and their low estimate of the antecedents of the
coastal rulers may have been in part a product of dynastic and political
rivalries. Undoubtedly some Islamic centres, such as Banten, Grisek, and
perhaps Demak, did break altogether with the Hindu dynasty, but most of
the larger states were anxious to preserve tradition not only in their chronicles
but in their court ceremonial, regalia, and etiquette. The magical aura of
sovereignty (*daulat*), which surrounded a ruler of the correct credentials, was
itself his major weapon in any contest for the throne. At least in the difficult
case of Java we must give some attention to the ways in which Islam may
have penetrated into the court circle itself.

ISLAM AND THE COURT OF MAJAPAHIT

According to Javanese traditions, recorded in a variety of forms from the
seventeenth century onwards, the major external sources of Islamic influence
were Champa and Pasai. The principal figure in these stories is the Puteri
Cempa, a daughter of a ruler of Champa who became the bride of the king
of Majapahit. According to the Javanese stories, the sister of this princes
married a wealthy Arab trader in Champa, from which union sprang one or
two sons who combined Islamic piety with the required exalted blood. The
eldest of these sons, in the versions where he appears, went to Java to become
imam of the mosque of Grisek. The younger (or only) son was the famous
Raden Rahmat, who visited his aunt at the court of Majapahit, where he was
received with great favour. Eventually he was allowed by the ruler to proceed
to Ampel, near Surabaya, to found a religious community and make converts
of anybody he chose (Graaf and Pigeaud 1974, 19–21; Raffles 1817, II: 115–
18).

In one tradition, the *Hikayat Bandjar*, Pasai rather than Champa is given
as the origin of Raden Rahmat. The Javanese traditions give Pasai as the
origin of two other famous *wali* (apostles) of Java, Maulana Iskak (father of
Sunan Giri) and Sunan Gunung Jati, the pioneer of Islam in Banten and
Cheribon. This connection, however, appears to be later than the Champa
one—early in the sixteenth century in the latter's case (Graaf and Pigeaud
1974, 170, 111–18).

The citations of Champa and Pasai in Javanese accounts of Islamization
are too frequent to be ignored, particularly as neither kingdom was significant
at the time the accounts were recorded. There is a problem however that the

dates even of Raden Rahmat and Puteri Champa, which Pigeaud and de
Graaf place in the middle of the fifteenth century, are too late to account for
the growth of Muslim centres at Grisek and Japara as recorded by the
Chinese, or for the Muslim graves at Troloyo near Majapahit, which cover
the period 1376–1475. The latter indicate that at the court of Majapahit in
this early period, there were Muslims of high status who were either Javanese
or at least Javanized foreigners (Damais 1954, 353–415; Robson 1981, 271–
2).

A factor not sufficiently considered in the discussions of this period in
Javanese history is the relationship between Majapahit's external relations and
Islamization. The evidence of the *Nagarakertagama* that tributaries of King
Hayam Wuruk extended as far as north Sumatra, Malaya, Champa, and
Maluku has been seen in terms of the possible influence of Java on these areas
(the list of tributaries is given in Pigeaud 1960, III: 16–17). We know,
however, from the "tributary" relationships of China, Siam, Melaka and
elsewhere that the exchanges were mutual. Regular and commercial relations
between Majapahit and these distant kingdoms certainly occurred, since these
are confirmed by the non-Javanese sources at the other end (the *Hikayat Raja-
Raja Pasai, Sejarah Melayu, Silsilah Raja-Raja Sambas, Hikayat Bandjar*) as
well as numerous oral traditions from the eastern islands. In view of the
predominance of Muslims on the trade routes of the Archipelago, these
relations cannot have been maintained without using at least some Muslim
ships, mariners, and traders. Some of the states claimed as Majapahit
tributaries were themselves Muslim, including Haru, Perlak, Samudra (Pasai),
Lamuri and Barus in Sumatra, and probably Terengganu in Malaya. In many
others there would have been a significant commercial minority of Muslims
likely to play a role in diplomatic as well as economic relations between the
states. Just as China under the Yung-lo emperor made use of Muslim admirals
and seamen to spread its influence abroad, Majapahit very probably
mobilized the Muslim shipping in many ports it conquered or influenced to
take part in missions yet further afield. One surviving example of the process
are the *orang Timur* of Jambi, said to be the descendants of men from
Sarawak and Brunei who came to Jambi as members of an invading
Majapahit army in the fourteenth century (Tideman 1938, 78). It may be
possible to explain the evidence for a superficial and short-lived Muslim
influence in fourteenth century Ternate (and much more problematically for
a similar phenomenon in Brunei and Sulu), a century before a continuous
tradition of Islam begins, by a burst of expansionist activity on the part of
Majapahit which made use of Muslim seamen and soldiers.

As the *Hikayat Raja-Raja Pasai* (161, Malay text, 102) reported of
Majapahit, "there was a coming and going of people from the territories

overseas which had submitted to the king". Some of these were certainly
Muslims, including the captives brought back by Majapahit's successful
expedition against Pasai:

> As for the Pasai prisoners, the Emperor made a decree ordering them to remain
> in Java but allowing them liberty to settle in it anywhere they pleased. That is
> why there are in Java so many *keramat* (holy graves) dating from the time of
> the conquest of Pasai by Majapahit. ("Hikayat Raja-Raja Pasai", 159, Malay
> text, 100)[6]

Although such captives undoubtedly contained men of high rank, it is not
there that we should look for the means by which Islam eventually penetrated
to within the highest Javanese court circles. In the dynastic marriages which
cemented relations between the most powerful "tributary" states and
Majapahit, on the other hand, this access could be expected. Although the
Hikayat Raja-Raja Pasai has a fanciful tale of the abortive suit of a Pasai prince
by a Majapahit princess, it is with Champa that these marriage relations are
most significant.

Just as Javanese records show the Majapahit king marrying a Cham
princess, it is Cham records which show the reverse process, in the marriage
of King Jaya Simhavarman III of Champa to a Javanese princess at the
beginning of the fourteenth century. These dynastic relations were close
enough for a Cham king to take refuge in Java after a Vietnamese attack on
his capital in 1318 (Robson 1981, 276).[7] The *Sejarah Melayu* (109–10) goes
further, claiming that a ruler of Champa journeyed to Majapahit to make his
homage, fathering there a child by a Majapahit princess who later grew up to
become the last ruler of Champa before its capital at Vijaya fell to the
Vietnamese in the mid-fifteenth century. Certainly relations between the
Cham court and the courts of Java and the Malay world appear to have been
exceptionally close, regardless of religion, and despite the earlier relation with
Java it was with Malayo-Muslim courts that the Chams became associated
after the fall of Vijaya. According to the *Sejarah Melayu* (110–11) the
defeated princes of Champa then fled to Melaka and Aceh, where they
became Muslim, while Makasar sources show Chams playing an honoured
role there among the Malayo-Muslim merchant group (*Sedjarah Goa*, 28;
Skinner 1963, 146–7, 269). In 1607 a Dutch fleet found that the vestigial
kingdom of Champa still had exceptionally close and cordial relations with
Johor, and that although the king was Hindu much of his court was Muslim
or pro-Muslim (*Begin ende Voortgangh* 1646, III: 120). The Cham aristocrats
who found refuge in fifteenth century Melaka became Muslim very readily
(although that state was alway tolerant of Hindus), yet they allegedly retained

a taboo against killing a cow or drinking its milk (*Sejarah Melayu*, 109, and 55 where the Cham *nakhoda* are given a very high ceremonial position at court). All of this suggests that even though the Champa court retained a high sense of the sacral purity required of a Brahmanic ruler, it was very closely tied to the Muslim commercial element both within its own kingdom and in the wider Malay world beyond. The Javanese story of Raden Rahmat and Putri Campa expresses exactly this situation, the marriage links leading from the Majapahit court to the Champa court to the Champa Muslim minority. It is in general through tribute and trading missions, and in particular through the Champa connection, that Islam appears to have gained respectability at the very heart of the Javanese state.

FORCE

Arnold's *Preaching of Islam* inaugurated a very salutary reaction against the crude caricature of an Islam spread by the sword. We risk distortion of another kind, however, if we overlook the extent to which relatively small but determined Muslim forces were able to impose their will on substantial areas of Southeast Asia. The chronicles themselves are usually not averse to emphasizing the victories of Muslim arms in the holy cause. In those areas where there was serious resistance to Islam, which included the whole of inland Java, South Sulawesi (with the Makasarese crusade against Wajo', Bone, and the other Bugis states), and Banjarmasin, war was required either to destroy the old dynasty completely or to persuade it to accept the new dispensation. Even in the Philippines the physical superiority of the Muslims did no harm to their cause. Without such wars Islam would have spread more slowly, and in such places as West and East Java might never have spread at all.

There are two elements in the superiority of Muslim arms against their Hindu-Buddhist adversaries. The first is the superior weaponry which wealth and international contacts made available to the Muslims. Some of the most spectacularly large cannon did come from the Middle East, like the Turkish cannon which helped Aceh win many battles in the sixteenth century. Yet most guns were probably either Chinese or home-made. Small Chinese brass guns, culverins, were in use by Muslims all over the Philippines, in Brunei, and probably in Melaka. Chinese Muslims themselves were often among the most useful gunners and manufacturers of guns in the Southeast Asian cities, notably in Giri, Gresik, and Banten. But from at least the sixteenth century the knowledge of gun-making was widespread among the commercial elements of Southeast Asia. When the Spanish sacked Manila in 1570 they found next to Raja Suleiman's house a foundry for making bronze guns. "Some small and large cannon had just been begun. There were the clay and wax moulds, the largest of which was for a cannon 17 feet long, resembling a culverin." ("Relation of the Voyage to Luzon", May 1570 in Blair and Robertson, III: 103) Similarly the Javanese in Melaka at the Portuguese conquest were reported to be active in "the making of arquebusses and all other kinds of firearms" (Barbosa 1518, 193). Traders were ready to defend their ships wherever they sailed, and many vessels appeared to be equipped with small guns. Foreign merchants were expected to assist the ruler of the port they were in during his campaigns, and of course proved useful allies. The Malays were often mentioned as prominent in the forces of Makasar, the Javanese and Gujeratis in Melaka, the Chinese in Java and a whole range of foreigners in Banjarmasin. Later, Europeans would find the same role expected of them.

The other element was the Muslim faith itself. Where Muslims were in a small minority their faith gave them both solidarity and the confidence that heaven was on their side. When we consider the very religious conception of power among all the peoples of Southeast Asia, this latter factor is not to be minimized. The magical potency of a ruler or war-leader, his skill at choosing auspicious days, invulnerable charms, and ritual preparations, had as much to do with success in battle as the weight of numbers or armaments. The first few casualties in a battle were therefore likely to decide the outcome. Whenever a determined force confident of its own destiny appeared in Southeast Asia, whether Muslim or Christian, it was able to achieve victories out of all proportion to its numbers. → how? was it that this confidence allowed them to battle more voraciously + intimidate their enemies?

THE MAINLAND EXAMPLE

Muslim trade also played a major role in Siam and Cambodia in the sixteenth and seventeenth centuries. The commercially-oriented Cham who fled their homeland and settled around the Cambodian capital near modern Pnompenh were all Muslim, or at least had become so by 1600. The western Muslims, particularly Persians and Chulias from South India, dominated the trade routes overland from Mergui, Junkceylon (Phuket), and Kedah to the ports on the east coast, and thence to Bangkok and Ayudhya. All along this route the governors of towns, nominally under Ayudhyan sovereignty, were Persian or Indian Muslims. In the middle of the seventeenth century a Persian Muslim, Okphra Sinnarat, was the dominant official in charge of commerce (Barcalon) even in the capital, Ayudhya. The third and most numerous Muslim element was the community of Malay traders conducting trade between the Siamese and Cambodian capitals and such ports as Patani, Johor, Aceh, Banten and Makasar. As the Dutch squeezed Muslim (and Portuguese) trade out of more and more centres in the Archipelago, Ayudhya and Cambodia tended to receive an increased number of politico-economic refugees.

The question therefore should be asked, why these ports too did not become Muslim in the seventeenth century. The factors which account for this difference shed a good deal of light on the process of Islamization in the remainder of Southeast Asia.

Firstly, it is of course true that commerce was less important to these two states than to those of the Archipelago. The option of closing themselves off altogether to outsiders, Europeans as well as Muslims, which the Mainland states eventually took in the late seventeenth century, was not really open to the Archipelago states—however hard Sultan Agung and his successors may have tried in Java. In the case of Siam, but not Cambodia, we would have to add that a higher degree of integration of the country around the central institutions of kingship and the Buddhist *sangha* had probably been achieved by the seventeenth century than in any Archipelago state. Yet even with these two factors taken into account, it was still an open issue whether these states would fall to the superior power of Muslim arms.

The Muslim element first showed its strength in the confused period in Cambodia following a Siamese invasion of 1593. Malays, Chams, Chinese, Japanese, Spanish and Portuguese were all competing for influence in the Cambodian capital in the decade that followed, though it was the European adventurers who behaved with the greatest violence and greed. In 1598 the Spanish briefly placed their candidate on the Cambodian throne, earning the particular enmity of the Malays and Chams who had previously formed the basis of the royal guard. When this king sent his European mercenaries against the Muslim group, led by a Malay Laksamana from Johor, the Muslims succeeded in first routing the Europeans and then killing the king himself. As the Cambodian chronicle put it: "The Cham named Chora and the Chhvea [Malay] named Laksamana, put the King to death." (Garnier 1871, 359) The Muslims had successfully foiled the Spanish bid for power, but no other force was strong enough to assume power until a measure of order was restored in 1602–3 by the renewed intervention of Ayudhya in support of a Siam-educated Cambodian prince (San Antonio 1914; Boxer and Groslier 1958; Morga 1609, 119–36).

The Muslim element had however emerged from this crisis with some claim to being the real defenders of Cambodian independence, and so they remained through much of the seventeenth century. Their principal antagonists now became the Dutch VOC, here as throughout Southeast Asia.

The regent in authority in Cambodia in the period 1625–42 leaned towards concessions to the Dutch, who of course wanted a monopoly position in Cambodia. He thereby alienated the Muslims, who supported a coup d'état against him in 1642. This placed on the throne a usurper apparently named Chan, who ruled in conditions of considerable disorder, leaning ever more heavily on his Muslim supporters, further wooed by taking a Malay wife. A party of Dutch traders was massacred in 1643, and Dutch attempts to obtain revenge either directly or by stirring up Cambodia's neighbours were not entirely successful. Heavily dependent on Muslim arms, the new king himself became a Muslim, adopting the title Sultan Ibrahim and establishing on the Mekong a replica of a Malay court. Eventually his enemies became too numerous, however. The Dutch forced him to sign a humiliating treaty in 1653, and internal Buddhist opposition increased. This made it easier for the Vietnamese in turn to intervene in 1658-60, replacing Sultan Ibrahim with another Cambodian prince who had a Vietnamese mother. Cambodia remained a battleground for the rest of the century, but Vietnamese and Siamese influence was now more important than either Muslim or European (Muller 1917; Garnier 1871, 364–6; *Dagh-Register* 1643–4: 17–18, 22-4, 42–3; 1656–7: 36–7, 118–19, 146–50).

Siam was of course in a better position to defend itself, yet the same pattern of rivalry between the Dutch and the Muslims for dominant external influence made itself felt there. Whereas Persians, Malays, and for that matter Portuguese, Chinese and Japanese, were willing to enter the service of rulers such as Prasat Thong (1630–56) and Narai (1658–88), the Dutch always loomed as a dangerous monolith working in the interests of monopolizing the trade of Southeast Asia for the VOC. This was a major reason why Siamese kings, among others, tended to lean towards Muslim traders who offered both economic and military support against the Dutch. Muslim influence appears to have reached its peak towards the end of Prasat Thong's reign and the beginning of Narai's. The major Persian source for events in Siam insists that Persians had a large part in Narai's seizure of power, and were leading this king towards Islam in the early part of his reign (O'Kane 1972, 77–8, 94–106). Okphra Sinnorat was regarded by the Dutch, even after his conversion to Buddhism, as the centre of a very powerful pro-Muslim lobby at court (*Records of the Relations*, II: 208–12). In 1668 ambassadors from Golconda and Aceh arrived in quick succession at the Siamese capital, both hoping that King Narai would accept Islam. They were well received with customary Siamese hospitality, leading to great concern on the part of French missionaries who had been led to hope for great things by that same hospitality (*Records of the Relations*, II: 92; Anderson 1890, 233; O'Kane 1972, passim).

There was apparently no overt military bid for Muslim power in Ayudhya, however, until it was clearly too late, with Muslim influence definitely on the wane. The supremacy of Constance Phaulkon at the Siamese court after 1680 with his pro-French policy, pushed the Muslims into a corner in a similar manner as had occurred in Cambodia almost a century earlier. As in the Cambodian case, there must also have been sympathy for the Muslim rebels on the part of factions at court who resented the strength of European influence, and who were to revolt successfully against that influence in their turn in 1688. The Muslim revolt, however, came two years too early, in 1686, and ended in disarray. Whatever help had been expected either from within the country or from Malay forces outside, it failed to materialize and the only effective rebel force became the small Makasarese refugee community, at most a few hundred strong. Even so, the remarkable success of the Makasarese in holding out for several days against the Siamese army and its substantial European reinforcements, indicates once again the military potential of a determined Muslim minority (*Records of the Relations*, II: 136–8; Turpin 1908, 53–64).

The Mainland evidence appears to suggest that without the complication of powerful foreign intervention, by Europeans, Siamese and Vietnamese in Cambodia, and Europeans in Ayudhya, the Muslim element might have played a similar role in these states as it had earlier in Java. By the seventeenth century European power was already in the ascendent and the Muslims were making their last stands at one point after another. We do not know whether or how far ethnic Thais and Cambodians were assimilating into the Muslim/Malay community of successful traders, as was happening elsewhere. Even if this were not occurring, however, the history of these countries confirms the importance of military power as one of the factors most critical in the rise of Islam in Southeast Asia.

In conclusion, then, we need to distinguish between the gradual progress made by Islam at a popular level, and its victory in the royal courts of the already Indianized states. The key factors at a popular level were the rapid social change Southeast Asia was undergoing and the ability of Sufi practice, as filtered through India in the thirteenth to sixteenth centuries, to cater for the world of spirits with which Southeast Asians were familiar. The fall of the Indianized courts to Islam, however, required some additional factors, including the network of commercial and tributary relations established by Majapahit, and the particular power balance prevailing in the Archipelago.

NOTES

1. Among an abundant anthropological literature, see especially Huntingdon and Metcalf (1979); Metcalf (1982); Motomitsu (1978); Schärer (1963); Loeb (1935, 74–93); Forth (1981, 83–103, 171–213); Stöhr and Zoetmulder (1968, esp. 219–26); Werner (1974); Koubi (1975, 105–19); Volkman (1979, 1–16). Since the original article was written the literature has grown much further. I will mention only Kipp and Rodgers (1987) and my own discussion in Reid (1993a, 132–73) and the literature cited there.

2. 2. The title by which Yusuf is known in Makasar, Tuanta Salamaka (our lord who preserves us) indicates the intentions of the hundred of visitors bringing offerings daily to his tomb.

3. I owe this point among others to Ann Kumar, whose then unpublished work (1985) stimulated my thinking on these questions.

4. I am grateful to M. Shalleh Putuhena of the IAIN Ujung Pandang for this information on practice in the Moluccas.

5. See Galvão (1544, 104–5). This text and other Portuguese sources date the introduction of Islam to Ternate at about 1460–70. The Ternate chronicles used by Valentijn and other Dutch writers, place the beginning of Islamic rule in the reign of Sultan Zainal Abidin (1486–1500?), though listing earlier fourteenth century chieftains also with Arabic names and Javanese connections. This may suggest a two-stage process of Islamization, the first being very superficial (Clercq 1890, 148-50; Manusama 1977, 6–7, 45–6, 86–7).

6. It seems possible that the writer of the original *Hikayat Raja-Raja Pasai* was himself among these captives, since his account of Pasai ends with a sympathetic account of the invasion of it by a glorious Majapahit, while the only known text was copied in 1814 from a text then in the possession of the *bupati* of Demak, one of the heirs of Majapahit's power in Java.

7. I cannot, however, follow Robson in accepting Maspero's dismissal of Islam in Champa before 1471 in apparent disregard of the contrary evidence assembled by Fatimi (1963, 42–57).

CHAPTER THREE

CHAMS IN THE SOUTHEAST ASIAN MARITIME SYSTEM

HISTORIOGRAPHICAL TRENDS

The past decade has seen a striking revival of interest in the maritime dimension of Asian, and especially Southeast Asian, history. For most of the previous century the emphasis of historiography had been all the other way. The exuberant diversity of Southeast Asian life was chopped up by European colonialism into a dozen colonial states with fixed borders. Colonialism and nationalism made common cause in establishing unified institutions and identities within these borders. New histories were created to link the states struggling into life from the chrysalis of colonialism with older kingdoms in imagined golden ages, whatever the perils of doing so for the minority peoples caught within the new borders. There was, moreover, a romanticization of the peasantry (itself a late nineteenth century invention) as the mystical heart of these new states, the "people" par excellence whom the national state was meant to serve. All this left little room for the multiplicity and mobility of identities which the Southeast Asian maritime world had always comprised. For peoples whose identity in no sense fitted the new boundaries, of whom the Chams are a prominent example, that historiographical tendency was particularly unhelpful.

Recent scholarship, however, has recovered the sea as a unifying principle in Southeast Asian history, and one which paid little heed to those boundaries which European colonial nationalism insisted on drawing on land. Following Braudel's work on the Mediterranean, a number of volumes appeared which considered the Indian Ocean, the South China Sea, and the Java Sea—as well as lesser areas such as the Sulu Sea—as unifying fields around which societies interacted (Chaudhuri 1985; Das Gupta, Ashin and Pearson 1987;

Chandra 1987; Reid 1988, 1993a; Lombard and Aubin 1988; Kathirithamby-Wells and Villiers 1990; Ptak and Rothermund 1991; Houben et al. 1992; Warren 1981). Two recent inaugural lectures by Southeast Asian historians, Professor Adri Lapian in Jakarta and Professor Kathirithamby-Wells in Kuala Lumpur, have stressed precisely this maritime theme. Within such a framework it was possible to understand and celebrate the groups which have helped create the modern world by mediating between peoples and places as traders, shippers, pilgrims, scholars, adventurers and warriors. Traders whose origins may have been in Canton, Fujian, Yunnan, Hadhramaut, the Coromandel Coast, Patani or Minangkabau, travelling scholars within the Muslim, Buddhist, Confucian or Christian traditions, functioned in Southeast Asia as brokers of goods and ideas, who enabled people to relate to one another. In the nationalist histories of past decades they appeared marginal or anomalous, but in the newer writing we see today they begin to emerge as pioneers of modern internationalism.

The revival of interest in the Cham is a reflection of this new appreciation of diversity and ambivalence in the region. The Cham were an embarrassment to both Vietnamese and Khmer nationalism, a reminder that borders had not always been where they came to rest in the colonial era, and that group identities were by no means fixed or immutable. They were a maritime and mobile people whose influence was felt as far afield as Java, Sulawesi and the Philippines, but who defied attempts to draw lines on the map indicating where they "belonged". In this they were characteristic of Austronesian-speakers, the mariners and rovers par excellence of the pre-modern world.

AUSTRONESIAN MARITIME IDENTITIES

Austronesian is the term preferred by linguists for the language family which appears to have developed in Taiwan between five and seven thousand years ago. Having brought agricultural techniques to that island from south China, adapted to island living, and learnt to navigate the Formosa Straits, from around the third millennium B.C. Austronesian-speakers must have carried techniques of shifting cultivation, boat-building and pottery-making southward to develop the Malayo-Polynesian sub-group of languages in or around the modern Philippines. By the first millennium B.C. western Malayo-Polynesian must have reached the modern Chamic area, as well as Borneo, Java, Sumatra and Sulawesi (Bellwood 1992). For a period probably during the first millennium A.D., this group of Austronesian-speakers travelled as far as Madagascar, not once but on a regular basis, to establish a western Malayo-Polynesian (Malagasy) culture which developed independently thereafter. Meanwhile an eastern Malayo-Polynesian group of languages developed on the coasts of what is now eastern Indonesia (Halmahera and Irian), whence it was carried throughout the Pacific, to Tonga, Samoa, Hawaii and New Zealand.

These amazing voyages made Austronesian the most far-flung language family of the pre-modern world. The pioneers who carried their languages across a third of the globe were pre-eminently people of the sea and coast, who understood wind and tide, the making of boats with outriggers, and who lived on a diet of cultivated tubers and millets, the product of palm and sago trees, and fish from the sea. They tied thousands of islands, and the parts of the Eurasian land mass adjacent to them, into a network of trading relations of interdependence. They were the pioneers who, already fifteen hundred years ago, knitted island Southeast Asia into a global system of trade which stretched from eastern Indonesia to China and Japan in the north and to Portugal and Ireland in the west.

While the tyranny of distance and the lack of any particularly valuable trade items tended to isolate the Polynesian islands, the world demand for east Indonesian spices ensured that the Southeast Asian Austronesians remained in contact with each other and the world. Cloves, nutmeg and sandalwood were sent to the north and west in small quantities from as early as Roman and Han times. Records of shipments reaching Europe are continuously available from only the tenth century, and they show a trickle of nutmeg and clove rising to a steady stream at the end of the fourteenth century. Austronesians, with intermittent stimulus from Chinese, were the carriers of these spices around the Archipelago, to entrepots such as Sri Vijaya, Melaka, Pattani and Banten. In a sense they colonized as far as Maluku and Timor, and kept them on the known map of world commerce. The Europeans and Chinese who had consumed the clove, nutmeg and sandalwood of the eastern Indonesian islands did not know where they came from until they themselves began making voyages to the island word. The Portuguese were of course the first Europeans to succeed in the long quest to discover the source of the spices, and one of them reported soon after reaching Melaka:

> The Malay merchants say that God made Timor for sandalwood and Banda for [nutmeg and] mace and Maluku for cloves, and that this merchandise is not known anywhere in the world except in these places (Pires 1515, 204).

In the perspective of Asian traders it was these islands which represented "the outer edge of the world" (Pinto 1578, 393; also Wolters 1970, 23–4), meaning the world of constant commercial exchanges. Of course there was some exchange across the Arafura and Timor seas, with a few slaves and birds of paradise from New Guinea and the surrounding islands being traded as far as Java. In comparison with the intense maritime commerce throughout the Austronesian areas of Southeast Asia, however, the low level of interaction beyond its boundaries was striking.

While linguists note the divergence over a thousand years ago of Taiwanese, Chamic, Philippine, western Indonesian and Madagascar sub-families of Austronesian, outside observers were struck at how much common ground there was between these groups in relatively recent times. In the eyes of Chinese, according to the seventeenth century Dutch traveller Wusthoff, "the inhabitants of Champa resemble the natives of Taiwan" (Wusthoff, 1642). In noting the skills of Javanese seamen, the Portuguese chronicler Couto noted:

> It is certain that they formerly navigated to the Cape of Good Hope, and were in communication with the east coast of the island of San Lorenzo [Madagascar], where there are many brown and Javanised natives who say they are descended from them. (Couto 1645, IV, iii: 169)

And around the coastal fringe of the Indonesian islands, a French traveller explained, "all the people of the parts beyond Melaka, and called by the Portuguese La Sonde [the Sunda Islands], differ nowise in features, colour, dress, language or customs—in fact they are the same people" (Pyrard 1619, II, i: 167). He went on to explain his theory that this was brought about through the frequency of their maritime interaction:

> The islands are fertile in peculiar fruits and merchandise, such as spices and other drugs that are found nowhere else; excepting Sumatra and Java which are fertile of all things the rest abound in only one particular thing and are sterile of all else. So this one product wherewith they abound must furnish them with everything else; this is why all kinds of food are very dear, save their own product, which is cheap, and why these people are constrained to keep up continual intercourse with one another, the one supplying what the other wants. (Pyrard 1619, II, i: 169)

Of course it must be said that Pyrard knew nothing of the interior peoples of all the larger islands, with their extraordinary diversity. His tribute is nevertheless a remarkable testimony to the interconnectedness of the trading centres throughout the Austronesian island world.

Involvement in maritime commerce was undoubtedly one of the themes that maintained a sense of common identity among Austronesians of otherwise diverse culture. As well as carrying their own produce into world markets, Austronesians commanded all the sea routes between east Asia and the rest of Eurasia. Whether shipping passed through the Melaka or the Sunda or the Lombok and Makasar Straits; whether portages were made across the Malay Peninsula from Melaka, from Kedah or from Tenasserim; whether traffic to and from China took on water and supplies along the Cham coast of Indochina and the east coast of the Malay Peninsula, or in the Philippines and eastern Borneo, or along the west coast of Borneo and Java, Austronesians were directly involved. In the long and often intense commercial and diplomatic relationship between Southeast Asia and China, it was Austronesians who took most of the initiatives at least until the Southern Sung dynasty (1127–1279) stimulated the creation of a Chinese sea-going fleet (Wolters 1970, 19–42). The Malay culture hero, Hang Tuah, was appropriately depicted sailing, trading and fighting for his king in China, India and the Middle East as well as Java and Siam.

While the Malay and Javanese maritime tradition is well known, it is worth recalling Dampier's praise also for some Hindu Chams, whose "very pretty, neat vessel" he encountered in the Gulf of Siam, carrying forty crew and a cargo of rice and lacquer to Dutch Melaka in 1687:

> They were of the idolators, Natives of Champa, and some of the briskest, most sociable, without Fearfulness or Shyness, and the most neat and dextrous about their Shipping, of any such I have met with in all my Travels. (Dampier 1697, 272)

CHAM CONNECTIONS WITH ISLAND SOUTHEAST ASIA

This common commitment to maritime commerce helps explain why many Southeast Asian Austronesians retained greater similarities in culture than would be expected by their wide dispersion. Relatively close contacts at periods during the last thousand years have made possible some cultural borrowings which bulk larger than the shared linguistic heritage of the remote past in contemporary construction of identity. The ports of Champa had some particularly strong connections which are explicable in terms of the trading system in the South China Sea.

The first point to stress is that China was the greatest centre of population and manufacture in the world throughout the period of Champa's prominence (roughly A.D. 300–1500). For Southeast Asian maritime states the exchange of their forest and sea products for Chinese metals and manufactures was always the readiest source of the material resources on which to establish a kingdom. Tribute relations with the Chinese court were the safest and most profitable means for rulers to engage in that trade. Indeed it gave rulers endorsed by the imperial court an enormous advantage over their rivals. Champa enjoyed the most fortunate location in Southeast Asia for this commerce with China. All shipping between China and the rest of the world (except the Philippine archipelago and Japan) hugged the Champa coast at least for the five hundred kilometres between Cape Varella and Culau Cham (just south of modern Danang) and usually, for those travelling from the Melaka Straits (and hence usually India) or Siam, for an equal distance southward almost to the Mekong Delta (Mills 1979, 73–5).

As the last port of call before this stream of shipping sailed across the Gulf of Tonkin to South China, Champa had to be heavily involved in the trade, tribute, and voyages of pilgrimage moving to and from China. Even hostile ships would stop at one of its natural harbours for water, and friendly ones would take on cargo, people, and ideas. Most of this shipping was manned by Austronesian-speakers. Not until the twelfth century did Chinese take a significant role themselves in the trade, and only in the sixteenth did they become dominant in it at the expense of Malays and Javanese (Reid 1993a, 36–45). As would be expected from its geographical position, as well as the need of rulers for Chinese assistance against local rivals and the ever-threatening Vietnamese, Champa shows in Chinese records as the most faithful sender of tribute missions whenever the state was well enough organized to do so. The pattern began as early as 284 A.D., when the Lin-yi (Champa) king sent an official embassy of tribute to China. In this he was no doubt aided by his chief counsellor Wen, a Sino-Cham or acculturated Chinese, who later travelled to China in 313 and 316, gained much from the experience, and took over the Lin-yi polity himself in 336 (Coedès 1968, 44–5). About twenty missions were sent in the seventh century, and a similar number in the ninth—far more than other Southeast Asian states of much larger population. Apart from a few periods of disturbance between 1391 and 1403, Champa sent tribute virtually every year from the establishment of the Ming Dynasty in 1368 until 1446, when the Emperor ordered that envoys be sent no more than once every three years because of the excessive expense (Wade 1991; Reid 1993a, 15–16).

The connections of Champa with Java and the Malay world, apparently strong though poorly documented, are best understood as a product of this maritime route for traders and pilgrims between India and Southeast Asia on the one hand and China on the other. For long-distance travellers, the other major Southeast Asian stopover was usually Java or Srivijaya, depending which was the more orderly. As early as the fifth century, for example, a Kashmiri Buddhist teacher named Gunavarman made converts in both Java and Champa as he travelled east by sea (Mabbett 1986, 295). During the substantial periods between the eighth and fourteenth centuries when Java was united and prosperous enough to send missions to China, it represented the strongest of Champa's Austronesian connections. The first presumed mention of Javanese in Cham inscriptions is usually taken as the raids by "ferocious, pitiless, dark-skinned sea raiders" against Cham towns in 774 and 787, and against Tongking in 767 (Coedès 1968, 91, 95; Lafont 1987, 76–7), though Hall (1992, 259) believes these are just as likely to have been local boat people. Either way it is an early indication of the frequently disturbed nature of this coast, on which passing traders often either engaged in a little piracy or defended themselves against it. From the eighth to tenth centuries the Mataram kingdom in Java was a great centre of Mahayana Buddhist influence with Tantric elements. This influence appears to have spread along the route to China, to Cambodia as well as Champa. Some historians refer to a "Javanese" stylistic period in Champa, and similarities are noted between the Mi-son temples in Champa and the Borobodur in Java. An inscription of 911 at Dong Duong records two journeys of the Cham courtier Rajadvara to Java to study its Tantric secrets of royal power (Coedès 1968, 123; Hall 1992, 258; Mabbett 1986, 297).

In the fourteenth century the connection between Champa and Java (now flourishing under Majapahit) was again close, and associated in Javanese tradition with the first appearance of Islam. The two states exchanged royal princesses and diplomatic missions, and King Che Nang chose Java as his refuge from Vietnamese pressure on the Cham capital in 1318 (Robson 1981, 276; Hall 1992, 258). Perhaps it is to these connections that the annual new year feast of *radja* among Vietnamese Cham Muslims relates. As described by Aymonier a century ago, a female shaman was the principal celebrant, interceding with a variety of spirits from beyond the seas, during the three days of feasting, dancing and praying on an elevated and decorated platform. A boat-like piece of wood was introduced and an envoy from Java descended from it to demand tribute. After much hilarity over the failure of the locals to understand Javanese, a tribute of eggs, cakes and bananas was finally placed on the "boat", along with a paper monkey (Aymonier 1891, 88–91).

Both Malay and Javanese traditions make much of the Champa-Java connection. The very pro-Javanese Banjarmasin chronicle, compiled long after these events, lists Champa (as well as, anachronistically, such seventeenth century kingdoms as Aceh, Patani and Makasar) as tributaries of Majapahit (*Hikayat Banjar*, 292, 416). Another key Malay text, the *Sejarah Melayu* (135), claims that a ruler of Champa journeyed to Majapahit to make his homage, fathering there a child by a Majapahit princess. This child grew up to become the penultimate ruler of Champa before the capital, Vijaya, fell to

the conquering Vietnamese. Majapahit itself, as reflected in the
Nagarakertagama, was certainly aware of Champa along with Cambodia,
Annam and China, but not necessarily as a tributary (Pigeaud 1960, 18, 98).
Indeed many of the traditions of Java suggest that dependence was the other
way around. At least one version of the legend of Aji Saka, the bringer of
Hindu civilization to Java, has it that Aji Saka stopped in Champa on his
way to Java, married a Cham princess there, and was later succeeded in his
civilizing role in Java by a son of this marriage, Pangeran Prabakusuma
(Lombard 1981, 286–7). More widespread traditions assert that it was
through a Cham princess married to the king of Majapahit, and her brother
Raden Rahmat, that Islam entered the Javanese court. To complete the
Austronesian triangle, Rahmat took as his wife a lady of Tuban named Nyai
Ageng Manila—perhaps evidence of Philippine birth (*Babad Tanah Jawi*,
20–1).

As Java fragmented and the Malayo-Muslim port-states became more
important in the fifteenth century, Champa's connections shifted to the
Melaka Straits region. Chinese records show that in 1418 envoys came
together to China from Champa, Melaka, Lamri (modern Banda Aceh) and
Shi-la-bei (another Sumatran state, difficult to identify). In 1438 the King of
Champa complained that the envoys he had sent to Samudra (or Pasai—
modern Lhokseumawe in northern Sumatra), the principal Muslim state in
Southeast Asia at that time, had been detained and prevented from reaching
their destination by the Siamese (Wade 1991). These precious fragments of
information help to sustain a presumption that the Malay (and in some
periods Javanese) ships which traded frequently to China up until the
sixteenth century (Reid 1993a, 38–40) called regularly at one or more Cham
ports, and that their crews intermingled with Chams all along this trading
route. Chams in this way became sufficiently familiar with Malay culture to
have adapted two of the most famous Malay epics, the *Hikayat Indraputra*
and the *Hikayat Dewa Madu*, into Cham, presumably between the fifteenth
and seventeenth centuries (Chambert-Loir 1987, 98–101).

Although there were certainly Muslims in Champa in the fifteenth century
and earlier, Islam was a consequence rather than a cause of the close relations
between Malays and Chams. As Chambert-Loir has pointed out, the Malay
texts were borrowed in pre-Islamic form without any of the later Muslim
alterations. The Cham ruling class was still Hindu at the time of the
Vietnamese conquest of Vijaya (Qui Nhon), which Vietnamese and Chinese
sources date in 1471. It is striking that the Malay Muslim author of the
Melaka royal chronicle identifies as Hindus the Champa nobles who took
refuge in Muslim Melaka and Pasai after the loss of their capital (*Sejarah
Melayu*, 136–7). There must have been a strong commercial and political

bond with the Malay world which overrode the difference in religion—
though the Chams did eventually become Muslim in exile. The king of
Champa, with his capital further south in Phanrang, remained a Hindu until
at least 1607, when a visiting Dutch admiral was told that the king's younger
brother and deputy "would like to become Moor but dares not for [fear of]
his brother". Champa was nevertheless then closely allied with Malay Johor
against Vietnamese, Khmer and Portuguese, and Islam was encouraged
among the coastal population through the building of mosques (Matelief
1608, 120–1; also Manguin 1979, 269; Lafont 1987, 78).

The other important maritime connection of Champa was eastward, to the
Philippines and Brunei. This requires some explanation. In early Ming times
when Chinese interaction with Southeast Asia was relatively intense, Chinese
shipping travelled to the south either by a western route via Champa or an
eastern route via southern Taiwan and western Luzon. When these routes
were both operating in the late fourteenth and early fifteenth century, and
again after 1567, there would have been little contact between Champa and
the Philippines. At an earlier period, however, before the eastern route was
developed, the Philippine trade and tribute does appear to have reached
China via Champa. The first tribute mission recorded from any Philippine
island, from Butuan in eastern Mindanao in 1001 A.D., gave rise to the
description of Butuan in the Sung Annals as "a small country in the sea to
the east of Champa, further than Ma-i [Mindoro], with regular
communications with Champa but rarely with China". In 1007 Butuan
petitioned the Emperor to be given equal status with Champa, but was sternly
told, "Butuan is beneath Champa" (cited Scott 1984, 66; also Wade 1993,
83–5). Scott believes that it was only about the thirteenth century that the
direct route between Luzon and Fujian became common, and that all trade
to China previously went by way of Champa along a route described much
later in the *Shun Feng Xiang Song* (Scott 1984, 67, 72; Mills 1979, 81).

In my view the contacts of Luzon (particularly the Manila Bay area) with
southern China became much more intense as a result of the numerous
Chinese missions along the eastern route to the Philippines between 1372
and 1427, when frequent tribute missions from "Luzon" and other Philippine
locations were recorded. While this period created a Chinese-influenced
commercial culture in the Manila Bay area, linked to others in Brunei and
Mindoro, its direct contact with China was lost in the mid-fifteenth century
as the Ming Emperors lost interest in tribute and banned private trade from
these regions. Trade was then redirected to Melaka, where the "Luzons" were
prominent traders at the time of the Portuguese arrival in 1511, sending their
ships on both the Manila-Brunei-Melaka and the Melaka-Champa-Canton
runs (Reid 1996, 34–5). There was therefore some connection between these

"Luzons" (Muslim Tagalogs or Sino-Tagalogs) and Chams, though an indirect one. It became closer when the old route between Champa (or at least Indo-China) was revived around 1500. Pires' statement (1515, 123) that "Chinese" had begun sailing direct to Brunei about this time should probably be interpreted to mean Chinese or Sino-Southeast Asians based in Champa or Siam. Neither the early Portuguese nor Magellan's expedition mention Chinese from China trading to the Philippines or Brunei, but Pigafetta (1524, 33) did come across a ship from "Ciama" (Champa or Siam) in Cebu. A Spanish source of the 1590s suggestively identified the source of Champa's Islamic influence as "Brunei and other Muslim countries" (Manguin 1979, 270). As late as the 1820s a knowledgeable British trader reported hundreds of vessels regularly sailing between the Cham coast and those of northern Borneo and the western Philippines (Dalton, cited Wade 1993, 85–6).

Though more complicated to explain, there were therefore close commercial connections between Philippine ports and those of the Cham coast in the eleventh to twelfth centuries, and again between about 1450 and 1567 (when the direct China-Philippines eastern route was permanently established). This may explain the connections with Champa which H. O. Beyer (1979, 11–12) found in Sulu sources, and which he attributed to the ninth to twelfth centuries. Still more interesting is the argument developed by Geoff Wade (1993) that the Indic scripts which were used by Filipinos at the time of the Spanish conquest are closer in form to Cham characters than to the Sumatran or Sulawesi alphabets with which they are usually compared. Wade argues that the failure of Filipino scripts to render consonantal endings of words could best be explained by the scripts having been brought from Champa by Chinese, who might have taught Filipinos to stress only the initial consonants when rendering their language into the script.

In the sixteenth and seventeenth centuries Champa continued to play a minor role in the affairs of Southeast Asia, but there was a more important element of Muslim Chams forming a kind of diaspora of traders, warriors and refugees. The group of "Malay" traders who were collectively given trading privileges and autonomies in Makasar in the mid-sixteenth century were reported to be from Johor, Patani, Pahang, Minangkabau and Champa (*Sejarah Goa*, 26–8; Reid 1993a, 126–8). Cham Muslims were among the multinational forces who were reported in the mid-sixteenth century battling the Portuguese in the South China Sea and aiding Demak's holy wars in Java, and in the seventeenth century helping even distant Makasar against the Dutch (Pinto 1578, 107, 386; Skinner 1963, 146–7). Malays and Chams were so closely aligned during the conflicts of seventeenth-century Cambodia that their Iberian enemies thought they were one people (Reid 1993a, 187–90).

It appears, then, that commercial links and a common orientation towards maritime trade linked the Austronesians along the trade routes of eastern Asia in advance of Islam. The spread of Islam to most of these areas can be seen as a consequence of this common involvement in maritime commerce, but it also served to strengthen a sense of common identity among them.

THE MANY-CENTRED POLITIES OF AUSTRONESIA

Reflecting on the ease with which authors like Heine-Geldern, Coedès, Majumdar and L. P. Briggs interpreted Southeast Asian inscriptions in terms of modern centralized states or empires, Herman Kulke has recently suggested that

> modern historians fell victim to a rather "sinister conspiracy" of ancient Indian and Chinese philosophers, historians and official scribes to conceal the historical truth, because it is well known that ancient Indian thinkers and their Southeast Asian contemporaries described the *sastric* theory of the state, whereas the court poets and authors of the inscriptions primarily aimed at a mastery of the highly-sophisticated art of poetry. None of them therefore cared for a (detailed) description of, for example, the actual structures of a state and its real borders. On the other hand, Chinese official scribes of the *Hung lu ssu*, the office which was responsible for "the reception arrangements for foreign envoys and also the recording of details about their countries," were certainly deeply interested in the actual situation among the "barbarians of the south". But in their reports, which they prepared for their emperor and which later on became available to historians, they "translated" the information not only into their own language but into their own officialese. Its idiom was deeply pervaded by the Chinese conception of their own centralized state. (Kulke 1986, 2)

Recent work has taken more serious account of the archaeological record, which shows a very different pattern of multiple settlements and shifting centres. Even such apparently impressive Southeast Asian capitals as Angkor, Funan and Majapahit have been looked at afresh as polycentric societies in fragile and temporary coalitions. Still more have the Austronesian societies scattered around island Southeast Asia shown a positive genius for resisting the claims of a centralized state. This recent reinterpretation of Southeast Asian history appears particularly helpful in attempting to understand Champa.

Let us examine briefly the other Austronesian systems of kingship in Southeast Asia, which ought to have had particular similarities with Champa.

Of these the most heavily Indianized, and the one in longest apparent contact with Champa, is Java. Its archaeological and historical record suggests a pattern of numerous kratons or court centres, owing tenuous allegiance to whichever capital managed to raise itself a little above the others. Temple complexes and inscriptions are dispersed in hundreds of places throughout the island. Although there are modest ruins of a Majapahit court capital at Trowulan, recent scholarship has pointed out that the real mystery of ancient Java, as of Sumatra and Bali, is how such apparently sophisticated Indian-influenced cultures developed without leaving the archaeological record of a central capital (Wisseman 1977, 1986; Kulke 1986, 3). Even during the heyday of Majapahit when tribute missions to China were frequent around 1400, the Chinese perceived two rival kingdoms over a long period in the Majapahit heartland itself, without even considering the diversities of Central and West Java. Once more detailed European accounts of Java become available, they reveal a dozen kings or princes warring with each other for all of the period 1500–1755 except 1620–60, even though one or two usually have larger claims to having inherited the mantle of Majapahit. Ricklefs has effectively shown that the Javanese sources dealing with this period acknowledge this diversity, even though they felt there "ought" to be one king—particularly of the lineage of the one for whom they were writing (Ricklefs 1992).

It is useful to look at Bali as a society which shared a common pre-Islamic culture with Java but preserved the essence of it until 1900, little affected by either Islamic or European conceptions of the state. After a brief period of apparent political unity at the same time as most other Indonesian societies at the peak of what I call the "Age of Commerce" (i.e. late sixteenth/early seventeenth century), Bali had returned to fragmentation by 1700. Although the nature of the Balinese state is complex and obscure, we know at least that the eight acknowledged Balinese polities of the eighteenth and nineteenth centuries were themselves internally diverse, with two kings at their centre, multiple intermarrying lineages, and strong institutions such as the irrigation cooperatives (subak) and bandjars over which the rulers had little control. As a puzzled Dutch official noted:

> Since my first arrival here, I have given myself the task of gaining a picture of
> the relationship between the rajas . . . the way of their government, their power,
> etc. The more I learned about it, the more I . . . became entangled in a labyrinth
> of complex family relations and interests (Schuurman, 1840, cited Schulte
> Nordholt 1993, 291).

Balinese culture was sophisticated and internally coherent—at least as much as stateless Batak or Minangkabau society. What held it all together, however, was not a centralized state of modern type, nor even (though this is closer) a ritual performance as sketched by Geertz, but rather a web of complex family and personal relationships, often supernaturally sanctioned.

[handwritten margin note: societies influenced by Indic models ⊕ pluralism becomes > marked]

As we move to societies less influenced by Indic models, the principle of pluralism becomes even more marked, and even more puzzling in its tenacity. Maluku (the Spice islands), now ably reexamined by Leonard Andaya, is a fascinating case because as the only source of the world's cloves and nutmeg until the late eighteenth century it had even more constant attention from outsiders than Java—or indeed anywhere else in Asia. If any area might have been expected to generate a strong state in order to deal with foreigners it would be Maluku. Yet despite all the attempts of first Muslims, then Portuguese and finally Dutch to manipulate one state to dominate the others, the Malukans remained resolutely, almost fanatically, pluralist. The two strongest states, Ternate and Tidore, were on tiny volcanic islands only five kilometres apart, yet throughout five hundred years of warring with each other and intriguing with foreigners, one never absorbed the other. Beyond this primary duality which spread itself throughout Maluku, there was a four-way division representing the cardinal points, which gave almost equal eminence to two other island kingdoms also within a day's sail of each other. The survival and interdependence of these states was seen as crucial to Maluku's well-being, even while they warred mercilessly against each other. Their necessary interdependence was spelled out in elaborate myths about the common origin of the two, four, or more kings. As Andaya points out:

> The Europeans were clearly puzzled by the relationship. Despite the sworn enmity between these two kingdoms, they continued to advise each other against any European activity which could threaten the other's well-being . . . Even in the midst of war, intercourse between the people of the two kingdoms continued. The dualism of Ternate and Tidore within the tradition of the "four" kingdoms was viewed as essential for the survival of the group. (Andaya 1993, 55)

The puzzlement of Europeans at the failure of Southeast Asian kings to fulfil their expectations of monarchy could be replicated all over the Archipelago. One of the first Spanish comments on Philippine social structure was similar:

> The inhabitants of these islands are not subjected to any law, king or lord . . .
> He who owns most slaves, and the strongest, can obtain anything he pleases . . .
> They recognize neither lord nor rule, and even their slaves are not under any

great subjection to the masters and lords, serving them only under certain
conditions. (Legazpi, 1569, cited in Blair and Robertson, III: 54)

Even Raja Suleiman, king of the nearest the Philippines offered to a state,
told Legazpi that in his domain "everyone holds his own view and opinion,
and does as he prefers" (cited Blair and Robertson, III: 325).

The major states which were generated in the eastern two thirds of the
Archipelago all had to incorporate the deep dualisms and pluralisms of their
environment. Makasar, the most powerful, was built on a contractual dualism
between the two states of Gowa and Tallo', which in turn were federations of
seven or nine lineages all with their clear rights within the united kingdom.
All Bugis and Makasar states were built on a contractual federal pattern
reinforced by solemn oaths, a system which proved exceptionally resistant to
centralized autocracy. The Dutch conqueror of Makasar, astonished at the
series of extremely complex rights, contracts and obligations to which he
became heir, noted that "The kings of Gowa and Tallo' cannot make one
false step once outside their own gates." (Speelman 1670). The Bugis
kingdoms which flourished in the eighteenth and nineteenth century had an
even more developed sense of contractualism among the local communities
who had formed a social contract of sorts to form the state. When enthroning
the king, the head of each constituting lineage ritually expressed his
autonomy: "I will conduct my own affairs, I will preserve my manners, I will
maintain my custom, only if I need it will I appeal to your advice." In return
the ruler declared to the assembly: "I will not oppose myself to your will; I
will not contradict your words; I will not prevent you from leaving Wajo' or
returning to it." (cited Pelras 1971, 173–5)

Sumatra, and the Peninsula opposite to it, provides perhaps the most useful
analogy to Champa in both ecological and economic terms. The Straits of
Melaka were, like the seas off the Champa coast, a passage through which all
shipping had to pass. It was certain that some maritime states would arise in
both locations drawing their sustenance from the traffic passing through. For
the same reason, however, both maritime zones were extremely attractive to
pirates, since the pickings were rich and the estuaries in which to hide were
many. The surviving records of both eastern Sumatra and of Champa suggest
an alternation between periods of anarchy and piracy, and periods in which
some state was able to profit sufficiently from the traffic to keep order in its
adjacent seas and require shipping to call at its port without the need for
violence.

Both regions offered a large number of rivers flowing from a hinterland
rich in forest produce towards the seaway. Each river had some maritime
settlement near its mouth with an ambition to become the major entrepot of

the region. Rather than any major centre of irrigated agriculture, the two zones offered "scattered communities that clung to the valleys and coastal plains" between sea and mountain, as Mabbett (1986, 291) writes of Champa. The history of Sri Vijaya and its Muslim successors in the Melaka Straits area would therefore be a valuable analogy for Champa even without the commercial contacts between them.

Sri Vijaya is now recognized to have exercised authority over the Straits of Melaka region at various times between the seventh and eleventh century. Yet it left no archaeological evidence of any major capital, and appeared to have been forgotten in Sumatra itself until French orientalists "discovered" it in the 1920s. As Wolters (1982, 22) puts it, "the notorious uncertainty about its geographical span and political identity is a striking instance of the amorphous nature of the great mandalas in earlier Southeast Asian history". Although a consensus is now emerging that its capital for much of the period must have been near modern Palembang, rival claims are made for Jambi in Sumatra, and various points in what is now southern Thailand. In more modern times the legacy of Sri Vijaya was spread among a great variety of small river-ports in both Sumatra and the Malay Peninsula. Even Melaka, the greatest port in Southeast Asia around 1500, could not begin to unite this "Malay" zone of the Melaka Straits, and it immediately returned to its natural fragmentation with the fall of Melaka in 1511.

In more recent times Sumatra was constantly frustrating to European officials who expected to make deals with kings which would bind their subjects. Kings there were in Sumatra, in some cases with a moment of effective central power during the peak of the age of commerce. But when the sources of that power faded, the inherent pluralism which seems so firm a part of Sumatran social structure reappeared. In each coastal sultanate there was pluralism at the very centre, represented by the *orangkaya* with a stake in commerce, without whose support the sultans could do virtually nothing. There was also another inherent dualism between the downstream (*hilir*) and upstream (*hulu*) arms of the state, the latter never having more than a very conditional reciprocity with the capital. The large number of substantial rivers ensured an almost equal number of small rulers of the river-mouth, who might sometimes send tribute to another ruler with greater charisma, but sometimes not. Beyond all this was the still more curious autonomy of self-governing Minangkabau *nagari* and Batak *huta*, which nevertheless were involved in sophisticated interrelationships of commerce, warfare and culture. They acknowledged the king of Pagarruyung as supernaturally powerful, to an extent which Europeans found hard to comprehend. Even the distant Bataks believed that if his status was challenged "their affairs would never prosper; that their padi would be blighted, and their buffaloes die", as

Marsden put it. Yet the authority of these kings was of quite a different character from that of the European Renaissance tradition. Lacking the economic or institutional resources to influence the behaviour of their subjects, it was their charisma which gave them importance. Like the Singamangaraja of the Bataks, the raja of Pagaruyung existed in a sphere which in no way curbed the complex autonomies of Sumatran society (Drakard 1993).

The social reality then was one of extreme pluralism, sometimes even to a dysfunctional degree. The ideology of kingship, however, did not so much celebrate this diversity as seek to disguise or absorb it into metaphors of oneness. One might almost say that the greater the contractual autonomies within society—as among the Minangkabau, Bugis, and Balinese—the loftier the assertions of kingly centrality in the relationship between man and the cosmos. The Minangkabau rulers claimed in their letters and seals to be equal heirs with the kings of China and Constantinople of the legacy of the world-conqueror Alexander the Great, to be the *khalif* (deputy) or shadow of God on earth (*zil'ullah fil alam*), to possess all manner of miraculous inheritances of past empires, and to be able to strike dead miraculously any who doubted these claims. As Jane Drakard (1993) has shown, these grandiose words were effective in projecting Minangkabau power outwards throughout Sumatra and beyond, though they appeared in no way (except occasionally in war) to limit the autonomy of the Minangkabau *nagari*.

One of the more interesting attempts to make sense of this pattern of internally plural states (which might better perhaps be called by another name) is Oliver Wolters' use of the Sanskrit *mandala* concept:

> the mandala represented a particular and often unstable political situation in a vaguely definable geographical area without fixed boundaries and where smaller centres tended to look in all directions for security. Mandalas would expand and contract in concertina-like fashion. Each one contained several tributary rulers, some of whom would repudiate their vassal status when the opportunity arose and try to build up their own networks of vassals. (Wolters 1982, 17)

To this I would add the essentially spiritual nature of power, which could make the name of a ruler potent over very long distances, at the same time as the vassals even within his reach in and near his capital were entirely autonomous in their day-to-day affairs.

I am inclined to endorse the view of Kenneth Hall that "the Cham polity was more like the Malay riverine states . . . than its mainland wet-rice plain neighbours to the west and north" (Hall 1992, 253). The internal diversity and flexibility characteristic of the other Austronesian states sketched above appears also to be a feature of Cham history. Hall presents a picture of "a weakly institutionalized" set of alliances in Champa, between rulers of different river systems, each of whom laid claim to spiritual and magical powers to endorse an authority which could not be guaranteed in other ways. Lacking a stable agricultural resource base, they periodically organized expeditions to acquire plunder which could be distributed to temples or individuals in order to shore up their fragile authority (Hall 1992, 252–60).

Hall's picture of a "plunder-based political economy" may be disputed for Champa at its more successful periods, as it could be for Sri Vijaya, Brunei or other Austronesian maritime polities. Much is gained, however, by seeing all these polities in their broader context.

Hall's view of Champa:
→ more like Malay marine states than mainland wet-rice neighbours
→ internally diverse; weakly institutionalised set of alliances between rulers of diff. river systems – each of whom laid claim to spiritual + magical power to endorse an authority not otherwise guaranteeable (plunder-based political economy)

CHAPTER 4

THE RISE AND FALL OF
SINO-JAVANESE SHIPPING[1]

[The Javanese] are all men very experienced in the art of navigation, to the
point that they claim to be the most ancient of all, although many others give
this honour to the Chinese, and affirm that this art was handed on from them
to the Javanese. But it is certain that they formerly navigated to the Cape of
Good Hope, and were in communication with the east coast of the Island of S.
Laurenzo [Madagascar], where there are many brown and Javanized natives
who say they are descended from them. (Couto 1645, IV, iii: 169)

The discrepancy is startling between the earliest European impressions
of Javanese shipping skills and those of the colonial era. When the
Portuguese reached Southeast Asian waters they found them
dominated by Javanese junks, particularly on the vital spice routes between
Maluku, Java and Melaka. Melaka itself was practically a Javanese city, with
skilled Javanese carpenters in the dockyard and Javanese *nakhoda* having a
great deal of say in the harbour and the market. By contrast it was notorious
by the end of the seventeenth century that the Javanese could not carry even
their own produce. While large-scale Banten shipping continued until the
Dutch conquest of 1684, the Batavia *Daghregister* reported in 1677 that "the
eastern Javanese of Mataram, besides their great ignorance at sea, were now
completely lacking in vessels of their own, even for necessary use" (cited
Schrieke 1955, I: 79).

Insofar as this extraordinary transformation has been discussed by scholars,
it has usually been seen as the destruction of a great maritime tradition in the
first half of the seventeenth century by the twin pressures of Dutch military/
commercial expansion and Mataram repression. Schrieke (1955, I: 49–79)
and Burger (1956) were the most influential authors to draw attention to

[handwritten margin notes: discrepancy between earliest European impressions of Javanese shipping skills + those of the colonial era: → b/c of Mataram repression + Dutch commercial/military expansion? or → b/c of changing European perceptions?]

such a development, and some of my writing has made the same point (e.g. see chapters 1 and 10). On the other hand the recent thesis of Luc Nagtegaal (1988, 12–14, 222–3) has argued that there was no fundamental change to Javanese maritime commerce, which remained viable into the eighteenth century. From time to time, moreover, doubt has been cast on the credibility of the earliest Portuguese accounts of huge and formidable Javanese ships, since the Portuguese appear to have defeated them with remarkable ease and may simply have been exaggerating the significance of their victories. Is it possible, then, that the disappearance of Javanese shipping is more a product of changing European perceptions, and the increasing size and efficiency of European ships as a base of comparison, than of any real collapse?

The whole issue needs to be examined thoroughly and systematically, as one of the most critical issues of Javanese history. This paper can only assemble some of the evidence, which I consider does show a spectacular flowering of maritime commerce based in Java during the fifteenth and sixteenth centuries. It is important, however, that ethnic labels such as "Javanese", change over time, and that the nature of the interaction between Javanese and Chinese is of great importance in understanding the changes.

"HYBRID" SHIPS OF THE SOUTH CHINA SEA

The famous outrigger vessel carved on the Borobodur is but one indication that ships and shipping played a large role in the affairs of Java and the Java Sea for many centuries before the fifteenth. Students of marine technology increasingly recognize a distinctive "Southeast Asian" or "Indonesian" type of vessel, still built in many parts of the Archipelago. Its hull was formed by joining planks to the keel and then to each other by wooden dowels, without using either a frame (except for subsequent reinforcement), nor any iron bolts or nails. The vessel was similarly pointed at both ends, and carried two oar-like rudders and a lateen-rigged sail. It differed markedly from the copiously described "Chinese" type of vessel, which had its hull fastened by strakes and iron nails to a frame and to structurally essential bulkheads which divided the cargo space. The Chinese vessels had a single rudder on a transom stern, and except in Fujian and Kwangtung they had flat bottoms without keels.

As Pierre-Yves Manguin (1984, 1985) has pointed out, however, this dichotomy has been undermined by the results of marine archeology over the past two decades:

Out of the dozen or so properly excavated shipwrecks in this area, seven so far have revealed hull structures that belong to a previously unheard-of

Fig. 1 Early European depiction of a 'hybrid' Sino-Southeast Asian junk
(J. Th. de Bry, *Pars Indiae Orientalis*, Frankfurt, 1599)

shipbuilding tradition that shares characteristics with both the "Chinese" and
the "Southeast Asian traditions" . . . up to now no large trading ship built with
either pure Southeast Asian or northern Chinese techniques has been reported
in wrecksites. (Manguin 1984, 198)

These wrecks, all dating between the thirteenth and seventeenth centuries,
have been found at various points around the South China Sea and the Gulf
of Siam. They appear all to have been involved in the trade between Southeast
Asia and southern China. Typically their hulls were fixed together by wooden
dowels in the Southeast Asian fashion, but with supplementary use of iron
nails to fasten the strakes to the wooden frames.

These physical finds provide a remarkable confirmation of the numerous
European reports of the sixteenth century about the large three or four-
masted cargo ships they unanimously call "junks" (Portuguese *juncos*, Italian
giunchi or *zonchi*). The word first appears unambiguously in the fourteenth

century travel accounts of Friar Odorico, John de Marignolli, and Ibn Battuta. In the sixteenth century we have much more precise descriptions, extolling the size and strength of these leviathans, and the workmanship which could construct them without nails from only the simplest tools— adze, drill and chisel in particular (Varthema 1510, 239; Empoli 1514, 48, 126, 131; Pires 1515, 194–5; Bochier 1518, 197–8; Pigafetta 1524, 59; Manguin 1980, 267–8) The first specifically Javanese junk described by the Portuguese was a vessel captured by them in 1511 on their way to Melaka, with four layers of superimposed planks which withstood the Portuguese cannon, an estimated six hundred tons burden, and a size that towered over the Portuguese warships (Albuquerque 1557, III: 62–3; Manguin 1980, 267). Once established in Melaka, the Portuguese identified Java as the home par excellence of the biggest junks:

> From the kingdom of Jaoa also come the great *junco* ships (with four masts) to the city of Malaca, which differ much from the fashion of ours, being built of very thick timber, so that when they are old a new planking can be laid over the former. (Barbosa 1518, II: 173–4)

Manguin (1980, 268) has taken the view on the basis of European accounts that the average burthen of the large freight junks would have been four to five hundred tons. The largest reported was an enormous troop-carrier of about a thousand tons, with several hulls superimposed for extra strength, built for the Javanese attack on Melaka in 1513—"beside it the *Anunciada* did not look like a ship at all" (cited Pires 1515, 152n).

Although it has been claimed that the origin of the word junk is a Chinese word for boat, *chuan*, the Javanese *jong* is a more likely candidate (Yule and Burnell 1903, 472). Manguin (1985, 24) holds that *jong* can be traced with the meaning of ship in an old-Javanese inscription of the ninth century. It had certainly entered Malay by the fifteenth century, when a Chinese word-list identified it as the Malay word for ship (Edwards and Blagden 1931, 734). The Malay Maritime Code, first drawn up in the late fifteenth century, uses junk routinely as the word for freight ships. The interesting point for my present purpose, however, is that the word was applied indiscriminately in the earliest sources to both Chinese and locally-owned vessels sailing in Southeast Asian waters.[2] If anything the latter were more impressive. Tomé Pires (1515, 122–3) was informed that authorities of Canton obliged foreign ships to anchor at an island off-shore "for fear of the Javanese and Malays, for it is certain that one of these people's junks would rout twenty Chinese junks".

The evidence of marine archeology is that the seas of Southeast Asia were dominated in the sixteenth century by large cargo ships of a common type, showing features predominantly Southeast Asian but with Chinese admixture. The literary evidence tells us that these were known as junks, with three or four masts and multiple hulls, and that they were operated by "Javanese", as well as by Chinese and Malays.

EARLY CHINESE INTERVENTION AND JAVANESE NAVAL POWER

This hybrid "South China Sea" junk, as Manguin calls it, dominated Southeast Asian waters in the sixteenth century, and according to the argument below it must already have been doing so throughout the fifteenth. To push the record back earlier than 1400 is to enter a much more speculative realm, where sources are very sparse. Few excavated shipwrecks have so far been dated earlier than the fifteenth century. There is, however, evidence that intensive interaction between Javanese and Chinese shipping traditions is at least as old as the thirteenth century, and this must be briefly considered.

Use of the word junk, as we have seen, goes back at least to the mid-fourteenth century. The hybrid type of vessel to which it referred in the sixteenth century seems remarkably similar to the ships engaged in the South China Sea trade which Marco Polo (1298, 213–15) described at the end of the thirteenth. The *Kidung Sunda*, celebrating a famous fourteenth century royal voyage from Sunda to Majapahit, explained that the king of Sunda travelled in a "*jong sasana*, such as was made in the land of the Tartars and was copied since the war of King Wijaya" (Berg 1927, 77). This war resulted from Kublai Khan's invasion of Java in 1293, the largest single Chinese intervention in Javanese history, during which Kertanegara's son-in-law Wijaya was able to manipulate the Chinese troops to his own advantage, and then harry them out of Java, leaving him on the throne. The Yuan dynastic history states that a thousand vessels carried twenty thousand Chinese soldiers from Fujian to Java to punish King Kertanegara for his insolence (Groeneveldt 1880, 21–7). "More than 3,000" soldiers were said to have been killed in Java, which makes it virtually certain that others were captured by the Javanese or remained voluntarily on Wijaya's side after his defection from the Chinese. This was therefore a highly probable time for an injection of Chinese technology and manpower into Java, which may have given rise to the hybrid ship type.

The story is more complicated than this, however. The Chinese ocean-going tradition was itself very new in this period. Up until the twelfth century, most of the trade between Southeast Asia and China appears to have been carried in Southeast Asian vessels. Only with the Southern Sung (1127–1279) was there a concerted Chinese effort to master the southern oceans (Wolters 1970, 36–42). Hence the Chinese ships built in Guandong and Fujian for southern expeditions may already have been based as much on the ocean-going ships arriving from Southeast Asia, as on the river-craft of northern China. What they introduced to ship design in Java in the late thirteenth century was probably limited to larger size, greater use of iron nails, and bulkheads dividing the cargo space (though not necessarily having the same structural purpose as on Chinese ships).

The Mongol military intervention was an isolated occurrence, but may have stimulated Chinese interaction with the Archipelago. The key evidence for this comes from the spice-producing islands of Maluku, which were first described in Wang Ta-yuan's account of 1349, apparently based on his travels in the 1330s. He made clear that it was Chinese traders at that time who were visiting Ternate and Tidore to buy cloves. "They look forward each year to the arrival of Chinese junks to trade in their country" (translated in Rockhill 1915, 259–60). This confirms the unanimous view of Portuguese writers, that it was the Chinese who pioneered the large-scale trade in cloves. As Barros (1563, III, i: 576–9) described it, the Malukans related that they had lived like savages and made no use of the cloves until Chinese, Malay or Javanese junks arrived, "but more affirm them to have been Chinese". They began selling the cloves to the Chinese, and obtained in exchange the Chinese *cash* which became their major currency. Eventually "the Javanese also responded to the commerce, and the Chinese stopped coming". Galvão (1544, 79–81) and the first Dutch account of Ternate (*De tweede shipvaart* 1599, 133) tell the same story.

Since the Chinese accounts derived from the Zheng He (Cheng Ho) voyages were unaware of Maluku, Chinese traders must have given way to Javanese on the spice route by 1400. The period 1331 to 1351 is that of Gajah Mada's expansionist policy, which according to the *Nagarakertagama* (1365) extended Javanese authority all the way eastward along the spice route to Maluku (Pigeaud 1960, 17). This period also saw the appearance of Islamic names in the king-lists of Ternate and Tidore (Clercq 1890, 148–9). Although more concrete information is lacking, something does appear to have happened about the middle of the fourteenth century which replaced the pioneering Chinese traders to Maluku with predominantly Muslim "Javanese".

Did the Javanese drive the Chinese out of the Malukan clove trade at this period? That is one interpretation, but not the only one. The success of Majapahit in dominating the Java Sea in the middle of the fourteenth century is difficult to explain without some incorporation into Majapahit designs of the existing seamen, pilots and ship-owners who plied these routes. Most of these appear to have been Chinese or Muslims (or both) by the mid-fourteenth century. The "tributary" relations which the smaller Archipelago principalities conducted with Majapahit brought diverse sailors, including Muslims and Chinese, to the ports of Java. Having come on the mixed political-commercial missions which tribute represented, they may often have been incorporated into further political-commercial expeditions from Java to other ports. The *Hikayat Raja-raja Pasai* gives some of this flavour when referring to the halcyon days of Majapahit around 1360, after Pasai itself had been conquered:

> People in vast numbers thronged the *negeri* (Majapahit) . . . There was a ceaseless coming and going of people from the territories overseas which had submitted to the king [*segala jajahan yang diseberang lautan*]. From the east they came from the Banda Islands, from Seram, and from K.r.ntok., bringing their offerings of beeswax, sandalwood, massoia bark, cinnamon, cloves and nutmeg piled high in heaps ("Hikayat Raja-Raja Pasai", 161, Malay text, 102)

That imperialism works both ways is shown by the same text's explanation that Java was studded with *keramat* (Islamic holy graves) because of the many Muslims brought there as captives after the conquest of Pasai, who were allowed to settle wherever they wished in Java ("Hikayat Raja-Raja Pasai", 159, Malay text, 100).

The maritime expansion of Java in the fourteenth century may best be seen as an incorporation into a Java-based political project of existing trade networks, in which Chinese and Muslim merchants had played key roles. "Chinese" merchants ceased to make the voyage between Java and Maluku, but largely because they ceased to be seen as such. They may have blended with the Muslim or Hindu-Javanese traders of the northeast coast of Java, or have become minor actors in the larger fleets which Gajah Mada put together to dominate the east. Wang Ta-yuan (1349) refers to Chinese traders frequenting Java but does not mention resident Chinese (Rockhill 1915, 237–8).

EARLY MING INITIATIVES IN SOUTHEAST ASIA

In the fourteenth century we are obliged to resort to conjecture, because trade was still relatively modest in scale, and the records very inadequate. With the advent of the Ming Dynasty in 1368, there is an upward leap in both respects. Mongol (Yuan) relations with the south had been military and spasmodic, and had shown little interest in private commercial activity which had therefore managed to continue. The first three Ming Emperors, on the other hand, suppressed private trade and replaced it by a sustained and vigorous series of diplomatic initiatives, designed to ensure that commercial exchange took place only in the form of frequent tribute missions from Southeast Asia to the Imperial Court.

The suppression of private trade may have been the reason why large numbers of Chinese merchant seamen took up residence in Southeast Asia at about the beginning of the Ming Dynasty in 1368, perhaps unable to return home or to conduct their former China-Southeast Asia trade without fear of punishment. Ma Huan, the Muslim chronicler of Zheng He's voyages, is the major source for this development, which appears to have begun before the admiral's official voyages to the south in 1405–21. Of Palembang, reported to be identical to Java in language, food and customs, he wrote:

Many of the people in the [Palembang] country are men from Guangdong and from Chang[chou] and Chuan[chou], who fled away and now live in this country. The people are very rich and prosperous . . .

Some time ago, during the Hung-wu period [1368–98], some men from Guangdong [province], Ch'en Tsu'i and others, fled to this place with their whole households; [Ch'en Tsu'i] set himself up as a chief; he was very wealthy and tyrannical, and whenever a ship belonging to strangers passed by, he immediately robbed them of their valuables. (Ma Huan 1433, 98–9)

Of the ports of eastern Java, Ma Huan reported (in Mills' translation):

Tuban . . . is the name of a district; here are more than a thousand families, with two headmen to rule them;[3] many of them are people from Guangdong [province] and Changchou [prefecture] in China, who have emigrated to live in this place . . .

From Tuban, after travelling toward the east for abut half a day, you reach New Village [Szu-ts'un], of which the foreign [Javanese] name is Gresik; originally it was a region of sandbanks; because people from China came to this place and established themselves, they therefore called it New Village; right down to the present day the ruler of the village is a man from Guangdong.[4] Foreigners from every place come here in great numbers to trade . . . The people are very wealthy . . .

[Seven miles further east] the ship reaches Su-lu-ma-i, of which the foreign

[Javanese] name is Surabaya . . . There is a ruler of the village, governing more than a thousand families of foreigners; and amongst these, too, there are people from China. (Ma Huan 1433, 89–90)

This is the most solid evidence for the importance of Chinese merchants in the life of the Javanese *pasisir* at the beginning of the fifteenth century. That importance must have been vastly increased by the activity of Zheng He's seven imperial fleets, each of which comprised more than a hundred vessels and tens of thousands of soldiers. Most of his voyages used the Gresik-Surabaya area to refit during a period of about four months, while awaiting an eastern monsoon in July to carry them to the Straits of Melaka (usually Palembang, Melaka and Samudra/Pasai) and across the Bay of Bengal. Specifically, these fleets were in eastern Java as part of the first five expeditions for substantial periods of 1406, 1408, 1410, 1414 and 1418, and during the seventh voyage in 1432. The sixth expedition, in 1421–2, was smaller and less well documented, but some ships may also have gone to Java (Ma Huan 1433, 8–19; Wang 1981, 70–4).

These unprecedented state trading expeditions caused a jump in the demand for Southeast Asian products. They not only brought large quantities of pepper, clove, nutmeg, sappanwood and other forest products to China, they also stimulated Southeast Asian production, and the distribution networks in the Archipelago needed to bring the prized items to market in east Java or the Melaka Straits. T'ien Ju-kang (1981) has shown that the leading products of the Nanyang trade, pepper and sappanwood, became for the first time items of mass consumption in China in the fifteenth century, and so abounded in government warehouses that they were used in part-payment of hundreds of thousands of Chinese officials and soldiers. The period from about 1370 also marked a steady upward movement in global trade, stimulated by a long-term increase in population and prosperity in both Europe and China following the ravages of the Black Death in the mid-fourteenth century. The collapse of the "Mongol peace" in central Asia moreover ensured that virtually all the increase in trade passed by sea routes through Southeast Asia, and not by the overland caravans. The Zheng He expeditions may fairly be taken as the starting point of Southeast Asia's "Age of Commerce", with a dramatic and sustained increase in the amount of shipping in the waters of the Archipelago (Reid 1990a).

SINO-JAVANESE COMMERCIAL ROLES IN THE FIFTEENTH CENTURY

In the short run this intense contact with China must have provided a more substantial injection of Chinese personnel and technology into the trade of Java than in the 1290s or any other period. Some of the Chinese who remained in Java helped to man the tribute embassies from Java to China which were the approved response to the early Ming initiatives. As with other Southeast Asian countries, the period 1369–1430 marked the peak in the use of tribute missions for economic and political purposes. The Ming Dynastic Chronicle recorded ten tribute missions from Java in the period 1370–1399, and an average of one per year in the first thirty years of the fifteenth century—more than from any other part of the Malay world (*Ming Shi Lu*; and cf. Groeneveldt 1880, 34–9; Kobata and Matsuda 1969, 151; Wang 1981, 70-8). In 1410 the Emperor instructed the Ministry of Rites to pay a higher allowance to Javanese envoys than to others (*Ming Shi Lu* I, 164), and they were frequently commended after this point for their special "loyalty" to the Middle Kingdom.

Many of the envoys whose names are recorded in the chronicles had a Chinese origin, even though they had been incorporated sufficiently into the Javanese court circle to carry the titles *patih* or *arya* (presuming these to be the probable titles represented by *pazhi* and *alie* in Chinese—see appendix). Something of the life of these Sino-Javanese cultural brokers emerges from a few particularly colourful careers. Chen Yen-xiang was among the first to initiate diplomatic relations between Southeast and Northeast Asia. He is first recorded in Korean records as an envoy of the Siamese king, arriving at the Korean court in 1394. He departed from Korea the following year, but was obliged to return after being attacked by Japanese pirates. He reappeared in 1406 as an envoy from Java to Korea, but his ship was attacked again by Japanese pirates at Kunsan island off Korea. Twenty-one were killed and sixty captured by the Japanese, but Chen was able to make his way to the Korean court with forty survivors. Although he no longer had any goods to offer, he was provided by the Koreans with a small vessel for the return journey to Java. Leaving soon after, Chen was wrecked on the coast of Japan, and again robbed of everything. This time it was the Japanese *bakufu* which provided a ship to get him back to Java. The voyage was successful, and it must have awakened in Java the desire to consolidate commercial and political relations with Northeast Asia. Some time later the Javanese kingdom sent a vessel to Japan with Chen again aboard, now proudly bearing the highest title of Javanese envoys, *arya*. Although it had to return to Java because of a storm, the vessel finally reached the Japanese port of Hakata in the seventh month of 1412. From there Chen wrote to the Korean court, saying that he wished to thank the Koreans for their help during his previous troubles, but since he was obliged first to go to Kyoto to express his appreciation to the Japanese court, he was sending his grandson Shih-chung to Korea (Kobata and Matsuda 1969, 149–50).

Another of the Java ambassadors mentioned in the Ming chronicles was Ma Yong-liang, by his name perhaps a Chinese Muslim. He told the Chinese court in 1436 that he was now representing Java with the highest title of *arya*, whereas on his previous mission he had carried the lesser Javanese title of *patih*. He again led embassies from Java to China in the years 1438, 1442, 1446 and 1447. On the 1438 visit, Ma told the Chinese court that he, as well as the two official interpreters travelling with him, were natives of Longxi in Fujian, who had accidentally washed up in Java on what was meant to be a fishing trip. It seems unlikely that this fishy story deceived anyone, but Ma was too important to be executed for the offence of trading privately to the South. He was allowed to revisit his native district, and encouraged to build a hall there to honour his ancestors. On the 1447 visit he reported that his ship had been damaged on the voyage, and the Emperor agreed to his request for Chinese wood and craftsmen to enable him to refit. Before he had returned, in September 1448, he was arrested in Canton because of a complaint from the Siamese envoy that during a previous 1444 tribute mission the Siamese interpreter Naiai[5] had stolen some of the royal tribute and absconded to Java with Ma. The last mention of Ma Yong-liang is in 1453, when on his return to Java he was entrusted with an Imperial message discouraging the Javanese ruler from sending frequent missions (*Ming Shi Lu*, II: 346, 352, 377, 387; see also Kobata and Matsuda 1969, 152–3).

There were certainly also indigenous Javanese among the envoys who went to China, since interpreters were included in every mission for translation. The frequency of these tribute missions, equipped and manned in the ports of Java albeit with a mixed crew, indicates the scale and sophistication of the Sino-Javanese trading world of the *pasisir* ports in the early fifteenth century.

CHINESE AND THE RISE OF *PASISIR* MUSLIM STATES

Controversial claims have been made for the leading role of Muslim Chinese in the expansion of Islam on Java's north coast during the fifteenth century, on the basis of evidence which is less reliable than the Chinese sources above. There is no doubt that many of the Chinese accompanying Zheng He shared the great eunuch's Muslim faith, as for example Ma Huan, a convert to Islam (Mills 1970, 34, 179). Others probably became Muslim by associating with

Muslim Chinese, Arabs and others in the ports of Southeast Asia. The only concrete indication of their relative strength is the categorization by Ma Huan (1433, 93) of the three types of people living in Java: "the Muslim people . . . from every foreign kingdom in the west who have migrated to this country"; the Chinese from Guandong and Fujian "who fled away and now live in this country . . . many of them follow the Muslim religion, doing penance and fasting"; and finally the savage Javanese, who worshipped devils and ate unclean foods.

The evidence which has been adduced for a dominant Chinese role in the building of the Muslim cities of Java's *pasisir* can be summarized as follows, in decreasing order of reliability:

1. The indication by Ma Huan and other Chinese sources that Chinese appear to have established the port-city of Gresik, and that a leader of Chinese descent was still playing a major role there in the second decade of the fifteenth century. Since Gresik was the oldest and most respected Islamic centre in the *pasisir*, this in itself suggests that the *peranakan* descendants of these Chinese may have been influential elsewhere.

2. The evidence from Ma Huan and others that there was a substantial Chinese community in Palembang, the head of which was seen by Chinese authorities as the effective ruler. In 1407 Zheng He established a Palembanger of Cantonese origin, Shih Chin-ching, in this role, and his daughters continued to exchange commercial/diplomatic missions with Ryukyu as late as 1440—though not with China, with which they seem to have had consistently bad relations (Ma Huan 1433, 98–100; Kobata and Matsuda 1969, 138–45). Palembang too played a prominent role in all Javanese accounts of the Islamization of Java's *pasisir*.

3. The Banten tradition, reported in both the *Sadjarah Banten* and the *Hikayat Hasanuddin*, that the military-commercial leader who built the greatness of Demak in the second half of the fifteenth century was descended from a prominent Chinese who became Muslim in Gresik (Djajadiningrat 1913, 21; Graaf and Pigeaud 1974, 34–9).

4. The Javanese (Mataram) tradition that the first ruler of Demak was a child of the last Majapahit king, Brawijaya, by a Chinese woman. (While Brawijaya's role is a transparent device to assert the legitimacy of the new dynasty, there was no advantage in "inventing" a role for Chinese).

5. The Javanese tradition that Kali-Nyamat, the royal and religious centre of the port-city of Japara, was established by a Chinese merchant named Wintang, who had been shipwrecked at Japara. He was converted to Islam by Sunan Kudus, and married a daughter of Sultan Trenggana of Demak who would later become queen of Japara in its commercial heyday with the title Ratu Kali-Nyamat. Wintang himself was reportedly killed in the

succession crisis following Trenggana's death in 1546 (Pigeaud 1968, II: 363; Graaf and Pigeaud 1974, 104).

6. The possibility that the style of the earliest Javanese (and other Indonesian) mosques was based on the multi-tiered pagodas of Chinese tradition, because they were built by Chinese architects (Graaf and Pigeaud 1984, 150–4).

7. The Parlindungan/Poortman text, of very uncertain origin and status, which posits a coherent network of Hanafi Muslim Chinese traders in fifteenth century Southeast Asia. This network, set in place by Zheng He himself, established the first Islamic communities in (in approximate chronological order) Kukang (Palembang), Sambas (Borneo), Gresik, Tuban, Jaratan, Lasem, Semarang, Ceribon, Ancol (Jakarta), Mojokerto. Zheng He's 1432 mission to east Java established a Muslim Chinese *bupati* ruling the Malang area (Tu-ma-pan/Tumapel?) on behalf of Majapahit. Tuban, with its Muslim Chinese leader Gan Eng Chu recognized as an intermediary by both China and Majapahit, was the headquarters of this network until about 1450, when contact with China was lost, and the Muslim Chinese community split, some abandoning Islam and turning their mosques into Sam Po Kong temples while others remained Muslim but became more Javanese. Leadership of the latter group passed to Gan's son-in-law Bong Swi Hoo, a Sino-Cham from Champa who had come to maturity in Palembang. Bong, presumed to be the Raden Rahmat or Sunan Ampel of Javanese tradition, led the forces of Islam from his base near Surabaya. The Raden Patah of Javanese tradition, warlike first ruler of Demak, was also a Sino-Javanese brought up in the Muslim Chinese circle of Palembang. He conquered Semarang in 1477, and Majapahit in 1478 and 1517 (Graaf and Pigeaud 1984, 13–36).

There is nothing inherently implausible about the picture presented by Parlindungan in the text de Graaf and Pigeaud believe to be based on a Semarang Sino-Malay original of the eighteenth century. More systematic research will have to be done, however, before it can be accepted as a credible source for the fifteenth century. Nevertheless the reason it was taken seriously by de Graaf and Pigeaud is that they knew how much corroborative evidence there already was for a large Chinese role in the building of the earliest centres of Islam on Java's north coast.

For my purposes here it is sufficient to conclude that the new Muslim ports of the Javanese *pasisir* were ethnically and culturally mixed in the first half of the fifteenth century, and that merchants, seamen and craftsmen of "Chinese" descent were the most important foreign element in them. The label "Chinese" here, it should be remembered, was no more clear-cut than the label "Javanese", as indicated by the use of "Tartar" or "Mongol" in the earliest Javanese references to them.

ISOLATION IN CHINA AND CHINESE ASSIMILATION IN THE JAVA *PASISIR*

The initiative of the Yongle Emperor during the first half of his reign was altogether exceptional in Chinese history. The first four massive Zheng He expeditions all took place in the period 1402–14, but there were also numerous other missions to specific Southeast Asian states. In total nine Chinese imperial missions went to Champa, eight to Siam, six to Melaka, six to Samudra/Pasai and ten to Java in the first eleven years of the Yongle reign. But as Wang Gungwu (1981, 70–4) has pointed out, the sense of purpose went out of Ming policy from the time of the fourth Zheng He expedition in 1413–15. As long as it looked as though China's occupation of Northern Vietnam was succeeding, Yongle's ambition seemed really to be "to protect the weak and deter the greedy" in Southeast Asia, as effective suzerain of the whole region. His stern letter of 1407 to the "western king"[6] of Java, whose men had killed 170 Chinese members of a mission to the weaker "eastern" king, is indicative of the spirit of this period:

> [We were] about to raise armies to punish [you], when your envoy A-lieh Chia-en arrived to admit your guilt. We note that you regret your actions and have for the time being stopped our forces. But thinking upon the 170 men who were killed for no reason, how can we stop there? [You should] immediately send 60,000 ounces of gold to compensate for their lives and to redeem your crime, so that you may preserve your lands and people. Otherwise we cannot stop our armies from going to punish you. The warning example of Annam is there. (*Yung-lo shih-lu*, translated in Wang 1981, 72)

After 1413, however, the only further Chinese initiatives in the region were the last three Zheng He expeditions in 1417–19, 1421–4 and 1431–3, and these were also more concerned with trade than with political arbitration. The rebellion in Vietnam, culminating in Le Loi's triumph of 1428, was one discouraging factor, and threats to the Ming from the traditional quarter, the north and northwest, was the other. In 1417 the emperor left Nanking to campaign against the Mongols in the north, and never returned. The capital was permanently shifted to Peking in 1421. Chinese policy thereafter moved from passivity to total isolation and disinterest.

As noted above, tribute missions from Java to China continued to be very frequent, since this was the only legal channel by which trade could be conducted and Chinese residents of Java could return home. Fifteen tribute missions were recorded in the 1420s, and Javanese continued to visit more frequently than envoys of any other part of Southeast Asia (except Vietnam) until the 1440s. In 1435 the Javanese envoy was given a large ship by the emperor with which to carry the envoys of eleven countries around the Indian Ocean (including Mecca and Aden) back with him to Java. When the expedition set off the following year, the king of Java was asked to send the others all back to their respective destinations, suggesting that Java was still seen in China as central to the maritime networks of the Nanyang (*Ming Shi Lu* II).

Javanese visits became too frequent for the Chinese, and in 1443, according to the Ming Chronicle,

> the Emperor wrote to the King of Java, Hyang Wisésa, and asked him to send tribute only once in every three years; and not to send any additional people beyond what was necessary to man the ship. The reason for this was that an official named Zhang Dan in Canton presented a memorial stating that missions from Java came too often, causing great expense to China, and that it was not beneficial to allow this to continue. (*Ming Shi Lu*, II: 366; see also Groeneveldt 1880, 38)

In 1453 the Emperor sent a similar message, thanking the king of Java for sending so many missions but urging him henceforth to spare them such trouble by sending fewer people less often (*Ming Shi Lu*, II: 387). Thereafter missions came very infrequently and at a low level (see table 5.1 in chapter 5).

Only five missions were reported from Java after 1453, as against forty-two in the first half of the century. Whereas previous Javanese envoys had been commended for their uprightness and loyalty, and in 1410 rewarded with higher allowances in China than other envoys (*Ming Shi Lu*, I: 164), the later missions were noted in the chronicles primarily for the violence to which they seemed particularly prone. In 1436, for example, a Javanese named Daxi killed a member of the Pasai tribute mission, whose family later petitioned the Emperor on behalf of his widow. In 1445 three members of the Java tribute mission named Pudala, Daluja and Misala were arrested for unauthorised trading with the Siamese mission, and sent for punishment to Beijing. There they quarrelled and Pudala killed Daluja. In 1460 the Javanese delegation got into a brawl in a hotel and killed six Buddhist monks (*Ming Shi Lu*, II: 370–1, 399). It seems likely that these were simple Javanese seamen insufficiently "Chinese" to cope with official requirements in China.

China's demand for Indonesian produce, and Java's need for the Chinese *cash* which had become its basic coinage, by no means abated. It now had to be met, however, by different means. Private trade remained illegal, and this was enforced with unusual strictness up to the 1450s. Two instances were recorded in the 1440s when Chinese authorities cracked down on traders who were evidently attempting to continue the trade by "smuggling". In 1444 it was reported from Guangdong Province that fifty-five men of the Chaochou region had shipped out to Java illegally for trade the previous year, and that twenty-two had remained in Java while the remainder came back. Some of them were about to return for another trip when the four ring-leaders were arrested. A thorough investigation was called for. The following year an imperial censor impeached the local authorities in Fujian for having allowed some traders of the Luhai district to sail to Java, posing as imperial envoys (Kobata and Matsuda 1969, 162). Between 1457 and 1520 the embargo against private trade was less strictly enforced, but it was easier for the merchants of Fujian and Guangdong to operate to nearby ports on the Southeast Asian mainland, under the pretext that they were simply engaging in coastal trade, than to clear on ocean voyages to Java (Wills 1974, 7; Mills 1979, 70).

This was one major reason that commercial exchange between the Indonesian Archipelago and China shifted to Melaka in the middle of the fifteenth century. The other was presumably the disturbed condition of Java, with its constant internal wars and lack of political or commercial centre, which contrasted with the stability of Melaka and the highly favourable conditions that port offered to Chinese. Melaka and Siam kept up their tributary relations with China more assiduously. Several Melaka junks visited a designated island off Canton each year (Pires 1515, 122–4). In return, Chinese junks regularly visited Melaka where they also anchored at an off-shore island (Pulau Cina). Five were there when Albuquerque's fleet arrived in 1511 (Albuquerque 1557, 97–9; Empoli 1514, 132–3).

Another means by which trade between China and the Indonesian Archipelago was able to continue was the intermediary role of the Ryukyu Kingdom (Okinawa). Its smooth tributary relations with both China and Japan enabled it to act as an entrepot for the passage of goods between these two manufacturing centres and Southeast Asia. Ryukyu records have been preserved for much of the fifteenth century, with the texts of diplomatic letters sent to Southeast Asian kings to facilitate trade. They show that it was the Chinese community of Palembang that initiated contacts by sending a vessel to Japan in 1419, the crew of which was sent home by way of Ryukyu and Siam in 1421. This initial contact appears to have stimulated Ryukyu to open commercial relations with Palembang in 1428, and with (eastern) Java in 1430. Sino-Javanese merchants probably managed the reception of Ryukyuan vessels in the Archipelago, and the accompanying correspondence in Chinese.

Six trade missions from Ryukyu to Java were recorded in the period 1430–42. Although the records of the subsequent two decades are missing, the direct relationship with Java, as with Palembang, probably ended in the 1440s. By 1463, when the *Rekidai Hoan* records are again available, Ryukyu trade had shifted sharply to Melaka, which became the entrepot for Northeast Asians trading with the Archipelago up until its capture by the Portuguese in 1511 (Kobata and Matsuda 1969, 131-63). Tomé Pires (1515, 130) reported that one, two or three Ryukyu junks reached Melaka each year.

In the second half of the fifteenth century, when direct contacts between Java and China had virtually ended, there was a marked assimilation of Chinese into the Islamic *pasisir* world. The shipping of Java was simply regarded as "Javanese" by Portuguese and other observers, with no mention of Chinese as a separate group. While this *pasisir* commercial element, which I have provocatively called "Sino-Javanese", now sent ships to China much less frequently, it expanded greatly in Archipelago trade, carrying foodstuffs and cloth to Maluku in exchange for spices, and food and spices to Melaka and Pasai in exchange for Indian cloth. "Javanese" became the major element in the population of the great emporium of Melaka, and the dominant influence in Maluku.

The Portuguese immediately encountered in Melaka both Chinese traders, moving back and forth on the route between China, Indo-China, Siam and Melaka, and Javanese traders in much larger numbers who dominated the route between Java and Melaka. By Javanese were meant people of the *pasisir* ports—Muslim, commercially oriented, and multi-ethnic in origin. When explaining the arrival of Islam in Java, Portuguese writers spoke of merchants coming there from Muslim countries—"Parsees, Arabs, Gujeratis, Bengalis, Malays and other nationalities" (Pires 1515, 182), since the Chinese they knew were not Muslim. When speaking more generally about the origins of *pasisir* dynasties and people, however, they gave Chinese the major role. Tomé Pires (1515, 182) had the excellent habit of reporting what he heard from local informants, even when it was contradictory or confusing. "They say," he wrote, "that the Javanese used to have affinity [*afenjdade*] with the Chinese". Some said that the king of Java was "a vassal, not a tributary, of the king of China" and that the latter sent his daughter to Java to marry the former, with numerous retainers and the *cash* which became the currency of Java, but that the Javanese "killed all the Chinese in Java by treachery". Others said that the *cash* came in simply because "the Chinese used to trade in Java long before Melaka existed. But now they had not been there for the last hundred years." (Pires 1515, 179). Describing the rulers of the Javanese port-states, he noted: "These lord patihs are not Javanese of long standing in the country, but they are descended from Chinese, from Parsees and Klings, and from the nations we have already mentioned." One example was the ruler of Demak whom he called Pate Rodim, whose grandfather had risen to power in Demak although originally from Gresik and variously reported as a merchant or a "slave" of the then Hindu lord of Demak (Pires 1515, 183–4). This enterprising grandfather is reasonably identified by de Graaf and Pigeaud (1974, 34–9) with the Chinese Muslim *patih* of Demak mentioned in the Banten chronicles.

Barros, whose information about Java was second hand, was even more confused about the curious relation between China and the Javanese *pasisir*. The Javanese, he reported, were

> the most civilized people of these parts, who according to what they say themselves came from China, and it appears that what they say is true, because in their appearance and in the form of their civilization they follow the Chinese closely, and have enclosed cities, and go by horse, and deal with the government of the land as they do. However since Moors from Melaka sailed there . . . and because of the war which the Moors made against them, they began to withdraw to the interior of the country near the mountains. (Barros 1563, II, ix: 352)

There must, however, have been some genuine oral tradition among Sino-Javanese families behind this Portuguese information. As Djajadiningrat (1913, 104–5) already pointed out, this was in an era before Muslim antagonism towards non-Muslim Chinese made the claiming of Chinese ancestry unfashionable. Even eighty years later, when the first Dutch fleet asked Javanese (presumably of the commercial elite) in Banten about their origins, they replied that a group of Chinese had fled the oppressive labour services of China to found a colony in Java, from which they were descended (Lodewycksz 1598, 99).

What seems clear is that the distinction between *peranakan* Chinese and *pasisir* Javanese had largely disappeared by 1510, and that the important distinction in the eyes of most was that between the Islamic/commercial *pasisir* and the Hindu/aristocratic interior. The "Javanese" whom the Portuguese encountered in Melaka, Maluku, and throughout maritime Southeast Asia were the former. They were notable for their skilled craftsmanship, their commercial habits, their proud demeanour, a social hierarchy based on trade-derived wealth, and the large number of slaves possessed by the leaders. Thus despite the lordly role of a figure like Utama di Raja ("Utimutiraja") in Melaka with his eight thousand dependent Javanese "slaves", many of them shipwrights and craftsmen, and his domination of the rice trade from Java, he was a self-made man through trade. A Javanese convert to Islam, "he was poor when he came to Melaka . . . he prospered well with his merchant trade, and became exceedingly rich" (Albuquerque 1557, 151).

This conclusion is based on sources better authenticated than the Parlindungan/Poortman text, to which I have so far avoided reference. If that text were to be admitted as based on independent evidence of the seventeenth century or earlier (which I continue to doubt), it would add substantial detail to the picture. In particular, Parlindungan/Poortman asserts that the *peranakan* Chinese community in Java split in the second half of the fifteenth century when contact with China was lost, the Muslim element becoming Javanese in culture, while another element moved away from Islam, turned its pioneering Hanafite mosques into Sam Po Kong temples, and retained its identity as a Chinese cultural minority centred around the temple and the dockyard of Semarang. Nevertheless this element cooperated closely with the Sino-Javanese Muslim elite of Demak in building and equipping its fleets, which were the most powerful in Indonesian waters at the time of the Portuguese arrival (Graaf and Pigeaud 1984, 27–30).

"JAVANESE" AND "MALAY" TRADE AROUND 1500

Ethnic labels vary over time, but also according to context. The "Jaoas" of early Portuguese writers meant firstly those from or based in the island of Java, and secondly these people or their descendants living in other ports of the region. It did not refer to language. The Javanese in Melaka certainly spoke Malay, and if Javanese was also spoken, as it must have been, the Portuguese were scarcely aware of it. "Malay" referred primarily to the ruling class of Melaka at that time. Pigafetta (1524, 88) specified that *cara Melayu* referred to the ways of Melaka, even for his Malay-speaking informants in Brunei. After the fall of Melaka in 1511, the term "Malay" expanded to indicate a real diaspora of Malay-speaking Muslims (undoubtedly of diverse ethnic origins) typically engaged in maritime trade and inhabiting numerous commercial centres of Southeast Asia. Undoubtedly, therefore, there was some shifting over time, with some of the "Javanese" of Melaka (whose forebears may have classified themselves as "Chinese" at an earlier period in Java) being identified as "Malays" later in the sixteenth century.

"Javanese" were certainly very numerous in Melaka in its heyday, to the point that a number of authorities referred to its population as predominately

Javanese (Varthema 1510, 226). In particular they were renowned as the carpenters and shipbuilders of the city. Albuquerque was so impressed with the skills of the Javanese craftsmen of Melaka that he took "sixty Javanese carpenters of the dockyard, very handy workmen" back with him to India to help repair Portuguese ships there (Albuquerque 1557, 168). When the Melaka chettiar Nina Chetu equipped trading ships to sail for Pegu, Pasai and South India under Portuguese auspices in 1512–13, Javanese also made up the majority of the crews (Thomaz 1966, 193–4; Bouchon 1979, 135). Javanese was well-enough known to the authors of the *Sejarah Melayu* for several lengthy dialogues to be quoted there.

The Melaka *Undang-undang Laut*, or Maritime Code, is the key indigenous guide to the system of trade and shipping in Melaka at its height. The code was originally authorized by Melaka's last ruler, Sultan Mahmud (1488–1511), but the text includes the following interesting passage about its authorship:

> These rules arise from the rules of Patih Harun and Patih Elias and Nakhoda Zainal and Nakhoda Buri [or Dewi] and Nakhoda Isahak. They were the ones who spoke. Then they discussed it with all the nakhodas; after they had discussed it, they went to Dato' Bendahara Sri Maharaja [who obtained the Sultan's approval] . . . Then titles were bestowed on all these nakhodas by Seri Paduka Sultan Mahmud Syah . . . Nakhoda Zainal was given the title Sang Naya 'diraja, and Nakhoda Dewa was given the title Sang Setia 'dipati, and a third was given the title Sang Utama 'diraja. (Winstedt 1956, 46)

Patih Harun and Patih Elias at least appear likely to have had Javanese origins, since *patih* was a title borne not only by the rulers of the Javanese *pasisir* port-states, but also by prominent Javanese merchant-aristocrats including many of the fifteenth century Javanese envoys to China and the Portuguese-appointed headman of the Javanese in Melaka's Javanese quarter of Upeh, "Pate Quedir" (Pires 1515, 182–8). If the man given the title Sang Utama 'diraja was still carrying it at the Portuguese conquest in 1511, this was the largest Javanese merchant in Melaka, an old man who had so prospered by dominating the rice and spice trade between Java and Melaka that he had eight thousand Javanese "slaves" with him in Melaka. His son was another *patih*, "Pate Acoo" (Pires 1515, 280–2; Albuquerque 1557, 151).

The Malay Maritime Code, then, was a collaborative effort in which the Javanese who were the most numerous Malay-speakers involved in the city's shipping played the leading role. One of the key concepts in that code is that of the *kiwi* (travelling merchant), who travels in a ship belonging to someone else and is therefore subject to the authority of the *nakhoda*. The *kiwi* had specified rights, however, such as to be consulted when cargo was jettisoned, or on other matters which would affect the commercial outcome of the voyage. After reaching port, the *nakhoda* was entitled to sell first the merchandise for which he was responsible; four days later the *kiwi* might begin to sell their merchandise; and two days after that the sailors could sell theirs (Winstedt 1956, 39, 44). *Kiwi* is no longer standard Malay, and appears to have been current only in the fifteenth and sixteenth century heyday of Malayo-Javanese commerce. It was borrowed from the Chinese term which in Amoy dialect is *kheh-ui* (*kewi* in pinyin), literally "passenger-space" (Douglas 1873, 125).[7] In the seventeenth century it appears to be less used in Malay, but the *Dagh-Register* of Batavia for 1624–9 (130), used it in the plural form "quewijs" for the forty merchants on a 450-ton Chinese ship.

Other commercial concepts taken into Malay and Javanese from Chinese in this period are better known. These include such measures as the *pikul* (Chinese *shih* or *tan*, about sixty kilograms) for the amount a man can carry with a shoulder-pole, or a *kati* (Chinese *kin*), for a hundredth part of a pikul, as well as the everyday word for a steelyard or weighing balance—Malay *daching*, Javanese *dachin*, from Cantonese *toh-ch'ing* (Yule and Burnell 1903, 175, 298, 690). The *kiwi*, however, was a particularly central concept in the way "Malay" trade was conducted during this expansive age which ended in the seventeenth century, so that the term is an even stronger argument for the partnership of Chinese and Indonesian commercial methods in the heyday of Malayo-Javanese trade.

THE DECLINE OF SINO-JAVANESE SHIPPING

To summarize, at the Portuguese conquest of Melaka in 1511, Malay and Melaka-based Javanese shipping was still frequenting Canton, and Javanese shipping was dominant on the routes within the Indonesian Archipelago. The size and structure of Javanese ships were comparable with Chinese ships sailing to the south. The question is, why was the situation so different at the time the Dutch provide relatively detailed descriptions at the end of the sixteenth century?

It is clear that while European ships trading to Asia grew much larger ion the sixteenth century, Southeast Asian ships grew smaller. One turning point was undoubtedly the expedition against Melaka of Patih Yunus of Japara in January 1513, in which according to one account there were "thirty-five large junks of five hundred tons each . . . and also seventy other smaller craft, and many small well-armed hulks" (Empoli 1514, 148). This attack was reported by Portuguese chroniclers as part of a strategy, predating the Portuguese capture of Melaka, to extend the power of the rising Javanese *pasisir* to the famous Malay port. Virtually the whole fleet was destroyed in a naval engagement off Melaka, with only the largest junk, a leviathan of perhaps a thousand tons, returning to be beached at Japara (Pires 1515, 188, 282; Cortesão 1944, 151–2, 282). This decisive engagement may well have convinced Javanese shipbuilders that their large but unwieldy junks were at too great a risk once the Portuguese had introduced European-style naval warfare into the Archipelago, so that their subsequent vessels were smaller and faster.

A particularly intriguing detail in Parlingungan/Poortman is the story of Ja Tik Su, a ship-owner of *Ta-shih* (west Asian) origins, whose ship was repaired in the Semarang dockyard in 1513, just after this Demak fleet had been destroyed. "The Ta-shih type of ship of Ja Tik Su was copied by Kin San[8] to increase the speed of the [existing] ships of the Chinese junk type, which were indeed large but very cumbersome" (Graaf and Pigeaud 1984, 30).[9] This is another startling piece of data which fits with modern scholarship but would have been most unlikely for a nineteenth or twentieth century amateur to have invented.

The first and one of the best Dutch chroniclers, Lodewycksz (1598, 130–3), noted in Banten that there were still Javanese junks, with three masts and the cargo space divided into partitions (*petak*). However he was much more impressed with the number than the size of Javanese ships—claiming he had not seen one which could take more than forty tons. In fact the biggest junks of this period, as earlier, were those which exported rice from Japara and Semarang, and Lodewycksz had no opportunity to see these leviathans. A later Dutch report estimated that the concentration of east Java ports in the Madura straits might have had a thousand ships of between twenty and two hundred tons, while Japara had at least one rice junk of four hundred tons ("Verhaal" 1622, 532, 540; also Leur 1934, 128, 372). The lesson of 1513 was repeated at Dutch hands, however. In 1618 a Dutch fleet attacked the harbour of Japara and either seized or burned all the junks there, including one large one which had about three hundred tons of rice aboard (Coen 1919, I: 419–20). Javanese ships tended to be regarded as fair game by the VOC after about 1613, particularly if they were involved in the spice trade from Maluku or the rice trade to Portuguese Melaka (Meilink-Roelofsz 1969, 277–8).

The damage the VOC wrought on the trade of the Javanese ports, particularly with Maluku, certainly weakened them in the life-and-death struggle in which they were engaged against a rising Mataram. The Dutch were not yet strong enough to threaten the major states militarily, but their attacks on the centres of commerce did alter the delicate balance of power in

Java at a critical time. Just as in Burma in the same period, military power shifted to an interior capital safe against depredations from the sea. Mataram was able to conquer and destroy Lasem in 1616, Tuban in 1619, Gresik in 1623, and the whole complex of east Java ports depending on Surabaya by 1625. Japara tried hard to show its loyalty to Sultan Agung, and it was the Dutch who ensured its destruction as a major international port. Coen ordered two attacks on the port, in 1628 and 1629, burning all the junks, destroying the English lodge, killing all Gujerati merchants who could be found, and carrying off the Chinese by force to Batavia (Meilink-Roelofsz 1969, 291). Thereafter the maritime pressure of the VOC and Sultan Agung's suspicion of any rival centres of power combined to reduce Japara to little more than a subjugated outlet for Mataram's royal monopoly of rice exports.

Agung's successor Amangkurat I (1646–77) had his father's ambitions without his father's military skills or charisma. He tried to keep the unprecedented empire of Agung together by unprecedented terror, military levies, and the destruction of any *pasisir* trade not under his direct control. In 1651 he prohibited his subjects from travelling abroad, and in 1655 he closed all ports and ordered the destruction of all Javanese vessels.

Of course Javanese commerce did not die without a struggle. It had to adopt different methods, essentially by using different ports and smaller vessels. Javanese ports were no longer safe for substantial Javanese merchants with their capital in highly vulnerable junks. There was a shift to much smaller and faster vessels—the *pangajava* or *balok* of later periods—which could outrun the Dutch ships or escape them in rivers and mangroves (Meilink-Roelofsz 1969, 293). Larger merchants moved to ports which could protect them, in Banten (until 1684), in Makasar (until 1669), in Portuguese Melaka (until 1641), in Aceh, Palembang, Banjarmasin, or smaller ports around the Archipelago such as the metalworking island of Karimata, and of course in the Dutch ports themselves. In all these places, however, they assimilated into the earlier diaspora of Melaka traders, and so were typically known as Malays.

THE BIRTH OF DUALISM BETWEEN CHINESE AND JAVANESE

Direct relations between China and Java were in virtual suspension from about 1450 to 1567. Throughout that whole period the extensive trade between the two societies took place primarily through intermediate ports. Melaka was the most important, but after its fall Patani, Johor, Pnompenh and Ayudhya also played a role in this intermediate trade. Descendants of the Chinese of Java, without significant new arrivals or hope of returning to China throughout this long period, had every inducement to intermarry with and integrate into the commercial world of the Java coast and the Java Sea.

In 1567, however, a new Emperor, Mu-Tsung, came to the Chinese throne. He broke with Ming tradition by yielding to the repeated appeals from the authorities of Fujian that junks be allowed to trade legally and thus bring profit to the government. Fifty junks a year were initially granted licenses (*wen-yin*) to trade in Southeast Asia. In 1589 this number was raised to eighty-eight, in 1592 to one hundred and in 1597 to 117. Of the eighty-eight junks licensed after 1589, half went to the "eastern ocean" (the Philippines and Borneo) and twenty-four to ports in Indo-China and Siam. This left twenty vessels destined for ports in the Malay world, including eight to West Java—four to Banten, three to Sunda and one to Kelapa (both presumably representing Sunda Kelapa, later Jakarta) (Zhang Xie 1618, 131–2; also Innes 1980, 52–3; Chen 1974, 12).

The fact that it was western Java which first enjoyed the stimulus of renewed direct visits by the larger Chinese junks had something to do with disturbances further east, but was primarily because of west Java's proximity to south Sumatra and the Malayan Peninsula, which had never lost contact with China to the same degree. Moreover the vast expansion of pepper-growing in Sumatra during the sixteenth century made entrepots in the western part of the Archipelago more attractive for the Chinese. Despite the crusading spirit in which Banten had been founded in the 1520s, when the Hindu-Buddhist ports of Sunda Kelapa (Jakarta) and Banten were overrun by forces from Demak, Banten maintained good relations with the Portuguese and other non-Muslim merchants. Mendez Pinto (1614, 391–8) and Henrique Dias (1562, 104) reported regular Portuguese voyages from Banten to China in the middle of the century, presumably carrying pepper. It would be surprising if there were not also Chinese who visited Banten from bases in Johor, Patani or Palembang. The legalization of the junk trade to Banten in 1567, however, meant that much larger vessels carrying hundreds of Chinese "kiwi" could again frequent Java ports.

By 1596, when the first Dutch voyage provided detailed descriptions, Chinese junks were visiting Banten regularly and had largely driven the Portuguese out of the pepper trade to China (Lodewycksz 1598, 105). From Dutch reports it appears that annual Chinese fleets to Java remained of a similar size through the first three decades of the seventeenth century—about eight junks divided between Banten and Jakarta/Batavia, each of five or six hundred tons (*De eerste shipvaart* 1597, 25; Coolhaas 1964, II:1; Meilink-Roelofsz 1969, 398; Blussé 1986, 109–15). Though similar to the "hybrid"

Southeast Asian junks of a century earlier, these were now markedly different from Javanese ships, and would become more so as the century progressed.

In contrast to the situation encountered by the Portuguese, the Dutch and English found a large and very distinct colony of Chinese in Banten. About three thousand strong, they lived in a separate quarter outside the city wall to the westward, in brick houses quite different from the Javanese style; they had their own temple, distinct funerary customs, their own language and writing, their opera groups and various other performers; they dressed in distinctive gowns, with their hair kept long and wrapped up in a knot on the head; they reportedly sent much of their profits back to China; there was considerable social tension between them and the local population (Lodewycksz 1598, 99, 121–5; Scott 1606, 97, 169–76). In modern terms it was a predominately *totok* community. Although these Chinese too acquired concubines or temporary wives among the Indonesian population, they expected to leave them eventually and return home. Many still did adopt Islam, but this was now a deliberate step from one culture and loyalty into another. As Scott (1606, 174) put it, Chinese were never too proud to accept any kind of profitable work, "except they turne Javans (as many of them doe when they have done a murther or some other villanie)". They then cut their hair, changed their dress, became as haughty as the Javanese, and abandoned any thought of returning to China.

The expansion of this community in seventeenth century Java has already been well documented (most recently by Nagtegaal 1988, 110–11). Despite his suspicion of the Chinese, Coen went to great lengths to lure or force them to move to Batavia, and the Dutch city soon became dependent on them as small traders, craftsmen, labourers, market-gardeners, bakers and practically every other productive role. In Batavia the Chinese were allowed to settle inside the city walls, where they represented 39 percent of the inhabitants in 1699 and 58 percent in 1739 (Blussé 1986, 84). Chinese had the great merit of being not only industrious but peaceful, posing no threat to the Dutch position in Java. The number of Chinese migrants increased rapidly in the last decades of the seventeenth century with the arrival of many who had supported Zheng Chenggong (Koxinga) in his long resistance to the Manchu regime, and of others who found they could leave China much more easily when foreign trade was finally opened in 1684. With the fall of Banten in the same year all the centres of Chinese economic and cultural life in Java were Dutch-controlled. From these culturally pluralistic bases Chinese commercial activity spread to all parts of Java.

The establishment of the Dutch in Batavia helped to move the interaction between Javanese and outsiders towards a more dualistic one, in which the economic activity of Europeans and Chinese increasingly diverged from that of Javanese. It was convenient for the VOC that the Chinese should remain distinct from Javanese, and therefore useful as intermediaries unlikely to form a combined resistance. Hoadley (1988) has shown how in Cirebon at the end of the seventeenth century Dutch policy deliberately encouraged the separation of *peranakan* Chinese from Javanese elites by classifying *peranakan* as Chinese and excluding them from holding office. It became difficult to remain culturally ambivalent, and those who wished to remain commercially active had to opt for calling themselves Chinese.

RETROSPECT

The intense interaction between Chinese and Javanese technology and enterprise in the period between about 1290 and 1450 gave rise to new forms of Java-based commercial activity. In the following century, contact with China was broken. The new *pasisir* culture was fully domesticated as Javanese, and temporarily assumed the dominant role in Javanese politics. The renewal of direct contact with China after 1567 recreated a *totok* community in Java, which gradually made its base in the Dutch entrepots and thus resisted assimilation into Javanese life. The seventeenth century therefore saw a new separation of functions. Commerce became identified as the sphere of culturally distinct Chinese (and to a lesser extent "Malays", Arabs and others), making it easier for Javanese and Dutch rulers jointly to suppress the "Javanese" commercial dynamism of the *pasisir*.

APPENDIX: TRIBUTE MISSIONS FROM (EASTERN) JAVA (*CHAO-WA*) DURING THE EARLY MING.[10]

Names marked with an asterisk * can be presumed to be Chinese, either from the name or from other data in the chronicles.

Year	King	Envoy
1370	Xi Li Ba Da La Pu[11]	
1372		
1375		
1377	Ba Da Na Ba Na Wu	
1377	Wu Lao Bo Wu ("western king")	
	Wu Yuan Lao Wang Jie ("eastern king")	
1379	Ba Da Na Ba Na Wu	
1380	Ba Da Na Ba Na Wu	
1381		
1382		
1393		
1394		
1403	Du Ma Ban[12] ("western king")	
	Bo Ling Da Ha ("eastern king")	
1404	western and eastern kings	
1405	Du Ma Ban ("western king")[13]	*Pazhi* Chen Wei Da* (Sep)
	Du Ma Ban ("western king")	*Arya* An Da and Jia Li Qi (Dec)
	Bo Ling Da Ha ("eastern king")	Ma Li Zhan (Dec)
1407	Du Ma Ban[14]	*Arya* Chia-en
1408	Du Ma Pan	*Arya* Chia-en
1410	Du Ma Pan	*Arya* Su Mu Ni
1411		
1413	Du Ma Pan	*Arya* Sha Ma Ye
1415	Yang Wei Xi Sha[15]	*Arya* Sha Ma Ye
1416		
1418	Yang Wei Xi Sha	*Arya* Wei Shu
1420	Yang Wei Xi Sha	*Arya* Tian You
1422	Yang Wei Xi Sha	*Arya* Tian You
	Yang Wei Xi Sha	*Bati* Xiao Ma Mo
1425	Yang Wei Xi Sha	*Arya* Huang Fu Xin*
		Bazhi Wei Su
1426	Yang Wei Xi Sha	*Arya* Fu Mu (Sept)
	Yang Wei Xi Sha	*Arya* Guo Xin* (Nov)
1427	Yang Wei Xi Sha	*Bazhi* Wei Kai (May)
	Yang Wei Xi Sha	*Arya* Xu Li Man[16] (Nov)
1428	Yang Wei Xi Sha	*Arya* Chang Xan Wen* (interpreter)
1429		*Arya* Chang Sun (Feb)
	Yang Wei Xi Sha	*Arya* Ma Mo and Li Tien Yang (July)
	Yang Wei Xi Sha	*Arya* Gong-yi Shan (Aug)
	Yang Wei Xi Sha	*Arya* Guo Xin* (Sept)
	Yang Wei Xi Sha	*Arya* Gong-yong-cai* (Nov)
1430	Yang Wei Xi Sha	*Pazhi* Zong Jing (interpreter)
1435		*Pati* Ma Yong Liang*[17]
1436		*Alie* Ma Yong Liang* and *Pati* Nan Wu (June)
		Arya Gao Nai Sheng* (July)
1437	Yang Wei Xi Sha	*Arya* Lai Zhe (June)
		Arya Zhang Wen Xan (July)
1438	Yang Wei Xi Sha	*Arya* Ma Mo
		Arya Ma Yong Liang*,
		interpreter Yin Nan* and Wen Dan*
1440		Interpreter *Pazhi* Zhao-yang
1442	Yang Wei Xi Sha	Ma Yong Liang*

Year	King	Envoy
1443	Yang Wei Xi Sha	Li Tian Fu*
1446		Ma Yong Liang*
		Pazhi Ma Mo
1447		Ma Yong Liang*
1452	Ba La Wu[18]	*Arya* Mai Sheng Geng
1453	Ba La Wu	Interpreter Lin Xuan*
1454	Ba La Wu	Zheng Duan Yang and *Arya* Gong Ma
1460	Tu Ma Pan[19]	*Arya* Guo Sin*
1465		*Arya* Liang Wen Xuan*
1495	Bu La Ge De Na Mei[20]	

NOTES

1. Chinese sources in this paper have been translated for me by Li Tana and Mo Yi-mei, to whom I am most grateful. Dr J. Noorduyn, Dr Robert Cribb, Brian Moloughny and Professor William Jenner made very valuable comments on the first draft of the paper.

2. Even Arabic sources used the unfamiliar word junk (*znk*) to refer to the ships of the two fleets of Cheng Ho to reach Aden, in 1419 and 1432 (Serjeant 1988, 74-5).

3. Rockhill (1915, 240) translates similarly, but Kobata and Matsuda (1969, 130) render this as "more than one thousand families, all under one chief", and Groeneveldt (1880, 47) agrees.

4. Rockhill (1915, 241) gives a similar meaning, but Kobata and Matsuda (1969, 130) translate this as "The wealthy people are Cantonese, and there are more than one thousand families" and Groeneveldt (1880, 47) broadly agrees.

5. This Naiai was evidently an enterprising rascal, for he appeared again in the Dynastic records in 1456 as envoy of Melaka, accused of embezzling pearls from the Melaka tribute. He ended by taking his own life as a result of an involvement with a Chinese woman in Guangdong (*Ming Shi Lu* II, 390).

6. Though it is not clear to what the "western" and "eastern" kings refer, this was almost certainly an internal Majapahit dispute within east Java. Today's West Java was not referred to by the Chinese as part of *Chao-wa* at all.

7. I am grateful to Chen Xiyu of Xiamen University for drawing my attention to this point while a visitor at ANU.

8. According to Parlindungan/Poortman, Kin San was *bupati* of Semarang, then the Demak ship-building centre.

9. Parlindungan equated Ja Tik Su with Sunan Kudus, a west Asian who reformed Central Java Islam and built the Kudus mosque at about this time (but who was not known as a merchant). De Graaf and Pigeaud prefer to identify him with the Chinese merchant Wintang who in the Javanese *babad* tradition was converted by Sunan Kudus, married the daughter of King Trenggana, became Sunan Kali Nyamat, and died in the succession dispute following Trenggana's death. This last point indeed coincides with a detail in Parlindungan/Poortman. It should be noted, however, that de Graaf and Pigeaud overstate the case for the equivalence of the shipwrecked Chinese Wintang with the west Asian shipowner Ja Tik Su by translating Parlindungan's "*kapalnya rusak dan diperbaiki di galangang kapal Semarang*" with "[Ja Tik Su] was *shipwrecked* and his ship was under repair" (de Graaf and Pigeaud 1984, 30–31, 102–104, 116, 162–163).

10. Most of this information is taken from *Ming Shi Lu Chong Zhi Dong Nan Ya Shi Lao*, as translated by Li Tana, to whom I am greatly indebted. For the years 1370–1420 my first point of reference was the reading of the *Ming Chronicles* by Groeneveldt (1880, 34–6); and Kobata and Matsuda (1969, 151), though I have supplemented their data and used pin-yin throughout.

11. Sri Bhattara Prabhu ("the august sovereign"), title of the King of Majapahit, who at this time was the great Hayam Wuruk (1350–1389).

12. This seems likely to refer to a prince of Tumapel, a common title of royal princes. Noorduyn (1978, 213–115, 250) argues that a son of King Wikramawardhana (1389–1429) who predeceased his father about 1427 first bore this title, and that it later passed to the king's youngest son, Kertawijaya, who became king in 1447–51. The Chinese data suggests a Prince of Tumapel challenging for the succession in 1403, prevailing by 1407, and assuming a more august title in 1414.

13. Under this date the chronicle records "From this time they brought tribute continually, sometimes once in two years and sometimes more than once a year, and the eunuchs Wu Pin and Zheng He (Cheng Ho) visited their country repeatedly" (Groeneveldt 1880, 37).

14. After noting the arrival of the envoy of the western king, Du Ma Ban, the chronicle adds, "Before this the western and eastern kings fought, and the western king was victorious".

15. Hyang Wisesa, one of the titles of King Wikramawardhana, who according to Noorduyn (1978, 250) ruled Majapahit from 1389 to 1429 (though if so, through a period of great internal upheaval). The Chinese chronicle notes in relation to this tribute mission "The western king of Java, Yang Wei Xi Sha, sent *Arya* Sha Ma Ye to bring tribute of horses and other things. Yang Wei Xi Sha was the new name of Tu Ma Ban" (*Ming Shi Lu* I, 202). This implies that the same Prince of Tumapel who re-united the (Majapahit) kingdom in 1407 continued to rule as Hyang Wisesa until at least 1442, a period which covers most of the reign usually allotted to Queen Suhita of Majapahit (1429–47 in Noorduyn 1978).

16. Presumably Suleiman, the most obviously Muslim name in the list.

17. Though not listed under 1435, Ma referred in his memorial to the court in 1436 to his role in the previous year's mission.

18. Perhaps *Prabhu*, a title of Javanese kings. Noorduyn (1978, 250–1) gives this as the reign period of King Rajasawardhana, Dyah Wijayakumara (1451–3).

19. This may again refer to a past or present prince of Tumapel.

20. This would be a poor rendering of Girindrawardhana, who was ruling Majapahit or some part thereof in 1486 (Noorduyn 1978, 246–51).

CHAPTER 5

DOCUMENTING THE RISE AND FALL OF AYUDHYA AS A REGIONAL TRADE CENTRE

The collective memory represented in chronicle traditions of Ayudhya, as of other early modern Southeast Asian states, has provided a narrative of battles, religious foundations and successions, and a sense of which rulers were successful and which not. Some reigns appear to be filled with temple-building, conquest and lawgiving, and others with grave instability or defeat. Such memories do not, of course, necessarily imply that ordinarily people were particularly prosperous in the "glorious" periods, or that the economic conditions of the country were really strong. It seems increasingly clear, in other Southeast Asian cases, that periods when royal power was curbed by that of the merchant-aristocrats, such as the lengthy minorities in Banten (1580–1624) and the period of female rule in Aceh (1641–99), were often marked by relative prosperity and technical innovation even though royal chronicles found them flawed. On the other hand reigns remembered as glorious periods of conquest and expansion, such as those of Sultan Iskandar Muda in Aceh (1607–36) or Sultan Agung in Mataram (1613–46) were often unfavourable or even disastrous for the economic fortunes of the state.

The only substantial quantitative indices we have for the pre-modern period as a check on such collective memories are those of foreign trade, usually collected at the other end of the transaction. Fortunately much attention has already been paid to such data for Ayudhya by a number of scholars, including Sarasin Viraphol, Yoneo Ishii, George Vinal Smith and Suebsang Promboon. It begins to be possible to assemble the figures over a longer term to try to establish how Ayudhya fared at different periods in its attempts to dominate the maritime trade of at least Mainland Southeast Asia.

CHINESE TRIBUTE AND THE RYUKYU TRADE, 1370–1500

Charnvit Kasetsiri (1976) has gathered effectively what evidence we have about the beginnings of Ayudhya as a political and economic centre in the middle of the fourteenth century. It does not really appear in the external record as an international trade centre, however, until a maritime Chinese embassy reached the new port in 1370, and recognised it as the Hsien-lo of earlier periods. In particular Sukhothai had conducted a busy tribute trade to China in the period 1280–1323, after which Siam had disappeared from Chinese records for a half-century. The first ruler of the Ming Dynasty, the Hung-wu Emperor, pursued an unprecedentedly vigorous policy of sending missions to Southeast Asian ports for reasons which remain controversial. Those Southeast Asian port-states which most successfully exploited this novel policy by the Middle Kingdom came to dominate the early phase of Southeast Asia's "age of commerce". They drew very substantial direct benefits from their relationship with China in the form of gifts from the Emperor which outweighed the tribute sent to the capital (then Nanjing), and the ability to trade during the period of the trade missions. Indirectly the tributary relationship gave the states sending it a privileged access to the most important international market of the period, ensuring that other areas not so blessed could only export to China through their ports. The frequency of the tribute trade in the period 1370–1430 is therefore a useful guide to the importance of different ports in becoming entrepots for the wider region.

Siam responded to the 1370 Ming initiative with extraordinary enthusiasm, sending twelve tribute missions to China in the five years 1371–75 alone (Promboon 1971). This dynamic response makes clear that Ayudhya must already have had some advantages enabling it to mount such missions—undoubtedly including a sizeable Chinese community with literate members able to formulate the necessary tribute letters, a king sympathetic to this community and probably related to it (though not so "Chinese" that he seemed to visiting Chinese missions as no more than an upstart Cantonese pirate, like the ruler of Palembang), and a fleet of ships (probably also Chinese) capable of making the journey to Canton. It undoubtedly also had trade goods, sappanwood in particular, acceptable as tribute and useful for trading in conjunction with the tribute missions.

During the period of the first three Ming rulers, 1370 to 1433, the South China Sea was extraordinarily busy. Large missions were sent out from China and tributary missions responded in much great numbers from a dozen Southeast Asian states and settlements. Siam sent thirty-six missions to China in the period 1371–1404, more than one every year on average, and twenty-two missions in the Yung-lo reign, 1405–33, or slightly less than one per year. In this flourishing system of eastern Asian trade and diplomacy, Siam, Champa and Java were the Southeast Asian heavyweights, with Melaka some distance away in fourth place. The smaller ports—Cambodia, Brunei and the Philippines—dropped out of the game after about 1425 as China's enthusiasm lagged.

TABLE 1 FREQUENCY OF SEABORNE TRIBUTE MISSIONS TO CHINA

Period	Siam	Cambodia	Champa	Java	Melaka	Pasai
1369–99	33	13	25	11		1
1400–09	11	4	5	8	3	3
1410–19	6	3	9	6	8	7
1420–29	10		9	16	5	5
1430–39	4		10	5	3	3
1440–49	3		9	7	2	
1450–59	2		3	3	3	
1460–69	1		4	3	2	1
1470–79	4		3		1	
1480–89	3		3			3
1490–99	3		3	2		
1500–09	1		2		2	

Sources: 1300s: Wade (1991); 1400s: Reid (1993a, 160).

Table 1 indicates that Ayudhya emerged very rapidly as the major Southeast Asian port for the east Asian trade under Kings Boromaracha I (1370–88), his nephew Ramesuan I (1388–95) and the latter's son Ramaracha (1395–1409), even though the chronicles suggest each of these short reigns began and ended violently, and that they were chiefly concerned with wars in the north (Wyatt 1982, 67–9). In the period 1410–30 Siam slipped into second place behind Java but ahead of Champa, while the order was Champa-Java-Siam in the middle of the century. In 1450–69, during the flourishing days of Sultan Mansur, Melaka became important enough to beat Siam into fourth place. In the last three decades of the century, however, Melaka and Java declined in importance due to internal conflict. Siam and Champa then remained the most important senders of tribute by sea, in a system rapidly declining in commercial importance.

As a proportion of all the seaborne tribute missions to China from Southeast Asia, including the smaller players not listed above, Siam bulked largest in the last decades of both fourteenth and fifteenth centuries, representing over one third of the total in both periods. In the intervening period there was a downward trend from 28 percent in 1400–9 to only 9 percent in 1460–9.

The absolute number of Siam's missions to China went into a decline after 1421, the last year in which more than one mission was sent. Since this pattern was broadly shared by its rivals, it seems probable that Ming policing of private trade (including that via Ryukyu) was less effective in the latter part of the century, so that the tribute missions represented a diminishing share of the total trade. Towards the end of the century the whole tribute system may have declined beyond the point when it was an accurate index of commercial dynamic. The trend continued in the following century, Siam averaging only one mission every 5.4 years through the period 1503–1619 (Promboon 1971).

The number of envoys comprising a mission, sometimes listed in Ming records, may be another index of their relative commercial importance. When given for Siam this was:

1418	100
1420	80
1421	60
1428	45

This seems to put Siam in the middle range compared with Java and Champa, though the royal missions sent by some of the smaller states were generally the biggest (e.g. Sulu 340 in 1418; Melaka 228 in 1434). Some of the Java missions were much bigger (e.g. 250 in 1422) but some smaller (Wade 1991, 79).

The early Ming rulers accepted only memorials written in Chinese or *fan* (Arabic) script. In 1487, however, it was recorded that a gold-leaf missive was received from Ayudhya, and that the envoys who brought it claimed that in the past both their own country's (Thai) script and Arabic had been used in letters to China. The imperial court ruled, however, that only Arabic could be used, since the other script was "hard to read". But in 1490 a proposal was made to the court in Beijing that the Translators' Institute should be reformed, included the addition of a Thai and Burman translator (Wade 1991, 80–81). This provides confirmation that at that period Siam was more important as a tribute and trade partner for China than were Java or Melaka, whose languages were not so recognised.

It might be argued that tribute missions provide a better index of the strength of a literate Chinese commercial element at the capitals of different states, rather than of the overall importance of the port, since many of the envoys recorded in the *Ming Shi-lu* had clearly Chinese names and identities. This is less true for Siam than for most other maritime states, however. Chinese names were considerably more common among Javanese than

Siamese envoys (Reid 1996, 27). Identifiable Chinese were prominent among Siamese envoys only at the beginning of the Ming dynasty, notably in the missions of 1381, 1391 (twice), 1405, 1410, 1426, 1427 and 1438 (deputy envoy). Thereafter there appear to be no explicitly Chinese envoys, which may of course simply mean that the pattern of assimilation of bilingual Sino-Thais into the Siamese aristocracy was smoother than the analogous process in Java (Wade 1991, 117).

Fortunately there is another index of the relative importance of fifteenth century Southeast Asian ports available in the *Rekidai-hoan*, the Ryukyu records of trade missions to China, Japan and Southeast Asian ports. As a strategically placed autonomous tributary of both China and Japan, Ryukyu was able to make itself a crucial entrepot between these two important markets and the tropical produce coming from Southeast Asia. While the Chinese records are silent or sternly disapproving of ports such as Palembang and Patani which they regarded as upstart nests of Chinese renegades and pirates, Ryukyu had no compunction about opening trade relations with any port where its merchants could identify a profit. The records pertaining to Southeast Asian ports have been carefully edited in English by Kobata and Matsuda (1969) and used by a number of other scholars, notably Yoneo Ishii for Siam. Unfortunately the records are missing for the two decades 1443–63, and are of relatively little use after 1544 when Japanese control intensified and Ryukyu shipping went into sharp decline. For most of the period between 1419 and 1543, however, they provide an excellent supplement to the more continuous Chinese tribute record.

TABLE 2   RYUKYU SHIPPING TO SOUTHEAST ASIAN PORTS

Period	Siam	Patani	Melaka	Total	
1419–42	29	0	0	40	(incl. Java & Palembang)
1443–63	—— gap in records ——				
1464–80	11	0	16	30	
1481–1508	0	2	2	4	(fragmentary)
1509–43	19	9	3 (1509–11)	34	
1544–64	3	0	0	3	

Source: Ishii (1988).

These data make even stronger the case for Ayudhya's pre-eminence as a Southeast Asian hub for the east Asian trade in the early part of the Ming period, attracting almost three quarters of the total Ryukyu trade on Southeast Asia in the period 1419–42. As with the Chinese data, there is a marked slump in Siam's relative as well as absolute position in the third quarter of the fifteenth century. Melaka under Sultan Mansur appears clearly to have become a more important port than Ayudhya in this period, with Siam's share of the Ryukyu trade down to 37 percent. The reign of the great Siamese law-giver, Boromotrailokanat (1448–88), appears not to have been a happy one for the maritime economy of Siam, however celebrated for establishing a *sakdina* bureaucracy.

SIXTEENTH CENTURY TURBULENCE

The Portuguese conquest of Melaka in 1511 may have benefitted Siam, in that it made Melaka much less attractive as a trade base for Muslims. When Portuguese attempts to trade directly with China ended with their expulsion from the Chinese mainland in 1522, it was also clear that Portuguese Melaka would be much less viable than Malay Melaka had been as a base for trading with China (Chang 1969, 69). Some other alternatives to Melaka developed in Aceh, Patani and Pahang, but none of these approached Ayudhya in importance as an entrepot for the trade between China, Southeast Asia, and the Muslim trade in the Indian Ocean. This favourable trend is indicated in the return to Siamese dominance (56 percent) of the Ryukyuan Southeast Asia trade in the period 1511–43, when its only remaining serious competitor, Patani, attracted less than half as many ships (table 2 above).

During this favourable period I believe Siam may even have become an important base for Chinese trade to Borneo and the Philippines. The direct "eastern route" of Chinese navigation from Fujian to Luzon and beyond appears to have been abandoned in the late fifteenth century, and replaced by a route via Melaka. With the fall of Melaka to the Portuguese in 1511, Ayudhya may have seemed a more appropriate place for transshipment of Chinese goods for these eastern islands. A Chinese navigation route from Siam to Mindanao was outlined in the late Ming *Shun Feng Xiang Song*, while Magellan's expedition encountered "a junk from Ciama" in Cebu, central Philippines, in 1521 (Reid 1996, 34–6). The Portuguese themselves acquired much of their Chinese export produce in the Siamese capital, and even occasionally traded to China in disguise aboard Siamese ships (Chang 1969, 71). Many Portuguese served in the military forces of King Chairacha (1534–47), for whom Portuguese Melaka was more like a tributary or dependant than a trade rival. Ayudhya appears to have been one of the biggest cities in Southeast Asia in this period,. The fifty thousand armed men referred to by Barros (1777, III, i: 161) and the 10,050 houses burned in a fire of 1545 according to the Luang Prasoet chronicle, would both suggest at least two hundred thousand inhabitants.

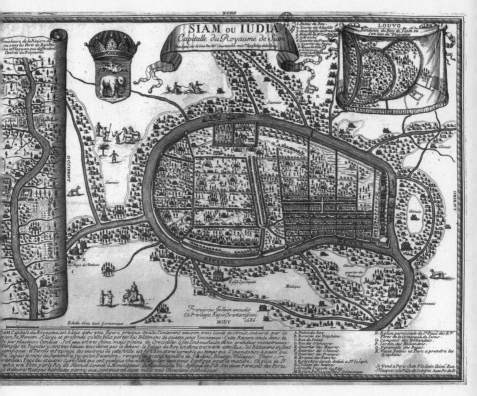

Fig. 2 French map of Ayudhya, 1686, with as insets the lower course of the Chaophraya River (left), and the royal retreat of Lopburi (Louvo) (upper right).
Cartes et Plans C27964, Bibliothèque Nationale, Paris

With the death of Chairacha in 1547, however, Siam entered on a period of turbulence and disaster, culminating in the destruction of Ayudhya by the Burmese in 1569. This period coincided with a great improvement in the fortunes of Portuguese Melaka as a trade port, with access to China restored and a much improved system of customs administration (Thomaz 1979; Ferreira Flores 1989). Banten, in west Java, also arose in this period as a major pepper port for the China trade, while much of the China-Southeast Asia trade previously centred on Ayudhya was dispersed to Cambodia and the small ports along the "Champa" coast of what is today southern and central Vietnam. Finally the direct Chinese route to the Philippines and Borneo was vigorously reestablished.

The next major indicator of the relative standing of Southeast Asian ports in the China trade is the list of licenses (*wen-yin*) issued to Chinese junks by Chinese port authorities in 1589 and 1592, after Chinese private trade to the south was legalised in 1567. Not surprisingly, this list showed that Ayudhya had lost its earlier pre-eminence, with only four of the eighty-eight licenses issued being specified for Siam. Manila, with its vast supply of silver flowing in from the new world, was now much the largest destination for Chinese shipping to Southeast Asia. Of the remaining ports, Banten was effectively issued seven passes (Banten four plus Sunda three), Palembang (another new pepper port) four, Cambodia and Champa three each, while the smaller ports on the way to becoming the southern Vietnamese state of Cochin-China (or Dang Trong) also received four in total (two for Thuan-hoa, one for Quang-nam, one for Qui-nhon) (Innes 1980, 53). The earlier Siamese dominance of Southeast Asian trade to eastern Asia had been so dissipated in the collapse of the 1560s that Ayudhya would never be able to recover the same centrality.

WESTERN DOMINANCE AND MONOPOLIES, 1600–88

The arrival of Dutch and English ships in Southeast Asian waters around 1600 changed the balance of trade profoundly. Their capacity quickly outstripped that of the Asian traders in the Indian Ocean region, and their competition for pepper and the spices of Maluku (clove, nutmeg and mace) enabled Europe to displace China as the primary market for Southeast Asian goods. The Dutch Company (VOC) set out to achieve monopolies of whatever branches of trade it could, succeeding totally with Malukan spices by mid-century, and partially with pepper and tin. In 1664 the VOC established also a monopoly in the export of deer hides from Siam to Japan. In general Ayudhya survived this reorientation better than most other Southeast Asian ports, but its overall share of the trade sank considerably. By the 1630s Batavia and Manila were Southeast Asia's two most important international ports, and the dominance of Batavia (but not Manila) continued to grow through to about the 1670s. Ayudhya was able to survive by concentrating increasingly on the China trade in which the Dutch were weakest, and by acting as a refuge for all the other elements excluded by Dutch monopolies—the Muslim traders, the English, the Portuguese and the French.

In the East Asian trade where Siam's position was strongest, the most revealing comparative figures for the early part of the century are those given for the Japanese Red Seal ships then being licensed to sail to the south. The Japanese ships were particularly interested in the mainland ports of Cochin-China, Cambodia and Siam, importing their deer and cowhides, as well as the sappanwood and ivory which were royal monopolies in Siam. Since these mainland countries had a similar set of exports, their relative standing in Japanese trade is probably significant, particularly in the period 1604-16 when the Japanese data is reliably complete.

TABLE 3 RED SEAL SHIPS SENT OUT BY JAPAN

| | Licensed to: | | | | | |
Period	Siam	Patani	Cambodia	Cochin-China	Luzon	Total
1604–07	12	5	17	1	15	98
1608–11	11	0	3	7	7	34
1612–16	13	2	4	25	12	63
1617–20	2	0	3	18	7	45
1621–24	6	0	3	7	9	39
1625–28	8	0	4	3	0	27
1629–31	3	0	2	3	0	17
1632–35	1	0	8	8	2	33

Sources: Iwao (1976, 300–1). See also table 2 in Reid (1993a, 18).

This pattern suggests that Ayudhya recovered quickly under the warrior brothers, Naresuan (1590–1605) and Ekathotsarot (1605–11), so as to become again a major player in the east Asian trade. Ekathotsarot was particularly anxious to attract foreign traders (Wyatt 1982, 107; Jarric 1614, 887), and in his reign Ayudhya retrieved from Cambodia the position it had lost as chief exporter of Southeast Asian hides, sappanwood, lacquer and ivory to Japan. But the Cochin-China port of Hoi An (near modern Danang) became overwhelmingly the favoured port for Japanese ships in the second decade of the century, and kept that position as long as the Japanese ships sailed south. Siam lost out almost completely in the Japan trade in 1629, when the shogunate banned trade to

Ayudhya in protest against Prasat Thong's usurpation of the throne and maltreatment of Japanese (Smith 1974, 227–36).

A similar pattern may have obtained in the more important China trade, though we unfortunately lack any single source of oversight of it. It appears that Chinese junks must also have deserted Ayudhya after the defeat of 1569, making use of Patani and Cambodia as alternative ports, so that by 1600 the number of junks had still not reached the six or seven a year reported a century earlier by Pires (1515). By 1610, however, the Dutch reported much increased activity on the Ayudhya-China run—again confirming Eka-thotsarot's reputation as a friend of commerce (Smith 1974, 236–39). In 1622, according to voc sources, three Chinese junks had been authorized to trade to Siam, as against only one each to Patani and Cambodia (but

seventeen to Cochin-China), and in 1625 the record was four junks to Siam
and three to Cambodia (Meilink-Roelofsz 1969, 398). By contrast in 1639
the VOC reported that China had licensed only two junks to Siam, the same
number as to Cambodia (Coolhaas 1960--, II: 1). We should probably
multiply all these figures by at least two to reflect the unlicensed trade, but it
is the relative standings which are important here. In relation to the much
larger numbers of junks licensed for Manila, Batavia and Hoi An in this
period, these admittedly inadequate figures suggest that Ayudhya under King
Songtham (1611–28) held the upper hand in the Gulf of Siam although not
a major player in the larger Asian contest for trade. Under Prasat Thong this
position seems to have declined significantly in the China trade as in the
Japanese.

The shipping in Chinese junks to the Japanese port of Nagasaki after 1640
is fortunately much better documented. Only Chinese (*Tosen*) and Dutch
ships were permitted to trade with Japan after 1640, and the Chinese had
much the larger share of all items in the Siamese export trade except hides
after 1664, when the VOC established a monopoly on the export of this item.
Table 4 shows the strong relative performance of Ayudhya during the reign
of Narai (1657–88), even though the total number of ships being accepted
by Japanese authorities in Nagasaki was in gradual decline.

Although in mid-century, Cambodia was more important and Patani
almost as important as Siam in supplying Japan, these two rivals declined
drastically during Narai's reign. Ayudhya maintained its number of junks on
the route better than other ports in this reign, so that its share of the
Southeast Asian shipping rose from 19.6 percent in the 1650s to 28 percent
in the 1680s. Ayudhya remained less important than Hoi An in this trade
throughout the period. On the other hand the reign of Narai undoubtedly
saw the reassertion of Ayudhya's domination of the Gulf of Siam and the
Mekong drainage area, which it may again have lost to Cambodia during the
reign of Prasat Thong (1629–56). Certainly van Vliet (1636, 90, 93) gave a
bleak picture of the way that king manipulated the market and demanded
unreasonable prices so that "nobody comes to Siam unless compelled to do
so". But of course the Japan branch of trade must have suffered more than
others during Prasat Thong's reign because of the Japanese court's boycott of
the "usurper" king.

An important feature which emerges clearly in this period was that the
majority of junks on the Siam-Nagasaki route were built, manned and
equipped in Siam rather than South China. Seventy percent of the junks for
which such data are recorded were based in Siam, whereas all other sectors of
the Southeast Asia-Japan trade were dominated by China-based vessels.
Although all of these ships were manned overwhelmingly by ethnic Chinese

(*tōjin* in the Japanese reports), a third of them were owned by the king (the proportion rose to more than half in the bleaker times after 1688) and a larger proportion had a few Thais aboard to look after royal or aristocratic interests in the trade. These Siam-based junks were larger than most for the period,

TABLE 4 NUMBER OF CHINESE JUNKS FROM SOUTHEAST ASIAN
PORTS TO JAPAN BY DECADE

Period	Tongking	Hoi An	Cambodia	Siam	Patani	Melaka	Batavia	Banten	Total
1651–60	15	40	37	28	20		2	1	143
1661–70	6	43	24	26	9	2	12		122
1671–80	8	41	10	26	9		38	1	133
1681–90	12	25	9	31	9	4	19	1	110
1691–1700	6	29	22	19	7	2	16	1	103
1701–10	3	12	1	11	2	2			31
1711–19	2	5	1	4			1		13
1720–24		4	1	2					7
Total	52	199	106	147	56	10	88	4	662

Sources: Reid (1993b, 19, based on readings by Li Tana 1992, 70), Ishii (forthcoming).

carrying an average of eighty-seven men and probably therefore weighing over two hundred tons (though ship size was not recorded, see Reid 1993b, 19–21). The establishment (or perhaps definitive re-establishment) of this very strong Siam-based Chinese trading community was to be the most important commercial legacy of the Narai period.

As Smith has well shown, the VOC trade with Siam did not flourish under Narai, showing a 28 percent drop in export value between the 1633–63 and the 1664–94 periods (calculated from Smith 1974, 252). But it is clear that the Company only did well where it could obtain the very high profit margins that came with monopolies, and hence its performance may have an inverse relationship with that of the overall Asian trade. The English reported in 1678 that Dutch trade had declined because Indian Muslim traders were coming in greater numbers to Tenasserim with much cheaper Indian cloth than the Dutch had been able to supply earlier (Anderson 1890, 427). Smith himself accepts that there was an "overall expansion of trade during the reign of King Narai", but believes it to have been caused primarily by the growth of Ayudhya's role as a Southeast Asian entrepot, exchanging Chinese and Japanese goods for Southeast Asian and Indian ones, rather than by expansion of the internal Siamese market (Smith 1974, 259).

This is indeed what one would expect, since the factor subject to most rapid change was always this fickle entrepot trade, always ready to move elsewhere in response to insecurity or oppression in a particular port. Though Narai was not perfect in this regard, he undoubtedly profited at the end of his reign from the Dutch conquest of Makasar (1669) and Banten (1682), together with the decline of Aceh's ability to deliver tin and pepper to foreign traders in the 1660s. After 1682 Ayudhya had few remaining competitors as a Southeast Asian entrepot independent of Dutch monopolies.

In 1678 the English report on Ayudhya's trade already makes clear that a large part of it was entrepot trade which in other circumstances could have taken place at Aceh, Melaka, Johor, Banten, Patani, Cambodia or Hoi An. Thus silks were imported from China for re-export to Japan; Indian traders brought textiles both through Tenasserim and directly to Ayudhya for the China, Japan and Manila markets; while "the Malays in small prowes" brought sandalwood, pepper, birds-nests and camphor from the Archipelago for sale here to the Chinese vessels (Anderson 1890, 424–6). Our Nagasaki reports confirm the picture for the 1680s. Thus a 1686 ship reported that as usual, "the Moors are coming overland to Siam for trade", while "In addition, a number of small ships arrived in Siam". In the following year, although complaining that business was not good (mainly because of restrictions in Japan), the *Tosen* ship reported that "Ships from various countries are incessantly visiting Siam" (Ishii forthcoming, *Tosen* I: 20 and I: 21). A final indicator of Ayudhya's important entrepot role in this period was the commencement of direct trading between Ayudhya and Manila in Narai's reign (perhaps a re-commencement of the Chinese Siam-Philippines route of the early 1500s), with twenty-five ships from Siam being recorded in Manila port records during the thirty years for which there is information in 1657–88 (Chaunu 1960, 148–75).

DECLINE OF AN ASIAN ENTREPOT? 1688–1765

There has been some interesting debate in recent years about the economic significance of 1688 for Ayudhya. Where older writers such as Hutchinson and Hall tended to see the overthrow of Narai as a retreat into isolation and economic self-sufficiency, Sarasin Viraphol (1977, 54–55) argued that the loss in European and Indian trade after 1688 was made good by an increase in Chinese trade. Dhiravat na Pombejra (1993, 1994) has examined Dutch and French records carefully to show that the court under Phetracha (1688–1703) continued to seek commercial contacts overseas, and that the Chinese hold on the Siamese economy did indeed grow markedly under this and the following reign. In quantitative terms, however, Dhiravat's data do seem to confirm an overall decline after 1688, even in the Chinese branch of trade which Sarasin believed to be on a marked rise. My own judgement, with the benefit of Dhiravat's first paper but not that of 1994, was that "Trade did continue, but it both declined in overall volume and shifted towards the East Asian pattern of overwhelming dependence on the Chinese junk trade" (Reid 1993a, 308).

Since the case for no decline or minimal decline rests primarily on Chinese shipping, it is particularly important to assemble a time series for the number of junks on the China-Siam route. Although from different sources, of which the European ones are not always clear whether they include junks from Japan and Vietnam, table 5 does give some indication of the trend.

TABLE 5 CHINESE JUNKS REPORTED VISTING SIAM

Year	Number	Source
1657	10	VOC (Coolhaas 1968, 193)
1659	10 (only 5 from China)	VOC (Coolhaas 1968, 257)
1688	15–20	French (Gervaise 1688, 76)
1689	14–15	*Tosen* I: 26 of 1690 (Ishii forthcoming)
1695	20	VOC (Dhiravat 1983c, 263)
1695	8	*Tosen* reports (Viraphol 1977, 55)
1696	13	*Tosen* I: 40 and 41 of 1696 (Ishii forthcoming)
1697	10	VOC (Dhiravat 1983c, 263)
1697	"at least 4"	*Tosen* reports (Viraphol 1977, 55)
1698	7	*Tosen* I: 45 of 1698 (Ishii forthcoming)
1699	6	*Tosen* I: 46 and 47 of 1699 (Ishii forthcoming)
1700	3–4	French missionary (Reid 1993, 308)
1701	1	*Tosen* reports (Viraphol 1977, 55)
1703	10	*Tosen* I: 49 of 1703 (Ishii forthcoming)
1733	18	VOC (Dhiravat 1994, 10)

Taken overall these figures do tend to suggest a rising trend under Narai, a falling one under Phetracha and again a rising one under Thaisa. The first Chinese reports reaching Nagasaki after the 1688 coup were very negative, suggesting that there was much resistance against the usurper and that trade was at a standstill. By contrast the ship of 1690 sent by a Chinese official of Siam presented a pro-Phetracha version of the coup and insisted that after some initial turmoil, "peace prevails over all the land. Thus trading ships enter Siam from various countries as before. Last year also from the great Qing [China], from Guangdong, Zhangzhou, and Amoy as many as fourteen or fifteen ships visited Siam which by now have returned home" (Ishii forthcoming, *Tosen* I: 26 of 1690). Although this upbeat tone was intended to restore confidence in Ayudhya as a trading centre, the overall impression given by the *Tosen* reports was of reduced trade opportunities during Phetracha's reign.

There appears no doubt that Ayudhya's entrepot role as a venue for commercial exchange between South Asia, East Asia and the Archipelago underwent a decline after 1688. But given that virtually all major ports of the region except Batavia were in crisis at some point in the second half of the seventeenth century, and that levels of external trade everywhere were drastically affected by changes of Chinese and Japanese policy over which Southeast Asians had no control, the more important measure for Ayudhya is its relative standing against other ports. Thus the sudden emergence of Cambodia as a more popular port than Siam during the 1690s in table 4 is the surest sign that the 1688 upheaval had been disastrous for Ayudhya's ability to channel the produce of the Chaophraya and Mekong watersheds towards Japan and China.

On the other hand, as Dhiravat, Sarasin and others have made clear, the reign of King Thaisa (1709–33) was marked by the domination of Siamese commerce by the Chinese Phraklang and his associates, and a definite rise in the volume of Siam-China trade. Dhiravat na Pombejra (1994) has labelled this "the first great Chinese phase in Siamese political and administrative history". The first mention of Siamese rice exports to China is in 1722, at a time of rice shortage in southern China. Shipments certainly remained fitful until Beijing's temporary bans on overseas trade were lifted in 1727, but thereafter became an annual affair (Viraphol 1977, 83–106). The figures we have are far from satisfactory, but they seem to point to a significant increase in Ayudhya's export trade to China in the reign of Thaisa, probably continued after initial interruption under Boromakkot (1733-58).

I am not aware of evidence that Siam was able to recover its primacy as a regional entrepot, however. Since the most important factors encouraging the China trade in this period—China's acceptance of rice imports, her gradual recognition of the legitimacy of foreign trade in general, and the prosperity of the Middle Kingdom under the Qienlong Emperor—were unrelated to Siam, it is likely that any gains made by Ayudhya were also made by her rivals. Hatien, Saigon, Brunei and Johor were all flourishing as centres of the Chinese trade in the middle of the eighteenth century, and probably at least held their own against Ayudhya. Like most other aspects of the eighteenth century, however, this needs much more systematic attention.

OVERVIEW

Since this paper has taken a long-term perspective, it may be useful to try to summarize what the evidence suggests about Ayudhya's relative stature as a Southeast Asian port at different periods. Like the Bangkok dynasty which succeeded it, Ayudhya appears to have begun very strongly, asserting its primacy over all other Southeast Asian ports in the East Asian system in the period 1370–1410. This position gradually eroded in subsequent decades, ceding first to Java and Champa but eventually to Melaka in the 1450s and 1460s. Ayudhya came back strongly to reassert its dominance in 1500–40, but appears to have been losing this position thereafter even before the disaster of 1569. By 1610 it had recovered to become again the major port in the Gulf of Siam, though worsted by Hoi An as a centre for China-Japan exchanges in the subsequent two decades.

Prasat Thong's reign appears to have set Ayudhya back again as a regional entrepot, but this loss was made good under Narai, when Ayudhya became for a time the strongest remaining non-European port in Southeast Asia. After 1688 the Siamese capital appears to have lost much of its entrepot role in the Asian trading system, though as an exporter to China it became more important in the eighteenth century. Nevertheless the emergence of Bangkok as the major Southeast Asian hub of Chinese international trade at the beginning of the nineteenth century was not something for which the last Ayudhyan reigns appeared to have prepared the way.

At the outset of each period—at its foundation, and after the two Burmese conquests of 1569 and 1767—Siam began very strongly as a pre-eminent centre of the Southeast Asian trade with China. After these strong beginnings in each case it gradually lost this position to its rivals. Should we see this as a characteristic sign of vigour at the beginning of each dynasty? Or is it rather that when leverage over the interior was minimal each dynasty sought support by allying with the Chinese international trade, whereas better-established kings tended to squeeze the port disastrously in the service of extravagant wars? The phenomenon appears to deserve some attention from Thai historians.

CHAPTER SIX

THE RISE OF MAKASAR[1]

The rise of Makasar to political and economic dominance in eastern Indonesia is one of the most rapid and spectacular success stories which Indonesian history affords. It occupied hardly more than a century, from the first evidence of a kingdom in any significant sense under Tumapa'risi' Kallonna (c.1511–48), to its flowering in the first half of the seventeenth century.

Since there are virtually no written sources on Makasar or the surrounding area of southwest Sulawesi prior to 1500, we will do well to begin with the origin myth of the Gowa dynasty, which is repeated with only slight variations in many oral and written traditions. The events are held to have occurred seven generations before Tumapa'risi' Kallonna, but since nothing but the name is known of most of the intervening generations, we are probably not justified in placing the foundation of the dynasty any earlier than 1400.[2]

The central element in all versions of the myth is that a beautiful nymph, Tumanurunga ("she who has descended"), came down from heaven in what is now the sacred core area of Gowa, a low hill just north of the Jeneberang river known as Tamalate or Kale Gowa. She took as her husband a mortal named Karaeng Bayo, who is described in some versions as the king of Bantaeng (Blok 1759, 7), in most others as a man from Bantaeng or a man from the south, though in the *Sedjarah Goa* as a man "whose country was not known" (*Sedjarah Goa*, 10). Tumanurunga was accepted as ruler by the heads of nine local communities, who became known as the *kasuiang salapanga* (nine retainers) or later *bates salapanga* (nine banners) and by their spokesman, who held the title *Patcalla*. Tumanurunga eventually returned to heaven as mysteriously as she had come, after leaving behind a son,

Massalangga Baraya, who possessed all sorts of magical powers, such as being able "to hear a hair cut in Java, to smell a dead buffalo in Selayar, and to see a pigeon in Bantaeng" (*Sedjarah Goa*, 11). Massalangga Baraya and his successors on the throne of Gowa were provided with various sacred objects by their forebears, however, which would ensure the power of the dynasty. Tumanurunga herself left half of the gold chain she had brought with her from heaven, known as *Tanisamanga*; the other magical bequest was the short sword named *Sudanga* left behind by Lakipadada, the younger brother of Karaeng Bayo, who had arrived in Gowa with the latter and eventually disappeared again with him. These two items were the most ancient and sacred of the regalia (*kalompoang* or *gaukang*) of Gowa, and the power of sovereignty resided within them. Equally essential for later kings were the places in Tamalate associated with Tumanurunga—the coronation stone on which she had been seated when she came from heaven, and the well from which Karaeng Bayo had drunk when wandering about in search of water. (For versions of this myth see *Sedjarah Goa*, 9–12; "Makassaarsche Historiën", 112–14; Blok 1759, 7–8; Abdurrazak 1969, 2–7; Friedericy 1929, 365–6; Erkelens 1897, 81–2; Eerde 1930, 820–1).

If we consider only the human elements in this story, they point in four directions which need to be pursued for clues as to the origins of Gowa and later Makasar. Firstly there are the original inhabitants of the area, represented by the "nine retainers". Then there is the link with Bantaeng, which seems unlikely to have been invented during the last three centuries when Bantaeng has been seen as subordinate to Gowa. Thirdly we have the Bajau, nomadic sea-people whose role is almost certainly represented by the name Karaeng Bayo, Makasarese for "King of the Bajau". Finally, most curious of all, we have the figure of Lakipadada, who plays a major role in the mythology of the Sa'dan Toraja but does not appear at all among the intervening Bugis. It will be helpful to consider each of these in turn.

THE MAKASAR/UJUNG PANDANG AREA

Christian Pelras is undoubtedly correct in insisting that the "Makasar" of the fourteenth century *Negarakertagama* "must not be prematurely identified with the present Ujung Pandang"[3] (Pelras 1981, 154). I think we can go further, to say it is unlikely there was any major power centre in the region of Ujung Pandang prior to the rise of Gowa around 1500.

Since its rapid growth around 1600, the city of Makasar has always been concentrated on the beach ridges which almost exactly coincide with the pre-1971 territory of Makasar city, with its eastern border near Jalan Veteran.

This area is elevated, flood-free, relatively flat, sandy and easy to dig for wells—a natural site, in other words, for a maritime city. The beach ridges were built up by wave action carrying the silt deposited by the Jeneberang river at a time when its outlet was several kilometres further to the north-east. The emergence of the beach ridges is geologically recent—at least since the end of the last major rise in global sea-levels (the Holocene Glacioeustatic transgression) about five thousand years ago.

This area may have taken its present shape only within the last thousand years, explaining why the "nine flags" of early Gowa appear to be located along the higher banks of the Jeneberang river, not on this coastal ridge strip.

During Makasar's heyday, as well as during colonial times, one of the city's major assets was the proximity of large fertile areas of wet-rice cultivation, notably in Maros and Takalar. It is not clear when these low-lying areas were drained and formed into permanent sawahs, but the indications we have suggest that they were not cultivated on a wide scale until the sixteenth century. Of Maros, Speelman reported that

> these lands were all conquered under the rein of Tunijallo' [1565–90] . . . and divided out among the Makassar notables by villages and lots, who each promoted their plantations here, insofar as they had men available, each successive year. (Speelman 1670, 11)

Of the rulers of Gowa themselves, we hear praise in the chronicles for the way the rice-fields flourished under Tumapa'risi' Kallonna and some later rulers, but rice is not mentioned in relation to any of the sixteenth century rulers (*Sedjarah Goa*, 19). The *gaukang* or regalia of Gowa itself, and of the other petty kingdoms of the area to its south (in present Takalar), are typically formed of magical weapons, and there are few examples of the ploughs or other symbols of agriculture so prominent among the regalia of the Bugis kingdoms further north. Finally it is notable that in the contract reportedly agreed between the "nine retainers" (*kasuiang salapanga*) of Gowa and their first rulers, Tumanurunga and Karaeng Bayo promise not to take the chickens, the eggs, the coconuts or the betelnut of their subjects, whereas nothing is said about rice (Abdurrazak 1969, 5).

These clues, together with the evidence of in-migration below, suggest that before the sixteenth century the area around Makasar/Ujung Pandang was still largely brackish swamps not yet intensively cultivated, and that the petty states conquered at the beginning of Gowa's sixteenth-century rise were none of them very significant either economically or politically.

BANTAENG

In modern times the boundary between Makasar and Bugis populations in South Sulawesi has been very indistinct, with a great deal of overlapping and intermingling both in the west (Pangkajene and Maros) and in the southeast (Bantaeng, Bulukumba and Sinjai). By contrast the situation in the twelfth to fifteenth centuries appears to have been one of quite separate development before Gowa's wars on the Bugis in the sixteenth and seventeenth centuries, and the Bugis incursions southward under Arung Palakka and subsequent Bone rulers. In contrast to the similarity between all the other South Sulawesi languages, especially the Bugis-Enrekang-Toraja-Luwu group, "Makassarese shows very low [lexico-statistical] percentages with all the other languages, implying a long separation" (Mills 1975, 217). The pre-Islamic burial practice of the Bugis aristocracy appears to have been cremation, whereas the Makasarese had an elaborate burial similar to modern Torajans (Pelras 1981, 170; Raffles 1817, II: clxxxvi). Most remarkable of all, the Makasarese know nothing of the Bugis *I La Galigo* epic so important to all Bugis royal courts,[4] and Makasar place names and characters appear to be almost absent in that great saga. While the only Makasar place name clearly identifiable is one unhelpful reference to "Mangkasa" (Kern 1939, 724), one of the wives of La

Fig. 3 Stone figures on the royal graves of Binamu (Jeneponto), South Sulawesi
(Photo by A. Reid)

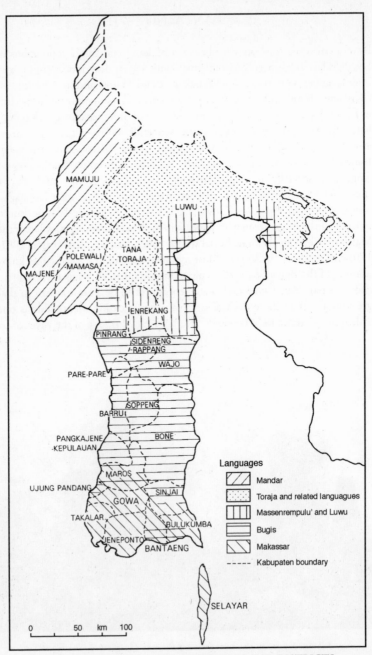

MAP 4 SOUTH SULAWESI LANGUAGES AND DISTRICTS

Galigo has the undeniably Makasar name of Karaeng Tompo'. She is a princess of Sunra (also called Pujanati), a kingdom variously described as three or seven days' sail westward of Cina (Wajo), with its capital a river-port visited by a merchant from Minangkabau (Kern 1939, 626–53). Pelras (1977, 246) has suggested the Pangkajene-Maros-Gowa area for this port; to my mind it could at least as probably be in the Bantaeng region.

The reason for the very low level of interaction between Bugis and Makasar prior to the sixteenth century may be geographic. Pelras (1977, 239–42; 1981, 162) has argued that the present heartland of the Bugis (Bone-Soppeng-Sidenreng/Rappang-Pinrang) was still largely under water in the era of the *I La Galigo* (perhaps fourteenth century). The main action of the epic, and the undoubted centres of Bugis kingship at that period, were in Luwu and Cina (Wajo). The cordillera of the southwestern arm of Sulawesi was virtually an island, probably Makasar territory for the most part, but with its main centres on the sea-route along the southern coast.

Although little scientific study has been possible on the grave-sites which have yielded so much Sawankhalok and Ming porcelain in recent years, the basic pattern seems clear from information provided by the (illegal) dealers. Apart from a few spectacular finds in Luwu, very few of these grave-sites have been uncovered in the present Bugis area—no doubt partly due to the factors mentioned above. The great majority of porcelain finds are at the head, pelvic area, and feet of skeletons, sometimes in wooden coffins, found usually in slightly elevated ground just back from the coastal plain, in an arc stretching from Pangkajene in the west, all along the southern coast to the Bira peninsula and the island of Selayar in the southeast. This coincides remarkably with Makasar territory.

There is no evidence of any Chinese traders visiting South Sulawesi prior to the seventeenth century, and we must assume that most of this porcelain was brought by Javanese and Malay traders on their way to obtain the spices of Maluku—a route open since at least the fourteenth century. Other early Javanese trade-routes may have led to the Malili area of Luwu[5] and to Luwuk/ Manggai, probably outlets for the nickeliferous Sulawesi iron necessary for making the famous krisses of Majapahit (Rouffaer 1904, 107–8; Noorduyn 1983, 111; Pelras 1981, 177). For all this shipping it would have been logical to stop for supplies along the southern coast of South Sulawesi, while some Javanese vessels, then as now, probably had the misfortune to be wrecked along the coast.

Aside from these physical remains, most of which appear to date from a period between the thirteenth and the sixteenth centuries, there are a number of other indications of Javanese commercial contacts along the southern coast of Sulawesi.

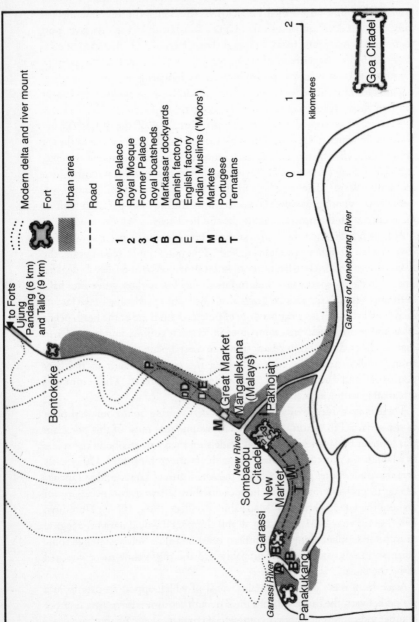

MAP 5 MAKASAR ABOUT 1650

Firstly we have the evidence of the fourteenth century *Nagarakertagama*, which lists three places—Bantayan (Bantaeng), Luwuk (probably Luwu, but perhaps the Luwuk of eastern Sulawesi), and Uda (unidentified)—as all being part of one island, with Bantaeng the principal place in it. This would appear to be Sulawesi, or at least its southwestern arm. In addition a number of separate islands are listed, including Selayar, Buton, Banggai, and "Makasar", of which more later (Pigeaud 1960, II: 17). Then in early accounts there are such place names as Sorobaya (Takalar and Bantaeng), Jipang (Takalar) and Garassi' (Grisek) (at the mouth of the Jeneberang), all names of north Java cities likely to have sent merchants in this direction (Goedhard 1920a, 337–8; 1920b, 166).

In Selayar some remains have been reverently preserved of a wooden vessel, with a beautifully carved winged *naga* motif on its bowsprit, and the clearly legible words "Sultan Abdul Malik Tuban" carved beneath the rudder support. Tuban was the last of the Muslim north Java ports to remain loyal to the Hindu kings of the interior of Java, and we may reasonably ascribe these remains to a Javanese vessel of the fifteenth or sixteenth century. In Bira, the shipbuilding centre at the southeastern peninsula of South Sulawesi, oral and written traditions ascribe the origins of the community to a group of wealthy Javanese traders shipwrecked nearby (Rizal 1978, 8). Similarly a legend once popular in Bantaeng ascribed the seven districts of Bantaeng to seven sisters, all of whom were taken to Java by the king of Java who wanted to marry the youngest of them, though they subsequently all returned to Bantaeng (Matthes 1943, 245–46; Goudsward 1854; Ulaen 1979, 21). The *gaukang* of Bantaeng, at least in the nineteenth century, was a golden Hindu statuette, perhaps also obtained from Java (Kooreman 1883, 188).

It seems clear, then, that before the rise of Makasar in the sixteenth century, there were already Javanese commercial contacts at many points along the southern coast. Among the finds in grave-sites in this area, some stand out as so valuable that they are likely to have originated from a wealthy dynasty. To my limited knowledge, this would apply to some finds near Tanahberu in the Bira Peninsula, to Bantaeng, and to the Pangkajene area north of Ujung Pandang which Pelras has shown to be the centre of a once-flourishing port of Siang (Pelras 1977, 252–5). In particular, two remarkable gold death masks have recently been uncovered, one from Pangkajene and one from Bantaeng.[6] The likelihood is that significant states existed in these areas, with some outside contacts, before the rise of Gowa.

It is the internal myths which lead us to believe that Bantaeng was a more important influence on Gowa than was Siang/Pangkajene. In addition to the Gowa origin myth, described above, we have the story of how Bajeng, in the Limbung (Polombangken) area, came to be the most powerful of the small

Fig. 4 Dutch sketch of Makasar in 1638 (Algemene Rijksarchief, Kaartenafdeling, The Hague)

states of Takalar before all were conquered by Gowa in the early sixteenth century. The first ruler descended from heaven with six brothers at Tanabangka in Bantaeng (perhaps a reflection of the Bantaeng legend of seven sisters, the youngest of whom was called *Bungko*). These brothers wandered about to the westward of Bantaeng looking for an appropriate place to settle, until at last they came to the Takalar area, where each founded a settlement. Since all were of heavenly descent (*Tumanurung*) each bore the title Karang Loe ("Great King"), which was also the title of the revered founder of the Bantaeng dynasty. The eldest of the brothers settled at Bajeng, but became especially powerful because of a magical blowpipe (or spear in other versions) which became the *gaukang* of the state. Only when King Tumapa'risi' Kallonna of Gowa obtained this *gaukang* by a trick was he able to defeat Bajeng and thus incorporate the whole Takalar area into the kingdom of Makasar (Tideman 1908, 488–500; Goedhard 1920a, 342–3; *Sedjarah Goa*, 20).

THE BAJAU

Bajau is the name usually given by Malay-speakers to those speakers of the Samal group of languages who still live primarily on their boats. Though linguistically similar, they are widely dispersed throughout the coasts of Sulawesi, eastern and northern Borneo, the southern Philippines and parts of Maluku. Their gradual settlement on land and absorption into the dominant Muslim populations of these regions has been proceeding for centuries. Nevertheless the characteristic features of the Bajau are still held to be a life spent predominantly in their small boats, a total dependence on the sea for a livelihood, and an animistic religion. These features have given the Bajau a low status in the dominant societies of the major land masses, yet they have nonetheless been indispensable servants of the major ruling dynasties—in Sulu, Bone, Luwu and Makasar as related groups were for the Sultanates of Melaka and Johor. They appear to have been the messengers, fishermen, and seamen of kings, at a time when few other ethnic groups had fully mastered the sea.[7]

Most Bajau oral traditions collected in the Sulawesi area agree that there was an initial relationship with the kingdom of Luwu (thus probably in the fourteenth/fifteenth centuries), which was subsequently transferred to Gowa (Makasar) and later still to Bone. Many myths point to an origin in Johor or elsewhere in the Melaka Straits, prior to a dispersal which brought them to Luwu. A few versions of the story have the Bajau coming directly to the Makasar area. But all agree that a sacred contract was made with the king of

Gowa, after he had taken a Bajau woman as his wife before he realized her ethnic identity. This is presumably the mythic explanation why the Bajau, although in a sense outcast, are yet closely tied to the ruler. Once the Bajau woman's identity is discovered, she is sent off again with her royal son, but only after an agreement that Bajau adat will be respected, in return for an annual tribute of sea-produce the Bajau will deliver to the king (Pelras 1972, 157–9; Soesangobeng 1977, 42–4). Speelman, the conqueror of Makasar, noted the value that the Bajaus still had for Makasar:

> The people that men call Badjous, living here in fairly large numbers before the war, under the jurisdiction of Makassar, mostly had their residence on islands before Labakkang [Pangkajene] and particularly . . . on Salemo . . . They also travel to all the islands lying further out to sea, to gather tortoise-shell from them, which they are obliged to deliver to the King of Makassar; and moreover they must always be ready to go with their vessels in any direction they are sent, wherever the King from time to time sees some advantage, being the type of men known as slaves of the King, *Amba Radja* . . . They are a very useful people. (Speelman 1670, I: 43)

The favourite locations of Bajau sea-people have always been clusters of small islands, large enough to provide well water, but not so large as to attract the attention of land-based peoples. The archipelago of coral islands which spreads out to sea in front of Ujung Pandang and the coast to the northward must have been the most attractive location in the whole of Sulawesi. There are upwards of fifty small coral islands within a day's sail of Ujung Pandang, most of them less than a kilometre across, but very well provided with water, with breadfruit trees, and with a fish life of extraordinary abundance. At least at two of these islands (Kodingareng Lompo and Balang Lompo) which are today the most heavily populated with Makasarese, local tradition concedes that the original inhabitants were Bajau (interviews; also Sopher 1965, 145). It seems more than likely that the Bajau were in fact the first to exploit the prolific marine resources of this archipelago.

The only certainly-dated account of early Bajau activity is that of Tomé Pires, written just after the conquest of Melaka in 1511:

> The islands of *Macacar* are four or five days journey beyond the islands we have described [southern Borneo], on the way to the Maluccas. The islands are numerous. It is a large country. One side goes up to Buton and Madura and the other extends far up north. They are all heathens. They say that these islands have more than fifty kings. These islands trade with Malacca and with Java and with Borneo and with Siam and with all the places between Pahang and Siam.

They are men more like the Siamese than other races. Their language is on its own, different from the others. They are heathens, robust, great warriors. They have many foodstuffs.

These men in these islands are greater thieves than any in the world, and they are powerful and have many *paraos*. They sail about plundering, from their country up to Pegu, to the Moluccas, and to Banda, and among all the islands around Java; and they take women to sea. They have fairs where they dispose of the merchandise they steal and sell the slaves they capture. They run all around the island of Sumatra. They are mainly corsairs. The Javanese call them *BaJuus*[8] and the Malays call them this and Calates. They take their spoils to *Jumaia*, which is near Pahang, where they sell and have a fair continually.

Those who do not carry on this kind of robbery come in their large well-built *pangajavas* with merchandise. They bring many foodstuffs: very white rice; they bring . . . some gold. They all wear krisses. They are well-built men. They go about the world and everyone fears them, because no doubt all the robbers obey these with good reason. They carry a great deal of poison[ed weapons] and shoot with them. They have no power against the junks which can all defend themselves, but every other ship in the country they have in their hands. (Pires 1515, 226–7, 451)

There is obviously some confusion in this description, between the seafaring Bajaus, who traded, marauded (notably, in more recent times, the Balangingi Samal of the Sulu area, see Warren 1981, 182–4), and were widely dispersed throughout the Archipelago; and the Makasarese, who were well-built, great warriors, and sometimes likened to Siamese (because of their physique and non-Muslim culture). Nevertheless it is important to note that it was Bajau seafarers who first made the Makasar area known in the Malayan area, and that their preference for island-dwelling led Pires (like other Portuguese and Arab writers) to think of *Macaçar* itself as a collection of islands. At this point we should look again at the *Nagarakertagama*, for it too, specifies "Those that are (enumerated) island by island (are): Makasar, Buton, Banggai, Kumir, Galiyao and Selayar, Sumba, Solot", thus clearly differentiating the smaller islands on the route to Maluku, from the three previously-named places all forming part of one island—Bantaeng, Luwuk and Uda (Pigeaud 1960, III: 17).

In the light of Pires' information, the story of Karaeng-Semerluki in the Melaka chronicle *Sejarah Melayu* (Brown 1952, 99–100) becomes easier to understand. Semerluki was a prince of Balului, represented as the most powerful city/state in "Tanah Mengkasar". Because of an illicit love for his aunt, the youngest of seven wives of his father the king, he was sent off to "Ujung Tanah" (Johor) to plunder the land and find a wife there. With his fleet he ravaged the coast of Java, Malaya, and Sumatra, before being worsted by the Laksamana of Pasai, and being forced to return to "Tanah Mengkasar". This was said to occur in the reign of Melaka's Sultan Mansur Shah, thus about 1440. Whether or not Pelras (1981, 154) is justified in reading Semerluki as "Same ri Luk" (a Samal prince of Luwu), we do seem to have to do here with a Bajau fleet similar to those described by Pires.

This evidence seems to suggest that the term "Makasar" first emerges into the consciousness of people elsewhere as the island base of the Bajau seamen. In the first instance these islands may have been used by the Bajau as a gathering point for voyaging much further afield, in all directions. Increasingly, however, they must have exported the produce of the immediate Makasar mainland, making agreements to this effect with the various petty *karaeng* of the Pangkajene-Gowa-Takalar area. In this context it is easy to understand the role the Bajau must have played in the rapid rise of one particular state, Gowa/Makasar, to predominance in this area.

LAKIPADADA AND THE TORAJA ENIGMA

Apart from the role of Lakipadada as the brother of Karaeng Bayo and provider of the sacred sword Sudanga in the Gowa chronicles, he makes only one appearance in all Bugis and Makasar texts, as far as I know. This is in Selayar, where "Lalakki Padada" is given as the name of the heaven-descended man from Makasar or Bantaeng, who founded the statelet (*negeri*) of Buki and later the senior statelet in Selayar, Bontobangun (Donsellar 1857, 284–5). Lakipadada does not appear in Bugis literature, but in the mythology of the southern Sa'dan Toraja he plays a very prominent role. He is a kind of Ulysses figure, who journeys across the ocean and to heaven itself in search of immortality, only to fail at the final test. After many adventures he arrives at Gowa, demonstrates his remarkable powers, and is allowed to marry the raja's daughter. From this marriage are born three sons, whom their father endows with dominion over Gowa, Luwu, and Tana Toraja respectively, giving to each a powerful weapon. Gowa, as in the story with which we began, receives the sword *Sudanga* (Nooy-Palm 1979, 148–51).

It is impossible to be sure whether the Lakipadada myth was borrowed by Toraja from Gowa, either during the seventeenth century period when Makasar had some influence there, or even more recently, or whether there was really some Toraja contact at about the time of Gowa's rise. If the latter is the case, the key probably lies in metal technology. The Lake Matano area of Luwu was the principal source of iron in eastern Indonesia, and the Toraja with the people of Seko and Rongkong to their east were acknowledged as the first in South Sulawesi to master the art of forging and weapon-making (Abendanon 1918, 1352–4; Noorduyn 1983, 111; Zerner 1981, 95–6). The biggest Bugis iron-working centre, at Massepe (Sidenreng), attributes the origin of its craft to a Toraja from Sangala' named Panre Baka (Isa 1979, 54–5). Since Lakipadada is noted in the Toraja legend for having collected a number of swords from all his travels, he may personify the spread from Toraja to Gowa of the ability to manufacture swords and spears.

The other curious factor, noted above, is that pre-Islamic Makasarese had a burial practice very similar to that of modern Toraja, whereas Bugis aristocrats appear to have been cremated, and their ashes buried in urns. Moreover a part of the *Kale Gowa* or Tamalate area where the kings of Gowa are buried is known as Lakiung, and Karaeng Lakiung was a title borne by two of the early rulers of Gowa (Tunipalangga and Mohammed Said). The word *Lakiung* appears to have no meaning in modern Makasarese, but in Sa'adan Toraja *Lakkian* is the elevated house-like structure in which a corpse is kept during a death-feast. This may be a clue to the origin of the unique royal graves of South Sulawesi, in the form of a stone or mortar edifice inside which a man can stand. Before Islam there may have been already a practice of building wooden house-like structures, perhaps called *lakiung*, over the graves of kings—such as still occurs in parts of Tana Toraja where there are no suitable cliffs for rock burial. Also suggestive are the human figures, in stone, still standing guard over some of the royal graves of Binamu, in the southern Makasar area (see figure 3)—reminiscent of the wooden *tau-tau* so famous in Tana Toraja.

Perhaps all that we are saying here is that Torajans and Makasarese shared aspects of a common South Sulawesi culture, from which in some respects the Bugis diverged as a result of Indic influences operating through Luwu. Perhaps also, however, there were, in the days before the Bugis expansion southward, some channels of direct contact between Torajans and Makasarese.

GOWA AND TALLO'

From all the above we may conclude that the Makasarese of the southern coast had had some fitful contact with Javanese traders for several centuries before 1500, and that significant states emerged in Bantaeng, Siang, and perhaps elsewhere. The small village units of the lower Jeneberang river appear to have profited from ideas of kingship from the Bantaeng area, and from the relatively strong naval power of the Bajau on the islands offshore, to give rise to the Gowa state. This may have occurred at the beginning of the fifteenth century or even earlier, though we have no definite evidence of the existence of Gowa as a significant state until the reign of Tumapa'risi' Kallonna (±1512–48), whose conquests are mentioned in the local traditions of the Takalar area as well as in Gowa chronicles.

The Gowa chronicle declares that Tumapa'risi' Kallonna was the raja who first compiled a code of laws and the manner of declaring war; that the *syahbandar* of this raja was named Daeng Pamatte'; that he was *syahbandar* and also *Tumailalang* (liaison between king and *bate salapang*); and that it was this Daeng Pamatte' who created Makasar writing (*Sedjarah Goa*, 18).

The mention of the Persian term *syahbandar* or harbour-master means that foreign traders were for the first time doing substantial business with Gowa during this reign. This is confirmed by a Portuguese visitor, Paiva, who moved his ships south from the established port of Siang in 1544 to "the great city of Gowa, where the ships were better protected against the wind" (Schurhammer 1977, 528). The Gowa chronicle agrees that Tumapa'risi' Kallonna was the first Gowa king to be visited by the Portuguese (*Paranggi*) while he also had a skirmish with a *Jawa* (Javanese or Malay) force (*Sedjarah Goa*, 22, 19).

The Portuguese sources of the 1540s tell us much more about the port and state of Siang (Pangkajene), "seven leagues" north of Gowa, which Pelras has convincingly shown to have been a major commercial centre already visited by Malay traders in the period around 1500 (Pelras 1977, 243, 252–3). The Portuguese and Makasar sources agree that Gowa had some military victories over Siang in the reign of Tumapa'risi' Kallonna, though Gowa's dominance over its older rival was not established until the reign of his successor (*Sedjarah Goa*, 18; Pelras 1977, 252–5).

One of the factors aiding Gowa in the contest to attract the patronage of Malay traders was the role of the Portuguese in Christianizing the ruler of Siang, thereby presumably driving the Muslim traders to seek allies elsewhere. Another factor must have been the tiny state of Tallo'. Whereas Gowa's capital was six kilometres from the sea, the first ruler of Tallo' had established his capital at a good anchorage at the mouth of the next river northward. As the Tallo' chronicle relates it, Karaeng Loe ri Sero' moved to the river-mouth because his previous home had been "inappropriate, being neither beside the sea nor in the foothills" (Rahim and Ridwan 1975, 6). The new location enjoyed the natural protection of the sea on the north, the river on the east and south, with low-lying marshland almost closing off the western side.

Tallo' appears to have been a maritime state from its foundation, probably owing much to Malay, Javanese, and Bajau traders. Karaeng Loe himself is said to have established Tallo' only after returning from a visit to "Jawa" (meaning western Indonesia in general). His son is said to have voyaged to

Melaka in the west and to Banda in the east. The wives of this second ruler were all from coastal, trading communities—from Garassi' at the mouth of the Jeneberang, from Siang, and a half-Javanese woman from Surabaya (Rahim and Ridwan 1975, 5–7). The third ruler, Tunipasuru', was said to have sailed to Melaka and to Johor, where he collected an outstanding trading debt (Rahim and Ridwan 1975, 9).

Tunipasuru' was contemporary with Tumapa'risi' Kallonna of Gowa. After one unhappy attempt to resist that ruler's military expansionism, Tunipasuru' invited him to Tallo' and established a close alliance with him. The two rulers and their *gallarrang* (local chiefs) solemnly swore that whoever attempted to divide Gowa and Tallo' would be cursed by God (*Sedjarah Goa*, 21). To this marriage Gowa brought its increasingly effective military power and its local alliances; but Tallo' brought its links with foreign traders and their advanced technology—Tunipasuru' is said to have presided over the first making of guns. Tallo' also took part in conquering the Jeneberang port of Garassi' for

TABLE 6 RULERS OF GOWA AND TALLO'

(following Sedjarah Goa; Sedjarah Kerajaan Tallo'; and Ligtvoet 1880)

GOWA	TALLO'
G 6 Tunatangka'lopi	
G 7 Batara Goa (son of G 6)	T 1 Karaeng Loe ri Sero' (son of G 6)
G 8 Tunidjallo'ri Passuki' (son of G 7)	T 2 Tunilabu di Suriwa (son of T 1)
G 9 Tumapa'risi' Kallonna (son of G 7) r. ±1512–1548	T 3 Tunipasuru' (son of T 2) allied with G 9
G 10 Tunipalangga (son of G 9) b. ±1512; r. 1548–66	T 4 Tumenanga ri Makkoayang (son of T 3) b. ±1521; r. 1547–77 Baligau of Gowa 1566–77
G 11 Tunibatta (I Tajibarani) (son of G 9) r. 1566 for 40 days	
G12 Tunijallo' (son of G 11) b. 1546; r. 1566-90	T 5 I Sambo (daughter of T4; wife of G12) r. 1577–90
G13 Tunipassulu' (son of G 12 and T 5) b. 1576; r. 1593–1639	T 6 Karaeng Matoaya, Tumenanga ri Agamanna, Sultan Awwal-ul-Islam (son of T 4) b. 1573; r. 1593–1637; Pabicara Butta of Gowa 1593–1637
G14 Tumenanga ri Gaukanna, Sultan Alauddin (son of G 12 and T 5) b. 1586; 5. 1593–1639	

the joint kingdom, which we can now call Makasar (Rahim and Ridwan 1975, 9).

The chronicles of both Gowa and Tallo' place a good deal of stress on the sanctity of the Gowa-Tallo' relationship. Both insist, for example, that the founder of the Tallo' dynasty was a brother of Batara Goa, the still shadowy seventh ruler of Gowa—a common means of symbolizing the fundamental equality of allied rulers. Both chronicles appear to have been written under the influence of the brilliant Tallo' figures, Matoaya and Pattingalloang, who are frequently quoted in them. We should probably understand these chronicles are in part a plea for the maintenance of the Gowa-Tallo' relationship, much as the *Sejarah Melayu* pleads for the relationship between Sultan and Bendahara as a fundamental pillar of Melaka's sovereignty. The marriage of Gowa and Tallo' was indeed a brilliant success, but a temporary one brought about by two or three outstanding personalities and a great deal of luck. Bugis-Makasar culture does make checks and balances against arbitrary power possible, notably by the sacred and binding nature of oaths taken before the spirits of the ancestors. Nevertheless there are plenty of examples in Makasar and other South Sulawesi societies to show that power corrupts there as it does anywhere else.

The first Tallo' ruler to play a major part in the joint kingdom was Tunipasuru's successor Tumenanga ri Makkoayang (±1547–77). Because two Gowa rulers died within three months of 1566, during a bitter war against Bone, this Tallo' ruler was able to take charge of the Makasar camp and arrange the succession. He placed Tunijallo' on the throne of Gowa, married him to his own daughter and eventual successor I Sambo, and retained considerable influence over the young ruler as his *baligau* or chief minister (*Sedjarah Goa*, 29, 39–42, 49; Rahim and Ridwan 1975, 10–11). The Tallo' chronicle quotes his son:

Karaeng Matoaya said, "In the time of this raja it was said that there was only one subject and two kings [*se'reji ata, narua Karaeng*]." People who dreamed of dividing Gowa and Tallo were put to death. (Rahim and Ridwan 1975, 11)

The partnership appears to have worked smoothly as long as Tumenanga ri Makkoayang lived, though once again we may have a deliberately idealized picture from the chronicles. This ruler's death left his daughter I Sambo on the Tallo' throne, and her husband Tunijallo' on the throne of Gowa— probably not a good formula for a long-term stable relationship. When Tunijallo' died about 1590, the dualism of the kingdom was thrown sharply into question, for the new king laid claim to Tallo' from his mother as well as Gowa from his father. This apparently headstrong young king was later

called Tunipasulu' ("he who was driven out"). He was the only Makasar ruler
in our period to be deposed, and the only one whom the chronicles judge
negatively. The major reason appears to be that in violating the duality of the
state he was held to have ruled tyrannically. As well as becoming king in
Gowa and Tallo', "he it was who forbade the subject [ata] to be loyal to two
masters"—presumably a direct repudiation of Matoaya's statement about the
previous reign. Moreover in his reign, "innocent people were suddenly simply
killed" (Sedjarah Goa, 55). The revolution against Tunipasulu' after only a
three-year reign was led by the brilliant Tallo' prince Matoaya, who took over
the endangered Tallo' throne and became chancellor of Gowa with the new
title pabicara butta for the next forty-five years (1593–1637). During the
most spectacular period of Makasar's growth as an international centre,
therefore, the dualism of Gowa and Tallo' became a sacrosanct article of
constitutional faith.[9]

TRADE AND THE TRADERS

When the Portuguese visited Siang in the 1540s, they found the principal
traders established there were from Ujung Tanah (Johor), Pahang and Patani,
and that they had been trading to the area for the previous fifty years
(Schurhammer 1977, 528; Wessels 1925, 8; Pelras 1977, 166). Probably
these Muslim Malay merchants, originally established in Melaka before its
1511 conquest by the Portuguese, had followed the route pioneered by the
Bajau to south Sulawesi. They appear not to have been on their way to the
spices of Maluku, as the Javanese traders who called at points further south
and southeast had been, but to have collected local south Sulawesi exports:
sandalwood, sea-produce (especially tortoise-shell), rice and slaves.
    At least by the reign of Tunipalangga (±1548–66), these Malay merchants
shifted their base of operations to the Gowa-Tallo' area. The chronicle relates
that this ruler was approached by a trading ship's captain from "Jawa" named
Nakhoda Bonang, a title which recalls the famous Islamic mystic of northeast Java, Sunan Bonang. After presenting the ruler with various gifts, Bonang
asked permission for the Malay community to settle in Makasar under four
guarantees of freedom. The Makasarese would not 1) enter the Malay
compounds; 2) go into their houses; 3) divide their children according to the
nigayang custom; or 4) seize their property as a result of some offence,
according to the nirappung custom (Cense 1978, 230, 590). These privileges
were granted, after establishing that they would apply to "all we who wear a
tied sarung [as opposed to Makasar trousers with loose sarung?], that is the
people of Pahang, Patani, Campa, Minangkabau, and Johor" (Sedjarah Goa,

28; "Kapitein Melajoe" 1929, 109). As far as I know this is the only pre-European case in Indonesia of specific written guarantees for foreign merchants, and it must have contributed much to Makasar's outstanding reputation as a country "kind to strangers". A regular system of weights and weighing was also organized under Tunipalangga (*Sedjarah Goa*, 26).

The Malay community grew steadily, especially as Makasar began to make itself a major collecting centre for the exports of a much wider region. Crucial in this regard was the route to the eastward. Tumapa'risi' Kallonna is already reported to have imposed some tribute on Bulukumba and Selayar, but a closer control over the whole southern coast was established under his two successors, aided by the Tallo' ruler who took part in expeditions against Binamu (Jeneponto), Bulukumba and Selayar in the 1560s and 1570s (*Sedjarah Goa*, 18, 25; Rahim and Ridwan 1975, 10–11). The Bira area of Bulukumba was essential as a ship-building centre. Together with Selayar, it also provided Makasar's major manufactured export—white and checked cotton cloth. "Selayar cloth", sometimes known as "Makasar cloth" became the Indonesian-made cloth in greatest demand throughout the Archipelago (Rouffaer 1904, 4; Speelman 1670, II, 241; Stavorinus 1798, II, 261–3).

This coast was also the first step on the route to Maluku, to which some Malay vessels must have been travelling for spices before the end of the sixteenth century. By the first decade of the seventeenth century we know that Karaeng Matoaya kept an agent in Banda, and the trade to exchange Makasar rice and cloth for Malukan spices was well established (see chapter 7). In 1625 Sihordt estimated that about forty junks each year were sent to Maluku by "Malays from Patani, from Johor and other places who lived in Macassar in many thousands" (*Dagh-Register* 1624–29, 125). The constant Makasar struggle to establish its supremacy in Buton, against the claims of Ternate and later of the Dutch, is part of this steady push towards dominating the spice route. The growing importance of Makasar as a source of spices and a market for Chinese and Indian goods also attracted the Europeans to the city. The Portuguese appear to have begun coming in substantial numbers at the beginning of the seventeenth century, as the Dutch were making it difficult for them to trade directly to Maluku. In 1625, according to Sihordt, there were between ten and twenty-two Portuguese frigates visiting the port every year, and up to five hundred Portuguese sometimes gathered there. After the fall of Portuguese Melaka to the Dutch in 1641, Makasar became the principal haven for Portuguese in the Archipelago, with as many as three thousand Portuguese living in the city. The English established a factory in Makasar in 1613, the Danes in 1618, while Spanish and Chinese traders began to appear from 1615 and 1619 respectively (see chapter 7).

The reason for this influx of foreign traders was not simply trade, but also the freedom and security of foreigners and their property in the city, constantly remarked upon in the English and Portuguese despatches. Long before the kings of Makasar became Muslim, Tunijallo' (1566–90) encouraged the Malay merchants to establish their mosque at their centre of Mangallekana (*Sedjarah Goa*, 50). Similarly, long after Islamization, the Portuguese were permitted to establish as many as four places of Christian worship in the 1640s (Meersman 1967, 115–19). A number of prominent refugees made their home in the city. Around 1620 an uncle and a sister of the queen of Patani established themselves in Makasar after some internal conflict in Patani.

The uncle, Maharaja Lela, became thenceforth the leader of the Makasar Malays ("Kapitein Malajoe" 1920, 109–10; Cense 1978, 425–6; cf. Skinner 1963, 240). Subsequently a very substantial Indian merchant (one of the Malabar Moplahs?) whom the Makasarese knew as Mapule and the English as "Mopley", established himself as one of the leading financiers and traders of the city, and his followers and descendants also came to regard themselves eventually as "Malay" (Cense 1978, 424–6). Similarly one of the most outstanding Portuguese merchant-diplomats in Asia, Francisco Vieira, decided to take his Cambodian elephants to Makasar instead of fulfilling his mission by presenting them to the Spanish viceroy in Manila, once he discovered that his country was again at war with Spain. The Makasar diary recorded that the first elephant was seen in the city on 16 May 1642—"a gift from Wehara (Vieira)". He went on to build up a major trading network based in Makasar (Boxer 1967; "Makassaarsche Historien" 1855, 121). In contrast with the intolerance with which Europeans treated each other in Asian waters, Makasar was a remarkable example of hospitality to all.

THE GEOGRAPHY OF MAKASAR CITY

The two oldest centres of government in the Makasar area are Kale Gowa (Tamalate), on elevated ground on the north bank of the Jeneberang about six kilometres from its mouth, and Tallo' at the mouth of the Tallo' river. These two sites appear to have similar features to the old fort of Siang described by Pelras (1977, 243). The walls encompass a very large area, with a total perimeter of two kilometres or more in each case. The central elements still to be seen are the sacred coronation stone on which new rulers took their oaths of office; a well or spring, often also held to be sacred; and the tombs of the rulers. Gowa, Tallo' and Siang are all featured in the earliest Portuguese descriptions and maps dating from the 1540s (Pelras 1977, 243–6). For

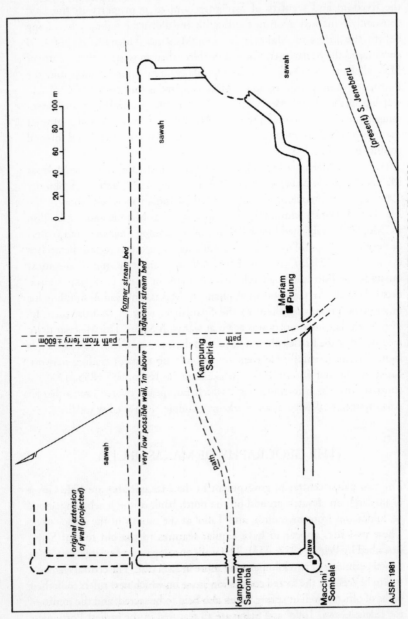

MAP 6 RECONSTRUCTION OF BENTENG SOMBAOPU

Gowa we are told the walls were built under Tumapa'risi' Kallonna (1512–48) (*Sedjarah Goa*, 67; Blok 1759, 9), though we presume the dynasty had established itself there considerably earlier. All of these three sites have yielded considerable finds of Chinese and Sawankhalok porcelain, presumably from the sixteenth century and earlier.

The Malay merchants who made their compact with King Tunipalangga (1548–66) were allocated a site at Mangallekana, on the coast just south of the Jeneberang river. That this must have become a centre of trade is confirmed by the title of the Shahbandar of that period, I Daeng ri Mangallekana (*Sedjarah Goa*, 25, 50; Noorduyn 1956, 249). The new role of Makasar as a trading centre must have required a capital nearer the commercial centre, and Tunipalangga is credited also with building the brick walls of the fort of Sombaopu, on the coast about a kilometre north of the outlet of the Jeneberang at that time (*Sedjarah Goa*, 26).

During the long duumvirate of Sultan Ala'uddin and Karaeng Matoaya (1590–1637) Sombaopu became the heart of Makasar, while the old Gowa must have become primarily a sacral centre for inaugurations and burials. As Kerckringh noted in 1638, "The King and nobles live in Sombopo, in houses built on thick pillars" (Tiele and Heeres, *Bouwstoffen*, II, 335). As is clear from the excellent Dutch maps drawn on a model from the 1630s, there were scores of separate houses in the rear (east) and northern side of the fort, grouped around the royal buildings in the southwest—two enormous wooden palaces, storehouses, and a mosque. Outside the fort were the two major markets to north and south respectively, the houses of the commoners, and, stretching north along the coast, the Portuguese and Indian quarters and the European factories.

Additional forts were built of brick during this reign—at Tallo' (presumable replacing an earlier earth wall), at Panakkukang just south of the Jeneberang mouth, and at Ujung Pandang (the later Fort Rotterdam) (Rahim and Ridwan 1975, 17). The two first-mentioned may well have been built to meet an expected Dutch attack in 1615, when the English agent reported "all the whole land is making of bricks for two castles this summer to be finished" (*Letters Received*, III: 150–1). In 1634 there was again a massive effort at building, primarily against the Dutch threat. Ujung Pandang was in that year provided with a brick fortress, Panakkukang was reinforced, and an earth wall was built to stretch all along the sea-front of the city for over ten kilometres, from Panakkukang past Sombaopu and Ujung Pandang to Ujung Tanah, where the coastline turns eastward toward Tallo' (Ligtvoet 1880, 94–5; Speelman 1670, I: 10–11). Later other forts were added along this defensive wall, at Barombong (near Panakkukang), at Sambong Jawa (between the English factory and Sombaopu) and at Ujung Tanah itself. All of these forts were destroyed either as a result of the Bungaya Treaty or the subsequent war in 1669, and their bricks were used either in Dutch buildings or in making wells and house foundations for the local population. The best indication of what they were is visible at the ruins of the sea-wall of Tallo', now exposed by the encroaching sea at many points. This was about two metres wide, with large stone blocks forming the inner and outer surfaces, and presumably earth and rubble in the middle.

Of all these fortifications, Sombaopu is the best known from contemporary sources, and yet the most difficult to locate today.[10] The reason is the build-up of the delta which has left it remote and inaccessible from either land or sea. The shoreline further north, including the mouth of the placid Tallo' river, appears to have been stable for centuries. The Jeneberang, on the other hand, has been pushing its delta further out to sea at a rate of several metres a year, and changing its outlet with every flood. It has thus become difficult to relate the seventeenth century maps and descriptions to the site which local inhabitants insist is that of Sombaopu, in Maccini' Sombala', Kampung Sarombe, on the island formed by two major mouths of the present Jeneberang river.

Aerial photographs however enable us to resolve the apparent discrepancy. Among the many earlier beds of the Jeneberang there is a clear one to the south of either of the present mouths, looping southward just before it enters the sea in a northerly direction, leaving Panakkukang on a peninsula on its southern bank (see map 5). The delta formed by this outlet must have formed the southern promontory of the deep bay shown in Woldemar's 1660 drawing (reproduced in Boxer 1967), in the 1669 drawing reproduced in Bassett, and in the 1693 "Carte ende Tykeninge van Macassar", which is abstracted in Leonard Andaya (1981, map 9) and partly reproduced in Skinner (1963). The northern promontory of this bay is formed by Ujung Pandang, and Sombaopu lies at the base of the bay, though nearer to its southern end. All the seventeenth century maps also show a smaller river running only a hundred metres or so to the north of Sombaopu, whereas the main river is much further away to the south (see figure 4). How this pattern came about is explained by Speelman's description, from south to north, of the coast of Makasar after his conquest of it:

> At the time of the overrunning of Panakkukang in 1660 the Garassi' [Jeneberang] River had its outlet close by this [Panakkukang] fortress, but the King of Makassar had it re-dug subsequently by force of men, and brought the mouth of the river to where it now is; an island, named after the negeri which is situated upon it, is now situated between the new outlet and the old, which still brings down a lot of water in heavy rain . . . The names of all the small,

burned-out negeris [are] Patto . . . Bontokeke, a larger village than many others
on the bank of the Garassi' River. I skim over all the pools or fishponds.

Then comes Sombaopu, now razed and thrown into chaos. As you look at
it, along the north side flows a river, named the new river or Binanga-beru,
because this was dug by the father of Karaeng Pattingaloang, Tumenange ri
Agamana or Karaeng Matoaya, from this bank to Sambong Jawa and further
to the north of Sombaopu to the Portuguese quarter. The area from Sombaopu
south to the Garassi' River should properly be called the city of Makassar,
although it is nevertheless divided by the Makassars themselves into various
villages, which bear their own name rather than any large one. (Speelman 1670,
II: 9–10)

The "new river" built by Matoaya shows on the maps of the 1630s as large
enough to harbour ships, and unbridged even though it virtually divided the
heart of the city from its very extensive northern suburbs. The river may in
fact have been intended to be a potential defence against the foreign residents,
almost all of whom were housed to the north of this river. The change
wrought by Hasanuddin in the channel of the main river is clearly shown on
the 1693 map as a straightening of the previous southward loop. It too was
presumably intended to shorten the defensive perimeter of the core city.
Although seemingly minor in comparison with Matoaya's project, it was
Hasanuddin's canal-digging which earned the legendary bitterness of the
Bugis captives forced to work on it (Emanuel n.d.).

At some stage subsequent to the Dutch destruction of Sombaopu in 1669,
flooding must have turned Matoaya's new channel into the main one, so that
the delta began to build up further to the north, around Sombaopu itself.
Meanwhile, the new colonial city, initially far smaller than the old one, grew
up seven kilometres further north on the northern side of Fort Rotterdam
(Ujung Pandang). Sombaopu was totally neglected, until today, and the
remaining bricks of the old walls were gradually removed by the local villagers
for use in their own building purposes. As far as I am aware, the only surveys
of Sombaopu in modern times have been one by Professor Mattulada (whose
publication on this I have not been able to locate) and one rather cursory
survey in 1977 by the Unit Penelitian Arkeologi Islam in Jakarta (*Berita
Penelitian Arkeologi* 26, 1980).

Fortunately what appears to be one bastion of Sombaopu has been
protected from further damage in modern times by the erection on it of a
holy tomb. This is now a mound 6.5 metres high and thirteen metres in
diameter, standing well above the surrounding delta. It is known as *Maccini'
Sombala'* ("the sighting of sails"), or sometimes simply as *Tompo' Bataya* ("the
highest brick-formation"). *Maccini' Sombala'* was once also the name of the

124

CHAPTER SIX

royal palace within Sombaopu, built on 26 August 1650 to replace a palace which had been pulled down, and ceremonially occupied by the king eighty days later (Ligtvoet 1880, 110). Its name may have lingered in the adjacent bastion. From this overgrown mound there extends in a northerly direction a still clearly evident though overgrown wall 150 metres long, and two to three metres in height and width, broken after sixty metres by what is now a village road. Similarly to the east of Maccini' Sombala' there extends another clear but overgrown wall, broken by flooding at many places, for about five hundred metres. This wall is now between one hundred and two hundred metres north of a new arm of the river now called the Je'ne' Beru (New River), though not to be confused with the "New River" of Speelman's day. The rear, eastern wall of the fort is also traceable, though it meanders strangely. More difficult is the wall on the remaining, northern side, which was once very strong. What is today pointed out as this wall, extending for about five hundred metres in a straight line, might equally be the bank of a small stream which at some time cut through and washed away the northern part of the ruined fort (see map 6).

From the Dutch maps and descriptions of Sombaopu in the 1630s we know that the seaward wall had a substantial bastion at each corner, and two entrances spaced along the wall, each protected by a fortification before it. Since there is now only one gap in this best-preserved wall, and no remaining northern bastion to match Maccini' Sombala' in the south, we conclude that the 150 metres now remaining is only two-thirds of the original wall, from the Maccini' Sombala' bastion to the second of the two gates. The remainder of this wall, the northeast bastion, and the whole northern wall would then have been washed away by one of the river outlets, since this area is now all low-lying ground. If our supposition is correct, this would give the original Sombaopu dimensions of about 240 x 500 metres, which is compatible with seventeenth century maps and only a little smaller than Gowa and Tallo' forts.

On 15 June 1669, after months of bitter fighting, the Dutch managed to undermine and blow up a gap about twenty metres long in the walls of Sombaopu. The following day the fighting for this famous fort was "so heavy 'that old soldiers have perhaps never heard its like in Europe itself', with the Dutch musketeers firing thirty thousand bullets that day" (Krucq 1941, 74). Only ten days later was the ruined castle fully in Dutch hands, and so ended "perhaps the heaviest and fiercest war ever fought by the [Dutch] Company" (Krucq 1941, 74). It is strange that so little attention has been paid by either side to the strongest fort ever built by Indonesians, the scene of one of the bitterest battles they ever had to fight.

NOTES

1. I am extremely grateful to Pam Millwood for drawing the maps in this paper, and to Alex Leget, Abdul Muttalib and Jo Jennings for help in understanding the land forms around Makasar. Local words are in Makasarese unless otherwise indicated. Place names are in modern Indonesian form.

2. Some versions of the chronicles add four earlier generations of rulers, beginning with the God-man Batara Guru, none of whom left any trace on earth. This must derive from a subsequent attempt to link Gowa with the Indic myths of Luwu or perhaps Java—but it is little help for our purposes.

3. Makasar was renamed Ujung Pandang in 1971.

4. The only Makasar region acknowledging any influence from Luwu, as far as I know, is Selayar, where a Luwu-derived dynasty on the east coast was later displaced by a Makasar/ Bantaeng one on the west (Donsellar 1857, 284).

5. The contacts of the Luwu area with Majapahit on the one hand and the Moluccas on the other are apparent in references to seafarers from Jadjapai' and Djawa, and warriors from Maloku and Teranati, occurring in the *I La Galigo* (Kern 1939, 180–5, 412).

6. The Pangkajene mask is described in Pelras (1975, 26). The Bantaeng one left Indonesia in the 1970s and may be that displayed in Jessep (1990, 223).

7. For a discussion of the Banjau-Samal role in the Sulu area see Nimmo (1972) and Warren (1981, 67–74, 182–4) and for the wider relations of *orang laut* throughout the whole Archipelago, see Pelras (1972), Sopher (1965) and Palleson (1978).

8. Cortesão has further confused a complicated issue by rendering BaJuus into English as Bugis. While the earliest European writers may well have sometimes confused the two peoples, there is little doubt that it was Bajaus with whom Pires was coming into contact in the waters of Melaka.

9. This question, and the later development of the Gowa-Tallo' partnership, are more fully treated in the following chapter.

10. The hope of the author in first publishing this chapter in 1983, that Sombaopu might again become a source of local pride and interest, has been abundantly fulfilled. Excavation and restoration of the site began in 1989, and it is now a significant tourist attraction and theme park.

CHAPTER SEVEN

A GREAT SEVENTEENTH CENTURY INDONESIAN FAMILY: MATOAYA AND PATTINGALLOANG OF MAKASAR[1]

F OR most Indonesians, and not only Indonesians, the past is remembered primarily through its great men. It has long been this way—the holy graves, *kramat*, of the great are everywhere venerated, and chronicles celebrate the deeds of saints and mighty rulers. The preoccupation of the nationalist movement and subsequently the Indonesian government with defining *pahlawan* (heroes) suitable to be upheld as paragons of the national struggle, has ensured that history has continued to be seen by the Indonesian schoolboy as a progression of great men (and recently of a few women).

Not surprisingly, given the priorities of the nationalist movement and the Dutch education of its leaders, the majority of the officially sanctioned heroes of modern times have been prominent opponents of the Dutch—many featured in colonial textbooks precisely because they were the losers in some significant Dutch victory. They have not always been historical models appropriate for the more complicated tasks of modern development, nor have they necessarily been people much loved by their subjects at the time.

This is particularly true of the seventeenth century, which threw up a number of very powerful Indonesian military rulers, who sought to unify their conquered domains by all means possible, and to concentrate economic as well as political power in their own hands. The pre-eminent cases in point are Sultan Agung of Mataram (1613–45), Sultan Iskandar Muda of Aceh (1607–37), and to a lesser extent Sultan Abdu'l Fatah of Banten (1651–83). I have argued elsewhere (see chapter 10) that the nature of the concerted monopolistic attack the Dutch were launching on the Asian trading system was probably a factor which encouraged the emergence of these centralizing rulers in the seventeenth century. All of them were intolerant of the private trade of their own subjects, and sought to obtain a position where the court alone would be able to bargain with the powerful foreigners over the terms of trade. They thereby established large fortunes and powerful armies, centralized power in their own hands to an unprecedented degree, and at their best imposed more predictable legal processes. But these changes never survived the death of the over-mighty monarch in whose hands all power resided.

Personally these famous rulers hardly offer an attractive example for young Indonesians. Iskandar Muda filled those around him with terror of sudden death, and devised hideous tortures and humiliations for all who failed to please him. Generals who failed were frequently emasculated and forced "to eat a plate of turds" in public, while one nobleman whose fighting cock defeated one of Iskandar Muda's reportedly suffered an even more humiliating death (Broecke 1634, I: 175–6; see also Best 1614, 172; *Letters Received*, III: 196; VI: 74, 78; Beaulieu 1666, 58–63). Sultan Agung has similarly been described as "a ruthless and brutal king" (Ricklefs 1978, 5) as well as a highly effective one. He too brought terrible destruction to all the areas he conquered, in particular the once flourishing cities of Java's north coast.

The historian might be inclined to excuse such tyrannical excesses on the part of a Shih Huang-ti, an Ivan the Terrible, or a Henry VIII on the grounds that these rulers were dragging their reluctant subjects along a path which we could later see to be leading towards the modern nation state. In the case of Iskandar Muda and Agung we have to record the opposite verdict. They appear to have ruled not by establishing enduring political institutions but by personal terror, which provoked a natural reaction in the opposite direction after their deaths. Aceh moved as far as an oligarchic style of government under a successions of queens—"the very name of kinge is long since become nautious to them, first caused through the Tyrannical Government of theire last kinge, and indeed, by the accompt they give of him, he was the cruelest Tyrant that many ages afforded" (Bowrey 1680, 296). Agung's empire similarly appears by historical hindsight as "a fragile construction basically held together by the threat of defeat and devastation" (Ricklefs 1978, 5), so that much of the turbulence of the succeeding century might be attributed to the reaction against the artificial centralization he had imposed. Moreover, Agung completely destroyed the vigorous commercial and maritime spirit of the Javanese, condemning them to isolation from the major technical and economic innovations of the seventeenth and later centuries.

Part of the problem for the modern national historian is that too little is known about the more quietly creative figures in Indonesian history to bring

them out of the shadows. Happily, however, there are a few personalities even
in the seventeenth century about whom we have sufficient data to show them
as both personally attractive and historically creative. The most striking, to
my mind, were members of the ruling family of Tallo', in South Sulawesi,
particularly Karaeng Matoaya and his son, Pattingalloang. They laid the basis
for the greatness of seventeenth century Makasar through not ruthlessness
but rather an extraordinary combination of intellectual eminence and
political wisdom.

Of course the expectations of kings were already very different in South
Sulawesi, where the obstacles to tyranny were many and strong. South
Sulawesi society is based on a very strong tradition of autonomy on the part
of the *wanua* or local community, which is united around some sacred objects
which are, like the chiefs who serve them, of heavenly descent. The customary
rulers of the political units which formed in the fifteenth-seventeenth
centuries out of federations of these *wanua* lost validity if they ruled otherwise
than in accordance with the *adat,* and the *adat* itself insisted that the
autonomy of the *wanua* be respected (L. Andaya 1975; Pelras 1971).

Within this tradition Gowa (Makasar) is usually considered the ruling
dynasty most influenced by outside ideas of exalted kingship. Nevertheless
the rise of Gowa to hegemony in South Sulawesi and beyond was marked
not only (as in other maritime states) by conquests made possible by the
technology and wealth derived from foreign trade, but also by a series of
solemn contractual engagements with other local communities.

For our purpose the most important of these relationships was that with
Tallo', only a few kilometres to the north. The traditions of both Gowa and
Tallo' trace the origin of the Tallo' dynasty back to a brother of the Gowa
ruler Battara Gowa, an origin which fitted the requirements of the later
political relationship very neatly (*Sedjarah Goa,* 13–14; Rahim and Ridwan
1975, 5–6). The reliable history of Tallo', however, goes no further back than
about 1500. The early sixteenth century rulers of Tallo' appear to have been
distinguished by their international travels and must have been more closely
connected than Gowa's with the trading community which linked the spice
islands in the east with Melaka and Java in the west (see chapter 6).

The third Tallo' ruler, Tunipasuru', made a solemn treaty with the
expansionist ruler of Gowa, Tumapa'risi' Kalonna (1512–48), after warring
against him for some time without success. Thereafter Tallo' participated in
all Gowa's wars, which were rapidly carrying it to pre-eminence in the
Makasarese area of Southwest Celebes. "Anyone who brought animosity
between Goa and Tallo' would be cursed by God", declared the chronicles
(*Sedjarah Goa,* 21).

We do not hear of any decisive Tallo' influence upon the affairs of the kingdom, however, until 1566 when the Gowa King, Tunipalangga, died in the third year of his war against the leading Bugis state of Bone. Tunipalangga's brother took over command of the armies, but was killed in battle forty days later. At this point the Tallo' ruler, known posthumously as Tumenanga ri Makkoayang, took charge. He arranged the succession of the slain king's twenty-one year old son, Tunijallo', a choice certain to please Bone, since Tunijallo' had spent two years at the Bone court hiding from the wrath of his father, one of whose women he had abducted. Not surprisingly, a peace was quickly negotiated between Gowa and Bone which would last for eleven years. The king of Tallo' formally installed the young Tunijallo' on the Gowa throne, married the new king to his daughter, and in return was appointed as *Baligau,* or chief minister, of the Gowa kingdom (*Sedjarah Goa,* 29, 39–42, 49; Speelman 1670, I: 51). This role of far-sighted diplomacy, particularly towards the Bugis, was to be a hallmark of the Tallo' family through the next three generations.

While Tumenanga ri Makkoayang lived, the influence of Tallo' in the affairs of the joint kingdom was great. At his death (probably in the 1580s), however, the very existence of a separate Tallo' dynasty became threatened. Tumenanga ri Makkoayang's heir and successor was his eldest daughter, the wife of the Gowa ruler Tunijallo', and the Tallo' chronicle records that, "they ruled together as husband and wife" (Rahim and Ridwan 1975, 14). Tunijallo' was killed in 1590 by one of his immediate followers, after having recommenced unsuccessfully the old bloodstained policy of warring on the Bugis. His successor was the eldest son of the Gowa-Tallo' marriage, a headstrong young man known to history as Tunipasulu' ("he who was overthrown"). He presumably attempted to unite the two dynasties in his person, and appears to have trampled on the treasured autonomy and privileges of the Makasarese chiefs. The Gowa chronicle records that he "also became raja in Tallo'", and that he "forbade subjects to honour two masters". Moreover, it was not only Tallo' liberties which were threatened. The Malay trading community, key to Makasar's wealth, began to move away from the port, as did many members of the Makasarese elite. "In the reign of Karaeng Tunipasulu', innocent people were suddenly just killed . . . He did many other evil things, which are better not to be discussed" (*Sedjarah Goa,* 55–6; see also Speelman 1670, I: 52; Abdurrazak 1969, 18–19).

In this way the Gowa chronicles explain and endorse the only recorded overthrow of a Gowa ruler, when Tunipasulu' was forced to flee to Luwu in 1593. While the chronicles are universally hard on Tunipasulu', however, they equally agree in their praise for the man who organized his overthrow, Karaeng Matoaya[2] of Tallo'.

Matoaya was therefore the second great Tallo' figure, after his father, to play a dominant historic role in the affairs of Makasar. Born about 1573, he was the son of Tumenanga ri Makkoayang by the latter's fourth wife, a Bontomanai woman of the *gallarrang* (village head) class (Rahim and Ridwan 1975, 13). His dynastic credentials to the Tallo' throne must therefore have been modest, and certainly less than those of his older half-sister I Sambo, daughter by a Gowa princess, who had succeeded to the Tallo' throne and married King Tunijallo' of Gowa. Nevertheless Matoaya must have been a capable and ambitious youth, for at the age of sixteen he was already given responsibility for organizing the system of obligatory service for King Tunijallo'. At the latter's death in 1590 Matoaya, though about the same age as the youthful new king, appears to have been given further responsibility as effective chief minister of Gowa (Rahim and Ridwan 1975, 14–15).

Matoaya must therefore have been a party to many of the policies which shook the constitutional basis of the state under the headstrong Tunipasulu'. Although Matoaya presumably reaped the goodwill of chasing out the arbitrary king, he did not reverse all the changes which had taken place. For example, the Gowa chronicle declares that Tunipasulu' "was the first (Goa ruler) to be made raja by the Maros people" (*Sedjarah Goa*, 56). Maros was the great rice bowl to the north of Makasar, which, according to Speelman, was entirely subjected, and "shared out in villages and allotments among the Makassarese nobility, who have each developed their plantations here insofar as they had men available each year". (Speelman 1670, I: 11, who attributes this to Tunijallo', though from the chronicles it seems likelier that the subjection took place in two stages). If this subjection really occurred under Tunipasulu', it certainly was not reversed by his successors.

Similarly Tunipasulu's short and seemingly violent reign is credited with institutionalizing the *Bate Selapang*, the nine traditional chiefs who formed the original kernel of the Gowa state, giving each a fixed jurisdiction and a banner *(bate)* (*Sedjarah Goa*, 55).

It is difficult to understand this except in the sense that the challenge Tunipasulu' posed to traditional autonomies gave rise to a new insistence on defining them clearly, perhaps in solidarity against him.

Undoubtedly the short reign of Tunipasulu' did involve considerable upheaval, and resulted in a monarchy both stronger and more centralized, now drawing much of its economic strength from the Maros area. This greater centralization probably explains why the Gowa chronicles conclude that the two following rulers, who appear the most cultivated and mild of Makasar kings, were "beloved by the village heads *(gallaranna)* and by the people, but the princes *(rianna' karaenga)*, high state officials *(tumailalang)*, and great men *(tumalompoa)* preferred Tunijallo'" (*Sedjarah Goa*, 61; also 69–70).

After arranging the overthrow of Tunipasulu', Matoaya placed on the throne of Gowa the seven year old I Mangngarangi (ruled 1593–1639), more conveniently known by his later Muslim name Ala'uddin. The youngster was a brother of Tunipasulu', a son of Tunijallo' by the same privileged queen, Matoaya's half-sister I Sambo. At the same time, according to the Tallo' chronicle, I Sambo herself "yielded the kingdom of Tallo" to her younger brother, so that Karaeng Matoaya became king in Tallo' (Rahim and Ridwan 1975, 14). As ruler of Tallo', chancellor *(Tuma'bicara-butta)* of Gowa, and guardian of his young nephew, Matoaya was now in a completely dominant position in Makasar. It was he who laid the foundations of the seventeenth century greatness of Makasar, guiding the state through Islamization and the arrival of the English and Dutch. But because he sought not personal glory but to build abiding conventions, his influence endured. He was the primary architect of the Gowa-Tallo' dual monarchy, as well as the policy which respected the autonomy of the Bugis states.

Like his father, who had established the first peace between Gowa and the Bugis, Matoaya continued this policy of seeking alliances rather than conquests. During Tunijallo's reign, wars against the Bugis states had resumed, and in 1582 the leading Bugis states of Bone, Soppeng and Wajo' had concluded the so-called Tellumpocco alliance of mutual support against Makasar. Wajo' had previously been a conquered state, "the slave of Gowa", so its defiance attracted the special wrath of Tunijallo'. With the death of this king, peace was again restored. Wajo', the former vassal, now became a true and loyal ally of Gowa.

The Wajo' chronicles place this new alliance in the short reign of Tunipasulu' of Gowa (1590–3), but significantly they credit Matoaya, not Tunipasulu', with bringing it about. Karaeng Matoaya journeyed to Wajo' to visit the old and greatly respected Arungmatoa (elected king) of Wajo'. He addressed the Bugis elder statesman:

"I have come here, father, because it is said that you are a hero, that you have reached a great age, and that your crops are always abundant, that you have children and grandchildren. Do me the favour of accepting a small token from me, two armbands, and accepting me as your son, and teaching me, so that we may be fortunate; [tell me] how I too can reach such a great age, produce such abundant crops, and obtain children and grandchildren, for I am the Karaeng who looks after the affairs of the country there in Goa."

The Arung-matoa [of Wajo'], To U'da, said, "How can the will of God be understood, in order to lengthen our lifespan and obtain abundant crops? As for your desire to be accepted as my child, that I shall do only when the countries of Goa and Wajo' are allies".

Karaeng Matoaya replied, "Just for that reason have I come here, because I want to unite the lands of Goa and Wajo' in an alliance, and also because I want to be accepted as your child".

The Arung-matoa said, "The one God *(Dewata)* is a witness of this. I say this to you: because I have been upright towards God and my fellow men, I have reached a great age and obtained children and grandchildren. And I have good rice-crops because I make no threats to God".

Karaeng Matoaya asked, "What is it, father, to be upright towards God and our fellow men?"

The Arung-matoa replied, "This is my uprightness towards God: that we do no evil towards what he has created. If we do evil against his creation, God is angry with us. And this is uprightness towards our fellow men: if they do evil towards us, we forgive them and admonish them, for we and our fellow men wish each other no evil. If I go to war, I pray about it to God, and it happens as God wills. And this is not to threaten God: that it is fixed in our hearts that we only exist because God has made us; that it is fixed in our hearts, that we can only do something when we are convinced that God approves it". (Noorduyn 1955, 259–61)

This remarkable exchange was probably not committed to writing for more than a century after it took place. We should not therefore be surprised if it belongs later than (as the context suggests) the beginning of Tunipasulu's reign, nor if the wisdom of the old Arung-matoa became refined over the years into the collective wisdom of Wajo' political experience, with more of Islam in it than was really probable before Wajo' had any substantial contact with any of the great world religions. Nevertheless it is highly significant that the chronicler chose to embody this advice to future generations of statesmen in a dialogue between the greatest of Wajo's leaders and the Karaeng Matoaya, undoubtedly the Makasar prince most widely respected in South Celebes as a whole. The Wajo' writer is clearly saying that Matoaya could not have achieved such wisdom; and could not ultimately have led South Sulawesi towards the truths of Islam, had he not had the good sense to sit at the feet of the great Arung-matoa of Wajo'. The exchange also helps to explain to later generations the basis of the Gowa-Wajo' alliance which began with these two statesmen and endured until Makasar fell almost a century later. It was the happiest example of cooperation between Makasarese and Bugis on a voluntary basis, and we may trust the chronicler when he puts much of it down to Matoaya's tact in approaching the Arung-matoa as his "father".

If Karaeng Matoaya of Tallo' expressed this agreeable filial respect for the Wajo' ruler, he himself enjoyed it from his nephew, the young King of Gowa whom he had placed on the throne. He did indeed "look after the affairs of the country", which now included the whole Makasarese-speaking area, from his position as chancellor. According to the later conqueror of Makasar, Speelman, a new understanding was formed between Gowa and Tallo' in his time, under the formula *dua raja satuan* (two kings in one). Tribute from conquered areas was to be divided into five parts, with two shares each for the Gowa and Tallo' courts and the fifth allotted to whoever was the older of the two rulers—which for the next half-century meant Tallo' (Speelman 1670, III: 57).

Although the Gowa ruler had formal primacy as sovereign (the English later referred to him as "the Great King" or sometimes "emperor"), this was largely balanced by Ala'ud-din's respect for Matoaya as the more wise and experienced.

The first substantial European account of the relations of the two rulers is a Dutch one of 1607, when the Gowa ruler was just nineteen. It reports:

> The King of Tello, who is the most respected there (although there are many kings there), is a fair-skinned man about forty years old; he is very industrious, which he shows in the building of fine houses, and fustas. He is also one of the most politic there are in this land, which he shows in his government. He has his subjects in greater subjection; also the nobility, and other people who are also kings, whom he manages so to draw to him by his amicable conversation that they love him like a father, as the King of Battergoa [i.e. Goa] (who is higher in birth than he) himself said to us, that he regarded him as a father, because of the good advice he daily had from him. He demonstrated that he is gifted with intelligence and understanding through various discourses which they had with him, in which he frequently astonished them. (Hagen 1646, 82)

Six years later, when the Englishman Jourdain described Makasar, Ala'ud-din had taken over sufficiently to be regarded as "the King of Makassar" at least in foreign eyes, but still, "The uncle of the King, the King of Tello, had been the King's protector in his minority, and therefore the King doth much honour him, and will do nothing without his council" (Jourdain 1905, 292–3).

It was during the regime of Karaeng Matoaya and his protégé Ala'ud-din that Makasar became not simply a minor Indonesian port and the strongest of several South Sulawesi states but the most important power between Java and Luzon, with hegemony over most of Sulawesi, eastern Borneo, Lombok and Sumbawa. That this occurred at a time when the arrival of the Dutch and English companies brought great disruption to the pattern of Southeast

Asian trade and politics is no small tribute to the sagacity of Matoaya and his colleagues.

In terms of export produce Makasar was not particularly well endowed. Its major asset at this time was the rice of the Maros area, which appears to have been developed under Matoaya's guidance so that a substantial marketable surplus was regularly available. The Dutch source quoted above relates of Matoaya:

> Throughout the whole country in every town and market-place he has erected fine barns full of rice, which is not allowed to be sold until the new crop is in, so as to suffer no shortage in any unseasonable year. He is very diligent in drawing trade to his country, to which end he expressly keeps an agent in Banda whom he provides every year with rice, cloth, and everything which is required there in order to get as much mace in his country as possible, and so to draw some merchants to him. (Hagen 1646, 82)

The Tallo' chronicle credits Matoaya with developing artificial water-courses, perhaps also in the interests of a rice surplus (Rahim and Ridwan 1975, 16). The fertility of the fields was always a test of a good ruler in South Sulawesi, and Matoaya received more than conventional praise: "During the government of this raja rice flourished, crops flourished, fishing was abundant, there was plenty of palmwine." (Rahim and Ridwan 1975, 18)

Together with slaves, rice had already been the major South Sulawesi export in the 1540s (Schuurhammer 1977, II: 522–3; Wessels 1925, 6–7). For the sixteenth century Portuguese only the slaves were of real interest, but it was the rice which provided the basis for the more crucial Malay trade with Maluku. An increasing number of Malay traders, predominantly from Patani and Johor, made Makasar their base for acquiring the rice which they would exchange in Maluku for the nutmeg, mace and cloves which were the great items of world trade. The enormous expansion of this Makasar-based spice trade in the early seventeenth century, to fill the gap left by the collapse of Javanese trade to Mauuku, was therefore made possible by Matoaya's encouragement of rice production in the Makasar area.

Although the growing Malay community of Makasar (in practice of very diverse Indonesian and Indian origins, but defined at least by speaking Malay and practising Islam) dominated this trade, Matoaya made sure that the Makasarese themselves played an increasingly active role in it. "The King of Makasar" himself (Matoaya or Ala'ud-din?) was in Banda on a trading mission in 1609, and ships belonging to Matoaya were reported trading to Melaka in the west and Ambon in the east (Wybrandt van Waerwijck 1646, 35; Broecke 1634, 58).

Around 1600 a number of factors caused major changes in the pattern of Southeast Asian trade from which Makasar was able to benefit. The Portuguese lost their most reliable base in Java when Balambangan fell to a Muslim force. With it went their major source of rice for Melaka and the Malukan trade. Makasar was a logical alternative, and Matoaya made the Portuguese welcome. It became still more necessary to the Portuguese as Dutch pressure on them in Maluku intensified. By 1607 the Dutch had taken the major Portuguese bases in Maluku, and Makasar became the safest place for Portuguese to buy the nutmeg and cloves they required.

The bitter enmity which the Dutch bore the Portuguese posed problems for every major Southeast Asian port, and not least Makasar. The consistent policy of Matoaya and his protégé, however, was to maintain an open door to all traders, and forbid any the monopolistic position they sought. When the Dutch made their first contact by letter in 1607, they received the reply that they were most welcome to come to Makasar to trade provided it was without any armed force, for the news had spread of Dutch attacks on the Portuguese wherever they found them. The Dutch opened a factory in Makasar the same year, but their efforts to stop the Makasarese supplying rice to Portuguese Melaka and supporting the free spice trade with Maluku were firmly resisted. In a meeting between Matoaya, Sultan Ala'ud-din and two Dutch envoys, Ala'ud-din insisted, "My country stands open to all nations, and what I have is for you people as well as for the Portuguese" (Stapel 1922, 11–12).

A few years later, in 1615, when a Dutch envoy tried to tell the Makasarese that the Dutch had a monopoly in Maluku and Makasarese trade was forbidden there, he received the famous reply from the king:

> God made the land and the sea; the land he divided among men and the sea he gave in common. It has never been heard that anyone should be forbidden to sail the seas. If you seek to do that, you will take the bread from the mouths of people. I am a poor King. (Stapel 1922, 14)

This was a clear declaration of a *mare liberum* principle, but also of a policy vital to Makasar. Makasar was becoming the major market in Southeast Asia for Malukan spices, especially valuable to Portuguese, Spanish, English, Danish, Chinese and Indian merchants who found themselves subject to Dutch attacks if they ventured to Banda or Maluku to collect the spices at source. Makasar became the champion of an open-door policy of free trade, which it was the intention of Coen and the VOC to crush. The Malay and Makasarese traders based in Makasar took the risks of running the Dutch "blockade" to buy from Maluku, who in turn took great risks to defy the

Dutch stranglehold. As some Muslims of Hitu stated, they would prefer to sell their nutmeg for one quarter *real* to the Makasarese than for two *real* to the Dutch, so hated did the latter become (Stapel 1922, 17n.). The English records are filled with testaments to the hatred which the Dutch drew upon themselves by their ruthless bid for monopoly. An old *orangkaya* of Banda, for example, told George Cockayne

> that it makes old men to weep, and will the child that is unborn, saying as God hath given them a country to them & theirs so He hath sent the Hollanders as a plague unto them, making wars upon them and by unjust proceedings seeking to take their country from them. (Cockayne to Smythe, 16 July 1615, *Letters Received*, III: 140)

Where Aceh had responded to Portuguese and later Dutch attempts at monopoly by trying to establish a counter-monopoly of its own, Makasar under Matoaya committed itself firmly to this free trade principle. It thereby won the support not only of the Malukan traders seeking to escape the Dutch, but also of foreign buyers. The English established a factory in 1613, the Danes in 1618, while a Chinese junk reached the port the following year—the first of many *(Letters Received,* III: 136–7). Later Golconda and Aceh also established their agents in the city, the Portuguese presence grew into a sizeable colony, while a Spanish official representative from Manila was in the city at least around 1615 and in the 1640s.

It was no accident that the friendly hand offered to the Dutch to trade on similar terms should ultimately be rebuffed. Already in 1614 a VOC commissioner to Makasar recommended that the factory be withdrawn and Makasarese trade in Maluku attacked whenever possible. Before this recommendation could be put into effect, however, a violent incident speeded the outbreak of hostilities. In April 1616 the Dutch factor, Abraham Sterck, boarded a visiting VOC vessel determined to leave the city because of the king's alleged failure to protect him from insults at the hands of the Spanish. Before withdrawing the Dutch factory, however, he wanted to force the king to repay certain debts, and conspired with the ship's captain to lure some Makasarese nobles on board and seize them as hostages against the debt. When the Makasarese resisted, about seven were killed, including a nephew of the king. Two survivors, the *shahbandar* of Makasar and another relative of the king, were taken off to Banten with the Dutch factors (Stapel 1922, 13–14; *Letters Received,* III: 132–5, 146–7, 273, 286–9).

The anger of the Makasarese at this outrage risked involving more than the Dutch alone, since the English factor unwisely identified with the Dutch and sailed off with them. Furious at the tragic effects of these quarrels among

Christians, Ala'ud-din reportedly "made a vow that never any Christian should have trade in his country" (Skinner to Denton, 12 July 1615, *Letters Received*, III: 134). The English and Portuguese spared no efforts to assuage the ruler, however, and soon returned to Makasar where they slowly learned to live in peace with one another. With the Dutch, on the other hand, war was virtually inevitable. Sultan Ala'ud-din told the English factor that he wanted to avoid further violence and would let no Dutchman ashore in future, for "the commonalty will not be pacified but would willingly . . . put them all to the sword" (Cockayne to Jourdain, 17 August 1610, *Letters Received*, III: 157). Sure enough, when fifteen men of the *Eendracht* (the ship which had just discovered Australia) went ashore in Makasar not knowing what had happened, all were killed (Stapel 1922, 14–15).

Whatever the skill of Matoaya and his young protégé in diplomacy, they lived in a dangerous world at a particularly dangerous time. Had they not been able to muster one of the most formidable military forces in Southeast Asia there is no doubt that their attempts at even-handed diplomacy would have come to naught, and the Dutch in particular would have made short work of Makasar. The restless energy and curiosity of these two rulers were therefore directed most urgently towards mastering European military techniques. As a result of the crisis of 1615 in relations with the Dutch the English factor found himself:

> called every day to the King or else he comes to our house to have me resolve him as well as I can of such questions as he doth propound unto me. The King is much grieved in mind and maketh much preparation for war; all the whole land is making of bricks for two castles this summer to be finished; in the armoury is laid ready 10,000 lances, 10,000 cresses [*kris*] with bucklers to them, spaces [*spata*, a type of lance] as many, pieces 2.422; 800 quoyanes of rice for store; all this is to entertain the Flemings . . . Yesterday in my sight the King, to see his force and how many men he could make, at an instant were mustered 36,000 able men. (Cockayne to Jourdain, 17 August 1615, *Letters Received*, III, 150–2)

The building of brick walls for defence purposes was a sharp break with older Indonesian methods of warfare (see chapter 10) but one of great importance in discouraging a major Dutch attack. Although some brickworks had been built in the sixteenth century, presumably with Portuguese guidance (*Sedjarah Goa*, 26), there is no doubt that Matoaya was responsible for greatly extending them during this period. The Tallo' chronicle credits him with building the fortresses of Tallo', Ujung Pandang, and Pannakkukang (Rahim and Ridwan 1975, 17; cf. Ligtvoet 1880, 95, which dates the Ujung Pandang walls at 1634), leaving only Sombaopu and Gowa as the work of earlier Gowa kings. The same chronicle insists that Matoaya was responsible for introducing the manufacture of cannons and small muskets to Makasar, while he himself was "skilled at making gunpowder, fireworks, flares, and fireworks that burn in water, as well as being an accurate marksman" (Rahim and Ridwan 1975, 16, 18).

Shipbuilding was another area in which the Makasarese had much to learn from the Malays, Chinese, and Europeans in their midst, and once again Matoaya is given much of the credit for technical innovation. The chronicle notes:

> This was the first raja who had supports made for the mast in the [type of prahu called] *banawa,* and who for the first time had men make the *bilu* [royal yacht]. In his time too, prahus were for the first time nailed together with large iron nails; for the first time the Makassarese were able to make the war *prahu* called a *galle* [galley]. (Rahim and Ridwan 1975, 16–17)

Of Matoaya's interest in shipbuilding we have confirmation from the Dutch, who noted on their 1607 visit that he,

> is very industrious, which he shows in the building of fine houses, and *fustas* otherwise called *korakara* [sailing galleys with outriggers], which are so large and smartly made, that all our carpenters who have been there affirm, that there are no masters in our country who would be able to make them. (Hagen 1646, 82)

While the arts of war were critical for Makasar's survival, Matoaya's interests by no means stopped there, and the chronicle is generous in praise of his knowledge of handicrafts, dancing, and so forth. One of his most remarkable innovations was the minting of coinage both in gold (the *dinara* or *mas)* and in lead (Rahim and Ridwan 1975, 18; Netscher and Chijs 1864, 185). Makasar appears to have been the only pre-colonial Southeast Asian state except Aceh to have its own gold coinage, and Makasar's was the only coinage of which the originator is personally known. In terms of the establishment of a reliable basis for commerce and capital accumulation this was of profound importance. It is significantly not until the influence of the Tallo' family was declining in the late 1650s that we see any significant devaluation of the Makasar *mas,* which kept its value for several decades at four English shillings or 0.8 Spanish real (Bassett 1958, 26–7; Makasar to Banten, 22 July 1658, IOL G/10/1: 148).

ISLAMIZATION

Matoaya's intellectual curiosity, and his energetic determination to put his country in the forefront of economic and technical developments, are apparent from all the above changes associated with his leadership. His name is especially revered in South Sulawesi, however, for an innovation of a different kind—the adoption of Islam. Once again we are in a position to know more about the individual personality behind this portentous change than in any other case of Islamization in the Archipelago. Makasar did not formally adopt Islam until 1605 (or 1606), the height of Matoaya's influence, and at this comparatively late date the city's contacts with both Muslim and Christian foreigners were already well developed.

The period of Matoaya's effective rule (1593–1610) had seen extremely rapid growth in the city's size and sophistication. By 1615, when 1260 houses were destroyed by fire without leaving a ruinous impact and when thirty-six thousand fighting men could be called up at twenty-four hours notice (IOL G/10/1: 5, 9; and see above), the city must have had close to fifty thousand inhabitants, some thousands of them Malay and Portuguese traders. But unlike the pattern in so many other trading ports of the Archipelago, the foreign element had in no sense overtaken the vigorous animist culture of South Sulawesi. The love of pork and alcohol in feasting, the sacral role of female and transvestite shamans, the topless style of dress for both sexes, and the insertion of balls or pins permanently in the penis, were features familiar to the animist "little traditions" of rural Southeast Asia, but they were rather startling in a cosmopolitan urban context. The first Dutch visitors in 1607 have already been quoted (chapter 2, p. 25) in this context.

Whereas other trading centres in the Archipelago adopted an Arabic, Roman, or Sanskritic script to cope with the new legal and commercial demands being placed on a written language, the Makasarese (and the Bugis after them) alone developed the indigenous Indonesian script into a vehicle for modern purposes. This relative success in adapting their animist culture to the needs of a modern city is part of the explanation for the surprisingly late religious change of Makasar. The other factor is that Makasar was faced with a real choice between the Malay/Muslim and Portuguese/Christian models, rather than having to approach the wider outside world solely as it was presented through one of these windows.

Makasar needed both Malay and Portuguese traders, and it learned much from both sources. Both Christian and Muslim dating systems were in use at the court, and Matoaya's decision for Islam is itself most frequently dated in terms of the Christian system—as 22 September 1603 (though most commentators have reinterpreted this to 1605 or 1606). Matoaya himself was assiduous in learning all he could from the Portuguese, Dutch and English, as well as from the Muslim traders. Pelras' suggestion (1977, 248–56) that Matoaya's father was a Christian convert is difficult to reconcile with Makasar sources, but it is clear at least that the family was familiar with Christian ideas. The contest for the soul of Makasar was remembered in a very strong tradition among the European community of Makasar, recorded at least from the 1640s. This had it that the leading men could not agree which of the new faiths to adopt, but feared the effects of religious division. They therefore decided to invite Aceh to send a Muslim theologian and Melaka a Christian one, and to accept that whichever arrived first in Makasar must have God's support (Hertz 1966, 207; Navarrete 1962, I: 113; Boxer 1967, 3n.; Gervaise 1701, 124–9). The idea of such a "race" is almost certainly apocryphal, but its probable basis is that Matoaya was sufficiently interested in Christian doctrine to invite the Portuguese to send a priest to him, which Melaka failed to do much to the chagrin of the Makasar Portuguese.

From what both the chronicles and European observers tell us, we know Matoaya to have been thoughtful, studious, and intensely energetic in the pursuit of new knowledge. Though the Tallo' chronicle is certainly not impartial about its hero, its description of Matoaya's character is of considerable interest:

> This king was a man of thought and of bold action, a learned man, a man of renown, a man of many talents, he was a skilled worker and had good hands for both men's and women's handiwork, he was known to all as upright and good-natured, genial towards anyone who wanted to receive him; he was quick to understand a person's feelings and a good mixer, he knew how to listen to people; he fully understood how to conduct correspondence, and his opinions were judicious; he was adept at reading *kitab* [Islamic books], and from the time he adopted Islam until his death he never once missed the time of prayer; only at the time his foot swelled up and an Englishman treated him by giving him alcohol did he not pray for eighteen days; he performed many *sunat* prayers. (Rahim and Ridwan 1975, 18–19, my translation, primarily from Abdurrahim's Indonesian)

As Noorduyn has already emphasized, such a man is likely to have decided for Islam only after considerable thought and study (Noorduyn 1956, 263).

There is confirmation from a Wajo' chronicle that Matoaya must have weighed the rival claims of Islam and Christianity, after coming to the view that the old animist faith was not adequate for the new needs of his country. This chronicle reports a second visit by Matoaya to the wise old ruler of Wajo' just before the latter's death in 1607. Matoaya reportedly asked the old man:

"You are very ill, father. Do me the favour of telling me how many gods there
are".

The Arung-matoa said, "There is only one God *(Dewata)*, but there are many
emissaries of God".

The Karaeng [Matoaya] asked, "Does this one God have no mother and no
father?"

The Arung-matoa said, "Just for that reason is he called the one God, that
he has no mother and no father". (Noorduyn 1955, 263)

This exchange suggests, as Noorduyn has again pointed out, that Matoaya
was considering the merits of Islamic arguments that the Christians were not
true monotheists. Eventually he decided to embrace Islam, especially as it
was presented by a learned ulama, Abdul Makmur Khatib Tunggal Dato' ri
Bandang, a Minangkabau who had apparently studied or taught in
Palembang, in Giri (East Java), and in Kutai where he is also credited with
the introduction of Islam. But whatever the merits of Dato' ri Bandang, the
chronicles insist that it was Matoaya himself who was primarily responsible
for spreading Islam to the whole of South Sulawesi: "It was this raja who
Islamized the Makassarese in the whole Makassar area, and Islamized the
Bugis in the whole Bugis area, except for the people of Luwu [who had been
Islamized earlier]." Rahim and Ridwan 1975, 15)

Matoaya's acceptance of Islam is clearly dated 22 September in all
chronicles, though there is much more doubt about the year. We may accept
Noorduyn's argument for 1605 as the most convincing, though a case could
also be made from the evidence for 1603 or 1606 (Noorduyn 1956, 248–66;
cf. Ligtvoet 1880, 86, and the statement of the Dutch visitors of 1607 that
the King had adopted Islam four years earlier). Matoaya underlined his
momentous change of faith by adopting as his Islamic name Sultan Abdullah
Awal-ul Islam (the slave of God, the first Muslim).

The conversion of two whole peoples as traditionally proud, warlike, and
autonomous as the Makasarese and Bugis by no means followed
automatically. It is possible that Matoaya's young ward, the king of Gowa,
became a Muslim under his influence at almost the same time, adopting the
name Sultan Ala'ud-din. However the first solemn celebration of the Friday
prayer in a Makasarese rather than "foreign Malay" context, at the court of
Tallo', occurred only two years later (probably 1607, see Ligtvoet 1880, 86).
There was strong opposition from many quarters, particularly on the part of
highly placed women, the traditional repositories of the older religious
knowledge. However we have it on the evidence of a hostile Christian source
(Gervaise 1701, 129) that Matoaya resisted the suggestions of his new
religious advisers that he should impose Islam by force, and instead relied

upon the influence of his example, persuasion, and favour towards those
quick to convert. The Makasarese accepted the religion of the Prophet
voluntarily, thereby ensuring the retention within Makasarese culture of more
pre-Islamic elements than among most other coastal Indonesians.

When his own Makasarese aristocracy had followed him into Islam within
three years, Matoaya turned his attention to the Bugis of the South Sulawesi
states. For the first and only time in his long political career, Matoaya
abandoned the policy of peace with the Bugis for what he evidently believed
to be the greater good of conversion to Islam. He first appealed to Soppeng
and Bone to accept Islam on the basis of a long alliance with Gowa. When
they predictably declined, Matoaya marshalled the forces of Makasar to attack
them in what became known as the "Islam war". According to Bugis sources,
the first Makasar attack was directed towards Soppeng in about 1608-9, but
was driven out after three days' fighting by the combined forces of Bone,
Soppeng, and Wajo'. Matoaya himself, the same sources allege, only escaped
death through his "fortunate constellation" (Noorduyn 1955, 94–5).
However the unity and strength of purpose was evidently much greater
among the Makasarese than the Bugis, and the Bugis alliance began to
disintegrate only three months after this initial success. A second Makasarese
attack then found a number of Bugis states on its side, while a third, the
following year, led to the death of the ruler of Soppeng and the defection to
Islam first of the Sidenreng people and then of the Soppengers. In the next
dry season the campaign was directed against Wajo', and now there was little
sign left of cooperation between the non-Muslim Bugis states—presumably
because of the mild terms consistently offered by Matoaya. After a few initial
defeats, the Wajorese sued for peace (Noorduyn 1955, 95–7).

As the Wajo' chronicle tells it, Matoaya simply asked the Wajo' leaders:

"Do me the favour of accepting a small token from me, that you follow Goa
into Islam and that you all offer homage to the one God".

To Appamole [the Wajo' leader] replied to King Matoaya, "We have made
the profession of faith, Your Majesty, and we all offer homage to the one God.
I request that my rice be not torn out, my mats not opened, and the mice not
cut out from the folds of my sarung. So will I follow Goa; when Goa goes to
war we will follow as Goanese, and I will bring my victuals in my sleeves, one
for the journey out and one for the journey home. When Goa is victorious in
war, so is Wajo also victorious. If you go by ship then we will not follow, for I
cannot sail. I will then sit in my house hoping that you win, and if Goa wins
then Wajo wins also. Only then will Goa and Wajo be divided, since God has
divided them".

The King said, "I agree with what you have said. Wajorese, I grant what you

request, as you make an effort to offer homage to Allah ta'ala and to follow the
Prophet Mohammad s.a.w." (Noorduyn 1955, 266–7)

Matoaya then presented the leading Wajo' men with clothes appropriate
for the Muslim prayer, and again according to the Wajo' source he accepted
their understandable wish to have a final magnificent feast on their
slaughtered pigs.

Next it was the turn of Bone, the strongest Bugis state, which similarly
sued for peace in 1611. Once again, according to the Bone chronicle itself,
the victorious Matoaya made no demands whatever save that the Bone leaders
make the profession of faith in Islam.

The ruler of Bone, although selected specifically to resist Islam, was so won
over that he became a great friend and pupil of Matoaya (Noorduyn 1955,
98; Bone chronicle as translated by Campbell Macknight). The Tallo'
chronicle, which makes of Matoaya a source of wisdom for later generations,
says of this "Islam war" that,

> he did not plunder, he did not levy any indemnity or impose any tribute, he
> did not want to do so. Tumenanga ri Bonto Biraeng [Matoaya's son
> Pattingalloang] used to say, "King Matoaya said to me, when I defeated the
> Tallumbocco alliance [Bone-Wajo'-Soppeng] I did not even pluck the leaves
> of the trees; I did not want to do so; I distributed about three hundred *kati*, I
> gave it in the form of presents of porcelain." (Rahim and Ridwan 1975, 16)

After all the major Bugis states had accepted Islam, Matoaya attended a
conference with their leaders, at which the terms of alliance were agreed. He
gave them each a ring as a symbol of alliance, and urged them to avoid
internal quarrels, "for the enemies of the Karaeng [Matoaya] are enemies who
come by sea" (Noorduyn 1955, 268–9). The peace thus established endured
throughout the rest of his lifetime, a rare period in the generally stormy
relationships between South Sulawesi states. Wajo's relations with Makasar
became particularly close, and we know of at least one internal Wajo' dispute
which was successfully referred to Matoaya to settle (Noorduyn 1955, 112).

How much this Islamic fervour had to do with the further extension of
Makasar authority by sea we do not know. As Makasar's importance as the
major entrepot of eastern Indonesia grew rapidly under Matoaya, and its fleet
expanded to the point it could equip expeditions of up to a thousand vessels,
political influence was bound to follow. Typically tribute was offered in trade
goods—tortoise-shell from Northern Sulawesi, slaves, wax and sandalwood
from the Lesser Sundas—as acknowledgement of Makasar's primacy as trade
centre, arbiter and protector. At least two texts explicitly credit Matoaya with

the conquest of the island of Sumbawa (Ricklefs and Voorhoeve 1977, 99; Rahim and Ridwan 1975, 17), although the earliest dates for expeditions of conquest are 1617 and 1618 (Ligtvoet 1880, 87), when Sultan Ala'ud-din was already sharing power with him. Makasar rule overseas appears to have been relatively mild, typically relying on a subordinate Muslim trading centre—Bima in the south and Mandar in the north—to extend both religious and political influence on its behalf. By the time of Matoaya's death in 1636 Makasar's hegemony had extended in this way to embrace almost the whole coast of Sulawesi, the east coast of Borneo, and the Lesser Sundas from eastern Lombok to parts of Timor. Despite the eagerness of the Dutch to find potential rebels against Makasar, only strategically-located Buton had to be reconquered on numerous occasions (notably 1626, 1655). We know that Matoaya (then aged fifty-three) and the Sultan both took part in the massive expedition which conquered it in 1626 (Ligtvoet 1880, 89–90; IOL G/10/1:39 refers to eighty thousand men and 1,900 vessels). The rulers must have gone too far with Bima too, in 1632, in appointing Ala'ud-din's brother-in-law to rule directly there. The Bima people threw the Makasarese nominee out, and in consequence had their lands laid waste (Stapel 1922, 25; Ligtvoet 1880, 93). Thereafter Bima remained a great centre of Makasar influence in the Lesser Sundas.

As the champion of Islam in South Sulawesi and beyond, we might expect Matoaya after his conversion to be hostile to the influence of the Portuguese and English. However, much had changed in Southeast Asia since the antagonisms of the previous century, and Makasar became the most striking example of religious tolerance in a generally tolerant Archipelago. As Jourdain remarked less than a decade after the city had accepted Islam, "It is a very pleasant and fruitful countrye, and the kindest people in all the Indias to strangers . . . The King is very affable and true harted towards Christians." (Jourdain 1905, 294–5) As we have seen both Matoaya and Ala'ud-din were extremely anxious to learn all they could from the Europeans, both before and after they converted to Islam. They were particularly beholden to the Portuguese, who supplied most of the Chinese and Indian manufactures needed in the region and represented a substantial colony—rising to several hundred by the 1620s and perhaps three thousand after the fall of Melaka in 1641 (Navarrete 1962, I: 114n). Matoaya, as we shall see, must have had his favourite son largely educated by the Portuguese. Ala'ud-din, who spoke a little Portuguese himself, appears to have gone further. Among his forty-odd wives were many foreigners, and one was reportedly a "Westerner" (*Sedjarah Goa*, 60). It was probably he (rather than his son Mohammad Said, born only in 1607, cf. Navarrete 1962, 118; Boxer 1967, 17n) who was the father, by a Portuguese woman, of Francisco Mendes, who became an invaluable, bilingual, link between Makasarese and Portuguese, a member of the Order of Christ, and "Portuguese secretary" to the Gowa court from about 1637 to 1656. Here at least such things were possible, leading a Spanish Dominican later to bemoan as "deplorable . . . that Christian men kept Mahometan women, and Mahometan men, Christian women" (Navarrete 1962, I: 122–3).

In 1614 Ala'ud-din even wrote to Manila to invite the Franciscans there to establish a house in Makasar, presumably to cater for the resident Portuguese rather than as a means to conversion. Significantly this request was declined not because the Makasarese were Muslim but because they had received Dutch ships—a more serious offence. Five years later some Franciscans did reach Makasar, and Christian services continued to be celebrated openly there (Meersman 1967, 91–7). With the fall of Melaka, Makasar became the principal Southeast Asian base for the Portuguese, and the Franciscans, Jesuits and Dominicans each had houses there in addition to the main Church operated by the former diocese of Melaka (Meersman 1967, 115–19). The Viceroy of Goa commented in 1638 that "in all the Southern Archipelago there is no other ruler who protects the Portuguese with greater firmness and allows conversion to the Christian faith" (cited Boxer 1967, 4). Certainly the contrast with the Dutch seemed striking to the Portuguese, but the viceroy's words should not be taken to mean Makasarese could freely convert to Christianity. The "Articles of Agreement" between the Makasar rulers and the English Company in 1624 explicitly forbade that (IOL, G/10/1: 35–6), and Catholic missionaries frequently complained that they made no progress with the native population (Meersman 1967, 97, 118–19). Conversions in the other direction were much more common, particularly on the part of slaves who used this device to escape their Christian masters (Navarrete 1962, I: 122). Nevertheless there was sufficient tolerance to permit a very extensive exchange of ideas, and we know that at least a few prominent Makasarese enjoyed attending the occasional sermon.

The state which Chancellor Matoaya had created, then, was a beacon of hope in Southeast Asia. Its policy of even-handed free trade for all appeared to provide a brilliant formula for dealing with the dangerous new interlopers. The English and Portuguese, even when at war with each other, accepted that they had to bury their swords in Makasar:

> The King requires that both may be alike free in the port of Makassar, but is loath to displease either, and his affection is very constant to the English, so as no politic prince in Europe could do more, but his country cannot be supplied without the Portugals, so the best we can expect is to stand in equal balance,

and that neither shall annoy the other in the King's havens. (Batavia to E. I.
Co., 18 July 1627, in *Calendar of State Papers, 1625-9:* 368)

The Dutch too, despite their bitter competition with Makasar-based traders
in Maluku, were treated with exemplary courtesy when they called at
Makasar, and given no pretexts to precipitate the war they saw as ultimately
inevitable. From Banten, Mataram, Aceh, Golconda, Ayudhya, Cambodia,
Denmark and France came envoys and traders.

For the people of South Sulawesi Matoaya remained the great Makasarese
hero, the bringer of Islam, the pioneer of many innovations, the builder of
Makasar's greatness. His words of advice to his son Pattingalloang were
passed down as the foundation of Makasarese statecraft (Matthes 1875, 12).
Although the ruler of Tallo' (where a handsome grave is also claimed as his),
he was honoured in Gowa almost like the founder of a dynasty, for all the
seventeenth century Gowa rulers were buried alongside him in tombs
modelled on his. Even in the chronicles of the Bugis he conquered there is
nothing but praise for Karaeng Matoaya.

PATTINGALLOANG

Matoaya appears to have had ten wives, of whom at least one was a favoured
slave, and another, having evidently displeased the chancellor and been
divorced, was killed at his death on 1 October 1636. He had lived long and
fruitfully, and prepared the way effectively for his departure from the scene.
He sired at least twenty-nine children, of whom seven were sons by his
principal wife, Iwara, the only daughter of King Tunijallo' of Gowa. The
first of these died at age seven, and it was the second who would succeed him
on the throne of Tallo' as Sultan Mudhaffar. Matoaya evidently groomed
him for this task, as he himself moved away from the Tallo' palace to a quieter
retreat in 1634, and had Mudhaffar formally enthroned eight months before
his own death (Rahim and Ridwan 1975, 19–24; describes his family in
complex detail). This son was principally noted for leading the Makasar
expedition which conquered the coastal ports of Timor in 1641, though he
died on the return journey (Rahim and Ridwan 1975, 26–8).

However it was as *bicara-butta* or chancellor of Gowa that Matoaya had
been able to play his unique role in the making of Makasar's greatness. He
had gradually and graciously moved out of the limelight as Ala'ud-din grew
into his role as sultan, ensuring an effective division of powers between the
two men. It seems probable that he had schooled his second surviving son,
Pattingalloang, to take over the chancellorship, but when he died Ala'ud-din

appears to have continued to rule alone until his own death less than three years later, in 1639. The Makasarese saw the two rulers as inseparable. The Gowa chronicle points out that 986 days after being deprived of Matoaya, the people were deprived also of Ala'ud-din. But there is no doubt that it was the former to whom the rise of Makasar was primarily attributed (*Sedjarah Goa*, 61, 65).

The new king of Gowa was Sultan Mohammad Said, the thirty-two year old highest-born son of Ala'ud-din. He is reported to have told the chief officers of state that he would only accept the throne if Pattingalloang "sits beside me in government, and leads the people as a whole" (*Sedjarah Goa*, 65–6). In all probability the new chancellor had already become virtually indispensable as the successor of his father in military and diplomatic affairs. The little the chronicles tell us of Pattingalloang before he assumed the chancellorship at the age of thirty-nine indicate that he was particularly close to both Matoaya, whose words he is often depicted quoting, and to Ala'ud-din, whose virtual adopted son he is shown to be (*Sedjarah Goa*, 60). From later reports we know that he must have been a brilliant youngster, exceptionally fluent in Portuguese and Spanish as well as Makasarese and Malay, and possessing his father's intellectual curiosity in almost every field. Already as an eighteen year old he was pestering the English for novelties aboard their ships (Staverton to Ball, 18 May 1618, in *Calendar of State Papers, 1617-21:* 166). By dint of these talents combined with his high birth he must already have accumulated numerous functions before the change of rulers. In 1632 we know he was entrusted with the Ujung Tanah area of the city as a kind of personal fief, with 1,584 subjects directly under him (Ligtvoet 1880, 93).

Because of his fluency in European languages Pattingalloang emerges more fully as a character than any other Makasar leader of his day. Most unusually, Western visitors were unanimously laudatory about him, even including the Dutch. The fullest descriptions come from Catholic missionaries in the city, and particularly Alexandre de Rhodes, who visited in 1646.

> The high governor of the whole kingdom . . . is called Carim Patengaloa, whom I found exceedingly wise and sensible, and apart from his bad religion, a very honest man. He knew all our mysteries very well, had read with curiosity all the chronicles of our European kings. He always had books of ours in hand, especially those treating with mathematics, in which he was quite well versed. Indeed he had such a passion for all branches of this science that he worked at it day . . . and night. To hear him speak without seeing him one would take him for a native Portuguese, for he spoke the language as fluently as people from Lisbon itself. (Hertz 1966, 208–9)

Some years after his death Pattingalloang's library of European books, "which was considerable", was still kept by his son and continued to excite the admiration of visitors (Navarrete 1962, I: 115).

Like his father, Pattingalloang was particularly anxious to keep abreast of European technical innovations, and he is the first Southeast Asian we know of to have seen the importance of mathematics for the applied sciences. There were few Europeans in Makasar in a position to instruct him, but he seized greedily on the rare visitor as learned as Fr de Rhodes:

Seeing that he was pleased to talk of mathematics, I began conversing with him on the subject, and God willed him to take such pleasure in it that he wanted to have me at his palace as a matter of course thereafter.

It happened that I predicted an eclipse of the moon to him a few days before it took place. I described it all to him exactly as he saw it later. This so won him over he wanted me to teach him all the secrets of the science. I, who had in mind teaching him the science of going to heaven rather than the courses of the stars, never saw him without always throwing in many things that might move him to conversion, and even when he sometimes changed the subject I never failed to return to my objective . . .

On my return to our house he sent me a Portuguese who was his great confidant, who made me a thousand protestations of friendship on his part and brought me various gifts along with a memorandum of curious articles he wanted me to bring him back from Europe, adding finally that he very much wanted to see me return and that he implored me to pass through his territory again, where I would always find proof of the high regard in which he held me. I had to be satisfied with these compliments and make him a return in kind. (Hertz 1966, 209–10)

Alexandre de Rhodes was not the only visitor to be importuned for books, maps, and rarities from Europe. It became well known to traders that such gifts were especially welcome to Pattingalloang, along with the horses, antelopes, elephants and weapons which were the more common means of impressing Asian monarchs. In 1644 the chancellor sent to Batavia a lading of sandalwood to pay for "various rarities, including two globes, a large world map or mappamundi, with the description in the Spanish, Portuguese or Latin language, a book describing the whole world, atlas in Latin, Spanish or Portuguese with its maps" (Wessels 1925, 22; also Stapel 1922, 40–41).

Three years later the Dutch in Batavia were still complaining that some of this order had not been supplied from Holland, notably "two globes of 157–160 inch circumference, of wood or copper, from which the north and south poles can be placed" (Coolhaas 1960-, II: 314). Eventually a "magnificent copper globe" was sent, and must have contributed to Pattingalloang's reputation in Holland, where the greatest poet of the day, Joost van den Vondel, devoted some lines to him:

> Dien Aardkloot zend 't Oostindisch huis,
> Den Grooten Pantagoule t'huis,
> Wiens aldoorsnuffelende brein,
> Een gansche wereld valt te klein
> (East India House sends a globe to the great Pattingalloang,
> whose endlessly curious brain, finds a whole world too small.)
> (Quoted in Valentijn 1724, 147)

While the Dutch were the unrivalled map-makers of the period, Pattingalloang evidently persuaded the Sultan to approach the English for help in astronomy. In 1635 Ala'ud-din gave the English factors 2-1/2 *bahar* (about half a ton) of cloves with which to buy a number of rarities including "one prospective glass, the very best that may be bought for money" (Banten to E. I. Co., 31 January 1636, IOL, E/3/15: f151v.). This appears to have been a very long time coming, perhaps having to be carefully constructed in England for the purpose. In 1652 a ship finally delivered a "Galilean Prospective Glass", to a new King of Gowa, evidently for a much inflated sum. When we recall that Galileo's first telescope was completed only in 1609, and there were still relatively few operating in Britain, Makasar was doing its best to keep abreast of the Renaissance explosion of knowledge. It seems unlikely that Sultan Mohammad Said himself had much understanding of astronomy, but in any case he died soon after its delivery, so that both the telescope and the debt for it were taken over by Pattingalloang. Unfortunately the great chancellor himself died the following year, and there being no-one else in the city with the necessary knowledge and money, it was returned to the English (IOL, G/10/1: 93 ff.).

It is extraordinary enough that there was a scientific mind of this quality in seventeenth century Makasar, but this assumes special importance in the person of the dominant political figure in the state. It is certain that Pattingalloang's habits of rational enquiry influenced the culture of Makasar in this period, and lay behind many of the innovations to which it gave rise. Some of these deserve special attention. Firstly, the only Indonesian translations we know from European technical treatises probably occurred at his behest. A sixteenth century Spanish text on gunnery, allegedly by "Andraes of Monyona", was summarized in Makasarese in 1635, and translated in full in 1652, shortly before Pattingalloang's death. A number of other translations on gunnery, gunpowder and arms manufacture, were translated from Spanish, Portuguese, Turkish and Malay authorities, although many of these survive only in imperfect Bugis retranslations of later date (Matthes 1875, 54, 58; Ricklefs and Voorhoeve 1977, 29, 31). Secondly, the Bugis' skill in making and copying maritime charts, also unique in Indonesia, has been traced back not unreasonably to the original enthusiasm of Pattingalloang (Le Roux 1935, 699–701).

The remarkable chancellor must also have had a role in the unique development of South Sulawesi historical writing. That he was extremely interested in the recording of history we know from the frequency with which he is quoted in the Makasar chronicles, and from the *Hikayat Tanah Hitu,* the writing of which he commissioned from an Ambonese refugee to whom he had given hospitality in Makasar (Manusama 1977, 1–2, 223–4). We appear to possess no documents definitely written by Pattingalloang, and can only infer that the most striking innovations from Western literary models probably took place under his guidance. The tradition of chronicle-writing was itself not very old in South Sulawesi, having begun in the mid-sixteenth century (*Sedjarah Goa,* 50). However, the most unique feature of South Sulawesi historical writing, the carefully dated diaries of important events, appear to have developed during the time of Pattingalloang's influence. The diary of Gowa-Tallo' has its first entry dated 1545, but all the early entries are calculations obviously made much later. Typically they give a date on which a well-known dignitary was "probably" born, based on calculating backwards from his age at the time of his known death. Only in the late 1620s does the detailed sequence begin which indicates that events are being recorded as they occur (Ligtvoet 1880, 85-90; also Noorduyn 1965, 149). Each major state occasion is written down under both its Christian and its Muslim date, in a straightforward, factual style quite unlike any other form of Indonesian writing. Others could have been responsible for this innovation, but there is no likelier candidate than Pattingalloang.

Like those of his Renaissance counterparts in Europe, Pattingalloang's scholarly interests were linked to very practical purposes. As leader of his people in war and peace, he was particularly concerned with military technology.

Whensoever he saw a sword, he would handle it, and enquire of the Quality of it. He once took a Portuguese's Sword in his Hand, and understanding from him that it would pierce a double Buff Coat, he made him try it immediately, which the Portuguese performed, tho he hurt his Hand with the great force he put to pierce the Buff, which was upon a Chair.

Patin Galoa seeing that done, ask'd for his Bow, and adding one fold more in the Buff Coat, made such a furious shot, that he pierc'd the three Folds. All that were present stood astonish'd. (Navarrete 1962, I: 121)

In foreign policy the Chancellor was complete master, handling the most difficult problems arising from European strength and rivalries with particular skill. Despite his ties with the hated Portuguese the Dutch treated him with great respect.

He governs the kingdom and can do us much good or harm, while the King spends his time trafficking and gambling . . . Karaeng Patengalo had very familiar and politic discussions with Vlamingh about the peace between Portugal and the Spanish crown, showing himself to be a man of great knowledge, science, and understanding. (Generale Missive of 19 December 1651, Coolhaas 1960-, II: 497–8)

Stapel, the chronicler of the Dutch war with Makasar, attributes the one real period of peace between the VOC and Gowa-Tallo', between 1637 and 1654, largely to the wisdom and effectiveness of Pattingalloang during these years. He always received Dutch envoys well and left them convinced that war would be more dangerous than peace for both sides (Stapel 1922, 34–5). The eventual conqueror of Makasar recorded that Pattingalloang was still regarded fifteen years after his death as "the idol" and "the father" of Makasar (Speelman 1670, I: 11; Stapel 1922, 35n). His fame reached as far as Borneo, where the *Hikayat Banjar* records (479) a mission from Pasir to Makasar "in the time of Karaeng Pattingalloang" as if that in itself explained the shift of allegiance of the eastern Borneo states from Banjarmasin to Makasar.

Pattingalloang's obvious admiration for and familiarity with many aspects of European culture led a number of missionaries to believe that he was on the brink of conversion to Christianity. According to Navarrete (1962, I: 120), he had read all the works of the celebrated Spanish Dominican, Luis de Granada (who was also translated into Japanese) and was intellectually convinced of the merits of Christianity. Navarrete claimed that he "was wont to say that Many went to Hell out of Reason of State, and that he was one of them" (Navarrete 1962, I: 120; also Wessels 1925, 32–3). However, Navarrete reached Makasar only after Pattingalloang's death when legend was beginning to take over from fact, and we need probably take this wishful thinking no more seriously than in the case of Pattingalloang's contemporary, King Narai of Siam. The flavour of his relations with Christianity is reliably given by Alexandre de Rhodes, who spared no pain to try to bring about his conversion.

He was so well informed on all points of our religion that he often argued them against heretics and routed them completely. He attacked the Dutch particularly on the authority of the Pope and ridiculed them for trying to create a body without a head, proving to them clearly that it could only be a monster

I neglected nothing that might win for Christ this man on whom the conversion of the entire kingdom depended. He never held it against me, but he didn't thereby change for the better. I was never able to discover what this came from, because from all appearances his life wasn't bad. He had no entanglements with women. I simply came to the conclusion that I was too big a sinner to bring so excellent a project to fruition.

When I was on the point of leaving I went to tackle him one last time on the subject of his salvation. As I took leave of him I spoke with many tears and proposed to him reasons quite sufficient to touch his heart; but after my talk, which was rather long, he replied to it all with nothing more than these few words, "Well done, Father, you have discharged your duty very well." With that he bowed to me many times and kissed me several times, but on the most important subject he said not a word. (Hertz 1966, 209–10)

The Gowa chronicle says that under King Mohammad Said, in whose name Pattingalloang governed, Makasar "never experienced plague, serious war, or serious misfortune" (*Sedjarah Goa*, 69). Undoubtedly in comparison with every other reign this must have seemed a time of extraordinary peace and prosperity. Nevertheless Pattingalloang's handling of the critical Bugis question, though it appeared brilliantly successful at the time, must be seen as contributing to Makasar's ultimate destruction.

Since under Matoaya Gowa had defeated Bone in the name of Islam, it was perhaps poetic justice that Bone should seek to disturb the status quo thirty years later also in the name of Islam. An unusually devout and intransigent ruler of Bone, Arumpone La Ma'daremming, made a number of bitter enemies in the early 1640s by attempting to apply the law of the Prophet rigorously. Although slavery was central to the whole South Sulawesi social system, he began to insist that all slaves should be freed unless they were born in that condition. The Arumpone's own mother fled to Makasar to protest about this novelty. Pattingalloang or his Sultan reportedly sent to ask the reformist Arumpone whether he was acting on the commands of the Prophet, on the basis of old custom, or according to his own whim. According to the Bone chronicle it was the Arumpone's failure to answer this letter which led Makasar to declare war on him. Still more serious, however, was Bone's attack upon Wajo' and Soppeng in the name of this fundamentalist view of Islam, leading to the death of the Aru Matoa of Wajo' and a grave threat to Gowa's position as *primus inter pares* of the South Sulawesi states (Noorduyn 1955, 116–17).

Pattingalloang therefore led forty thousand Makasar troops into the field against Bone in October 1643. According to the English factors they were up against twice as many Bugis, who were creating havoc and devastation quite close to the city limits, but the superiority of Makasar arms ensured a complete victory within a month (Banten to E. I. Co., 9 December 1643, IOL G/10/1; Ligtvoet 1880, 105). The intransigent Arumpone fled towards Luwu. The Gowa chronicle relates that Pattingalloang then instructed the Aru Pitu (council) of Bone to find another ruler from among the Bone royal house, but the councillors came back with the request that the Raja of Gowa or Pattingalloang himself should rule over them since there were no others capable. The chronicle has Pattingalloang reject this with the words: "There is a custom that if we choose a raja, the Bone people have nothing to do with it, and if the Bone people choose a raja, we similarly have nothing to do with it" (*Sedjarah Goa*, 71). In the event it seems that no king was installed, but a prominent Bugis named To Bala' was appointed as regent or Kadi of Bone, depending on the source.[3]

The Gowa chronicles may have put these and other moderate words in Pattingalloang's mouth to emphasise that the subsequent humiliation of Bone was no part of his intentions. Similarly the chronicle goes on to have him warn the Bone Council, "if you choose a king and do not inform us I will not shield you from danger, and we will attack you" (*Sedjarah Goa*, 71–2). Since the Bone people are portrayed doing just that three years later, their downfall is identified as entirely their own fault. The truth of these allegations is impossible to verify, but the chronicle makes clear that the ruling circles in Makasar, and notably Pattingalloang himself, were well aware that the autonomy of the Bugis states could not lightly be breached.

In any event, Bone did rebel under To Senrima, and was utterly defeated in April-May 1646 by a large Gowa force under Pattingalloang, supported by Wajo' and Luwu. Now for the first time the Raja of Gowa was himself proclaimed King of Bone, with To Bala (or Karaeng ri Sumanna', according to *Sedjarah Goa*) to represent him there. Even the main Gowa source concedes that for the first time Bone was plundered, "although the plunder was returned to them because it was judged that only the Arumpone was disgraced" (*Sedjarah Goa*, 72–3). Speelman, writing from a viewpoint closer to Bone's, relates that Makasar "stripped Bone of all dignity, made the whole country subservient to it, and took away all the notables" (Speelman 1670, I: 54; see also Ligtvoet 1880, 107; Noorduyn 1955, 118). Undoubtedly the power to which Makasar had risen made it difficult to maintain the traditional autonomy of a proud and warlike neighbouring state. It was, however, the bitterness of conquered Bone, skilfully exploited by the relentless VOC, that made possible the Dutch-led conquest of Makasar twenty years later.

By then, of course, Pattingalloang was no more. He died on 15 September 1654. He left an able son, Karaeng Karunrung (1631–85), to carry on the brilliant tradition of the family into the fourth generation. Karunrung was also fluent in Portuguese and Spanish, valued his father's fine library, and was among the outstanding Makasar statesmen and warriors (Navarrete 1962, I: 114; Skinner 1963, 283–4). However he was never in a strong enough position internally to ensure continuity of policy, and lacked the sure touch of his father at least in dealing with foreigners.

Only a month after Pattingalloang's death, the new king of Gowa, Hasanuddin (Mohammed Said having predeceased Pattingalloang by a year), declared that he would be his own chancellor (Ligtvoet 680, 113). The quasi-constitutional division of authority which had been the hallmark of Makasar's rise over the previous sixty years was at an end. Makasar came to suffer from the principal problem of the other mercantile states of Southeast Asia—concentration of inadequately defined powers in the hands of a frequently arbitrary ruler. In the years that followed we hear for the first time a string of complaints about dissensions among the ruling elite, endemic rebellion among the Bugis, and arbitrary and covetous actions by the ruler damaging the attractiveness of Makasar for traders (IOL, G/10/1: 149, 163, 181–2, 193–4, 261–2). Makasar remained a great city until the Dutch conquest (1660–9), but it no longer had the unity nor the foresight in its direction to withstand the threats to it.

NOTES

1. I am most grateful for the comments of Campbell Macknight, Christian Pelras and Abdurrahim on earlier versions of this paper.

2. In reality this title was not used until after the acceptance of Islam fifteen years later, but it is convenient to stick to it in view of the succession of titles he bore: Palakkaya, I Mallingkaang, I Daeng Mannyonri, Karaeng ri Kanjilo. Karaeng ri Segeri, as well as the later Islamic title Sultan Awal-ul-Islam (the first Muslim), and the posthumous one of Tumenanga ri Agamana.

3. *Sedjarah Goa* (71), and the Gowa Diary (Ligtvoet 1880, 105) both have To Bala appointed Kadi, and the former adds that Karaeng ri Sumanna' was appointed regent. The description of subsequent events by the *Sedjarah Goa* makes it seem likelier that by Kadi was meant the person responsible to Gowa for Bone affairs. We are inclined therefore to follow Noorduyn (1955, 117), and Speelman (1670, I: 54), in regarding To Bala as effectively regent.

CHAPTER EIGHT

EARLY SOUTHEAST ASIAN CATEGORIZATIONS OF EUROPEANS

S OUTHEAST Asia was not "discovered" by world trade systems. It lay athwart the sea route between India and China. For centuries before 1500 it had exported spices to the whole of Eurasia, and imported cloth, political systems and religious ideas from India, porcelain, technology and people from China. A substantial sea voyage lay between these places and Southeast Asia, but there had for over a millennium been traders, adventurers and pilgrims (to the holy places of India and Sri Lanka) who thought that effort justified. Europeans, therefore, were initially just one more strand in the already complex fabric of Asian maritime trade.

CATEGORIES OF OTHERNESS

Many Southeast Asians of the sixteenth century shared a religion with those outside (Buddhism, Islam, or for Vietnamese, Confucianism). Within these larger worlds they distinguished themselves in geographical terms. Vietnamese saw themselves as a distinct "southern" country equal in civilization to China in the north, the constant point of reference.[1] The remainder of coastal Southeast Asia, particularly those parts touched by Malay culture, identified themselves as "below the winds" in relation to India and all points west, which were "above the winds". Barros (1563, II, vi, II: 4) was the first western writer to record this distinction, but William Marsden (1812, II: ix–xiii) was more perceptive about its meaning. He argued that it was analogous to "us-them" distinctions such as Greeks and Barbarians, Jews and Gentiles, Arabs and others (*arabu ajem*), except that unlike these phrases, or similar distinctions made by Chinese, Christians, Muslims and others, there was no presumption of moral or cultural superiority involved. The Malay-maritime culture of coastal Southeast Asia was itself too ethnically varied, too open to external influences, to be inherently exclusive in that way. When conflict led to polarization against Europeans, as we will see below, the exclusive terminology of believer and infidel became more useful.

Chinese and Japanese were outside the "above the winds" category, since they came from a different direction, with different monsoon winds, and had cultures very distinct from those of the Indian Ocean. Europeans, however, even when they came across the Pacific as the Spanish did, were quickly understood to be part of that world "above the winds", in which Hinduism, Buddhism, Islam, and such powerful associated symbols as Alexander the Great and the empire of "Rum", all had their origin.

"Below the winds" located Southeast Asians geographically, notably in relation to a set of Indian Ocean ports which already had many points of reference in common. The same points of reference—commerce, cosmopolitanism, affluence, lavish dress, diplomatic decorum, a strong Islamic presence—implicitly juxtaposed the whole universe of Indian Ocean exchange against tribal shifting cultivators of the interior.

Foreign writers no doubt exaggerated the stories they heard in the cities about the savages of the hills. Ma Huan (1433, 92), for example, distinguished three types of people in Java in the early fifteenth century. Both the Chinese residing temporarily and the Muslim traders from every quarter who had taken up residence there more permanently were clean and civilized. The natives of the interior, however, were dirty, worshipped devils and ate unclean foods. Chou Ta-kuan portrayed an even more stark gulf between the civilized lowland Khmers of Angkor and their slaves taken from savage highlanders.

> They constitute a race apart known as the *ch'uan* [Ch'ong] brigands. Brought into the town, they do not dare to come and go outside their houses. In town, if in the course of a dispute one calls one's opponent *ch'uong*, he is suffused with hatred to the marrow of his bones, to such an extent are these people despised by other men . . . Males and females couple with each other, but their masters would never have sexual relations with them. If by chance a Chinese arrives and, after his long enforced celibacy, should inadvertently have intercourse just once with one of these women, and the master finds out, then the next day the latter will refuse to sit down in the newcomer's company, because he has had intercourse with a savage (Ian Mabbett's translation from Pelliot's French in Reid 1983a, 44).

A succession of visitors to northern Sumatra, from Marco Polo onwards (Polo 1298, 225–7; Gubernatis 1875, 35), made similar points about the contrast between the civilized Muslims of the ports and the savage cannibals of the interior who lived like beasts.

Although local residents must have been the sources for these sharp distinctions, Southeast Asian writers themselves were more ambivalent about the dichotomy. Almost every lowland people had to deal with adjacent upland people, and often also "sea-gypsies" (usually ethnically Bajau-Samal), whom they regarded as lacking civilization and religion and therefore fit to be enslaved. Yet at the same time they were seen as the original inhabitants, often having a special (if servile) relation with the coastal ruler and mysterious, even magical, powers over the natural and supernatural forces of forest and sea. Their rare appearances in Archipelago sources, therefore, are chiefly as direct servants of the king (Matheson and Hooker 1983, 192–9) or as magically potent individuals (Iskander 1958, 91–2). The riverine kingdoms of Mainland Southeast Asia all saw themselves surrounded by "wild" upland peoples, potentially able to be brought within the ever-changing boundaries of lowland royal control and settled wet-rice agriculture (see e.g. Than Tun 1983, I: 13). The interdependence in trade between the upstream and downstream populations ensured that each side incorporated the other into the myths which expressed their world-view.[2]

Nevertheless this dichotomy between civilized/cosmopolitan peoples of the cities and coasts, and barbarous/isolated people of the interior or of remote islands, was certainly part of the thinking of the former. It finds one form of expression in the contrast of the Javanese (and Thai and Cambodian) theatre between *halus* and *kasar*, that is the refinement proper to the court and city as against the gross appearance and behaviour of rustic folk, people from the *sebarang* (places outside Java), and demons. It also helps account for the credence given to stories of bizarre savages in some more distant island or mountain valley, whom nobody had seen but all had heard tell about. Some had tails; others had ears so long they could wrap themselves up in them at night; in one mysterious island there were only women, who became pregnant by the wind and put their male children to death.[3]

In this context one can also understand the response of Raja Soliman, the Muslim ruler of Manila, to the aggressive approach of the first Spanish fleet under Legazpi, in 1570. Manila was already the most important port of the Philippines, but a somewhat tenuous Muslim enclave in an animist Archipelago. Its commercial links with China and the other Muslim ports of the Archipelago were as vital as those with its unruly hinterland. When the Spanish somewhat peremptorily summoned Soliman to talks, therefore,

Fig. 5 French officers depicted in a seventeenth-century Thai watercolour panel from Wat Ban Koing, now in Suan Phakat palace, Bangkok
(No Na Paknam, *Farang Nai Sinlapa Thai*, Bangkok, 1986)

Soliman assumed an air of importance and haughtiness, and said that he was pleased to be the friend of the Spaniards, but the latter should understand that the Moros [Muslim Tagalogs] were not painted Indians [i.e. tattooed Visayans]. He said that they would not tolerate any abuse, as had the others; on the contrary they repay with death the least thing that touched their honour (translated in Blair and Robertson 1903-9, III: 95).

FIRST CONTACTS: "WHITE BENGALIS" AND "IRON HEADS"

Europeans were often astonished at what they found in Southeast Asia, a place of fabulous wealth, mysterious herbs and poisons, and strange sexual customs. It was certainly no less remarkable to them than Africa, the Pacific, or the New World of the Western Hemisphere.

But the surprise was not reciprocated. In a region of enormous diversity, accustomed to having its ports crowded with people of every kind, Europeans represented just another element. Foreign ships were always welcome, for they represented wealth and power. Every coastal ruler wanted to have them calling at his own port and not his rival's. The initial reception Europeans encountered was therefore uniformly agreeable. Even in relatively remote Samar, Magellan's first Southeast Asian landfall in the eastern Philippines, "their chief went immediately to the captain-general, showing signs of joy because of our arrival" (Pigafetta 1524, 23).

Foreign merchants were acknowledged and honoured figures in the diplomatic practice of the region. They were allowed to build temporary houses on shore, to acquire temporary wives, to mingle freely in the marketplace. Their leading figures had much better access to the ruler and his circle than did most natives, for they brought him extra prestige. If they carried a message from their ruler, as most substantial merchants took care to do, they were mounted on richly-decorated elephants or galleys to ride in solemn procession to the palace, where they were entertained with feasting and dancing.

Language was not a major barrier. Linguistic diversity was part of the everyday experience of Southeast Asian commerce, and virtually all had to resort to some lingua franca. Arabic was one of them, because of Islam, and provided a key for the earliest European visitors—Italians travelling overland through the Middle East, Portuguese and Spaniards with a long history of interaction with "Moors". The most valuable lingua franca was however Malay, which foreign traders including the Europeans were quick to pick up. The first two non-Portuguese expeditions to reach the region already had Malay-speaking interpreters on board who facilitated their early encounters. The Spanish fleet in 1521 made use of Magellan's Sumatran slave as interpreter in the Philippines (Pigafetta 1524, 26), while the French expedition of the Parmentier brothers in 1529 carried two Malay-speakers who had been in the East with the Portuguese (Parmentier 1883, 63, 67).

Women were the crucial cultural intermediaries with the earliest Europeans, as with generations of foreign traders before them, though their role is seldom acknowledged in the literature of either side. It was not simply that temporary marriage was accepted in Southeast Asia, that divorce could be readily undertaken by either party, and that wealthy foreigners were acceptable marriage partners (except for high-born women) in most coastal centres. Retailing, small trade and money-changing were seen as the domain of women and some very large commercial transactions were handled by them. In all the ports of the region it was accepted practice that visiting traders took a temporary local wife, who was at the same time a commercial partner able to provide local market information, sell foreign goods in the market, and buy and sell trade goods on behalf of her partner during the monsoon period when he was away (see Reid 1988, 155–6). As a seventeenth century Chinese visitor to Hoi An (Central Vietnam) matter-of-factly put it: "The women are very good at trade, so the traders who come here all tend to marry a woman to help them with their trading." (Da San 1699, IV: 9, as translated by Li Ta Na) This practice was especially highly developed by Chinese, but there is no doubt that Europeans also profited from it.

Such relationships began very early, and provided the mechanism whereby Portuguese learned the language and culture of their Asian environment, and the local community domesticated newcomers and learned their languages. Among the tiny proportion of such relationships which happen to have found their way into the literature, some occurred at the very beginning of Portuguese contact. The first European fleet to reach Southeast Asia, that of Lopes de Sequiera in 1509, was reportedly saved from a Malay surprise attack by the timely warning of a local Javanese woman who swam out to alert her lover on one of the Portuguese ships (Albuquerque 1557, II: 74). Among the Portuguese captured in Melaka from that fleet, nine escaped the city with the help of the daughter of the aristocrat to whose custody they had been assigned (Barros 1563, II, vi, II: 28). In Maluku, the "Spice Islands" proper, the first Portuguese commander was Francisco Serrão, sent there by Albuquerque in 1511. Pigafetta, who arrived in Maluku two years after Serrão's death in 1521, happened to report that he had left two children by a woman he had married in Java, presumably during that first voyage from Melaka in 1511 (Pigafetta 1524, 66–7). We have to assume that the harshness of the initial Portuguese irruption into Southeast Asia was very quickly modified by relationships such as these.

Regrettably few indigenous documents have survived from the early sixteenth century, and later reconstructions often carry the burdens of another age. Moreover the impact of the early encounters appears to have been far greater on the Europeans, for reasons sketched above. Except in the cases where they achieved spectacular military victories, Europeans are largely ignored by indigenous chronicles until the eighteenth century. What follows, therefore, is limited to a narrow range of Southeast Asian literature, supplemented by European descriptions.

The few Europeans who reached the region before Vasco da Gama, like the Jews of Cairo or the Armenians of Persia, usually travelled with Persian or Arab vessels and were identified with them. Nicolo Conti, for example, was a Venetian who learned Arabic as a young merchant in Damascus, travelled to Baghdad in an Arab caravan, and subsequently learned Persian in the ports of Ormuz and Calacatia. There he threw in his lot with some Persian merchants, "having first taken a solemn oath to be faithful and loyal companions to one another" (Major 1857, 5). He sailed with them to India and eventually Southeast Asia in the 1430s. Towards the end of the century, Hieronomo di Santo Stefano of Genoa travelled overland from Cairo to the Red Sea port of Cosseir with an Arab caravan, and then sailed in Arab vessels to India and Sumatra. The people he identifies as having rescued him from disasters were the Muslim *kadi* of Pasai (Sumatra), presumably a learned Arab trader, who knew some Italian as well as Arabic, and some Arab merchants from Damascus whose service he entered in India (Major 1857, 8–9). In the first decade of the following century Ludovico di Varthema learned his Arabic in Damascus, and must have passed as Muslim since he joined a caravan to Medina and Mecca. He found the Persian merchants of Shiraz "the best companions and the most liberal of any men who inhabit the earth", and formed a contract with some of them to explore the world together. Thus in Burma, for example, he was simply a Persian (Varthema 1510, 102–3, 220–2).

Europeans may typically have been a shade paler than Arabs and Persians, but the physical dividing line was not a fundamental one. Both the Russian Athanasius Nikitin and Ludovico di Varthema claimed that their relative whiteness was a source of interest in southern India and Burma. There were places, not easy to locate from their accounts, where women were said to offer themselves readily to the white men, or be offered by their husbands. Whatever the truth of such stories, it is significant that both authors granted that no distinction was made between themselves and their Muslim travelling companions (Varthema 1510, 202–4; Major 1857, 10). The Portuguese conquistadors routinely described their Gujerati or Arab antagonists as "white", as well as the Chinese and Ryukyuans with whom they had better relations—implying that European skin-colour was not seen as novel by either side (Alboquerque 1557, III: 69; Empoli 1514, 132; Pires 1515, 130).

The early Portuguese fleets, carrying hundreds of Portuguese with little prior experience of non-Christians, were of course perceived differently from individual traders. The Portuguese began by attacking Muslim ships, which confirmed the earlier idea of Muslims in the Indian Ocean that these were

"Franks", the same people who had attacked the holy places during the Crusades (see below). They now demanded to be classified as distinct from other visitors, especially Muslims. Some Malay accounts of their arrival grant this distinctiveness, though it has to be remembered that none date from before 1536, a generation after the Portuguese had demonstrated a certain uniqueness by conquering and fortifying Melaka.

The first direct impact of these "Franks" (Malay: *Feringgi*) in Southeast Asia was the mission of Diego Lopez de Sequeira, arriving in Melaka in September 1509. The chronicle of Malay kings, *Sejarah Melayu*, has this to say of the occasion:

> Then there came a Feringgi ship from Goa, and it came to trade in Melaka. The Feringgi saw that the city of Melaka was magnificent, and its port was exceedingly crowded. The people crowded round to see what the Feringgi looked like, and they were all surprised at their appearance. The Melaka people said, "These are white Bengalis!" Dozens of Melaka people surrounded each Feringgi; some twisted his beard, some knocked his head, some took off his hat, and some grasped his hand. The Captain [*kapitan*] of the ship then presented himself to the Bendahara [Chief Minister], Sri Maharaja. The Bendahara adopted him as his son, and gave him honorific cloths [the normal honour for ambassadors]. The ship's Captain presented Bendahara Sri Maharaja with a golden chain studded with jewels. He himself put it around the neck of the Bendahara. At that everybody was angry at the Feringgi Captain, but they were stopped by the Bendahara, who said, "Don't get carried away, for these are people who know nothing of manners".[4]

Though any European who has visited rural Southeast Asia will recognize the chaotic scene, we cannot be sure it all happened in 1509. The Malay account is primarily concerned to put the blame for the loss of Melaka on Sultan Mahmud, particularly by his execution of its hero, the Bendahara of the above account. According to the numerous Portuguese chroniclers (notably Barros 1563, II, i: 400–7; Pires 1515, 254–7), the respectful initial reception of Sequeira quickly turned sour, and he was lucky to escape with his life, leaving about sixty of his men ashore who were killed or kept captive. The *Sejarah Melayu* however turns this into two separate incidents, with Sequeira returning to Goa to explain the wonders of Melaka, and the viceroy (*wazir*), Albuquerque, then sending a fleet to try to take the city, which fails. Albuquerque wants at once to send a larger fleet, but is warned against this by his admiral (*Kapitan Mar*), who states prophetically, "Melaka will not fall if Bendahara Seri Maharaja is still there; no matter how great the force sent against Melaka, it will not fall" (*Sejarah Melayu*, 248–9; Winstedt 1938, 182; Brown 1952, 57–8).

Nevertheless there is much of interest in this account about Malay perceptions of the Portuguese in the sixteenth century. In likening them to Bengalis rather than Arabs, a put-down may have been intended. The latter had to be respected on religious grounds, however much laughed at privately, but Bengalis were more numerous and more resented in Melaka. Tomé Pires (1515, 93) noted "When they want to insult a man, they call him a Bengali", since these were a mercantile rather than a military people, alleged to be sharp-witted but treacherous. At all events the Portuguese seemed a variation on the Indian theme. They were a substantial group of over-dressed, round-eyed, relatively hairy males (Malays and Javanese carried women in their ships), coming from above the winds in well-equipped ships. The earliest Burmese references to the Portuguese also describe them as a kind of Indian: *Kala-pyu* (white Indians) or later *Kala-barin-gyi* ("feringgi" Indians) (Saya Lun 1920, 116–17; "History of Syriam" 1915, 53; Lieberman 1986, 244n).

After the Portuguese conquest of Melaka, some Malays made an analogy the Portuguese found more to their taste, with the Ryukyu traders who carried Japanese goods from Okinawa to Melaka. "The Malays say to the people of Melaka that there is no difference between Portuguese and Ryukyus, except that the Portuguese buy women, which the Ryukyus do not." Their country had wheat, meat and "wines after their fashion" as well as rice; they were truthful, non-Muslims, and far too proud to sell a fellow-countryman into slavery. "They are white men, well dressed, better than the Chinese, more dignified . . . If they are lied to when they collect payment [for sales on credit], they collect it sword in hand." (Pires 1515, 130)

The other area where the initial Portuguese impact could not be ignored was Maluku. Again there is a Malay account, written more than a century after the events by Rijali, a Muslim Ambonese taking refuge against Dutch depredations at the court of Makasar. He describes as follows the arrival in Nusa Telu, Ambon, of a small group of Portuguese under Francisco Serrão, shipwrecked nearby in 1512 after having made the first Portuguese voyage to Banda, further south:

> At one time a vessel from Sakibesi Nusa Telo went fishing to the Puluh Tiga Sea. Then they came and brought news to the Chief Minister [of Hitu] Jamilu, saying "In all our lives in this world we had never encountered people who looked like these. Their bodies were white, and their eyes were like cats-eyes. Then we enquired of them, but they did not know our language[5], and we did not know their nationality." Jamilu said to them, "Go, and bring them here." So they went back and brought them to the town, to Chief Minister Jamilu.

He asked them, "Where do you come from and what is the name of your country?" They replied, "We come from *negeri* Portugal with the intention of trading. The reason we came here was that we were lost and didn't know the route. So we were cast upon the coast . . . What will our fate be here?" Then they were given a place they could build a house. After some time they asked that half should stay and maintain the house, while the other half should take the news back to their superiors. When the time of the west monsoon came they arranged for a ship to come every year without interruption. So the market became busy at Hitu, and the whole of Ambon became renowned . . . At that time the name of Kapitan Hitu was famous from *negeri* Ambon to *negeri* Portugal. The King of Portugal gave him two names, the first Kapitan Hitu and the second Don Jamilu. (Manusama 1977, 167–8)

Just as the Bendahara was the central figure of the *Sejarah Melayu* account, Jamilu holds centre stage here, though he eventually comes to a bad end through pride, drunkenness and irreligion. Yet the Portuguese are clearly portrayed as an exceptional windfall, as Chinese and Javanese had been before them to the ports they had frequented. The Portuguese accounts of the early contact in Maluku are more graphic in showing the enthusiasm of the Malukans, much tested in later years, for alliances with the powerful foreigners. Portuguese chroniclers depict the rulers of Ternate and Tidore, rival centres of clove production, trade, and political influence, competing to bring Serrão's men to their capital, and thereafter to play the Portuguese card against their rivals. The same enthusiasm greeted the Dutch, the next unpredictable new factor in Malukan politics a century later.

Commercial wealth was one reason for this enthusiasm, but military prowess was the other. Galvão's view was that small-scale warfare was the favourite sport of the Malukans: "they are always waging war; they enjoy it; they live and support themselves by it". (Galvão 1544, 169) Foreign traders, with large ships, firearms and experienced fighters, were often a crucial factor in these wars. Portuguese immediately acquired a reputation everywhere as formidable warriors, but nowhere more than in Maluku where armour and firearms had previously been virtually unknown:

Formerly, upon seeing a man with a helmet, they said, "Here comes an iron head", and all of them ran away presuming that we were invincible and not subject to death. But at present they know that under that helmet there is a head that can be cut off, and a body that is not immortal. And seeing us fire muskets, they imagined that our mouths breathed out a deadly fire; and at hearing bombards shooting and the Portuguese being mentioned, pregnant women had a miscarriage because among them artillery was unknown nor had

they any inkling of it. But for a long time now [1544], they make war with us
and do not hold us in much esteem . . . They are men expert at arms. (Galvão
1544, 171)

Other Portuguese chroniclers relate that the Ternate ruler maximized the
effect of his new Portuguese allies by claiming they were the fulfilment of a
prophecy: "That the time would come, when Iron Men should arrive at
Ternate, from the remotest parts of the world, and settle in its Territory; by
whose power the glory and dominion of the Moluco islands should be far
extended" (Argensola 1708, 3, 6).[6]

In the bigger ports of the region firearms were already known, and the
surprise factor cannot have been as great. The Portuguese claimed, probably
with exaggeration, to have taken three thousand guns in their conquest of
Melaka, where "the gun founders were as good as those of Germany"
(Albuquerque 1557, III: 128).[7] These guns appear to have been highly
ornamented bronze culverins, introduced from both Gujerat and China.
They may have been intended to intimidate rather than to injure. In reality
it can only have been the way the Portuguese *used* their artillery so effectively
that surprised the defenders. The *Sejarah Melayu* account takes this further,
making play of the strangeness of the guns:

> On arrival at Melaka the ships forthwith opened fire with their cannon. And
> the people of Melaka were astonished at the sound of the cannon, and they
> said, "What sound is this, like thunder?" When the cannon balls began to arrive
> and struck the people of Melaka, some had their heads shot away, some their
> arms and some their legs. The people of Melaka were more and more amazed
> to see how these guns were made, and they said, "What is this weapon called
> that is round, yet is sharp enough to kill?" (Translated from Raffles 1817, 182
> with some deference to Brown 1952, 158)

There is confirmation in letters from two Italians in Albuquerque's fleet
that the fire from four hundred shipboard cannon was indeed exceptionally
intense, especially from a specially fortified junk which the Portuguese
anchored in the Melaka river, near its central bridge, in order to bombard
the town from very close quarters, "day and night" for twenty days before
the assault proper began. According to these accounts the fearful novelty of
this did encourage the defenders to treat for peace (Empoli 1514, 137;
Gubernatis 1875, 375–6). Yet it is curious that the Malay writers make this
alarming bombardment part of the fictional Portuguese attack between
Sequeira's visit and Albuquerque's conquest, and make the outcome of it a
Portuguese defeat. They wanted to show the Portuguese as a new and

different element in Malay history, but clearly they did not find their modern weapons a satisfactory explanation for the loss of Melaka.

In short, Europeans were initially perceived as another kind of people from "above the winds", who were distinguished by pale skins and round eyes but particularly by the effectiveness of their shipboard cannon, armour, and firearms. Although most indigenous sources took little account of them, they did have a major effect on the military balance in a number of areas and they greatly speeded the transformation of Southeast Asian warfare. In some areas such as Maluku and the Straits of Melaka, the Portuguese state enterprise became a significant player in inter-state rivalries. Elsewhere Portuguese individuals were much in demand as mercenary gunners. In 1550, for example, a Portuguese arquebusier killed one of the leading contenders for the throne of Pegu (lower Burma), and Portuguese mercenaries subsequently helped Bayinnaung to unite Burma by conquering the old heartland around Ava. A first-hand Burmese account of Bayinnaung's five-day bombardment of Ava city in 1555 makes no mention of Portuguese as such, but its amazement at the intensity of the bombardment ("cannon and muskets reverberated like Indra's thunderbolts . . . detonation followed detonation till it seemed a man's ears would burst") (Lieberman 1980, 215) is comparable to the Malay depiction of Albuquerque's onslaught at Melaka.

POLARIZATION

Despite the disaster the Portuguese inflicted on Malay kingship, Malay accounts of their arrival are morally neutral about the newcomers. The wars fought by the first generation of Portuguese were described as if they were fair contests between two honourable parties. The real villains of the story were not the Portuguese, but the Malays who let the side down—Sultan Mahmud himself, and Raja Abdullah of Kampar who foolishly believed Portuguese promises that they would help him become king of Melaka.

The contrast is striking with the outright hostility of their fellow-Muslims "above the winds", notably the Arabs of the Red Sea area: "The vessels of the Frank appeared at sea [in 1502] en route for India, Hormuz and tho · parts. They took about seven vessels, killing those on board and taking some prisoner. This was their first action, may God curse them." (Serjeant's translation of the Arab chronicle of Hadhramaut in Chaudhuri 1985, 65)

The Portuguese wasted no time in attacking the shipping of the "Moors", beginning with Arabs but quickly extending to the Gujerati Muslim traders who were a far bigger factor in Southeast Asia. Their reputation as fanatical enemies of Islam was carried ahead of them to the port · t the Straits of

Melaka region. When Lopes de Sequeira arrived in Melaka in 1509, according to Tomé Pires (1515, 255),

> first the Gujeratis went to the said king Mahmud with a great present, and also the Parsees and Arabs and Bengalis and many of the Klings [South Indians] reported to the said king together, that the Portuguese had reached the port, and consequently were bound to come there every time, and that, besides robbing by sea and land, they were spying in order to come back and capture it [Melaka], just as all India was already in the power of the Portuguese—whom they call *Framges* here—that because Portugal was far away they ought to kill them all here.

The first "ethnography" of the newcomers was undoubtedly provided to local rulers by Muslims in this way, and was not flattering. When Magellan's men reached the Philippines, the same thing happened: a Muslim merchant in the port of Cebu explained to its raja that these were the same *Feringgi* who had conquered Calicut and Melaka (Pigafetta 1524, 33). It was this Muslim term for Frank (Arabic *Faranj*, Malay *Feringgi*), carried by Malays or other Muslim traders, which came to characterize the Portuguese (and Europeans in general) almost everywhere. In Burma the term was *Balang-gyi* or *Bayin-gyi*, in Thai it became *Farang*, in Khmer *Barang*, and in Chinese *Fo-lang-ji*. Only Vietnam encountered the Portuguese without this Muslim mediation, through Macao-based trade, and used geographical terms such as "people from the sea" (*Yang Ren*) or "western sea people" (*Yang Tây Duong*). In the Philippines the Muslim filter was very temporary, and the Spanish were soon called by their own preferred term, *Castila*.

It by no means followed, however, that Southeast Asians, even when they were Muslim, would necessarily share the negative view of the Gujeratis and Arabs. The initial reaction was much more neutral or even positive, as we have seen. Only as Portuguese plundering appeared to confirm the unflattering picture given by the foreign Muslims did Southeast Asians range themselves in opposition to them. An Italian serving a Portuguese cause for which he had no special love, Giovanni da Empoli, gave a graphic account of this mounting hostility in northern Sumatra, where Albuquerque selected the reluctant Florentine as his trouble-shooter:

> the General [Albuquerque] was sending me to enemy territory [at Pidië] where there were, as well, people whose boats and belongings had been seized, and whose fathers, sons and brothers, etc. had been killed by us . . . and he commanded this like a man who had little regard for me . . . And while I was there, many people came by night with lights to see me, as if I were a monster;

and many asked how we made so bold as to pass through other peoples' territory plundering peoples and harbours (Empoli 1514, 125).

At both Sumatran ports Albuquerque visited on his way to Melaka, da Empoli was sent ashore to spy out the land and talk to the ruler, and in both cases he received a lecture on how foreign traders ought to behave: "that whoever seized his ships coming to his ports could not be deemed a friend, and that if he desired his friendship what had been seized should be returned" (Empoli 1514, 127–8).

The *Hikayat Hang Tuah* is the most timeless because the most popular of Malay epics. Its earliest versions must have been recited in the fifteenth century, but the versions that survive in written form were adapted and reworked in the following century and a half. It is the story of a warrior hero of the Melaka Sultanate who is the epitome of Malay bravery, loyalty, cultivation, physical attractiveness and mastery of the spirit world. All the other peoples with whom Melaka had to do are brought into this great epic. Hang Tuah travels to India, China and "Rom" (Byzantium/Turkey) to show the greatness of these countries, and the high respect they have for the Malays and their king. He is sent to Siam and Java to get the better of civilized and formidable rivals who have designs on the independence of Melaka. Europeans (*Feringgi*), however, appear only as antagonists for the Malay culture hero.

Chronological sequence is not of great concern in the story, and Hang Tuah first meets the Portuguese on his voyages on Melaka's behalf to India and China. In both cases the local harbour-master (*syahbandar*) asks the Malays to berth their ships adjacent to the Feringgi, who become angry at the approach of the Melaka vessels. The Malays reply: "Why should you forbid us? We too are merchants; wherever we are told to go, there we anchor. However if you want to fight with us . . . so be it." (*Hikayat Hang Tuah* 1966, 346, 364) In China the enmity appears more patent, and the Malays respond that they are ready to fight, "for the Feringgi and the Malays are enemies". (*Hikayat Hang Tuah* 1966, 364) It is forbidden to fight in a neutral Chinese port but the Portuguese, further humiliated by the magnificent reception given by the Chinese court to Hang Tuah, lie in wait for the Malays when they leave. The Portuguese guns prove useless when Hang Tuah reads his magic spell and the Portuguese are all killed or put to flight (*Hikayat Hang Tuah* 1966, 369–72).

News of these humiliations eventually reach the "Gebernador of Manila" (meaning this story at least post-dates 1571), who reports in person to the king of Portugal. The latter sends a fleet of forty well-armed galleys to attack Melaka in revenge. Although sick, Hang Tuah is there to drive them away with terrible casualties including the Portuguese commander (*Hikayat Hang Tuah* 1966, 428-35). Only after Hang Tuah's death do the Portuguese succeed in taking the city by stratagem. Not surprisingly, there are many to advise the ruler not to deal with them at all, because "the Feringgi are evil people" (*Hikayat Hang Tuah* 1966, 487).

The Portuguese, it seems, were simply like that—born enemies of the Malays. There is nothing in this or other early Malay sources to point to religion as the reason for this antagonism. Some early Portuguese sources, on the other hand, do impute the same religious motive to the Malays as to themselves. Tomé Pires, for example, related that Sultan Mahmud eventually sided with the anti-Portuguese lobby in Melaka in 1509, and told his ministers that the Portuguese "go about conquering the world and destroying and blotting out the name of our Holy Prophet. Let them all die." (Pires 1515, 256) But indigenous sources only picked up this theme in the second half of the sixteenth century, if at all.

A religious polarization between Islam and its enemies became established in Southeast Asia only after 1550. One reason may have been the Catholic Counter Reformation, the arrival of Francis Xavier and his Jesuit followers in 1542, and the beginning of a serious attempt by the Iberians to make conversion one of their major goals in the region. Another was the revival of the Islamic spice-trading route, shipping cloves, nutmeg and pepper directly from Aceh (Sumatra) to the Red Sea ports with increasing efficiency from the 1530s, in direct competition with the Portuguese route to Europe. A third factor was the rise of Turkey as a great Islamic power, commanding the western termini of this route, and able to challenge Portuguese dominance of the Indian Ocean in the name of Islam. Factors internal to Islam must nevertheless be given the greatest weight. In India, as in Southeast Asia, there was a steady shift towards militant orthodoxy during the century between 1550 and 1650. Orthodox Sunni Islam became the state religion not only of the Mughals, but also of southern states such as Bijapur, Golconda and parts of Kerala (Eaton 1978, 83-134; Aziz Ahmad 1964, 182-90; Dale n.d.). In Southeast Asia, states such as Aceh, Brunei, Banten, Makasar (Muslim from 1603) and Ternate were visited by a stream of reformist preachers and teachers from the Middle East, and began to generate revered teachers of their own, some of whom had spent long periods in Mecca and Medina.

Having arisen by uniting the northern coast of Sumatra against the Portuguese, the Sultanate of Aceh set the pace for this militant trend throughout the sixteenth century. Sultan Ala'ad-din Ri'ayat Syah al-Kahar (1539-71) was hailed by the Muslim historian Raniri a century later as "the very first who fought against all the unbelievers [*kafir*], to the point of going himself to attack [Portuguese] Melaka" (Nuru'd-din 1966, 31-´). He w also the chief beneficiary of the direct spice trade to the Red Sea, now a Turkish lake. Through this connection he received not only a succession of Muslim scholars, but also guns and men with which to fight the infidel (Reid 1969a, 395–414; Farooqi 1986, 267–9). Mendes Pinto put several militant anti-Christian speeches into al-Kahar's mouth, including one justifying his ferocious execution of the king of Aru on the grounds that this rival king had so far forgotten his religion as to ally with "those cursed dogs from the other end of the world who, by the most tyrannous means, aided by our sinful negligence, have become masters of Melaka" (55). Although Pinto's colourful writing must always be treated with caution, there is more direct evidence of the Sultan's thinking in a letter he wrote to the Sultan of Turkey in about 1565 which is recapitulated in the extant Turkish response of 1567.

> The Sultan of Aceh says that he is left alone to face the infidels. The infidels have captured islands, and taken Muslims. Merchant and pilgrim ships going from these islands towards Mecca were captured one night, and the ones they couldn't capture they fired upon, causing many Muslims to drown. And infidel rulers have conquered Ceylon and Calicut, where most of the inhabitants are Muslims. If we (Turkey) would send a fleet, all the infidel subjects of those lands would come to the true faith (Saffet Bey 1912, 606–8).[8]

There is no doubt that a militant Muslim "ethnography" of the Iberian Christians was making rapid headway here. An oral and written literature developed in Southeast Asian languages exhorting Muslims to holy war against them.[9] Similar ideas suffuse Rijali's chronicle about Maluku, the other area of intense Portuguese impact, written about 1650. After the good fortune represented by the initial Portuguese arrival, described above, the *Hikayat Tanah Hitu* changes mood to describe the constant wars against the infidel, and the succession of war leaders who distinguished themselves in them. Although this pattern of Muslim-Christian warfare was in many respects a continuation of traditional hostilities between rival Ambonese *negeri* (village communities), the chronicle portrays a situation of constant holy war (*perang sabilu'llah*) in the second half of the sixteenth century. All the dead who fell on the Hitu (Muslim) side were martyrs (*syahid*) guaranteed immediate entry into heaven (Manusama 1977, 169–71). The Iberians appear as the inevitable enemies of the faithful, now giving a wider meaning to the ancient cleavages within Maluku.

Muslim-Christian conflict affected most parts of the region in this period, with Catholic missionaries, and to some extent Europeans in general, seen by the mercantile Muslims of the cities as inveterate enemies of Islam. A Franciscan missionary, Francisco de Santa Maria, was killed by a militant

Muslim group in Brunei in the 1580s, while the first Dominicans to arrive in the Siamese capital in the 1560s were set upon by a Muslim mob who killed one and badly injured the other (Ribadeneira 1601, 457–60; *Exemplar literarum ex Indiis*, 1571). In the leading Islamic capitals such as Aceh, Banten, Brunei and Makasar, Europeans who broke laws or offended rulers were given the choice of conversion to Islam or death. Some of the Muslim scholars whose job it was to convince such Christians to accept Islam showed from their arguments that they had considerable knowledge of Christianity through an Islamic prism.[10]

The Theravada Buddhists of Mainland Southeast Asia had a tradition of tolerating the religious practice of others, and the friendly initial approach of the Iberians gave them no reason to change it. By the end of the sixteenth century, however, a bloody Spanish intervention in Cambodia and Portuguese military activity in Burma changed the perception of the Europeans.

Burmese chronicles have nothing good to say about Europeans, despite the crucial role Portuguese mercenaries played in helping Tabinshweti and Bayinnaung reunite the country and bring it to its greatest pinnacle of power. Of Tabinshweti (1531–51) it was recorded that "he gave himself up to the company of his favourite, a *Kala-pyu* adventurer, from whom he learned the habit of drinking. Addicted to hard drinking he began to lose his sense of morality, and had no scruple to commit adultery with the wives of his ministers." (Saya Lun 1920, 118–19)[11] More severe judgements were passed on Philip de Brito, the enterprising Portuguese who captured the port of Syriam (opposite modern Rangoon) on behalf of the King of Arakan in 1599, and managed to turn it into a powerful independent kingdom with some local Mon support. The Mon chronicle of Pegu was very Buddhist in spirit, and its main concern with de Brito was his inability to earn merit and ensure the kingdom's welfare because he was not Buddhist: "The ship commander, the *kala* Kappitan Jera [Captain General], was king again in Syriam. Because he was of Devadatta's company, a heretic, he had no opportunity of enshrining at the relic chamber of the pagoda." ("Slapat Rajawan Datow Smin Ron" 1923, 59) The chroniclers of the Burmese Toungoo dynasty, which took Syriam and executed de Brito in 1613, were even more hostile towards this foreigner. Although acknowledging that he made Burmese and Mon allies, including the ruler of Martaban whose son married his daughter, the major chronicles portray de Brito (whom they call the *kala baringyi* Nga-zinga) as plundering the Buddhist shrines and temples of their riches. "He removed the precious stones with which the images were adorned, melted down the gold and silver, and beat them into leaves which he sold to traders calling at the ports, Thus, he waxed very rich by this nefarious trade, and with riches came power and authority." ("Intercourse between Burma and Siam" 1959, 153; Kala 1961, III: 106–11)[12] After Toungoo had conquered Syriam, de Brito was publicly impaled in the town square because he was "a man who had destroyed religion". Between four and five hundred of his *kala baringyi* followers were sent to Ava as captives, where they eventually served the Burmese kings as soldiers ("Intercourse between Burma and Siam" 1959, 158; "History of Syriam" 1915, 53). According to Furnivall, de Brito was still remembered as "the destroyer of religion" in Syriam early this century ("History of Syriam" 1915, 57).

The lack of interest of the Dutch in spreading their own religion, together with their readiness to ally with all enemies of the Portuguese, undermined the simple polarization between Muslim and Christian. Yet because Dutch did establish a degree of military and economic hegemony which the Portuguese did not, opposition to them quickly became even more universal. One of the greatest VOC empire-builders in the east, Rijklof van Goens, conceded in 1655 that "There is nobody who wishes us well in all the Indies, yea we are deadly hated by all nations." (Quoted in Boxer 1965, 84) English observers make the same point (Dampier 1697, 82–3), and a Chinese memorialist, noting that of all barbarians Europeans alone should be feared as "the most evil and intractable", singled out the Dutch as especially insatiable.[13]

A good example of the mood of those who suffered from Dutch expansion was the *Sja'ir Perang Mengkasar*, a verse epic in Malay celebrating the fierce wars of the 1660s through which Makasar lost its independence to the Dutch (with much Bugis help). Its author uses the terms Hollander (*Welanda*) and infidel (*kafir*) interchangeably to suit his metre. Each term is invariably accompanied by some colourful epithet—"cursed", "devils", "fiendish", "renegade", "perfidious", "greedy", "thieving", "insane".[14] As others have pointed out, the term *kafir* was not in itself necessarily abusive (Skinner 1963, 11n; Skinner quotes Snouck Hurgronje on the same point). In referring to the English who supported the Makasar side as far as they could, the Malay writer noted, "their minds were as sharp as a *kris*; although they were crass *kafir*, they were unwavering, with upright hearts" (Skinner 1963, 144). On the Dutch, however, his judgement is clear:

> Listen, Gentlemen, to my request
> never make friends with the Dutch
> they behave like devils
> when they are about no country is safe (Skinner 1963, 214)

EMULATION

The Southeast Asian sources of the period show both neutrality and hostility toward the European, with the latter gaining ground over the former. Positive remarks about Europeans are extremely hard to find before the nineteenth century. Yet that cannot have been the whole picture. In the first century and a half of intense contact, before the gulf in power and wealth had become substantial, there were numerous Southeast Asians who responded enthusiastically to the new ideas introduced by Europeans. King Narai of Siam, Karaeng Pattenggalloang of Makasar and Raja Laut of Mindanao were three seventeenth century statesmen known from European sources to have read European books and creatively mediated European scientific and historical knowledge to their people (Reid 1988, 232–4). The conversion to Christianity in the short period 1570–1650 of the great majority of lowland Filipinos and substantial numbers of Malukans and Vietnamese, is evidence of a positive response at a mass level. How did such converts perceive the Europeans who presented the gospel to them? For the most part we can only guess, on the basis of missionary accounts, that they saw them as having the keys to a great source of power.

The only Filipino author who wrote in Tagalog and touched on the issue was Tomas Pinpin, a Tagalog printer whose *Librong Pagaaralan nang manga Tagalog nang uicang Castila* [Book with which Tagalogs can learn Castilian] was published in Manila in 1610. He took for granted that his fellow-countrymen wanted to emulate the Spaniards:

> No doubt you like and imitate the ways and appearance of the Spaniards in matters of clothing and the bearing of arms and even of gait, and you do not hesitate to spend a great deal so that you may resemble the Spaniard. Therefore would you not like to acquire as well this other trait which is their language? . . . it is this [Castilian] that is the source of a lot of other things and it is like the inside of things, and everything else is only its external covering. (Translated in Rafael 1988, 58)

The prologue of this work promised that learning Spanish would help or "cure" Tagalogs, and was sure to give pleasure. Vicente Rafael's intriguing analysis argues that Pinpin and his readers saw Spanish as a source of protection against the unpredictable shocks of the hierarchic system the Spanish sought to impose (Rafael 1988, 55–83). However Pinpin's complex text is read, it is almost the only extant Southeast Asian writing from this early period to the effect that the Europeans had introduced something of real importance.[15]

EXPLAINING EUROPEAN POWER

In every culture, perhaps in every soldier, there is a curious mixture of belief in technology and belief in fate. Few soldiers neglect to sharpen their swords or keep their powder dry before the battle, but equally few will explain their own survival or their comrade's death in purely material terms. In saying that Southeast Asians of the sixteenth century believed power to be essentially spiritual in nature, therefore, we are placing them on a continuum, not in opposition to Europeans. Portuguese too attributed their victories to divine help and the intervention of Santiago (St James). Their early victories were however partly attributable to the stronger conviction among their Southeast Asian antagonists that there was no use fighting if spiritual forces favoured the other side. Southeast Asian wars had often been decided like trials by ordeal, by an initial skirmish or battle between individual champions or leaders. If the spiritual preparation, moral worth, and reading of the signs were superior on one side than the other, one death could be enough to show it (Reid 1988, 121–9).

As we have seen, Southeast Asian sources refused to attribute defeat to inferior technology, even when they described the superiority of European firepower. As European power grew and the memory of its origins faded, stories were developed to explain it which were progressively more symbolic. The royal chronicle of Melaka, in the post-conquest versions that have come down to us, can be seen as a moral text on the theme that Melaka was made great by virtue and destroyed by vice. The dying testament of the penultimate ruler to his successor is that if you put your people to death when they have done no wrong, "your kingdom will be brought to nought". It is then made crystal clear that Albuquerque's conquest of the city was only possible because the great Bendahara Sri Maharaja and others were unjustly executed by the Sultan (Brown 1952, 124–5, 156–71). The best of nineteenth-century Malay historians, Raja Ali Haji, retold this story more simply: "According to the story, when His Majesty Sultan Mahmud killed Bendahara Sri Maharaja without just cause, by the decree of God Almighty the Portuguese came and attacked Melaka." (Haji ibn Ahmad 1982, 17)

In Malay texts intended more for popular entertainment than for royal instruction, explanations in the tradition of the beloved trickster tales play their part. These have nothing to do with the facts of Albuquerque's conquest in 1511, but draw inspiration from the tortuous attempts by later European companies to build permanent stone dwellings in the trading cities. Up until 1619 their requests were sometimes granted in return for favours rendered, but in that year the Dutch made themselves impregnable in their fort in

Jakarta, which they renamed Batavia and established as the headquarters of their Asian trade empire. The same mistake was not made again.

The main Javanese chronicle of the kings of Banten, suzerains of Jakarta, tells this story in realistic terms. Kapitan Jangkung [Jan (Pieterszoon) Coen] requested a piece of land from the Pangeran of Jakarta, and built a strong wooden fence around it. When goods were stolen, he was allowed to strengthen this fence. A large Dutch ship then sank in the harbour, and the Dutch received permission to unload it into their factory. Trade goods were unloaded by day and, unknown to the Javanese, arms by night. Approval was sought from Banten for this increasing strength, and the Banten authorities accepted Jangkung's argument that the Dutch would be a buffer against the greater threat of Mataram (which ruled central and east Java). However several ministers gave the prophetic warning: "The Dutch now were like a spark no bigger than a firefly. They must be smothered now lest that spark become a great fire which would destroy all." (Djajadiningrat 1913, 43–4).

The Batavia experience seems the likeliest origin for a trickster story which quickly spread around Southeast Asia and beyond. This has the Europeans requesting and receiving a plot of land no bigger than an oxhide. They then cut an oxhide into long strips, so that it embraces enough ground for them to build a great fort. This story is told of the Dutch occupation of Jakarta by several Javanese histories (Djajadiningrat 1913, 165; Raffles 1817, II: 154). It is also told of the Portuguese conquest of Melaka by a number of Malay texts, including the popular *Hikayat Hang Tuah* (see also Linden 1937, 31–7). While the borrowing of stories between Malay and Javanese texts is to be expected, it is surprising to find exactly the same story told to explain the power of the Portuguese in Cambodia and Sri Lanka (Ponchaud 1990, 3; Silva 1994, 320). The Burmese chronicle of Syriam uses the same legend to explain Philip de Brito's capture of that city. De Brito made the Burmese ruler numerous presents so as to be "allowed to found in our town of Syriam a village such as might be included in a hide. When this request had been granted, he drew out the hide like a wire and on the North, South, East and West, he measured out land." ("History of Syriam" 1915, 53)

Classicists will not need reminding that this is exactly the tale told by Virgil about how Dido established Carthage, by purchasing from the king of Libya as much land as an oxhide would cover, and then stretching the hide out in narrow strips. The story may be even older as a Phoenician legend, carried by them around the Mediterranean, and notably to the Iberian coast. Spanish and Portuguese folklore adopted it as a kind of origin myth of civilization, so that the Iberian Peninsula is still sometimes referred to as *la piel de toro* (the oxhide).[16] The Phoenician story could have been carried by Arabs into the Indian Ocean, but it seems more likely that it was the Portuguese themselves who took it to Sri Lanka and Southeast Asia, making it seem to Asians a particularly appropriate explanation of Portuguese conquests. At all events it must have been thought apt as well as entertaining, explaining as it did how a handful of people coming from the other side of the world, ostensibly to trade, could have ended by making themselves impregnable and strangely powerful.

In the colonial era the mental world of businesslike Dutchmen and mystical, hierarchic Javanese seemed poles apart, and theories of dualism were popular to explain how they coexisted without influencing each other. Looked at in the longer term, however, this dualism can be seen as an historical construct which suited the Dutch East India Company (VOC) very well. The earliest Dutch descriptions give no suggestion of such an opposition—indeed the Dutch were known to complain that "a Javanese would sell his own father for a little business" (Heemskerck 1660 in Jonge 1862–88, II; 451). But under Jan Pieterszoon Coen's guidance the VOC showed itself on the one hand absolutely ruthless towards its commercial competitors in the spice trade; on the other hand indulgent towards the symbolic claims of rulers in the interior to divinely-ordained and universal power. VOC factors at Semarang and Padang sent regular tribute to the "Emperors" of Mataram and Minangkabau respectively, addressed them in appropriately humble terms, and supported them against their more commercially oriented local antagonists. Although the military power of the Dutch was far beyond that of their Iberian predecessors, they used it for calculated commercial advantage, never for symbolic victories. In effect, if not in deliberate intent, they encouraged Southeast Asian rulers to retreat from economic and military concerns to symbolic and spiritual ones where they did not compete with Dutch ambitions.

Java was the principal battlefield where this symbiosis was hammered out, and it is to Javanese chronicle literature we should look for how it was perceived at the end of the day. Unfortunately almost all of this writing has come to us in versions written *after* the Gianti Treaty of 1755, whereby the Mataram kingdom was divided under Dutch sponsorship between Surakarta and Jogjakarta. To that extent it can be seen as a literature trying to make the best of a series of humiliating setbacks.

The only Javanese historical text definitely pre-dating 1755, the *Babad ing Sangkala* of 1738, treats very cryptically the failure of the Mataram expedition sent to expel the Dutch from Java in 1629 (Ricklefs 1978, 37). A much fuller account was given in the "Great Babad", the version of the *Babad Tanah Jawi* which did not achieve its definitive modern form until 1836 (though undoubtedly based on earlier texts now lost). This text has the great Sultan Agung sending one of his commanders, Mandura-Reja, with a vast army to drive the Dutch into the sea. While the battle rages at great cost to both sides, the Sultan sends a more trusted retainer, Purbaya, with instructions simply to scare the Dutch. Purbaya has some share in the supernatural powers of the ruler himself. He flies over Batavia, mocks at the Dutch and with a wave of his hand causes a breach to open in their fortifications. Then he returns to advise the Sultan to stop the war, "since the Dutch have only come here to trade". The king agrees. The Dutch coming was God's will, since he knows the future when they would assist his successors. "The reason I began this war," he says, "is only to make an example, so that in the future they will be fearful." The army is withdrawn and Mandura-Reja and other commanders are executed. The Dutch are of course relieved, but "all realize that this resulted from the desire of His Majesty, who had offered forgiveness to the Dutch. The Dutch thereupon sent an envoy to Mataram to present a great number and variety of gifts." (*Babad Tanah Jawi* 1987, 140–3)

Underlying this specific story of one defeat was a broader mythological theme used by a number of Javanese texts to legitimate Dutch power in Batavia as a successor to the Sundanese kingdom of Pajajaran in west Java. This Hindu kingdom, defeated in the sixteenth century by the rising Muslim power on the coast, was seen by Javanese as legitimately distinct from Javanese kingdoms (indeed early Portuguese maps, based on Javanese information, placed a waterway through the island separating Sundanese from Javanese territory). At the same time its dynasty was believed to possess great spiritual powers. From their line came the Queen of the South Sea (Nyai Loro Kidul), mystical bride of all legitimate Javanese rulers. The common element in all the stories in question is a beautiful Pajajaran princess so sacred (or perhaps accursed) that flames issue from her genitals whenever a normal mortal attempts to sleep with her.[17] Other rulers having failed to conquer her, she is exiled to the island of Onrust (off Jakarta), where a Dutch captain arrives and marries her—or more commonly buys her for the price of three magically powerful cannon. Their union is the origin of all Dutchmen, or at least of the Governors-General of Batavia, and explains why the Dutch are appropriate rulers of western Java and allies of the Javanese kings (Pigeaud 1968, II: 249, 333, 361, 463; Djajadiningrat 1913, 285–6).

While this story is usually but a small episode in mythical histories of Java, one cycle of stories set out explicitly to explain in extraordinary complexity who the Dutch were and why they were powerful. This is the story of Baron Sakender, whose name appears to unite a Dutch aristocratic title (familiar only from the time Baron van Imhoff became Governor-General in 1743) and the Javanese name of Alexander the Great.[18] In this text the princess with the flaming genitals is married by Sakender's brother, Baron Sukmul, who returns with her to Holland after his successful trading expedition to Java.

The son of this union is Jangkung (J. P. Coen), a famous warrior who determines to avenge the insult to his mother and her loss to the Muslims of her Pajajaran kingdom.

It is Baron Sakender who dominates the story, however, with a succession of superhuman exploits worthy of Ulysses or the Monkey King. Though these are too numerous even to summarize, some of them reveal much about the then perception of the Dutch. The first Dutch ruler is called Nakhoda (i.e. ship-owner or supercargo), who has eleven other sons besides Sakender and Sukmul, all of whom have the names of prominent Dutchmen in the east such as Speelman, van Imhoff, and (again!) Coen. After obtaining various magical powers and assistants, Sakender saves the kingdom of Spain from attack by all the other known kings of the world above the winds (Persia, England, France, China, the Arabs), and marries the king's daughter. The Spanish throne, now suzerain over all these countries, is repeatedly offered to Sakender, but he seeks more adventure and so bestows it instead on his father, Nakhoda, the king of Holland. Nakhoda regulates this great kingdom to be governed by his other twelve sons, who are the founders of the *Edele Heren*, the members of the Dutch *Raad van Indië* which ruled Batavia. He tells them:

> Suffer no misfortune in what you desire,
> even though it comes to thievery,
> These worldly goods I name, "The Company".[19]
> But to be consulted over by [you] twelve are all of its affairs:
> Commerce, war, the destroying of cities.
> These worldly goods be salaries then,
> But omit not to calculate,
> write up precisely
> the profits and losses (Ricklefs 1978, 396).

This is the foundation of the curious power of the VOC, so utterly at odds with eighteenth century Javanese ideas of what kingly power should be. The Company was ruled by a committee of men equal in rank, yet it was heir both to Dutch mercantilism and the world-empire of Philip II of Spain.

Baron Sukmul and his son Coen carry this power to Batavia to claim the inheritance of Pajajaran. It is not their firepower which gains them victory, but the characteristic trick of firing coins from their cannon, causing the defenders to become so distracted they can easily be killed. The truly powerful figure and hero of the story, Baron Sakender, appears to play no further part in advancing the cause of Holland or Europe. He flies off to see the wealthy land of Java, together with his magically powerful companions, the eagle Garuda and the horse Sembrani. In Java they appear to meet their match.

Their powers of flight are negated by some more powerful force. Alarmed, they disguise themselves in new curious forms and go to meet Senapati, the first ruler of Mataram (ruled 1600–13), whose service they enter. Attention then switches to Senapati, and a prophecy about the greatness of his dynasty, which will nevertheless fall after three generations.

By the time this tale was written, the power of the Europeans could not be ignored. Javanese attempted to domesticate it through myth; others saw it as a punishment by God, or a sign of the approaching end of the world. Curiously, it was not until European colonial power was at its arrogant peak, after 1890, that Southeast Asians could see in the ideas behind it a great source of new hope.

NOTES

1. The founder of the Lê Dynasty put it clearly after driving out the Chinese in 1427: "Our state of Dai Viet is truly a cultured land. Our mountains and rivers have long been different, as likewise have the customs of South [i.e. Vietnam] and North [China]". Quoted in Whitmore (1985, 128).

2. The upstream-downstream symbiosis was set out by Bennet Bronson (1977, 39–54). It has been sensitively explored in a Sumatran context in two recent studies: Jane Drakard (1990) and Barbara Andaya (1993).

3. Local informants of Pires put the people with long ears in Papua and the island of women off the west coast of Sumatra; those of Pigafetta put the former in the lesser Sundas and the latter south of Java (Pires 1515, 222, 162; Pigafetta 1524, 93, 95). The notion of an island of women somewhere in the Indian Archipelago was reported by Chinese writers as early as the sixth century, and Arabs in the tenth (Hirth and Rockhill 1970, 151–2).

4. I have translated this from the Shellabear text of *Sejarah Melayu* (1961, 248). The Raffles text, better known through Brown's translation (1952) is almost identical except for the omission of the final sentence of this paragraph.

5. The fishermen were therefore portrayed as simple folk who knew only their local language, and not the lingua franca, Malay, in which the Portuguese would have conversed to Jamilu.

6. A similar allegation is made by the major Burmese chronicler U Kala, with similar scepticism, that Mon monks had claimed that de Brito's advent had been prophesied in their religious texts, which foretold that "strangers with white faces and teeth [Southeast Asians blackened their teeth] and cropped hair" would have a period of ascendance (Lieberman 1980, 218).

7. The more balanced account by the Italian Giovanni da Empoli (1504, 136–7) confirms that Melaka did defend itself with cannons.

8. I am grateful to Professors Salih Ozbaran and Cornell Fleischer for the outline translation of this letter.

9. The oldest known version of the popular Acehnese *Hikayat Perang Sabil* [Rhymed chronicle of the Holy War] is dated 1710, but there were probably oral predecessors (Alfian 1987, 109–14).

10. Frederick de Houtman's account of his captivity in Aceh (1948, 96–100). A more fatal Catholic experience in Aceh is chronicled by Tres-saincte Trinité (1652, 496–515).

11. The adventurer in question was Diogo Soares. The rise and fall of this "lustful Galician", who was military commander and confident of Tabinshweti, but stoned to death by an angry crowd under his successor for his "abominable crimes", is colourfully told in Pinto (1578, 425–30).

12. I am grateful to Maung Maung Nyo for translating this last source for me.

13. Quoted in a letter from Beijing by the Jesuit de Mailla, 5 June 1717, in *Lettres édifiantes* (1781, 10–12). See also memorial of 17 January 1684 by Shih Long, translated in Fu (1966, 60–1).

14. *Kutuk, syaitan, iblis, murtad, dusta, bacil, pencuri, gila*, respectively.

15. As has been shown by Ileto, Filipino borrowing of Spanish motifs extended to the popular myths through which they expressed their longing to be free in later centuries. The holy week drama of the passion of Christ, and the heroic struggle of the Spanish millennial hero Bernardo Carpio, were rendered into Tagalog verse so emotionally powerful that it provided the language for nineteenth century liberation movements (Ileto 1979a; 1979, 379–400).

16. Personal communication from Dr Eduardo Aznar-Vallejo.

17. An established theme in Javanese mythology, since Ken Dedes in the sixteenth century *Pararaton* had the same miraculous power, which only the legitimate ruler Ken Anggrok could cope with.

18. The only scholarly edition of this epic is by A. B. Cohen Stuart (1850), which uses a text dated 1845. The same text was published with an Indonesian translation in Jakarta in 1978. I am indebted for what follows, however, to the lengthy summary and analysis provided by M. C. Ricklefs (1974, 377–407) based on an earlier British Museum text of about 1810.

19. *Kumpeni*, a term by which the Dutch were known throughout Indonesia until early this century.

CHAPTER NINE

SLAVERY AND BONDAGE IN SOUTHEAST ASIAN HISTORY[1]

These slaves constitute the main capital and wealth of the natives of these islands, since they are both very useful and necessary for the working of their farms. Thus they are sold, exchanged, and traded, just like any other article of merchandise, from village to village, from province to province, and indeed from island to island (Morga 1609, 274).

THUS does the most reliable of Spanish chroniclers describe perhaps the most important social institution found in the Philippines of the sixteenth century. His description is typical of scores of Western sources describing a varied range of Southeast Asian societies which they encountered in the sixteenth and seventeenth centuries. What is the historian or social scientist to do with such statements?

Everybody who writes in a language different from that of his subjects must be familiar with the problem. Can we free the most important terms from the associations and cultural bias of our own tradition and language and make them universally applicable? In particular, can categories derived from European history fit quite different historical traditions? Do we gain more explanatory power by emphasizing the relationship of an institution with similar institutions in other times and places, or by emphasizing its place within a range of related indigenous institutions?

There are few such institutions which appear to be so universal as "slavery". Yet many would have us abandon a term so laden with pejorative European-American associations. As soon as we replace it with "bondage", "dependency", "rights-in-persons" or "dyadic ties", however, we discover that we have exchanged a category with difficult boundaries for a category so broad as to be almost meaningless. Miers and Kopytoff (1977, 12) urge us to "discard Western concepts as we try to understand what it is that Western observers have, for various reasons, called 'slavery' in Africa. The position of the 'slave' must be examined in the context of the society to which he belongs." They are correct in urging the researcher to begin by seeing exactly what each institution means to the people within the system, yet as soon as we write about that system in English we begin the process of equating it with a larger set of categories outside. Miers and Kopytoff themselves rather shamefacedly use the word "slavery" throughout their theoretical introduction, though their contributors drop the inverted commas.

My own view is that slavery is one of the most important terms of comparative social and historical analysis, and must be rescued from the specific moral associations which nineteenth century reformers gave to it. When we define the term clearly, and examine the great variety of cultures and social systems within which it applied, we emerge with a much clearer picture of how far the Greco-Roman or American slave experience was a development, a variant or an exception to more general patterns. Moreover we find that the category slave becomes most important, and most clear-cut, precisely at the interface between two cultures, when labour is being transferred from relatively poor or weak to relatively rich or powerful societies. If we are to understand the nature of this exchange and what it meant for both sides, we must seek a serviceable definition which fits both buyers and sellers, both masters and victims. It transpires that Southeast Asia is a peculiarly fruitful place to examine the interaction of different concepts of servitude—Islamic, Indic, Chinese and modern European, as well as a range of indigenous forms—and thus to delineate the most useful boundaries of slavery as a global concept. Unfortunately, since Montesquieu (1949, 239) used Dampier's evidence about Aceh (Sumatra) to show that slavery can be relatively "mild" in the type of polity he labelled "despotic", the Southeast Asian evidence has been almost ignored in the general discussion of the subject.

The chief exception to this neglect is H. J. Nieboer, and it may therefore be no coincidence that I find his definition among the most useful: "We may define a slave in the ordinary sense of the word as a man who is the property of another, politically and socially at a lower level than the mass of the people, and performing compulsory labour" (Nieboer 1910, 5). Watson is surely correct in re-emphasizing persons-as-property and compulsory labour as central to any universal definition of slavery (Watson 1980, 8). The third of Nieboer's criteria, lower political and social status, is broad enough to accommodate both the explicit legal status of Roman law and the (possibly temporary) "outsider" status of a captive in many African and Southeast Asian groups who may eventually be assimilated, but equally may be used for a human sacrifice. Nieboer clearly does not mean, as McDermott (1981, 677) has claimed for the Chinese *nu-p'u*, that a group cannot be slaves if a few of them become rich and powerful. If that were true we would have to stop using the term slavery for the Ancient World and most of Asia (Watson 1980, 6; Caplan 1980, 192–3).

Although the boundaries are difficult, the theoretical concept of slavery is at least as clear as most of the categories historians use. It is the functions, the forms and, above all, the associations of the term that cause the difficulty. In the popular usage of European languages, it is probably true to say that the only historical term equally burdened with pejorative emotion is "fascism". This is partly, but not wholly, because of the value modern Western society puts on personal freedom. There is also the problem of what we would today call racism, but which historically we might consider as the category of the servile outsider.

It is a common enough phenomenon in history that, when a large category of impoverished or captive aliens becomes available as slave labour, indigenous slaves move up the social ladder to become a junior part of the dominant group—even if still under bondage. There are some examples of this in Southeast Asian history, particularly in the affluent Malays of the trading cities of Melaka, Aceh or Patani at their height. Of Melaka, de Barros reported, "you will not find a native Malay that will carry on his back his own or any other man's property, however much you may offer him for doing so" (cited Crawfurd 1856, 404). Similarly the Tausug of eighteenth century Sulu could assimilate second or third generation captives into the dominant group because there was always a supply of new captives.

While such dominance was always short term and limited in the kaleidoscope of Southeast Asia, it is not difficult to see in European history a gradual progression towards identifying the "in-group" as necessarily free from slavery—with the black-white dichotomy of North America and the West Indies as the ultimate crude expression of the trend. If we go back to biblical sources, we find a Hebrew pattern of familial slavery which is very close to that of many Southeast Asian societies in modern times. A range of types of servitude is described by the one word *'ebed*, including the bondage of Israel in Egypt and the bondage of Israel or of individuals to their God, as well as the familiar patriarchal picture in which male and female slaves form part of the household, being bought in good times and sold in bad (Leviticus 20, 10–11). Adultery with a freewoman is punished by death, but with a slave woman only by the offering of a ram—and the whipping of the unfortunate woman (Leviticus 19, 20–2). As in Africa and parts of Southeast Asia, the boundary with family is difficult, since men evidently sold their daughters and bought their wives also as *'ebed* (Exodus 21, 7–10). Yet the experience of bondage in Egypt and of the subsequent conquest of the Canaanites produced a clear disapproval of enslavement of the dominant children of Israel, not (yet) because they were free, but because they were the slaves of God, redeemed by him from Egypt. Therefore, "Both thy bondmen and thy bondmaids which thou shalt have, shall be of the heathen that are round about you; of them shall you buy bondmen and bondmaids" (Leviticus 25, 44; see also Davis 1966, 63–6).

Greek and Roman law eventually came to define the status of slave and free with much greater precision. Nevertheless, Greek *doulos* and Latin *servus* continued to be morally neutral terms covering a variety of servitudes. Plato thought slavery to be a perfectly natural outgrowth of the hierarchies of the patriarchic family, and the authors of the Greek and Latin Christian scriptures still saw no difficulty in identifying the righteous man as the slave of God. In Asia such language still presents no emotional difficulties, and no one objects to being called Abdullah (slave of God) or, in India, Das. Nevertheless, whenever there was an abundance of "barbarian" captives available as slaves, the slave tended to be seen also as outsider.

The process of evolution from slave to serf from the time of the late Roman empire is of course a very complex one. We might single out from the literature three important factors which are also present in the erosion of slavery in Southeast Asia in the seventeenth and eighteenth centuries: impoverishment (since slavery was an expensive way of maintaining labour), the growing power of the state, and universalist religion (Bloch 1975, 1–6; Westermann 1955, 108–59). The decisive upgrading of the Latin term *servus*, however, came with the introduction in the eleventh century of a new category of servile "outsiders", the Islamic captives of the Iberian Peninsula and the Russians exported to Germany. Two centuries later, Italian imports of slaves from the Black Sea expanded rapidly, and fixed some derivative of the ethnic label "Slav" (slave, esclave, esclavo, schiavo, sklav, slaaf), as the lowest servile category in all West European languages. Although serfs, the heirs (along with "servants") of the Roman *servus*, continued to suffer from many of the unfreedoms imposed by Roman law, the idea was now established in Europe that "true slaves" were or should be inferior outsiders. The 1611 English translation of the Bible shows how far English thought had gone already along this path, making it impossible for an English reader to identify with a slave (even of God) or a slave-based society. It is therefore not surprising that the European observers of slavery in Southeast Asia persistently comment on its mildness.

The idea that slavery is contrary to nature is surprisingly ancient in Western Europe. Henry VII of England reflected a strong medieval tradition in declaring that "in the beginning nature made all men free, and afterwards the law of nations reduced some under the yoke of servitude" (cited Davis 1966, 83). By the nineteenth century this belief had become the dogma of moral campaigners, who saw slavery as not only evil, unchristian and malevolent, but also (unlike Plato and Aquinas) as contrary to the natural and original state of man. Similarly Auguste Comte and Marx saw slavery as a development, though in their case a morally neutral one, away from an earlier more egalitarian system.

Nineteenth century European administrators and missionaries, on whom we rely for our knowledge of many Southeast Asian societies before colonization, brought these ideas with them. Thus Raffles, Crawfurd, Kruyt and many others tended to see the existence of slavery in Southeast Asia as some form of deterioration from an earlier state of relative equality. Crawfurd goes so far as to posit a Southeast Asian scale, in which "the more abject the state of man in the scale of social improvement, the freer the form of his government; and in proportion as he advances in civilization, is that freedom abridged, until, at the top of the scale, he is subjected to a tyranny where not a vestige of liberty is discoverable" (Crawfurd 1820, III: 4; see also Kruyt 1938, 500–9). It is hardly surprising that assumptions of this sort have found their way also into modern Southeast Asian elite perceptions of their own societies, as indicated by the Thai insistence that Sukhotai was the "pure" Thai state free of slavery (Kasetsiri 1976, 14; Chaloemtiarana 1978, 744–94); Hatta's attraction to the "original democracy" of Indonesia (Hatta 1953, 81–93); Rizal's idealized picture of the pre-Hispanic Philippines (cited Schumacher 1979, 273); and the recent trend among Vietnamese Marxists to reject slavery as a mode of production in their own past (information from Oliver Wolters).

HIERARCHY IN SOUTHEAST ASIA

While it is difficult to speak with any certainty about the more remote periods of Southeast Asian history, such assumptions do not help in understanding the role of slavery and bondage within the range of Southeast Asian institutions. All the evidence we have suggests that vertical bonding is very ancient and central to almost all Southeast Asian societies, and cannot helpfully be portrayed as an external or recent factor. What we have to try to understand is how this system of bonding operated in a wide variety of historical situations, and in which of them it can usefully be equated with slavery as we know it in other parts of the world.

As soon as Southeast Asians speak, they place themselves in a vertical relationship. Diller has cited fifteen alternative forms of the pronoun "I" in

Thai, and in all major Southeast Asian languages the second person pronoun is even more finely graded. The assumption behind these speech patterns is that society is naturally hierarchic, like the family, so that comfort and intimacy are best achieved when one can address the other party as an older or younger brother or sister, or as father, grandfather, uncle, boss or lord. Horizontal and superficially equal relations cannot in practice be avoided in the modern world, but this dilemma is frequently resolved by suspending pronouns altogether, at least until the relationship becomes clearer, or by substituting English "you". Among the most frequently used first person pronouns are the ordinary words in each language for slave or bondman, that is, Malay/Indonesian *saya*; Javanese *kula* or *kawula*; Thai *kha*; Khmer *khnjom*; Burmese *kyun-taw*; Vietnamese *toi* (Diller 1979, 26–9; Blust 1978, 2; Uhlenbeck 1978, 294–6).

This striking linguistic pattern suggests that vertical bonding is at the heart of many Southeast Asian social systems. Even today it continues to strike anthropologists as characteristic of the societies they study. In the Philippines (especially the Tagalog region) the system has now become well known by the description *utang na lo'ob*, debt of gratitude (Kaut 1961; Ileto 1979a). In Indonesia a prominent anthropologist has generalized it as simply an "excessively vertical orientation" in his country (Koentjaraningrat 1974, 47–56). Chabot (1950, 102), working among the Makasarese of Sulawesi, called it a "follower system": "The basis of this system is the awareness that a relationship of authority of high over low exists, accepted by the latter, and likewise the realization that high and low need each other in their striving for higher standing. This relationship is based on cooperation. The relationship between (almost) equal groups, on the other hand, is best described as opposition."

It requires effort for modern Westerners to understand a situation where unequal relationships can be both cooperative and intimate. The only example of such a phenomenon in the West is the nuclear family, and that too is under strain. We have to remember that in pre-modern Southeast Asia the family was a great deal broader and more porous, with a high level of temporary or permanent adoption, while at the other end of the spectrum the nation and its institutions, whose taxes and laws Westerners accept with little more than a grumble, were extremely weak. The unit formed by the patron and his varied dependants, both kin and non-kin, resembled what Tocqueville called "a sort of lesser country, more tangible and more cherished than the country at large" (cited Dumont 1970, 18).

The theoretical concept of human equality (although at least latent in the three major world religions in Southeast Asia) is not, as far as I know, present in the great texts of the Southeast Asian high cultures. What we do find

Fig. 6 Three slaves of the Raja of Buleleng, Bali, 1864 (KITLV 4392, Leiden)

celebrated there is a mystical unity between servant and master—*kawula* and *gusti* in the Javanese texts (Moertono 1968, 14–24). The masses are not forgotten in Southeast Asian drama and popular culture. They have their place as followers, dependants, servants or slaves of the great—portrayed often comically, with coarse speech and gestures, but possessing both loyalty and folk wisdom. Oral or written traditions of Thailand, Celebes and the Visayas, at least, trace the origins of slaves to the original divine dispensation. The first ancestor of the ruling dynasties descended from heaven already provided with slaves or dependants (Scott 1983; Reid 1983b; Pelras 1971, 177; Baas Terwiel, private communication).

What we are suggesting is that the various systems of bondage encountered during the last eight centuries of recorded history, including those we recognize as slavery, are indigenous developments having their origin in a characteristically Southeast Asian acceptance of mutual obligation between high and low, or creditor and debtor.

DEBT AND OBLIGATION

The key to Southeast Asian social systems was the control of people. Land was assumed to be abundant, and not therefore an index to power (with the partial exceptions of Java and Central Thailand in relatively modern times). It is this that distinguishes traditional Southeast Asian states from feudal ones. Society was held together by the vertical bonds of obligation between people. The wealth of the rich, and the power of the strong, lay in the dependant man- (and woman-) power they could gather around them. For the poor and weak, on the other hand, security and opportunity depended upon being bonded to somebody strong enough to look after them.

In this situation the important question was to whom you were bonded rather than the abstract legal quality of your bondage. The same words— *kyun, phrai, hamba, ata*—could mean in our terms subject, vassal or slave, since they expressed total obligation and fealty in any relationship.

These bonds, however, were transferable, and it is this that provides the overlap with slavery. Bondsmen might be presented as a marriage gift, donated to a monastery, offered as tribute, given as security for a loan, sold or inherited, without having any say themselves in such total disruption of their lives. Moreover the person was the ultimate security for a man's actions, so that his bondage had a clear monetary value. If a debt or fine could not be paid, the debtor or one of his dependants had to be transferred into bondage to the creditor. Similarly, people could be redeemed or bought, so that their obligations passed to the "buyer".

From very ancient times to surprisingly recent ones, men have worked for someone else because of an accepted obligation, and not in payment for a wage—even though in many cases labourers, even those most clearly in the slave category, did receive food and even "pocket money". If we seek a single origin for this system of obligation, it appears to be debt.

Even in relatively simple societies little penetrated by money, there were ritual needs for substantial expenditures—the payment of bride-price for marriage and the slaughter of a buffalo at the death of a family member. It is widely reported that such ritual needs are the most common reason why the poor become indebted to the rich (Leach 1965, 141–2; Kruyt 1938, I: 501–

6). In the Kei islands of eastern Indonesia, a type of bondage is described when a particular sub-clan is unable to afford the bride-price payments necessary to acquire wives, and so enlists a wealthy *maduan* (translated as master or owner) to pay the costs, the sub-clan all becoming his *koi* or bondsmen. The children of marriages so contracted are described as belonging to the *maduan*, and he can also repossess the wife he provided if his bondsmen fail to carry out their obligations to him (Wouden 1968, 12–13). A similar type of bride-service, sometimes involving bondage to the future father-in-law, is reported in the Philippines, Sulawesi, Sumatra and northern Thailand, and may once have been much more widespread (Miles 1972, 105–8; Kathirithamby-Wells 1977, 110–12).

Although there is of course a large gulf between this type of bride-service and a permanent class of slaves forbidden to intermarry with freemen in more developed wet-rice societies, there are also continuities. Thus a slave-owner was expected to provide a wife for his slave, which is one of the reasons the latter is often considered more fortunate than a poor freeman. At least in the Philippines and Sulawesi (Scott 1983; Sutherland 1983), domestic servitude at the beck and call of the master tended to be reserved for unmarried bondsmen, who were eventually rewarded with marriage, a house of their own, and looser bonds of obligation. Nevertheless, the children of such a marriage remained bonded to the master, provided he had met all the expenses, including bride-price (*Adatrechtbundels* 36, 254).

The imagery of bondage is most commonly that of the extended family. The words for bondsmen are often cognates of those for children, foster-children or nephews, and a slave is permitted a level of intimacy with his master which no one who was not a member of the household could dare assume (Kruyt 1938, 518; Leach 1965, 160–1; Bachtiar 1967, 373). Although, as we shall see, bondage took many forms including some very unpleasant ones, its prototype was junior membership of the household, doing all its most menial jobs, yet closely bound in intimacy to it and sharing its triumphs as well as its disasters.

Studies from a variety of Southeast Asian cultures make clear the close relationship between debt and obligation—obligation to serve the creditor in whatever manner is deemed proper (Reid 1983b). Self-sale and judicial bondage, although in places governed by specific regulations, can be seen as emanating from the same basic principle. Sale or commendation of oneself and/or one's wife and children to a wealthier person is reported in all societies, especially in times of severe hardship. Bondage was always preferable to starvation or beggary. Similarly, we hear examples very widely (Terwiel 1983; Goudsward 1854, 353; Wilken 1888, 563–4) of men gambling themselves into bondage, since gambling seems throughout Southeast Asia to have been

Fig. 7 A slave auction in Batavia, c. 1800 (KITLV, Leiden)

an abiding passion, especially in connection with cock-fights. Wilken relates that Toba-Bataks who expected to gamble on market day would go equipped with a special form of rope (*tali pasa*) as a sign of their good faith that their bodies were the surety for their gambling debts.

Similarly, much the most common judicial sentences were in a monetary form. The Melaka legal code was conscious that it frequently parted company from Islamic law ("the law of God") in preferring monetary compensation over Kuranic "eye for an eye and tooth for a tooth" principles (Liaw 1976, 31–2). While executions certainly occurred, notably for crimes against the ruler or against traditional taboos such as incest, ordinary murders were frequently punished only by a fine. In Banten it was twenty reals for a slave, fifty for a freeman and one hundred for an aristocrat (Scott 1606, 94). The nineteenth century European invention of the prison would have been seen as an extraordinary waste of valuable human resources. Frequently, of course, the fines could not be paid, and the condemned man, often accompanied by his dependants, became the bondsman of the ruler, of the injured party, or of whoever was able to pay his fine for him.

Islam's disapproval of interest (*riba*), and preference for profit-sharing arrangements between creditor and debtor, appear to have presented no problem to Southeast Asians. The payment of money interest on a debt was already a peripheral phenomenon among them, primarily used by foreigners in the cities. Pawning one's dependants or oneself (and in modern times one's property), or else entering a very unequal partnership with the creditor who became the patron if not the master, were the common Southeast Asian means of obtaining capital. In these relationships between debtor (or pawnee or criminal) and creditor, the labour service of the debtor was always seen as paying what we would call the interest on the outstanding loan—explicitly in the modern Thai case (Terwiel 1983) and implicitly in all others. Labour never paid off the loan itself. The debt never became reduced with time, therefore, and commonly assumed a permanent character, bondage being passed on from parents to children.

In the nineteenth century there was a marked tendency for the category of debt-bondage to be extended, distinguished from "true slavery", and in some cases regulated. The main reason for this was that Europeans and those who dealt with them could no longer openly countenance "true slavery", though a secondary reason may have been the diminution in the number of war captives owing to steadily more peaceful conditions. Those (chiefly Europeans) who sought to emphasize the distinction between debt-bondage and "true slavery" did so on the basis of the temporary and qualified nature of debt-bondage, since the debt-bondsman had a theoretical right to buy himself out. Nineteenth century Siamese law itself made a distinction of this type, while fixing the point at which a debt grew so big that a debt-bondsman became a "true slave".

We must insist, however, that this distinction is not of primary importance in the indigenous Southeast Asian context. Except in some exceptional urban situations which we will consider below, the abstract legal status of different types of citizens was not clearly defined. What was universal was the association between debt and bondage. With the exception of the Siamese, and possibly the Javanese, Southeast Asians did not themselves emphasize a distinction between bondsmen in terms of the route which had taken them into bondage, unless this happened to correspond with the socially (but not legally) important distinction between outsiders (usually captives in origin) and insiders (usually debtors). Even in the case of a manifestly permanent slave, his bondage could be redeemed if the price was right. In fact the debt-bondsman better fits the key element in our definition of the slave, his character as saleable property, than does the inherited domestic slave who is so intimately part of the family that he is highly unlikely in practice to be sold. The obligations of a newly acquired debt-bondsman were seen as having a very explicit cash value, so that this was probably the category of bondsmen most frequently traded and exchanged, as Sutherland (1983) shows for South Sulawesi. In Burma there were brokers who specialized exclusively in the hiring and selling of such bondsmen (Aung-Thwin 1983).

In normal times debt was certainly the most important source of bondage in Southeast Asia, and bondsmen with such origins made up a very large section of society. Pigeaud (1960, IV: 173–4) has suggested that they were the dominant social group in the Java of Majapahit, and Hoadley's evidence (1983) that debt was the basis of the *cacahkawula* category in Ceribon (Java) confirms the centrality of the institution four centuries later. Debt-bondsmen have been estimated as between a quarter and a half of the population of Central Siam in the eighteenth and nineteenth centuries (Terwiel 1983; Rabibhadana 1969, 109; Johnston 1975, 22–3). Having rejected a distinction between debt-bondage and "true slavery", do we then have to declare such societies veritable "slave systems", with a higher proportion of slaves than was common even in ancient Greece or Rome? (cf. Westermann 1955, 9; Sargent 1925.) I think not, since the legal categories of slave and free were not well defined, obligation and fealty were more central to the Southeast Asian system than status-as-property, while in certain cases serf seems a more appropriate English word than slave. There is, however, a very important area of overlap where slave is the most helpful word, as we will attempt to make clear below.

WAR CAPTIVES

Captives in war or raiding expeditions were usually enslaved, at least temporarily, and the legal codes we have do not distinguish between their status and that of other slaves. In practice, however, the fortunes of war made a considerable difference to the position of slaves in any given society—in Southeast Asia as in Europe or the Muslim world. In Angkor at its height in the thirteenth century, for example, a very large proportion of the population appear to have been slaves captured or bought from the surrounding hill-peoples or neighbouring states. As described by Chou Ta-kuan, the social gulf between these "savage" slaves and the dominant Khmer population was extreme even by the standards of the New World, since runaway slaves were tattooed or branded, and sexual relations with slave women were abhorred. In such a situation, where slavery becomes associated with alien "barbarians", the status of indigenous bondsmen will naturally rise to the point where "slave" is no longer an appropriate term for them. These situations, however, were usually temporary. Most war captives were culturally closer to their captors than this Angkor example, so that within a generation or two they shared the language, religion and lifestyle of the dominant population.

URBAN SLAVES

The Angkor of Chou Ta-kuan, where rich men had a hundred slaves and only the poor had none, is representative not only of a conquering state but also of a prosperous Southeast Asian city. Large cities of up to a hundred thousand population, as Angkor, Ayudhya, Melaka, Banten, Aceh and Makasar appear to have been in their pre-colonial heyday, required a large labour force to keep pace with their rapid expansion. This was provided not by spontaneous migration and wage labour, but by an influx on a large scale of people in bondage. Some came in the retinue of the traders and officials who flocked to the big cities; others were brought home as captives from military campaigns, to be distributed or sold, or to work for the king; others again were brought to the cities by slave traders. The merchants and officials who lived by the trade of these cities at their peak could afford an enormous retinue of slaves, and they maintained large establishments guarded and served by slaves. The most menial work was probably carried out by the most recent captive arrivals, and we know that there was a high rate of upward mobility in the subsequent generations. For the dominant classes it was imperative to do no manual work oneself, and to show one's status by the retinue of slaves on every venture outside the household.

It was also in these flourishing mercantile cities that the law codes which are among our most important sources were drawn up. It is easy to see why slavery was the subject of so much attention in most of these codes. Traders came to these cities from every part of the world, and they could not function effectively within the Southeast Asian societies unless they had men bonded to them. In a cosmopolitan commercial setting, however, the cultural assumptions that debt entailed obligation were not sufficient. Slaves were the most important single item of property. Laws were required to prevent them running away, to regulate compensation if they were killed, raped, injured or abducted, and to regulate the ownership of their children. Given the large number of foreign merchants involved, it is not surprising that these law codes owed much to foreign, especially Islamic, ideas of slavery. The codification of such laws must in itself have tended to create in these cities what we do not usually encounter in the countryside, an abstract status of slave as opposed to free, with a juridically defined position as inferior chattels.

A similar process in the Greek city-states had produced that first sharp antithesis between slave and free that the world knew. As Perry Anderson (1978, 22) comments, "The solstice of classical urban culture also witnessed the zenith of slavery; and the decline of one, in Hellenistic Greece or Christian Rome, was likewise invariably marked by the setting of the other." In Southeast Asia, too, a phenomenon which we are obliged to call slavery reached its peak during the high points of commercially oriented urban development (Reid 1980). Yet even in this urban situation, the Southeast Asian character of slavery always asserted itself: in the familial model for master-slave relations, in the freedom of many slaves to make extra income for themselves on the side, and in the tendency to free or assimilate the second generation of slaves into a more ambivalent form of bondage.

EUROPEAN-OWNED SLAVES

It was into this Southeast Asian urban culture at its commercial height that the Europeans came as traders and colonists—the Portuguese and Spanish in the sixteenth century and the northern Europeans in the seventeenth. Like the Indian, Arab and Chinese traders before them, they had initially to acquire labour on Southeast Asian terms. In the areas they came to rule directly, they eventually married their European concepts to the Southeast Asian social realities around them. Southeast Asia provides the most important evidence of European colonists taking over and interacting with an existing Asian system of slavery, rather than imposing their own system in a vacuum as in the New World or South Africa. We should therefore examine carefully how far the new patterns which emerged were determined by the masters or the slaves; by Europe or by Asia; by legal theory or by the political and social environment.

When the Europeans encountered Asia in significant numbers, they had already narrowed their conception of slavery to a relatively brutal type associated with captive "outsiders", and the social distance between European master and slave was already wider than was common in the ancient world (though it was to become wider still). These Europeans encountered a type of bonded labourer in the cities of Southeast Asia whom they called "slave", primarily, one must assume, because that was how these bondsmen were described by earlier inhabitants in the various languages they used as lingua franca—Arabic, Portuguese and Malay were the most common. The earliest word-lists between Malay and European languages gave *hamba* and *alipin* as slave (Pigafetta 1972, 151; Lombard 1970, 194). The Europeans immediately noticed, however, that most of these slaves were treated as well as servants in Europe, if not better. The Portuguese captain in Melaka cited by Manguin (1983) is an excellent example, complaining that one had to pamper each slave "so that he does not run away".

Laws existed in Southeast Asia law codes as well as European-colonial ones to prevent slaves from running away, but for the most part society was too fragmented to allow them to be rigorously enforced. Even relatively strong governments, like those in pre-nineteenth century Siam or seventeenth century Dutch Batavia, could not prevent slaves from fleeing to the jungle hinterland. In more pluralistic and free-wheeling cities, slaves could frequently abscond safely from one master to another, without even leaving the city. Because of the extremely high cost of "free" labour (meaning bondsmen hired from their master), the English and Dutch were obliged to buy slaves. Initially they sought slaves from as far away as possible—India, Arakan, Madagascar or New Guinea—so as to minimize the likelihood of slaves fleeing from anything they found unacceptable. Increasingly, however, they adapted to the Southeast Asian urban system in which slaves were either well fed and clothed in a domestic situation (which was therefore a luxury) or else were allowed to seek their own subsistence for a proportion of their time.

The European-controlled enclaves in Southeast Asia differed from all but the strongest Southeast Asian states in their ability to impose a uniform legal system on their inhabitants. In pre-colonial Banten, one source (Scott 1606, 170) reports that masters could execute their slaves "for any small fault", while another (*De eerste schipvaart*, I: 129) says this was only possible with the king's permission. What is clear is that the rule of law was less certain in Banten at that time than it became in nearby Batavia under Dutch control.

Anxious to prevent the dangers of revolt or large scale flight, the VOC in 1625 forbade Batavian owners to put their slaves in chains or to impose more than "civil and domestic" punishments without the express permission of the authorities (*Nederlandsch-Indisch Plakaatboek1*, I: 171). This did not prevent horrific punishments being imposed, but executions and floggings were in practice almost always carried out by the magistrates. In British Bengkulen there were also strict rules against abuse of slaves (Kathirithamby-Wells 1977, 130–1).

Probably much more effective in practice as a discouragement to mistreatment, however, was the reputation of slaves from the Archipelago for responding to ill-treatment with a murderous attack on the offending master, with complete disregard for the certain execution that awaited them thereafter. Stavorinus (1798, III: 392) was one of many who pointed out that barbarous ill-treatment of slaves was not common, because "those who are guilty of such conduct seldom fail of meeting their due reward, and are generally murdered, or poisoned, by their exasperated slaves; or else the slaves run away from their masters who thereby lose a valuable property".

In the Cape of Good Hope, Mauritius and Réunion, as at Batavia, slaves from the Archipelago had the reputation of being at once the most intelligent and agreeable domestic servants, and the most dangerous if provoked by insult or ill-treatment (Boxer 1965, 259–65; Kock 1971, 53; Gerbeau 1979, 12–14; Böeseken 1977, 46, 75). This was especially true of the Makasar-Bugis who were the most numerous Southeast Asian slaves in all these places. Could the prominence of Indonesians as domestic slaves at the Cape have something to do with the mild "Southeast Asian" type of slavery which reportedly obtained there, in contrast to the brutal type associated with Dutch colonies in the Americas?

In the earliest period of European colonies, when the labour system was still similar to that of the Southeast Asian trading cities which preceded them, much of the labour and retailing was still done by slaves, who frequently lived in their own houses owning their own property, including even their own slaves (Haan 1922, I: 457; Iwao 1970, 7, Sutherland 1983; and for the same pattern at the Cape, Kock 1971, 209). This phenomenon of slaves buying and owning other slaves is a feature also noted in indigenous centres as diverse as Angkor, Aceh, Sulu and Toraja. Once it is accepted that slaves can own property (though not legally inherit it), then ownership of other slaves is also logically possible. Presumably the acquisition of such slaves in effect freed a slave from burdensome labour, even if the bond with the master remained. A captive in Sulu was offered, as a reward for curing an influential man, "two slaves, with whom I could trade as if I were free" (cited Warren 1981, 227).

As in the Southeast Asian pattern everywhere, however, the most common

Fig. 8 A domestic slave of a large Dutch household supervising a sinjo *(young master)*
(Koninklijk Instituut voor de Tropen, Amsterdam)

purpose of European slaves was for domestic service, in particular to display
(and if necessary defend) the wealth and status of the owner. As the Dutch
(and Spanish) found cheaper ways to tap the labour of the hinterland through
a system of corvée, the domestic and luxurious character of slave-holding
became more and more marked, while the really vile work, like digging the
mud out of the canals, was reserved for the differently bonded *moddennars,*

Fig. 9 Two Toraja slaves being offered for sale in Palopo, South Sulawesi, 1895
(Sarasin, *Reisen in Celebes*)

sent for that purpose by the Javanese princes of the hinterland. Boxer (1965, 240) quotes a description by a young bride in Batavia of her household of fifty-nine slaves:

> Three or four youths, and as many maids, accompanied herself and her husband whenever they left the house. Another five or six serving men and maids stood behind their respective chairs at meals. They had a slave orchestra which played on the harp, viol and bassoon at mealtimes. Three or four slaves attended constantly on them indoors, and one slave always sat at the entrance ready to receive messages or to run errands. The remaining slaves were employed in various household, cellar, and buttery duties, and as grooms, cooks, gardeners and seamstresses.

Such a description is remarkably similar to those we have of large and wealthy households in the indigenous pre-colonial cities, where there were also dozens of slaves for entertainment, display, protection and running messages of every kind.

Another Southeast Asian feature of the colonial cities was the seemingly high rate of manumission of slaves, on the "open" pattern described by Watson (1980; also Reid 1983a). In Batavia, and also in the Cape of Good Hope, slaves were very frequently manumitted on the death of their masters, and also often succeeded in buying themselves out of slavery with the money they accumulated in their own time (Barrow 1806, 241; Böeseken 1977, 76–85; Iwao 1970, 7–9). For the Dutch, as for their predecessors in the Southeast Asian cities, slavery was a means of incorporating servile labour quickly into the urban setting, and it was primarily the first generation of slaves who occupied a truly menial position. The Dutch and British (the Portuguese much less markedly) differed from Southeast Asian urban slave-owners, however, in that they maintained a social distance from their slaves and made little effort to incorporate them culturally. Their slaves did become a part of the ordinary urban or suburban population within a generation or two, but not of its ruling white caste.

We are vastly better informed about slavery in the colonial cities than elsewhere because careful notary records were taken of sales, manumissions and mortgages involving slaves. The Dutch did carry something new into the East in "the Roman law regarding slavery in all its extent and rigour", as Raffles (1817, I: 76) pointed out. The practice of slavery in the Dutch and British colonies, however, as Raffles went on to concede, had nothing of the harshness of the New World about it. In other words, slavery in the European colonies owed more to the Southeast Asian environment than to European legal ideas.

ROYAL BONDSMEN, PRIVATE SLAVES

When the only index of power is control over persons, diffusion of power will be expressed in a multiplicity of centres of bondage. Much as feudalism limited the aggregation of power centres by segmenting control of land, systems of "private" slavery limited central power in Southeast Asian conditions. It is not surprising that slavery was most in evidence where power was diffused. This applies both in the "closed" slave systems like those of Nias and the Toraja, Kachin, Kayan and Kenyah, and to the port-states dominated by merchant aristocrats (Melaka, Patani, Aceh, Banten). Bali, South Sulawesi, the Philippines and Siam also appear to show clearer characteristics of slavery when competition between multiple power centres is most marked. Akin Rabibhadana (1969, 24–39) has pointed out for Siam what is certainly true for many other states, that there was a constant struggle between the king and the powerful nobles for control of men, the former seeking to maximize the number of people directly obligated to himself through corvée, and the nobles to withdraw men from the corvée system through a system of "private" bondage or slavery.

The extremely heavy burden of royal corvée in Burma, Siam and (at times) Cambodia put these states at one extreme of the Southeast Asian spectrum. For the ordinary men in these societies, there were only three real alternatives: bondage to the king through the corvée system; bondage to a monastery or religious foundation; and "private" bondage or slavery to a prominent or wealthy man. Of these three, bondage to the king was likely to be the most onerous, entailing one half of a man's labour in Siam. It is easy to see why Siamese reportedly sold themselves cheerfully into slavery, particularly in times of hardship, and why the term for buying a slave was "helping (the slave) by redeeming" (Rabibhadana 1969, 110). In the Malay world, on the other hand, the category of royal bondsman (*hamba raja*) was frequently a privileged one, because government was so personalized that much of the ruler's authority and inviolability rubbed off on his bondsmen.

Westermann (1955, 108–13) points out that the growing power of state slaves (*servi Caesaris*) under the Roman Empire was one of the factors which eventually altered the institution of slavery altogether. We have cases also in Southeast Asia, where a particularly vigorous ruler, like Iskandar Muda in Aceh (1607–36) or Ekathotsarot in Siam (1605–10), curtailed drastically the ability of citizens to control their own men, through slavery or bondage, to the exclusion of royal power. All strong powers, Asian as well as European-colonial, prohibited the export of slaves as an intolerable loss of the country's most precious resource. The expansion of the power of the state to control the lives of all its citizens in modern times is undoubtedly one of the reasons why slavery and related phenomena were abolished. This too applies as much to Siam under Chulalongkorn as to the European-colonial powers as they expanded in the nineteenth century.

Wherever "state slavery" is alleged to be the only type of slavery in existence, we will be well advised to avoid use of the term "slave" at all. "Slave" is also a word frequently misused, even by Southeast Asians themselves, to describe an essentially tributary relationship between a conquered state or an economically dependant hill people and the dominant lowland states. For slavery to exist, it must be possible for the slave to be sold or otherwise expropriated to another party; if the state has an effective monopoly over bonded labour, the bondsmen cannot be considered property in the same sense.

To return again to the cities, both European- and Asian-controlled, we can understand why slavery was most clearly in evidence in conditions of the most vigorous and successful international trade. All of the flourishing ports of Southeast Asia were dependant on attracting and retaining wealthy merchants of varied ethnic backgrounds, all of whom were (at least initially) forced to rely on their own bondsmen rather than on the indigenous bonding system for both labour and protection. Although kings often tried to humble these independently powerful merchants and deprive them of their slaves and retainers, they could never do so successfully without destroying the whole basis of the state's prosperity. In these cities, therefore, "private" slaves predominated over "state slaves" (including the VOC slaves of Batavia), so that even the latter category assumed the character of marketable property.

FREEDOM AND SLAVERY

An increasing number of modern historians (for example, Morgan 1975) have seen beyond the apparent paradox that slavery and the ideal of freedom went hand in hand in Ancient Greece and in Revolutionary America. M. I. Finley (1968, 308) and Perry Anderson (1978, 23) both argue that the concept of personal freedom can only arise, as an antithesis to slavery, in situations where other forms of servitude are subsumed into a clearly demarcated slave category. There is undoubtedly much truth in the proposition that the novelty of the Greek city-states in developing slavery into the single legal category of chattel made possible that other remarkable Greek discovery, personal freedom as a status guaranteed by law. As far as I know, however, there has been no attempt to investigate whether completely different cultures which developed slavery in the same direction may also have stumbled towards the idea of freedom.[2]

Finley (1968, 30) quite correctly points out that, because in most Asian systems of bondage, slavery was but one option among alternative forms of obligation, Asian languages developed no word until modern times which can translate the word "freedom". This is true also for most of Southeast Asia. The alternative to slavery was some other form of obligation, more or less burdensome, rather than any clearly defined rights as a "freeman". The terms currently used for political or personal freedom are relatively recent, and most of them are unrelated to any earlier slave-free distinction. Thai and Khmer, for example, use derivatives of Sanskrit *sri* (splendour, glory). Tagalog *kalayaan* has the root meaning "satisfaction of wants" or "parental pampering" (Ileto 1979a, 107–8, 331).

There is, however, one very important exception—the word *merdeka* in Indonesian and Malay. Its origins go back to a Sanskrit description of a person of great (spiritual) power or wealth (*maharddika*), and it appears to have been in use in seventh century Sri Vijaya as a chief or leader over a group of subjects or bondsmen (Hall 1976, 71, 99). In some form it spread as far as Sulawesi and the Philippines, where it was used to describe the class above the slaves, or people having slaves or bondsmen attached to them. When in the Malay-speaking cities of the fifteenth to seventeenth centuries a clear legal concept of freeman or non-slave did develop, it was the same word which was used. The Malay law codes refer frequently to crimes involving freemen (*merdehika*) as well as slaves. From there, laws were also drawn up to govern freeing (*memerdehikakan*) slaves. The Dutch in turn took over the word to refer to the freed slaves (*mardijkers*) who formed a large part of the population of Dutch settlements in Indonesia.

Unfortunately we are not in a position to say how far this word was used in a more abstract sense prior to its adoption by nationalists in the early twentieth century. In South Sulawesi, however, there is definite evidence that it was so used as early as the eighteenth century. The Bugis and Makasarese had a relatively sharp delineation, endorsed by law codes, between slave (*ata*) and free (*maradeka*). They also had a finely balanced political system, with numerous competing states and sub-states. The word for slave was used for the total subjection of a former vassal state which had rebelled and again been defeated (Andaya 1981, 111). In 1737, when Wajo liberated itself from such a subjugation to Bone, the word *maradeka* was used to describe the goal of its struggle (Noorduyn 1972, 62). These Bugis of Wajo developed a saying, "Free (*maradeka*) are the people of Wajo: their only master is custom" (Pelras 1971, 174). No more than Pericles in Athens or Jefferson in Virginia, of course, did they include their slaves in this splendid declaration. Perhaps because their wealth and power were securely based on their own *ata*, they refused to be the *ata* of their (elective) king. James Brooke, visiting Wajo in

1840, described how numerous slaves did all the productive work there, yet in the same breath he declared that "amid all the nations of the East—amid all the people professing the Mahometan religion, from Turkey to China—the Bugis *alone* have arrived at the threshold of recognised rights, and have *alone* emancipated themselves from the fetters of despotism" (Brooke 1848, I: 65).

THE LIFE OF THE SLAVES

Slaves were reported in every conceivable occupation, as rice farmers, cash croppers, fishermen, seamen, construction workers, miners, urban labourers, craftsmen of all sorts, textile workers, entertainers, concubines, domestic servants, retailers, traders, scribes, interpreters, surgeons, soldiers and even trusted ministers (Warren 1981, 221–8). If we are considering a "slave mode of production", however, we must distinguish between slave workers who were centrally managed and who thus made possible a scale of production not otherwise available in a household-oriented economy, and the majority whose bondage merged into a kind of serfdom or household membership.

The chief examples of the former kind must come from the cities, where the wealthiest commercial households were full of slaves who traded, carried, built and sailed for their lord. In terms of manufacture, much of the metal-working and other crafts connected with arms and warfare were performed primarily for the king, and thus on the basis of a relationship more akin to tribute than slavery. Weaving and textiles, on the other hand, seem to have been both the most important item of manufacture and the one most given to large-scale slave labour. The Dutch remarked of Banten that the slave women who were not busy marketing for their lord "sit at home and weave, while others spin" (Lodewycksz 1598, 129). Burger (1962, 108) comments that some Javanese regents around 1800 had weaving "factories" with as many as thirty or forty women debt-slaves working in them. It may therefore be significant that the areas of the Archipelago which had the largest export of textiles—South Sulawesi, especially Selayar, and Bali—were also noted for large accumulations of slaves. When John Anderson (1826, 312) visited the most flourishing textile-exporting centre in Sumatra in the 1820s, he noted that "In almost every house at Batubara is one or more looms; and the [chiefly Batak] slave girls spin, dye, and weave."

In agriculture, which is by far the dominant economic activity in Southeast Asia as a whole, it is much more difficult to speak confidently of a long-term slave system of production, even when our sources do so. In the nature of things the farmer had his own house and considerable freedom in the management of his own time. Typically he was married at the time he was put on the land. He worked harder but under freer conditions than a domestic slave. Warren (1981, 221–2) has suggested a "slave mode of production" in Sulu agriculture, and something rather similar appeared to exist among the Kachin (Leach 1965, 232), in Selayar (*Encyclopaedia van Nederlandsch-Indië*, III: 506) and occasionally elsewhere. Much more frequently slaves were put on a piece of hitherto unworked land, though in the absence of any concept of central management like that of a Roman *latifundia* or West Indian plantation their status quickly came to resemble that of serfs, who had to remit a proportion of their produce to their lord. We are inclined to take the view that a slave mode of production did not exist in the sense of a significantly different production system from that of serfdom, even though the labour mobility made possible by slavery was frequently used to open up new lands. The only definite exception to this point is the Dutch *perkenier* system for producing nutmeg in Banda with hundreds of slave labourers on large estates (Hanna 1978).

The most characteristic roles for slaves were as domestics and entertainers, in which roles their status as slaves was frequently emphasized precisely because it added to the status of their master. When the Dutch arrived in Banten, the merchant aristocrats of the place already had their slaves entertaining them at night with singing and dancing. The most exotic Persian dancing-girls in Banten had reportedly cost two to three thousand guilders each (Fryke 1692, 78). The nobles of Sulu and the burghers of Batavia equally valued their musically talented slaves (Warren 1981, 225–6; Abeyasekere 1983), and the special pleasure both took in the European violin helps to explain how that instrument spread so widely in the Malay world. The entertainment business has also been one of the last to give up its reliance on slave or semi-slave labour, whether in traditional forms like the Bugis *pajoge* (Kennedy 1953, 103–4) or Malay/Javanese *joget*, or in modern prostitution and bar-girl rackets.

The domestic role of slaves appears to dominant in the eighteenth and nineteenth centuries, particularly among Europeans. In consequence, the life of slaves probably became easier and more secure in a physical sense. The way upward for a slave had always been to attach himself to an affluent and influential master. In these terms the European slave-owners of Batavia, Melaka and Makasar, as a relatively stable monied class, represented some hope of advancement, although within the limits of a racial barrier which did not apply elsewhere.

Usually slaves were treated not very differently from other members of the lower orders of society at any given time and place. La Loubère (1691, 77) put the point well of seventeenth century Siam: "The master has all power over the Slave, except that of killing him; And tho' some may report, that Slaves are severely beaten there (which is very probable in a country where free persons are so rigidly bastinado'd) yet the slavery there is so gentle, or, if you will, the Liberty is so abject, that it is become a Proverb, that the Siamese sell it to eat of a . . . *Durion.*" Students of Southeast Asian history will never be able to compile statistics of welfare in the way Fogel and Engerman (1974) have done for the American South, but they have no reason to doubt those scholars' conclusions that in a material sense slaves were better off than the poorest freemen. To accept a slave was to accept the obligation to feed and clothe him. Of early nineteenth century Siam it was said that slaves were treated as well as, or better than, servants in Europe (Rabibhadana 1969, 110).

For the slave, the real relative deprivation was of neither his liberty nor his welfare, but the possibility of being sold to some distant land where a more terrible fate might await him. Slaves were sometimes sacrificed to meet some ritual need such as the funeral of a chief or the erection of a large building, in the Philippines, Sulawesi, Borneo, Nias, Burma, Cambodia and probably elsewhere. Usually recently bought or captured slaves would be used for the purpose, or else a local slave who had committed some crime. Even if this happened infrequently, the practice was well enough known in Sulu to fill many of those destined to be sold with terror that this might be their fate (Warren 1981, 199, 249). Accounts of the slave trade make it clear that those being transported away from their homes and possibly their families had to be chained up to prevent them rushing against their captors or flinging themselves overboard. It is in this tearing away from familiar surroundings that the nature of a slave as totally powerless chattel is most clearly expressed. Once the slave was acquired by an owner and put to work in a new environment, the bonds of iron tended to be exchanged for bonds of habit or even of affection. For every story of a slave attempting to run away, there is another of one who declined to run away or even to return home when the opportunity arose (for example, Warren 1981, 221, 231; Loh 1969, 193–4; Bigalke 1983, 355).

There are horrific stories from Batavia and Maluku of how the Dutch authorities of the seventeenth and early eighteenth centuries executed offending slaves in the most gruesome possible ways, but they appear to have meted out similar punishments to Indonesian freemen or rebellious Dutchmen. The stereotype of abuse of slaves, which nineteenth century Dutch reformers used to attack the whole system, was of a different kind. This was the diabolical torture meted out by the mistress of many Dutch households, usually scarcely different in education or lifestyle from the slaves who surrounded her, towards any of the slave-girls who were pretty enough to arouse her jealousy (Stavorinus 1798, I: 319; Haan 1922, I: 463). The misery caused by such jealousies became legendary in Van Hogendorp's play "Kraspoekoel", or Hardouin's portrait of the "Bathing Slave Girl" (Hardouin and Ritter 1855, 71–94).

CONCUBINAGE

The Parisian career of "Annah la Javanaise", Paul Gauguin's obsession, illustrates the horrified fascination with which late nineteenth century Europeans came to regard the sale of young Southeast Asian women. Nevertheless, the opportunities for upward mobility and an easier life had long been greater for bonded women than men (Warren 1981, 227; Lasker 1950, 290–1). Rulers and wealthy men surrounded themselves with numerous wives, concubines and female retainers, whose lives were both easier and more respected than those of farm women. To be taken into the palace was supposed to be an honour, and it was by no means only the most servile categories who experienced it. The use of palace women in the Malay world to bestow favours and mutual ties of obligation with those outside it was often misunderstood as prostitution by Europeans (B. Andaya 1993a, 57–60). Prostitution of a purely commercial kind was much less frequent than the use of bonded women as a means of attracting male retainers. The aristocrats of the court do frequently appear to have had their pleasure of the unmarried slave girls about the place. Those of lower social status in the retinue of a ruler or wealthy aristocrat could hope to be rewarded for their loyalty by being given one of the bonded women as a wife.

Although there are many sources which suggest that sexual relations between a master and his slave girls were normal (Scott 1606, 170; Lodewycksz 1598, 115; Matheson and Hooker 1983), this applied only to unmarried women. To interfere with a married slave was illegal in Siam (Rabibhadana 1969, 112), and highly dangerous and uncommon everywhere. This was true of European as of Chinese or Southeast Asian slave-owners. Slave marriages were everywhere recognized as valid.

Although prostitution was uncommon, there were vast numbers of single men in the port cities, particularly with the large-scale immigration of Chinese from the early seventeenth century. The needs of these men were met by the buying or hiring of a bonded woman, who served frequently as cook, commercial assistant and local informant as well as sexual partner (Dampier 1699, 248, 268). Scott (1606, 176) reported of the Chinese of Banten: "Their manner at Bantam is to buy women slaves (for they bring no women out of China) by whom they have many children. And when they return to their owne countrey . . . they sell their women, but their children they carry with them." Exactly the same pattern is reported of Batavia (Fryke 1692, 29; Abeyasekere 1983). European men naturally followed this example, although they reportedly demanded less physical labour from their concubines, and were probably also more inclined to free them than to sell them. The more the hopes of Chinese and European settlers of returning to the fatherland receded, the more likely they were to marry their concubines. At its best, therefore, the trade in women came to resemble a large-scale "marriage market" by the early nineteenth century. The slave trade appears also to have provided a large proportion of the female population of the British Straits Settlements at their foundation. John Anderson (1826, 298-9) could not conceal his reluctance to see the abolition of a system which "had nothing but the name against it". The slave women "contributed so much to the happiness of the male population, and the general prosperity of the settlement [and] . . . became wives of respectable Chinese." No doubt there were also terrible abuses. From the viewpoint of understanding the real contribution of Batak, Balinese, Nias, Bugis and other women to the Straits Settlements, however, this trade deserves to be better studied.

The growing importance of concubinage in the overall movement of slaves is apparent from the alteration in relative prices of slaves. In the seventeenth century and earlier, slave prices appear to have been determined primarily by age and physical strength, with no distinction between male and female (for example, Morga 1609, 273–4; Pelras 1981, 158–9; Böeseken 1977). This pattern continued until about the middle of the eighteenth century, presumably because it was the physical labour of slaves which was primarily valued. In the late eighteenth and early nineteenth centuries, however, the price of females became two or three times as high as that of males of the same age (Warren 1981, 203; Raffles 1817, II: clxxxix, ccxxxiv; Sutherland 1983). The likeliest reason for this appears to be the rapid growth of the male Chinese population in the middle and late eighteenth century. Batavia's Chinese population grew threefold between 1749 and 1789 (eleven to thirty-four thousand) (Raben 1996) and thereafter there was an equally rapid influx to the Straits Settlements, as well as to Riau and West Borneo. The really "fancy prices" reported for attractive young slave girls were, however, paid primarily by Europeans. Prices as high as a thousand Spanish dollars, over twenty times the normal male price, were quoted, for example for "a Nias maid, when all her points are good" (Barrow 1806, 240; also Haan 1922, I, 466; Lennon 1908, 273).

THE SLAVE TRADE

Before indentured labour was developed in the nineteenth century, the movement of captive peoples and slaves was the primary source of labour mobility in Southeast Asia. Typically it took the form of transferring people from weak, politically fragmented societies to stronger and wealthier ones. The oldest, and demographically most important, form of movement was the border raiding against animist swidden-cultivators and hunter-gatherers by the stronger wet-rice cultivators of the river valleys. Chou Ta-kuan shows this process in full swing in Cambodia about 1300, and at least up to the late nineteenth century the same process continued to occur in Cambodia (Comte 1976, 73–5), in Malaya (Endicott 1983), in Sumatra (Anderson 1826, 297–9, 315), in Borneo (Lasker 1950, 290–1), and in Luzon (Worcester 1913, 6-12). The dimensions of this process are naturally impossible to measure, but a rough comparison of the relative size of coastal Malay and *orang asli* populations between 1800 and 1900 in Western Malaya suggests that it could be of major proportions.

It is a little easier to measure the contribution of the slave trade to city populations, since these captives often came by sea in large shiploads. There seems little doubt that the majority of the Southeast Asian (that is, excluding Chinese, Indian, European, and so on) urban population prior to about 1820 was recruited in a captive state, either through the slave trade or war. For fast-growing indigenous cities such as Melaka and Aceh, there are numerous impressionistic sources to this effect, though few hard statistics. For the Dutch and British colonies we are better off.

As Sutherland (1983) shows, slaves were a majority of the population of Dutch Makasar in the seventeenth and eighteenth centuries. In Batavia, too, slaves were always a majority of the population inside the city walls, where free Indonesians were very scarce. As the eighteenth century city grew outside the walls, however, the slave population did not keep pace, largely because of the ever higher proportions of descendants of freed slaves assimilated into the Batavian population (Haan 1922, 1: 468; Blussé 1982). The total slave population of Batavia (inside and outside the walls) was relatively stable between twenty-four and thirty thousand from the late seventeenth century to the 1770s. In the latter decade it rose quickly to about thirty-eight thousand, but fell again after 1800 to reach about eighteen thousand during the English interregnum (Abeyasekere 1983; Raben 1996). A high rate of imports of slaves appears to have been necessary to retain these numbers, in part because of the frequency of manumissions (particularly in the late eighteenth century), but more still because of the extraordinarily high death rate for slaves (among others) in Batavia. In the years 1759–78, an average of

1,325 persons per year were buried in Batavia's two slave cemeteries (Blussé 1982). In the seventeenth century about a thousand slaves per year may have been imported on average, but in the eighteenth it probably averaged about three thousand. We have estimates of four thousand around 1770 (Haan 1922, I, 453); three thousand in 1776 (Stavorinus 1798, III: 390); and one thousand in 1792 (Barrow 1806, 239).

The biggest single contribution to the Batavian population appears to have come from South Sulawesi. During the first thirty years of Batavia's existence, Indian and Arakanese slaves provided the main labour force (Iwao 1970, 7; Haan 1922, I: 452; Sutherland 1983), but thereafter eastern Indonesia came to provide the great majority of Batavia's slaves—and subsequently freemen. Balinese appear to have been most numerous in mid-century, but Bugis-Makasar slaves far outnumbered them during the Makasar wars of the 1660s. Of almost ten thousand Indonesian slaves brought to Batavia in the two decades 1661–82, Schulte Nordholt has calculated that 4,110 (42 percent) came from South Sulawesi, while another 24 percent came from Bali and 12 percent from Buton.[3] Similar proportions occur among Indonesian slaves in the other Dutch posts in the Archipelago and at the Cape of Good Hope, where South Sulawesi contributed 46 percent and Bali 6.6 percent of the 166 Indonesian slaves imported in the last three decades of the seventeenth century (Böeseken 1977, 75). We are less well informed about the first half of the eighteenth century, but at the end of that century Bugis-Makasar slaves are again much the largest group, followed by Balinese (Abeyasekere 1983). On the other hand, an ethnic breakdown of the free Indonesian population of Batavia, most of whom (except the Javanese, Malays and Ambonese) descended from free slaves, shows Balinese to outnumber South Sulawesi people slightly in the second half of the eighteenth century. Over the five years 1786–90, for example, free Balinese averaged 13,319 (21 percent of the Indonesian population), while there were 3,912 Makasarese, 6,508 Bugis and 1,375 Mandarese, or 11,794 freemen in total (18 percent) from South Sulawesi, and another 1,452 (2 percent) from Sumbawa and 909 (1.4 percent) from Buton. These figures may suggest that imports of Balinese, the majority of whom appear to have been bought by Chinese, were less likely to be officially recorded than those from Dutch-controlled Makasar.

The extent of slave imports to the British settlements of Penang and Singapore is difficult to establish, since the trade in slaves had officially been abolished in 1807 and frowned upon for some time before that. Nevertheless Anderson (1826, 298) estimated the export of Batak slaves from Asahan alone to the Straits Settlements at about three hundred per year in the early nineteenth century; while Munshi Abdullah (1955, 161–2) describes a single Bugis shipload of three to four hundred East Indonesian slaves being sold in

Singapore. In the late 1820s Nias slaves were still being smuggled into Penang in large numbers (Reid 1973, 205–6), and the Dutch estimated that several thousand Bataks each year were being sold to the slave depots of Penang and the tin mines of Perak and Selangor in the 1860s (Schadee 1918, I: 129). Most of these slaves were women, and as Anderson (1826, 298) pointed out, the trade "was of immense advantage in procuring a female population for Penang." The 1830 census of Singapore showed 4,421 "Bugis and Balinese" women against only 1,048 men in the same category (Kathirithamby-Wells 1969, 71n), and there is little doubt that almost all had been brought in to be sold as wives and concubines for the male population.

There is an overall consistency in the pattern of the slave trade, which tended to take people from east to west, from small divided states (especially those prey to internal warfare) to larger wealthier ones, and from non-Muslim to Muslim societies. A number of states rose and flourished primarily on the traffic in slaves, many of them seized by raiding expeditions against coastal peoples in the Central Philippines, eastern Indonesia, New Guinea, Arakan or the Mekong delta. Aru (Sumatra) and Onin (New Guinea) had this reputation in the sixteenth century, Sulu, Buton and Tidore in the seventeenth, and Sulu in the eighteenth.

The overall pattern of the seaborne trade in slaves may be glimpsed at three different points in its history. In the early sixteenth century, according to Tomé Pires (1515) and other Portuguese sources, the cities of Melaka, Ayudhya (Siam), Pasai and Brunei appear to have been the largest importers of slaves, and Java—no doubt affected by the wars associated with Islamization—was the largest exporter. The non-Muslim ports of Sunda Kelapa in the west and Balambangan in the east were the largest exporters in Java, but Muslim Gresik appears also to have been a significant slave market (Jacobs 1979, 167). Further east, the Lesser Sunda Islands of Bali, Lombok and Sumbawa had already acquired a name as sources of slaves, while the earliest Portuguese reports on South Sulawesi relate that abundant slaves were also to be had cheaply there. In Sumatra the (possibly Karo Batak) centre of Aru was a major slave market, while Rokan and Palembang also exported slaves to Melaka. Melaka evidently re-exported slaves to Ayudhya.

Over a century later, Speelman's description of Makasar's trade in the mid-seventeenth century (Noorduyn 1983) can be combined with other sources to show the changes in the pattern. Sulu and Magindanao had by this time begun their history as major centres of slave raiding and redistribution, mainly at the expense of the Visayas, but also from northern Sulawesi and eastern Borneo. They exported slaves to the flourishing urban centre of Makasar, both directly and through the entrepot in Brunei. Further east, Manggarai, Timor, Alor and Tanimbar also sent slaves to Makasar, sometimes as tribute. By this time too Tidore was taking slaves from the Raja Empat Islands and the New Guinea coast, also frequently in the name of tribute. Buton was a major raiding centre and market, and sent nothing but slaves to Makasar. Makasar and Bugis people were no longer being sold overseas, but Makasar re-exported slaves or sent foreign captives as far afield as Palembang, Jambi, and Aceh in Sumatra, and in large quantities (up to eight vessels a year) to become pepper cultivators in South Borneo. Java had virtually ceased to export slaves, but Bali, and to a lesser extent the islands east of it, had now become major suppliers of Batavia. Further west, Patani was drawing its labour force from Brunei, Champa and Cambodia (Nieuhoff 1934, 85), while Aceh's slaves were "from every nation", many of them captives during the conquests of Iskandar Muda (1607–36), but thereafter chiefly commercial imports, primarily from the Coromandel Coast of India.

Finally, the careful work of James Warren (1981, esp. 208), makes it easier to grasp the scale of the slave trade at the end of the eighteenth century. Sulu and Batavia now dominated the picture in the Archipelago. Balangingi raiders probably brought between two and three thousand captives to Sulu each year, from voyages which focused on the Central Philippines, but also ranged at times over almost the whole of maritime Southeast Asia. Many were absorbed into the Sulu population, but many more were resold to rulers in Borneo or further afield. Batavia's supply of slaves, on the other hand, now came primarily from South Sulawesi, with large numbers also from Nias and Bali. With the increasing pressure from European governments against the slave trade in the early nineteenth century, areas outside European control, such as Nias, Bali and Sulu, became increasingly important as slave sources. Increasing numbers were taken illegally from these centres to the plantation economies of Mauritius and Réunion, deprived since 1815 of their "legal" sources in India (Kraan 1983; Lyman 1856, 377).

From the viewpoint of the societies supplying these involuntary migrants, the demographic consequences could be very large indeed. The Archbishop of Manila estimated in 1637 that the Muslim raiders from the Sulu area had taken thirty thousand Filipinos captive in the previous thirty years (Pastells 1933, VIII: li)—perhaps 4 percent of the then population. Warren (1981, 208) estimates that in the period 1770–1870 between 200,000 and 300,000 captives were taken to Sulu, most of them from the Philippines. The effect was profound on some coastal provinces such as Nueva Caceres, where 750–1,500 captives were estimated taken each year in the early nineteenth century (Warren 1981, 180). A student of Balinese history has estimated that Bali exported at least one hundred thousand of its population in the period 1620–1830 (Schulte Nordholt 1980, 40; also Kraan 1983). Nias must have suffered even more in relative terms, since it appears to have been losing between 800 and 1,500 of its small population each year in the period 1790–1830 (Milburn 1813, 345; Raffles 1835, II: 181; Lyman 1856, 377), or about 0.5 percent per annum. Bigalke (1983) calculates that Toraja lost 10–15 percent of its population through slavery in a few decades before 1905; while very high losses must also have been sustained by the Bugis-Makasar population at an earlier period.

THE "ABOLITION" OF SLAVERY

The decline of slavery as an institution had little to do with an increasingly sensitive moral conscience. Exemplary morality could be shown within the terms of vertical bonding as well as in combating that bonding in the name of equality. Two structural factors were of longer term importance. Firstly, the state, in both its colonial and national forms, increasingly demanded that control over all its people, in the areas of law, policing, military service and taxation, which the system of bondage had left to individual patrons. Secondly, the growing numbers of impoverished landless labourers made wage labour a cheaper and more efficient system of exploitation.

European governments began to take steps against slavery in their colonies at the beginning of the nineteenth century. The *trade* in slaves was theoretically banned by the British parliament in 1807, and a similar ban was imposed on the French at the Treaty of Vienna in 1815. The Netherlands moved in the same direction in its colonies in 1818.

The only economy in Southeast Asia seriously inconvenienced by these bans was that of the nutmeg-growing *perkeniers* of Banda (Hanna 1978, 102–11), thereafter obliged, like southern United States slave-holders, to rely on regeneration of their existing slaves and a little smuggling. The urgent demand for labour by the planters of Mauritius and Réunion also caused a boom in the smuggling of slaves to those islands from unpatrolled ports of Southeast Asia. This ended definitively with the abolition of slavery itself in Mauritius in 1835 and Réunion in 1848.

The Dutch did not make slavery illegal in their colonies until 1860. During the subsequent forward movement of Dutch, British and French into the remotest corners of Southeast Asia, the suppression of indigenous slavery was frequently used as a pretext for intervention, although colonial governments always took a more pragmatic view of the problem once they were in control. Only in 1910 did the Dutch seriously attempt to suppress slavery in the Batak area, while the British waited until 1926 to redeem the slaves of the Kachin-dominated Hukawng valley of eastern Burma. Siam made slavery illegal in stages between 1874 and 1905, thereby keeping in step with its European-ruled neighbours (Cruikshank 1975). The institution continues to exist even today, illegally and relatively harmlessly, in out-of-the-way corners of Southeast Asia.[4]

This gradual abolition of slavery by no means implied that a free market in wage labour was introduced to Southeast Asia. In so far as wage labour did become available in the nineteenth century, it was chiefly in the form of immigrant Chinese in the cities. Southeast Asians themselves appear to have continued to regard wage labour as alien and demeaning. Instead, traditional systems of bondage and obligation were redefined to the exclusion of those relationships closest to chattel slavery, which had in any case become both expensive and unnecessary by this time. Governments, both colonial and indigenous, gained in authority and sometimes revenue to the extent that they succeeded in replacing private slavery with state corvée, as the Spanish had done in the Philippines as early as the sixteenth century. Corvée and debt bondage became the dominant forms of labour in the nineteenth century.

It became an article of faith among Europeans and Chinese seeking to exploit Southeast Asian labour in the nineteenth and early twentieth centuries that wages were not the answer. Hugh Clifford (1897, 19), for example, painted his engaging Pahang Malay in terms of this stereotype:

> He never works if he can help it, and often will not suffer himself to be induced or tempted into doing so by offers of the most extravagant wages. If, when promises and persuasion have failed, however, the magic word *krah* is whispered in his ears, he will come without a murmur, and work really hard for no pay, bringing with him his own supply of food. *Krah* . . . is the system of forced labour . . . and an ancestral instinct, inherited from his fathers, seems to prompt him to comply cheerfully with this custom, when on no other terms whatsoever would he permit himself to do a stroke of work.

Colonial governments could exploit Southeast Asian labour through this system of corvée, most notoriously through the *cultuurstelsel* so profitable to the Dutch in Java. Traders and capitalists who did not have access to corvée found that they could achieve a similar result through a system of credit advances. Chinese traders used the system at least since Chau Ju-kua described it in the thirteenth century Philippines (Hirth and Rockhill 1911, 160). The Dutch called it the *voorschot* system and the British called it "trusting". All were surprised at the fidelity their Southeast Asian debtors showed in these relations. Labourers in European factories, mines and estates in the nineteenth century continued to be tied by advances which not only obligated them to labour for their creditor but also, they believed, obligated the creditor to guarantee their basic needs and security (Lasker 1950, 292–

311; Meyer Ranneft 1929, 79–80; Day 1904, 348–51; Wallace 1869, 73, 311-12). A similar characteristic of modern Southeast Asian social organization has been extensively discussed by political scientists under the rubric of patron-client ties (for example, Schmidt et al. 1977). Any synchronic discussion which ignored the background of that phenomenon in the system of obligation based on debt, however, would be superficial.

This system of obligation must once have been an appropriate response to Southeast Asian conditions, and its disruption, for example by the Spanish in the Philippines, may have brought about a real decline in productivity. What is clearer is that in the more intensive interaction with global capitalism in the nineteenth and twentieth centuries the system has tended to prevent Southeast Asians accumulating capital themselves, and made them vulnerable to exploitation by others.

CONCLUSION

I will conclude with two general points. Firstly, the labour system of Southeast Asia through most of its recorded history was based on the obligation to labour for a creditor, master or lord. Secondly, a form of bondage which must be recognized as slavery arose from within the broader basic pattern, assuming in certain situations a major role in economic and political life.

Because this slavery was never sharply demarcated from other forms of bondage, sometimes equally oppressive, it remained a "mild" variant of the universal genus of slave. This does not mean that slaves were not cruelly treated, but that the maintenance of a permanently inferior slave class was not of particular importance to the state, so that manumission or functional absorption into the master's household was frequent.

It means that Southeast Asia demonstrates very well the fundamental contradictions always inherent in slavery. The slave is a commodity and yet a human being; exploited and yet trusted to be loyal; inferior and yet intimate. These contradictions have ensured that no system of slavery can be "pure" or free from anomalies.

Nevertheless it is important to retain the term slave for those bondsmen whose character as property is most marked. This occurs especially at the point of sale, which emphasizes that the slave is both chattel and outsider. Through this process of sale, hundreds of thousands of Southeast Asians were transported to all points of the compass, as far afield as South Africa on the one hand and Mexico (Filipinos transported on the early Manila galleons) on the other. Slavery populated the most flourishing of Southeast Asia's cities.

It changed people's ethnic and cultural identities on a massive scale. It strengthened the power of merchant aristocrats against the crown.

Finally, slavery must remain as a cross-cultural concept because, like trade and warfare, it is one of the modes of interaction between peoples of different languages and cultures. It is always likely that the associations of slavery will be different between slave buyers (or takers) and sellers (or victims), but the transaction itself forces them to use a common concept. When complete outsiders came to the region, they in turn used their own time-honoured terms for the phenomenon they encountered, and for the people they bought: *'abd* in Arabic, *nu-pi* in Chinese,[5] slave or its cognates in European languages.

One of the countless Southeast Asians for whom slavery was the mode of interaction with different cultures was Surapati, the eighteenth century hero of resistance against the Dutch. His story, as related in east Javanese chronicles (Kumar 1976) illustrates both what is common to slavery everywhere, and what is characteristically Southeast Asian in the perception of it. As a young man, Surapati asked his ruler in Bali to sell him to a slave dealer, so that he could see the great city of Batavia (in other versions he was captured and sold to a Chinese). Once in Batavia, he became greatly valued and honoured by his Dutch master, to whom he brought miraculous good fortune. He bore arms with great success on behalf of his owner. Dutch women fell hopelessly in love with him, but he honourably refused their overtures. Before escaping to begin his career as a rebel king, he stole enough money from his master to redeem hundreds of other slaves and debtors in Batavia, so that their obligations were transferred to him, and he thereby had the nucleus of an army.

The career of Surapati cannot be understood without a concept of slave that is to some extent common to Javanese, Balinese, Dutch and English. But the definitional issue should be put behind us, so that we can pursue more interesting questions about the quality of that slavery, in which debt, loyalty, honour and charisma are so characteristically displayed.

We will thereby illuminate, in one of the few ways open to us, the lives of ordinary people from the large lower stratum of pre-modern Southeast Asian society.

NOTES

1. I am very grateful for the critical comments and assistance with this paper provided by Howard Dick, Brian Fegan, James Fox, Michael Vickery, Leonard Blussé and Henk Schulte Nordholt.

2. Since these words were written, at least two books have addressed that problem: Patterson (1991) and Kelly and Reid (1998).

3. I am most grateful to Henk Schulte Nordholt for making available these calculations of his, based on the Batavia *Daghregisters*.

4. Subsequent to the first writing of this chapter, the decline of slavery has been discussed by Anthony Reid for nineteenth-century Indonesia, and by David Feeny for the Thailand of Chulalongkorn, in Klein (1993).

5. The nomenclature used by Chinese travellers in Southeast Asia is of course more complicated. Chou Ta-kuan uses the most common term *nu-pi* (male and female slaves), while Chau Ju-kua (Hirth and Rockhill 1911: 31) refers to the Southeast Asian slaves on Chinese vessels as *kuei-nu* ("foreign devil" slaves). In at least one relatively recent text, the *Hai-lu* (Cushman and Milner 1979: 17), the retainers of eighteenth century Malay nobles and rich men are called by the more ambiguous term *nu-p'u*.

CHAPTER TEN

THE ORIGINS OF SOUTHEAST ASIAN POVERTY

THE poverty of contemporary Southeast Asia is a tragic fact. In relative terms the GNP per capita of Indonesia, Burma, and Indochina is half that of China, a fifth that of Turkey, a thirtieth that of Australia or New Zealand. In human terms a substantial portion of their people live in wretched health, makeshift housing, with neither land nor the opportunity to labour in order to provide themselves with adequate food.[1]

The causes of poverty are usually discussed by economists, sometimes by sociologists. Historians tend to avoid the long-term sources of the problem, perhaps because of an assumption that the problem is unreal. The origins of capitalism and of the industrial revolution lie in Europe, and therefore the causes for the enormous gulf in living standards between Europe and southern Asia in the twentieth century are also assumed to lie in Europe. The rise of European capitalism is the subject of a lively literature, although it can hardly be said to have resolved the question whether we should be looking to the growth of medieval cities, to a labour surplus in the feudal countryside, to royal or baronial initiatives, or to elements of Christian culture for the central key. The assumption behind this one-sidedness is that the dynamic of change lay in Europe while most of the rest of the world, including Southeast Asia, has been a sort of constant—relatively inert and unchanging.

In reality, change has been the rule in Southeast Asia as in Europe, and we must look at the pattern of this change to understand both the relative and the absolute dimensions of poverty. To understand either the increasing wealth of Europe or the increasing poverty of Southeast Asia we must look at both sides of the equation—not because they are necessarily dependent on each other (though some have argued that), but because we can only see what is significant and what is unique in the development of one corner of the world by looking at other corners which developed differently.

Needless to say we have no comparative statistics for the sixteenth century or earlier, and judgements can only be made on the basis of travellers' impressions. Fortunately we are relatively well endowed with such accounts for the period around 1600, and somewhat less well for the preceding century. We can assume that European and Chinese accounts which were written for readers at home tended to dwell on the things which struck them as unusual. When there is silence on an everyday aspect of life it can usually be assumed to be because the travellers found it unsurprising and similar to conditions at home.

On this basis it seems possible to surmise that around 1600 maritime Southeast Asians were roughly as tall and as long-lived as Europeans, and if anything rather more healthy. In the few cases where travellers mentioned the stature of Southeast Asians, they typically recorded them as being of "average" height but of unusually well-proportioned and athletic build. After eight years in eighteenth century Sumatra, Marsden "could scarcely recollect to have seen one deformed person among the natives", and earlier reports confirm this pattern (Marsden 1811, 44; Goens 1956, 185). Where the age-span of Indonesians and Filipinos is mentioned, it is almost always in envy of their apparently better prospects than Europeans. "The Javanese in general grow very old, the men as well as the women", reported van Goens in 1656, while a reliable Spaniard noted that the Visayans "reach an advanced age in perfect health". Maluku had a reputation for particular longevity in the sixteenth century, though the extraordinary bloodshed, destruction, and famine visited by the Dutch on Banda and to a lesser extent Ambon altered this reputation drastically by the mid-seventeenth century (Reid 1988, 48).

Since the average life-span of Europeans in this period is often estimated as only twenty or thirty years, we need not assume a remarkable degree of longevity on the part of Southeast Asians. What we know of the medical practices of the time would help to account for their relative good health, however. Europeans were astonished at the array of herbal remedies, as well as massage, in treating disease, while the Asians were spared the contemporary European reliance on bleeding and a great deal of clumsy surgery. As late as the early nineteenth century Crawfurd was still amazed at the absence of inflammation or infection associated with wounds—presumably because of the efficacy of herbal antiseptics (Crawfurd 1820, I: 31–2).

Still more striking is the absence of any mention of poverty on the part of early visitors to the Archipelago. There are references to the relative simplicity and primitiveness of the more isolated communities; and to the large proportion of people taken to be in a condition of slavery. The furniture of the poorer houses was noted as very simple, with the principal capital of the lower classes seemingly invested in gold ornaments and weapons. There is however no evidence I have found of famine, starvation, and wretchedness, as was frequently the case in India, China, or indeed Europe at the time. No doubt the reasons for this are clear enough. Rains were relatively dependable; population pressure was very low; and if the staple rice crop did fail there were numerous alternatives to fall back upon including sago, banana, coconut, fish and a variety of roots and fruits, all of which were accessible almost to anyone. Only as a result of the dislocation caused by war do we see large numbers of people dying of hunger—either as captives or as refugees.

At the other end of the spectrum there was the same opulence and extravagant consumption as was found in the courts and trading centres of other parts of Asia and the Mediterranean world. In Aceh and in Brunei the king entertained guests with feasts in which all of the dozens of dishes were served on gold. The Sultan of Ternate astonished Drake with his sumptuous gold-thread dress and the "chain of perfect gold" around his neck (Drake 1580, 70), while the opulent dress and jewel-encrusted krisses of the nobles of Banten, Makasar and other centres is frequently noted. The richest merchants of Melaka were reputed to have abundant gold; Sultan Iskandar Muda of Aceh kept three hundred goldsmiths in his household; a German surgeon was rewarded by one grateful merchant of Banten to the tune of three hundred rijksdaalders (*Sejarah Melayu*, 184; Beaulieu 1666, 90; Fryke 1692, 133).

This wealth derived directly or indirectly from trade. In this respect the cities and city-states of Southeast Asia in the sixteenth and early seventeenth centuries resembled Venice, Genoa and Antwerp more than Delhi or even Golconda. Even more strikingly than the Mediterranean was this a region "made for merchandise"—to borrow Tomé Pires' description of Melaka. It lay athwart the trade routes between China and Japan on the one hand, and India and the West on the other. Moreover in the spices of Maluku and the pepper of Sumatra it provided the items in greatest demand in world markets. Many of its people lived on the water, by fishing and by trade, and boat-building and navigation were among the most developed skills. As Pyrard noticed at the beginning of the seventeenth century, the whole region was interdependent, so that "these people are constrained to keep up continual intercourse with one another, the one supplying what the other wants" (Pyrard 1619, II: 169). Cities such as Melaka and Aceh, and islands like Ternate and Tidore, were almost wholly dependent on imported rice, which they could well afford to pay for through their export and trading activity.

In terms of their population and the extent of their trade, the cities of Southeast Asia appear to stand comparison with the most bustling cities of

Europe in the sixteenth century. It is difficult to escape the conclusion, if we compare all the available contemporary estimates, that Melaka had a population close to one hundred thousand around 1500, that Aceh and Brunei were at least half as large in the mid-sixteenth century, and that Aceh, Banten, Ayudhya and Makasar were all in the region of one hundred thousand in the first half of the seventeenth century. In sixteenth century Europe only Paris and Naples were certainly above the level of a hundred thousand, and many of the real centres of trade and capitalist growth, including London, Amsterdam, Genoa, and Lisbon, appear to have been smaller than fifty thousand in the sixteenth century.[2]

In terms of shipping, Ruy de Araujo's estimate that there were about a hundred junks in Melaka, of which at least thirty belonged to the Sultan and the local merchants (Sá 1954, I: 22), compares favourably with the merchant fleet of Venice, for which estimates vary between about twelve and thirty-five "large" ships, on average somewhat smaller than the five hundred tons which the Asian junks reached (Lane 1973, 480). A century later Aceh's war fleet comprised one hundred galleys, a third of which were said to be larger than any built in Europe (Beaulieu 1666, 106; Blair and Robertson 1903–9, IV: 134, 151, 161, 184). Of course the Malay *prahu* were far more numerous than these large ships—too numerous to be able to estimate even approximately.

Even if we cannot confirm Barbosa's claim (1518, II: 175) that Melaka was "the richest seaport with the greatest number of wholesale merchants and abundance of shipping and trade in the whole world", it was undoubtedly in the major league. Tomé Pires' figures for the value of annual imports from India alone total approximately six hundred thousand cruzados (Pires 1515, 269–72; Meilink-Roelofsz 1969, 87–8). This figure must at least be doubled to reach the total annual imports of the city, or quadrupled to 2.4 million cruzados to give the total volume of trade (imports + exports). If Braudel (1972, I: 439–41) is correct in estimating the volume of trade of Valladolid at 594,600 ducats = 560,000 cruzados (220 million maravadis) in 1576; of Seville at 4.297 million ducats = four million cruzados (1,590 million maravadis) in 1597; then it is clear that the trade of Melaka at the beginning of the century before inflation had begun, would have been one of the biggest in the world.

The manifest size and wealth of these cities should not lead us to ignore some profound differences with the cities of Europe, or indeed of China and the Middle East, however. Asian cities of the sixteenth century were typically bigger than European—Peking, Edo (Tokyo) and Constantinople were bigger than any cities in Europe—but as we know it was not from these large cities that modern capitalism was born. There are some very striking differences in the case of Southeast Asian cities which undoubtedly have a bearing on their relative performance in the more intense economic competition which was to come.

In the first place there was no barrier between city and countryside. Few Southeast Asian cities had a city wall, and where they did it was essentially to enclose the inner core where the ruler and his great nobles had their courts. Cities of any consequence almost invariably became capitals in every sense of the word. There is no capacity in most Southeast Asian languages to distinguish between city and state—they are one and the same. Above all, as a consequence of all this, the city could not be an autonomous world with its own liberties and responsibilities quite distinct from the countryside.

Secondly, it is not easy to draw a line between a land-owning nobility and an urban bourgeoisie. There was a great deal of upward mobility in the fifteenth and sixteenth centuries, as we see from the origins of three mighty men of the time of the Portuguese arrival. The Laksamana of Melaka and subsequently Johor was the grandson of a Palembang slave who became a favourite of Sultan Mansur of Melaka; the ruler of the flourishing city-state of Japara was the grandson of "a working man in the islands of Laue (Pontianak) with very little nobility and less wealth", who made his fortune trading in Melaka until he was strong enough to establish a new city-state in Java (Pires 1515, 187, 249). Similarly, the leading Javanese in Melaka, Utama di Raja, said to have six thousand "slaves" and enormous wealth, had come to Melaka about fifty years earlier as a poor man "of the lower class" (Albuquerque 1557, III: 151). Yet even if the mobility of these men as "foreign" traders in Melaka gave them a certain distance from the state, they could only retain their wealth and power over several generations by merging into the nobility of the city and holding a court function—if not by founding their own little state. Wealth alone was not safe from confiscation by the ruler, and eminence could only be safeguarded by a numerous armed following, or by making oneself indispensable to the ruler—or indeed both.

The system of dependency, generally called slavery by Europeans, was indeed at the heart of the functioning of these great cities. Land was abundant and considered to have no intrinsic value in the law codes of most Southeast Asian peoples. The climate, the insecurity, and the assumption of constant mobility, all militated against the accumulation of fixed capital in the form of buildings and furniture. It was manpower which was seen as the scarce resource and the key to wealth, power, and status. In Melaka, in Banten, in Maluku, and in the Philippines we are assured by the European sources that "their wealth lyeth altogether in slaves", and the attention given to the position of slaves in indigenous law-codes confirms this (Scott 1606, 142; Blair and Robertson 1903–9, III: 54, 197; Liaw Yock Fang 1976, 70–123).

It was not only western observers who were struck by the prevalence of "slavery". A Banten man taken to Amsterdam in 1597 expressed his surprise "that every man there was his own master, and that there was not one slave or captive in the whole land"; while eighty years later Evelyn records how two Banten envoys to London were "exceeding astonished how our law gave us property in our estates, and so thinking we were all kings, for they could not be made to comprehend how subjects could possess anything save at the pleasure of their Prince, they being all slaves." ("A True Report of the gainefull, prosperous and speedy voiage to Iava in the East Indies, performed by a fleet of eight ships of Amsterdam," 1599, in *De tweede schipvaart*, I: 36–37; Evelyn 1955, 286).

Finally we have to repeat the point that the wealth of the trading cities did not lend itself to the accumulation of either fixed or liquid capital, except in the hands of rulers or a select group (of *orang kaya*) strong enough to withstand the ruler's demands. Strong rulers put great pressure on resident traders, claiming the right to confiscate their estate at death, and sometimes even executing their wealthiest subjects in order to confiscate their property, as was reported of Sultan Mahmud of Melaka and Sultan Iskander Muda of Aceh (*De tweede schipvaart* 1942, II: 33; Blair and Robertson 1903–9, IV: 149; Beaulieu 1666, 108-9; Pires 1515, 258–9; La Loubère 1691, 42; Vliet 1636, 51, 96). Except for the favoured few in the court circle, therefore, Southeast Asian traders learned to operate without large accumulations of capital. Tomé Pires explained the longer duration of Malay trading voyages than Portuguese ones with the sweeping remark that "as they have little capital and the sailors are slaves they make their journeys long and profitable" (Pires 1515, 220). In Aceh it was noted in 1643 that "the buyers of goods in quantity are only such as belong to the Custome House . . . They pay not ready money (for any), and he that will reimburse himself with money must sell to shopkeepers, who buy only by the corge [twenty pieces] or half-corge, so they can sell the same day in the bazaar" (IOL, E/3/18, f.282v) The Dutch, the English, and the Chinese quickly found that the only way to do significant trade in most areas was to advance cloth to merchants, who would return after the harvest with the equivalent amount of export produce.

We cannot and should not, therefore, proceed from the size and wealth of Southeast Asian trading centres to attempt to place them on some linear scale of ascent towards capitalism of the western model. The Southeast Asian city was of a quite different type, and we cannot say with confidence what path it was evolving along at the height of its sixteenth and seventeenth centuries prosperity.

The most important point to make here is a different one. The one critical asset the commercial emporia of this period had which their successor nations lacked lay in the nature of commercially-oriented, cosmopolitan, urban life. These cities were in touch with the most dynamic growth points of the renaissance world, and were open to new ideas from within and without. They were prepared to adopt new techniques and technologies when these were manifestly superior in meeting their needs.

The rapid social and cultural change represented by the Islamization of the major trading centres of the Archipelago between about 1300 and 1600 is the most spectacular demonstration of this openness. Writing, arithmetic, political analysis, and a host of literary models were borrowed from the Arabs. Paper came from China and later Europe, though the Indian-derived systems of bundling up a small book of palm leaves by a thread tied through a hole in the middle was also continued for some time. The system of scales and weights was much influenced by Chinese practice, while accounting methods appear to have come from India, notably Gujerat. Arabic was widely spoken and studied, and by the mid-sixteenth century Portuguese was also spoken in every major city—though Malay of course remained the great lingua franca of the region. Perhaps the most telling factor of all comes from the court chronicles and the religious literature of this period, which is constantly aware of the international dimension in a way difficult to replicate in either Europe or China of the period. In the texts emanating from the port cities an index of prosperity and righteous government is often taken to be the large extent of foreign trade and shipping coming to the capital.

Except in the field of herbal medicine we cannot point to items of practical knowledge or technology in which Southeast Asia gave the lead to other parts of the world. But it is clear that discoveries elsewhere quickly found their way to the cities of the region. A Florentine merchant noted of the Gujeratis in Melaka before the Portuguese conquest: "They are astute and clever merchants, as good as us in all business matters; their cargo ledgers with their bales laded and discharged are all in perfection" (Gubernatis 1875, 375–7).

Military technology was the fastest to be borrowed because failure to do so had the most immediate disastrous consequences. From the Chinese and Gujeratis many Southeast Asian centres had already learned the art of casting bronze cannon before the European advent on the scene. The Portuguese claim to have captured three thousand cannon at Melaka in 1511, and the Spaniards 170 at Brunei in 1578, the latter being of great value to the hard-pressed Spanish in Manila (Albuquerque 1557, III: 127–8; Sande, IV: 126). The casting of much larger guns was learned by the Acehnese from their diplomatic relations with Turkey in the 1560s. Sultan Selim II sent a number of master gunsmiths to Aceh in addition to soldiers and gunners. Since Turkey was at this period producing monster cannon larger though less effective than the European variety, it was not surprising that the cannons

John Davis saw in Aceh were "the greatest that I have ever seen" (Davis 1905, II: 321; Reid 1969a, 395–414). In response to the European challenge and example, the manufacture of matchlocks became very well developed in West Sumatra, Bali, Java, and Sulawesi; many cities adopted a system of stone fortress construction; and the Portuguese chain mail, lighter and more flexible than the Japanese armour which had been used earlier, was adopted by some peoples. The only example we know of early translation from European writing, as opposed to Arabic, Sanskrit or Pali, is not surprisingly in the area of acknowledged European expertise—firearms. A Spanish text on gunnery dating from 1563 was summarized in Makasarese in 1635, and translated in full seventeen years later (Matthes 1875, 54, 58; Ricklefs and Voorhoeve 1977, 29, 31). The translation survived in various imperfect Makasarese and Bugis versions of much later dates, often in combination with works on the same subject by Persian, Turkish, and Malay authorities.

Our own prejudice tends to make us more appreciative of cultural and scientific borrowing from European than from Arab or Chinese traditions, and for this reason at least we must instance Karaeng Pattingalloang and his circle in seventeenth century Makasar. As described in chapter 7, he accumulated a considerable library of Portuguese and Spanish books, spoke Portuguese "as fluently as people from Lisbon itself", was expert in mathematics, and probably inspired the translations mentioned above. In addition he may have been responsible for the Makasarese innovation of keeping accurate records of state events in the form of a dated diary—something no other Southeast Asian culture appears to have done so early.

To live by trade, however, was to live dangerously, at least in the altered circumstances of the seventeenth century. As long as the commercial system was allowed to flourish, Southeast Asians were inclined to buy the new technology rather than to learn to make guns and machinery themselves. The most prosperous port-states, moreover, were not yet oriented to the full-blooded system of warfare of the Eurasian land mass. The tradition of warfare in the Archipelago in particular had tended to be sparing of lives, since manpower was the primary source of wealth to be safeguarded. Finally, those city-states best equipped to attract and safeguard Asian trade, by virtue of their relatively pluralistic structure where the ruler's power was held in check by a variety of powerful *orang kaya* dynasties, were not those best equipped to withstand a European military onslaught. These states were accustomed to asserting their suzerainty over weaker states by a mixture of military and commercial pressure, but not to the direct siege and assault tactics of the Portuguese.

The most flourishing of these open cities was the first to fall victim to the European onslaught. Melaka fell to the Portuguese in 1511, even though the real power of the Portuguese in sixteenth century Asia bore no relation to the magnitude of this extraordinary feat. The Spanish in 1578 launched an attack on Brunei which made it impossible for this state to continue its role as the centre of commercial activity in Borneo and the Philippines. Southeast Asian city-states were forced to adopt a more defensive posture to meet this new military threat. Some of the stronger cities, particularly on Java's north coast, adopted the system of stone or brick defensive walls as the Iberians themselves had done. Others, like Johor and Sulu, responded to the threat in a more traditional Southeast Asian way by moving their capital further inland, more remote from the European marauding fleets but also from the life-giving system of trade. The counter-crusading spirit of sixteenth century Aceh and Japara, and the piratic raids from Sulu and Mindanao which intensified at the end of the century, were other types of response to the European practice of using warfare as a means to trade.

Nevertheless, the military and commercial power of the Iberians was not particularly strong, and the Southeast Asian trading system quickly revived and expanded in a somewhat different form. Cash-cropping for export, and the lucrative trading system based on it, continued to be attractive occupations and the basis of most wealth, even in Maluku where the Portuguese impact was strongest. Only in Luzon and to a lesser extent the Visayas did the process begin in the sixteenth century of turning the inhabitants away from commercial and export-oriented activities. The Spanish system of levying a heavy tribute on any productive activity such as gold-mining or cloth manufacture quickly drove home the lesson that Filipinos were safer sticking to a more subsistence style of production.

The Dutch in the seventeenth century were quite a different matter. The vigour of Dutch commercial activity in the early 1600s, and the skill and determination with which they pursued their goal of monopolizing the key Southeast Asian exports, were unprecedented not only in Southeast Asia but in the world. Two years after the first Dutch fleet sailed to the Archipelago in 1596, twenty-two Dutch ships sailed in a single year. In 1601 the figure was sixty-five ships. The following year Dutch endeavours in Asia were centralized and coordinated in that remarkable joint-stock company, the voc, with an initial capital of 6.5 million guilders and the declared aim of monopolizing the most lucrative aspects of the trade in Asia. By 1622 the Dutch Governor General in Batavia had at his disposal eighty-three ships in Asian waters, all of them the most effective of their day in combining naval warfare with trade (Meilink-Roelofsz 1969, 194–5; Masselman 1963, 133–50). The most progressive capitalist cities of Europe had combined to produce a highly effective instrument to crush whatever embryonic capitalism existed in Southeast Asia. The preferred tactic of the Dutch in their first decades was to make an offer to an indigenous ruler to take all his pepper or spices on condition the rival European and Asian traders were altogether excluded. The most difficult society the Dutch found to deal with was Banda, which had no ruler but rather a merchant oligarchy uncomfortably similar to that of Holland. These were the Muslim *orang kaya* who financed the production and export of nutmeg, and who remained as a remarkably cohesive ruling class for over a century. The Dutch soon despaired of bribing or intimidating all of them into monopolistic agreements, and concluded that "one cannot hope for anything certain from that nation unless they be once and for all brought under control by warfare" (Coen quoted in Leur 1934, 183). Banda was conquered in a bloody battle in 1621, all the forty-five *orang kaya* captured were put to death, eight hundred Bandanese were transported to Batavia as slaves, and thousands of others were left to starve in the inhospitable interior of the major island. The most "republican" state in Southeast Asia had become the first victim of the power of the Dutch Republic. In Ambon and Northern Maluku the warfare the Dutch waged with Spaniards and Muslims for control of the spice-producing centres, and the eventual suppression of all production except that which the Dutch controlled, ensured that the blessing of having a crop in universal demand had by the mid-seventeenth century become a curse. The Malukans had to turn their attention to pure economic survival and subsistence.

The same phenomenon of maritime commerce in Asia turning sour with the advent of aggressive European fleets, particularly the Dutch, is apparent throughout the continent. The factors are undoubtedly complex which led to similar responses in different parts of the region: Japan closed itself off from overseas trade in the 1630s and forbade its citizens to go abroad or to build sizeable ships; Chinese interest in the outside world declined steadily during the seventeenth century; in both Burma and Java at almost exactly the same time during the early decades of the seventeenth century, a strong, agriculturally-based, inland and isolationist dynasty arose during the early decades of the seventeenth century while the once-flourishing port-state on the coast was in chaos. It is sufficient to say in passing that in relation to the experience of maritime Southeast Asia, the decision for isolationism by China and especially Japan does not look as historically disastrous as it is usually portrayed. Total isolationism, if it could be achieved, at least allowed the internal economy of the country to develop in a relatively balanced fashion.

In the Southeast Asian cases mentioned—Burma and Java—there is little doubt that the commercial and military role played by the Europeans did much to weaken the capacity of Pegu in Burma and of the coastal ports in Java to withstand the destructive fury of Toungoo and Ava on the one hand and Mataram on the other. In most of Southeast Asia, however, it was not possible by this means to exclude the Europeans altogether. Trade was too important and too persuasive. The contest continued until nearly the end of the seventeenth century, with such city-states as Aceh, Banten, Ayudhya, and Makasar attempting to beat the Dutch at their own game.

The monarchs of such states had of course not proved as easy to bribe or intimidate over the long run as the Dutch might have hoped. The lesson of Jakarta (Jacatra) was not lost on other states. There, in contrast to neighbouring Banten, the position of the ruler had seemed strong enough to ensure for the Dutch and English the monopolistic terms they wanted, and the main problem they faced was the competitive bidding between them. The Dutch had more than their money's worth, however, for the fortress which they began to build there proved impossible for the Jakartans subsequently to dislodge. As Sultan Agung of Mataram is reported to have remarked:

> Jacatra hath a thorne in her foote, which he himself must take the pains to plucke out, for fear the whole body should bee endangered. This thorne is, the castle of the Hollanders, who have now so fortified themselves (through bribery) that they regard not the king nor his country, but set him at defiance (Martin Pring, 1619, in IOL, E/3/6, f.292).

No ruler would make this mistake again. Nevertheless, the system of attempting to bribe or coerce rulers to exclude all merchants but the Dutch did have the effect of encouraging an absolutist, centralized trend in the Southeast Asian states. Some rulers, like the Sultan of Mataram when he was not at war with the Dutch, believed that he could eliminate the power of potential rivals and rebels by restricting all trade to that between himself and the VOC. Others, like Iskander Muda of Aceh (1607–37), Prasat Thong of Ayudhya (1629–56), or Hasanuddin of Makasar, imposed monopolies themselves on various items of export or insisted that European traders deal with them at fixed prices before going to the open market. Others still, pre-eminently Sultan Abufatah of Banten (1651–83) and Narai of Ayudhya (1656–88), made extensive use of English, French, Danish and Chinese merchants to conduct an extensive international trade on behalf of the crown.

In a more negative sense, the Dutch pursuit of trade by warfare obliged their opponents also to place more emphasis on military prowess than on peaceful trade. Makasar, for example, could only survive as an entrepot to the extent that its traders could fight their way through the Dutch policing fleets in Maluku. Banten also suffered intermittent Dutch blockades for most of the seventeenth century, making peaceful trade and cash-cropping a highly dangerous enterprise. The greater emphasis which had to be placed on artillery, on heavily-armed large ships, on foreign mercenaries, gunners, and navigators, all served to strengthen the position of the king in relation to his subjects. There seems little doubt that, even in the states which remained active in the competition for maritime trade, these trends served to weaken the elements of *private* capital and of non-royal commercial activity in Southeast Asian trade.

In any case, none of the great commercial states survived to the end of the century. Determined to be rid of its commercial rivals, the VOC threw all its resources into a successful campaign against Makasar in 1666-9, and against Banten in 1682–4. Both campaigns were extremely costly in lives and money, and neither would have been possible without the Dutch capacity to wait for signs of internal division in these states. The bulk of the conquest was of course carried out by Indonesian allies of the Company, Aru Palaka's Bugis and Captain Jonker's Ambonese, but the new element in the warfare was the tenacious and stable organization of the Dutch, seizing on every weakness in its antagonists. Ayudhya fell under the influence of a much less persistent foreign element in the French, and was able through an anti-foreign revolution in 1688 to rid itself of Europeans for over a century. The price however was a retreat like that of Burma into relative isolation and stasis. Only Aceh was able to remain as a major independent trading centre, but by 1700 it was much reduced in economic and military strength, no longer capable of directing the bulk of Sumatra's foreign trade through its port.

With these defeats, the last great defenders of indigenous trade in the political sphere were destroyed, as were the great indigenous centres of urban life. The message appeared to be clear that to base a state entirely on trade and cash-cropping for export was to invite ultimate destruction, either directly at Dutch hands or through the vagaries of a market now crippled by the Dutch monopoly. Already during every Dutch blockade of Banten, pepper trees had had to be cut down to promote subsistence in rice. The absolutist rulers of Aceh in the early seventeenth century had actually banned pepper cultivation in the central area of their kingdom, presumably in the interests of a more stable economic and political situation (Beaulieu 1666, 948–9; Broecke 1634, 175). The seventeenth century court chronicle of Banjarmasin, itself a great centre of pepper cultivation and export, seemed to express the perspective of a ruler tired of the unstable and vulnerable position in which cash-cropping appeared to place him:

> Let people nowhere in this country plant pepper, as is done in Jambi and Palembang. Perhaps those countries grow pepper for the sake of money, in order to become wealthy. There is no doubt that in the end these countries will be ruined; with much intrigue and expensive foodstuffs . . . The government will be chaotic because the people of the capital will not be respected by their

subjects; royal functionaries will not be feared by the pepper growing
population (*Hikayat Bandjar*, 330–1; see also, Siegel 1979, 101–2).

The chronicle noted later: "instructions would not be followed because the
masses (*orang banyak*) would be impertinent towards the raja" (Siegel 1979,
442–3).

It is significant that the same conservative chronicle warns that Banjarese
should adopt all the ceremonial and manners of the Javanese court, and not
imitate the dress or habits of the foreign merchants in their midst—
Makasarese, Acehnese, Malay or Dutch. For it was the rulers of Java who had
most wholeheartedly and successfully crushed the mercantile spirit of their
people. The mighty Sultan Agung (1613–45), who proudly told the Dutch,
"I am a prince and a soldier not a merchant like the other princes of Java"
(quoted in Masselman 1963, 313), decisively shifted the locus of power by
destroying or subordinating all the flourishing coastal cities, centralizing
power in his own hands, and monopolizing the country's principal export,
rice. Of his successor, Amangkurat I, van Goens tells us

> he exceeds his father in statecraft. He has forbidden any of his subjects to sail
> overseas, forcing all outsiders to come to his country for rice, well knowing
> that because Mataram is the rice bowl of Batavia, all goods which come to
> Batavia will come to him, without any of his subjects being able to trade for
> even a penny . . . I once made bold to advise the King that he should allow his
> subjects to sail, to become rich, but was given the reply, "My people have
> nothing of their own as you have, but everything of theirs comes to me, and
> without strong government I would not be king for a day" (Goens 1956, 200–
> 1).

Since the rulers of Banten, Makasar, and Ayudhaya had concentrated such
a great proportion of economic resources in their own hands, the eclipse of
these states as trading centres was a much greater disaster than the fall of
Melaka. The "Malay" mercantile class of that city had successfully moved its
operations to a number of other ports—Patani, Brunei, Aceh, and Pahang in
the first instance—whereas there was little left of such a class by the end of
the seventeenth century. Only Aceh survived into the eighteenth century as a
significant urban centre of international trade, but even here the change of
atmosphere was marked by the growing dominance of a rural elite based on
rice cultivation, by the appearance of Acehnese rather than Malay literature,
and by the relative isolation of even that city from the major world centres of
intellectual and technical innovation.

By 1700 the impoverishment of Southeast Asia was becoming a source of difficulty even for the Dutch who had done most to bring it about. The lucrative trade in Indian and Chinese cloth had always flourished not because Southeast Asians were unable to produce their own cloth, but because they could afford to buy the foreign luxuries. At each blockade of seventeenth century Banten and consequent decline in pepper production, Bantenese had gone back to producing their own cloth. A Dutch observer of 1705 noted: "it is nothing but poverty that is the true reason that the traffic in the finest [Coromandel] Coast and Surat cloths declines daily while by contrast their own weaving has increased more and more through the multiplication of poor people" (Chastelein quoted in Rouffaer 1904, 3). The Dutch and English now had to try to force Indian cloth on a less wealthy population by discriminatory tariffs against Indian cloths and raw cotton, or outright prohibition of them.

By the eighteenth century there was an economic gulf between Southeast Asians and the Europeans in their midst. Javanese chronicles began to characterize the Europeans as crude and greedy, but as a result of their greed "they are enormously rich and live in cities like heaven, the manifold luxuries of which could not be described even in a whole day" (Kumar 1979, 197).

In reality the majority of Southeast Asians of the eighteenth century and early nineteenth century were by no means in poverty, in relation to other parts of the world or to twentieth century conditions. Van den Bosch believed the poor of the Dutch cities he had studied were much worse off than Javanese peasants in 1830 (Vlekke 1959, 288; Crawfurd 1820, I: 40), and observers of the early nineteenth century were still more inclined to note the good health and abundant food supplies of Southeast Asian communities than their poverty. What had happened in the seventeenth century was that Southeast Asians had been driven away from the economic high points where they controlled trade, commanded substantial resources of good ships, and presided over bustling international entrepots. There were few wealthy Southeast Asians left outside the ruling courts, and these courts had either withdrawn altogether from trade (Java, Siam, Ava) or had become too weak to treat with European traders on a basis of economic or cultural equality.

The percentage of the indigenous population in urban centres must have decreased in these centuries—indeed there may well have been a decline even in the absolute numbers of city-dwellers. In the eighteenth and nineteenth centuries the largest cities became the colonial entrepots—Batavia, Manila, and later Singapore, Rangoon, Surabaya and Penang. Javanese were not permitted into Batavia at all in the seventeenth century, and these cities tended to remain culturally remote from their hinterlands, with Europeans and Chinese dominating the commercial and manufacturing sectors, such as they were. Bangkok, though nominally independent, was functionally little different. Thais played a small part in its economic life. Since the indigenous centres were stagnating in isolation, indigenous manufactures remained at the level they had been in the sixteenth century. Elaborate bronze and silver work, *kris* manufacture, and weaving on small inefficient looms were still being practised in the nineteenth century in the same places and with the same methods which had been developed during the heyday of urban growth three centuries earlier. Such production was more remote from developments in other parts of the world, more and more stylized for ceremonial functions, and less and less able to compete in price terms with foreign manufactures. We have seen how in the seventeenth century, indigenous cloth production provided the cheaper part of the market, but had to expand when the indigenous elite became less able to afford imports. The development of mechanized mass production in Lancashire changed this completely. As an English merchant testified, when the British occupation of Java began in 1811, "The natives were clothed in manufactures of their own, partly, and partly in the manufactures of British India . . . in 1828, when I left Java, the natives were almost exclusively clothed in British manufactures" (*Parliamentary Papers, House of Commons* 1830, 238). The same transformation occurred within the next few decades in every part of the region, the Philippines being the last to abandon its flourishing indigenous textile industry in the 1870s. Indigenous production was never improved, except in the Philippines where the Spanish had no interest in imported cloth. Instead it was pushed aside in the interests of greater trade with Europe, until it remained significant only as a quaint "craft" using antiquated labour-intensive methods to serve a shrinking, largely ceremonial market. The same was true of the once famous bronze, gold and other metal-work, typically centred in the remnants of once-great cities now isolated from the mainstream of commerce.

Until the twentieth century the trend was exclusively in this direction, with European traders and later colonial governments doing their best to encourage it. The case has often been made for India, how British manufactures aided by colonial pressure drove out indigenous manufacture. It is not sufficiently realized that the much greater importance of foreign trade in the economy of Southeast Asia rendered it more vulnerable to this process, and at an earlier date, than other parts of Asia. Already in 1830 John Crawfurd could claim with satisfaction that he knew of no people "that consume British manufactures more largely [than Siam], the population being considered, except probably the inhabitants of the island of Java" (from "China Trade", *Parliamentary Papers, House of Commons* 1830, 312).

The pattern then was one in which Southeast Asians were pressed more and more into purely agricultural activity where they had little capital or incentive to experiment. Even within this general picture there are of course a number of examples of creative adaptation to a market opportunity, with temporary prosperity as a result. We might instance the enormous pepper production of independent Aceh in the nineteenth century, the commercial rice-growing for export in the mainland deltas around the turn of the nineteenth century, the prosperity which came to underpopulated eastern Java in the early stages of the cultivation system, or the smallholder rubber boom of the 1920s in many parts of outer Indonesia. For the most part the wealth from these activities failed absolutely to reverse the long-term trend, or to give rise to indigenous centres of capital and large-scale modern production. In most cases this was because the colonial or semi-colonial framework ensured that this wealth would be channelled into the upper layers of the plural society—European and Chinese capitalists and an unproductive indigenous aristocracy. Where such commercial enterprise occurred in an independent context, leading Acehnese pepper-traders and Siamese or Lombok rulers to invest in schooners and steamships, this brought such states into direct conflict with the colonial powers. The impoverishment which came to the elites of Aceh, Lombok, Ava, and Vietnam as a result of the last phase of European aggression in Southeast Asia at the end of the nineteenth century was immediate and spectacular—reminiscent of the fall of Makasar and Banten in the seventeenth century. The Dutch forced a huge indemnity of four hundred thousand rijksdaalders from Lombok just before the final obliteration of that kingdom in 1893. In Aceh we are told that the population melted down all their gold ornaments to provide funds for the resistance, and the wealthy class which had financed cash-cropping, trade and craftsmanship was ruined by the war's end.

We would however distort history if we attempted to place all the historic burden of responsibility for Southeast Asian poverty at the feet of European trade and conquest. We have seen already that certain states *chose* to attempt to isolate their people from cash-cropping and commerce when this turned sour, while rulers persistently distrusted any of their subjects who became independently wealthy. Moreover the points above do not fully explain the failure of any class of substantial merchants or capitalists to arise, at least after the seventeenth century, despite some large infusions of wealth through cash-cropping (notably about one million Spanish/Mexican dollars a year to the Acehnese pepper industry for most of the nineteenth century) (Reid 1969b, 14–15).

We cannot ignore a persistent cultural preference for using wealth to acquire a personal following rather than an accumulation of capital for land. Historically we can explain this by the relative scarcity of labour in early Southeast Asia in comparison with other parts of Asia or Europe, and the abundance of land, which was therefore held to be of no intrinsic value. The change in these attitudes which was probably beginning to occur in the large trading cities of the fifteenth to seventeenth centuries was aborted when these cities were conquered or overtaken. Even as population pressure began to rise in the nineteenth century, therefore, the primacy of the personal bond of dependence remains marked. For the patron a dependent labour force continued to be the key to status, to power, and to comfort. For the client the insecurity of property and often of life itself disposed him to value the protection of a more powerful figure.

In my Acehnese pepper-growing example, therefore, or the pepper-growing of most other Sumatrans, it was only the chief who provided the capital for new plantations. Conversely, the person who provided the capital had to be the chief, the effective ruler of that area with the title of raja. We could replicate endlessly the following description of East Sumatran Malays in the early nineteenth century: "The moment a Malay becomes possessed of a little money, he entertains as many attendants as he can, and is accounted rich or respectable according to the number of his followers" (Anderson 1972, 268). The other side of this phenomenon is Clifford's description (1897, 19) of the absolute refusal of Pahang Malays to work for wages, whereas for someone they regarded as their chief they would work really hard, "for 60 hours at a stretch", for no pay at all and bringing their own food. In nineteenth century Siam too, bondsmen were valued more highly than capital. Creditors preferred to accept the debtor himself rather than his land as guarantee for a loan—so that debt slavery in one form or another continued to flourish. Some have argued that half the Siamese population was in a position of debt bondage to someone else when the system began to be abolished about 1870 (Terwiel 1983a). Even in the semi-urban manufacturing world of Surabaya, a mid-nineteenth century observer was convinced that the highly-skilled craftsmen would never become affluent because they worked only on the basis of an advance from the buyer: "When the workman has no further debt, he considers the relationship broken, and will not work again until he feels a need again to expose himself to new debts" (Hageman 1859, V: 142).

It is not difficult to see how the Dutch Cultivation System, using obligatory unpaid labour to produce export crops, profited from this cultural preference, intensified it, and thereby ensured that Java would be the least equipped of any Southeast Asian society to cope with the introduction of modern capitalism. Onghokham has recently extended Geertz's argument that the system artificially consolidated the predominance of the aristocratic class over an economically undifferentiated mass of peasants. The Council of the Indies judged in 1865, when the system was nearing its end, that "the Regents are the only group left in Javanese society with a high income, and it is wise of the Dutch to keep it so" (cited in Onghokham 1976, 143). Significantly it is in Java, in the 1840s, that one finds the first evidence of acute poverty and famine.

In 1830 the Javanese aristocracy of regents had apparently rejected a Dutch offer to provide them with private lands, preferring the traditional system of exacting labour and tribute from the whole populace (Onghokham 1976, 139ff, 341). In the long run, they therefore became wholly dependent upon the Dutch colonial government, and were easily transformed into a bureaucracy with no commercial interests at all. More independent princes in the outer islands, in Malaya, and in Siam, continued to dabble in commerce as they had in the past, but they too found that the reliance on patronage gave them a very weak basis from which to attempt to enter the capitalist world as either merchants or large landowners.

The Malay world in particular found itself therefore entering the twentieth century with nothing which even remotely resembled a middle, or propertied, class. Control of the bureaucracy had to be the key to the survival of the traditional ruling classes in independent Malaysia and Indonesia, and so it has proved. The functional middle class, in an economic sense, was everywhere occupied by a foreign, predominantly Chinese element, which in Muslim countries had minimal interaction with the value systems and political processes of the indigenous group. The Chinese of the Philippines, and to a lesser extent Siam, did on the other hand intermarry with the indigenous landed aristocracy of the late nineteenth century, producing a new dominant class much more attuned to capitalism and skilful in manipulating it in ways familiar to ourselves. Yet even in these countries, roughly twice as wealthy as Indonesia, the bulk of the peasant population remained remarkably isolated from the booming capitalism of the cities, and if anything, more preoccupied than ever with the grim struggle for daily survival.

NOTES

1. These lines were written in 1979. The subsequent improvement in living standards has fortunately made them much less appropriate for all of Southeast Asia except Indochina and Burma.

2. These estimates are more systematically placed in context in Reid (1993a: 67–77).

CHAPTER ELEVEN

CHANGING PERCEPTIONS OF THE "HERMIT KINGDOMS" OF ASIA[1]

TOKUGAWA HISTORIOGRAPHY IN ASIAN PERSPECTIVE

HISTORIANS of Japan need no reminding of the extraordinary change that has come over the historiography of the Tokugawa period in the last half-century. The debates of the 1950s revolved around whether the merchant class of that period was "progressive" or part of the essentially static feudal culture. Either way modernity was seen as coming to Japan with foreign intrusion and the Meiji restoration of 1866. For the dominant schools of history, Marxism provided the most influential explanation of how Japan fitted into a broader global historical evolution. In this pattern the Tokugawa era of relative isolation was interpreted as pre-modern and feudal—indeed as the closest approximation to European feudalism outside Europe. In isolating itself from the technological advances and social upheavals occurring elsewhere, Japan became locked into a social pattern from which Europe had escaped by the fifteenth century.

This picture (somewhat caricatured here in the first place, perhaps) was undermined first by the economic historians. C. D. Sheldon, Thomas Smith (1988) and Syd Crawcour (1961, 1963) played a role in mediating for non-Japanese readers the new thinking about the strength and diversity of the urban merchant class, and the increasing productivity of Japan's farmers, in the seventeenth and eighteenth centuries. As Tessa Morris-Suzuki (1993) has pointed out, a new historiography has gone much further. Emphasizing culture rather than economics and completely rejecting Marxist categories, some of the "Edo-boomers" now seek to find the roots of Japan's successful modernity precisely in the Edo period. Instead of being backward, hierarchic and isolationist, Tokugawa Japan is now seen as the key to Japan's modernity, and perhaps even to a new stage of modernity for the rest of the world.

The smaller states of eastern Asia—Korea, Vietnam, Burma, Siam, and to a lesser extent some of the Archipelago states—also withdrew into relative isolation from the mid-seventeenth to the mid-nineteenth centuries. The east Asian "Age of Commerce" of roughly 1400–1650 had seen an enormous expansion of involvement in maritime trade by not only Japanese but also Javanese, Malays, Mons, Tagalogs, Chams and the inhabitants of all of the trading cities which were the engines of growth in the period. The Ryukyus, Java, Siam and even Korea and Japan were linked by a Chinese or Chinese-mestizo diaspora in the fifteenth century, and many more players joined in the trade boom which followed in the late sixteenth and early seventeenth century. This increasing reliance on trade was drastically curbed in a crisis of the mid-seventeenth century, which saw the Dutch East India Company establish monopoly control over the Archipelago's most lucrative exports, while the leading Southeast Asian commercial centres were either destroyed (Brunei 1578; Pegu 1599; Tuban 1619; Surabaya/Gresik 1625; Makasar 1669; Banten 1684) or declined through loss of their vital trade. The capital of Java moved from the commercial north coast to interior Mataram (near Jogjakarta) around 1600. The capital of Burma similarly moved from the great maritime city of Pegu to Ava, taking permanent root there in 1635. The Siamese port-capital of Ayudhya was the last east Asian capital to retain a major stake in global trade, but after its "1688 revolution" it too turned its back on most Western and Muslim trade, leaving the Chinese and Dutch in command of a much reduced foreign commerce (Reid 1990b, 1993a).

Like Japan, these states were thought by Western historians of an earlier era, and by many of their own nationalists and Marxists, to have lost a great opportunity by turning their backs on commerce and new technology. Yet for these societies too this period of relative isolation is the source of most of what we today associate with their specific cultural identity. The dilemmas that face Japanese historiography, in other words, are shared by many other historiographies in the region. What distinguishes Japan is the new-found confidence of having to write the history of number one, and the consequent vigour in challenging historiographical categories designed to explain European progress.

"ISOLATION" IN SOUTHEAST ASIA AND KOREA

The period of relative isolation by Asian states has generally received a bad press from Western historians until very recently. D. G. E. Hall said of the move of the Burmese capital far into the interior at Ava (near modern Mandalay):

> It was a retrograde step, a surrender to traditionalism . . . Cut off from contact with the outside world, Burmese rulers came truly to believe that their palace was the centre of the universe, that building pagodas, collecting daughters from vassals, and raiding their neighbours for white elephants and slaves was the essence of kingcraft . . . The chief ingredient in the failure of the Burmese kingdom was supplied . . . by the intransigence and xenophobia which radiated from the court of Ava (Hall 1950, 66).

Even Siam, though retaining a capital dependent on maritime trade, had in the view of Hutchinson (1940, 192) surrendered to a "spirit of blind and arrogant self-sufficiency" after its change of direction in 1688.

It is hardly surprising that the Englishmen responsible for the conquest and reconstruction of Burma and the Malay States, the French in Vietnam and Cambodia, the Japanese in Korea and the Dutch in the Archipelago should have justified their actions by casting the respective *anciens régimes* in a negative light. When writer-activists such as Fytche, Garnier, Pavie, Brooke, Swettenham, Snouck Hurgronje, Liefrink and Colijn portrayed the nineteenth century kingdoms as tyrannical, chaotic, backward-looking and incapable of delivering welfare to their people, they were in part making the case for why these regimes had to be pushed aside.

There were however more fundamental mental attitudes in the nineteenth century which drove colonial-period scholars, including those deeply sympathetic to the cultures in question, to conclusions often even more negative than those of the first generation of activists. As Michael Adas (1989) has well shown, the eighteenth century marked a change in attitude of the West to the non-West, as the confidence born of technological superiority carried into the fields of statecraft and education. By the middle of the eighteenth century the fascination many earlier European intellectuals had felt for distant and exotic cultures was replaced by a growing conviction that "oriental despotism" kept these countries poor.

> This inertia or sluggishness from which the country [Burma] suffers in respect to invention and the progress of the arts may have many causes. But the principal one is the government itself, oppressor of any industry" (Mantegazza 1784, 103).

> These people's [of Magindanao, southern Philippines] laziness seems to proceed . . . from the severity of their prince, of whom they stand in awe; For he dealing

with them very arbitrarily, and taking from them what they get, this damps
their industry, so that they never strive to have anything but from hand to
mouth (Dampier 1697, 223).

In response to the European enlightenment this view became linked with a
theory of decline from an earlier period of stronger and more effective states.
There were at least three grounds for this theory. First, European standards
of what an effective state was had changed since the early travellers had
written enthusiastically about Pegu, Melaka, Brunei and Ayudhya. Second,
those early travel reports dated from the "Age of Commerce" in the sixteenth
and early seventeenth centuries, when many Asian states experienced a peak
of wealth and centralization. Third, Europeans began in the nineteenth
century to uncover ruins of the classic temple-building civilizations of
Angkor, Pagan, Champa and Java, which they could equate with the vanished
glories of Greece and Rome.

Raffles was the first and perhaps the most influential of the enlightenment
generation to be seduced by the romance of these overgrown monuments, as
he encountered them in Java. "The grandeur of their ancestors", he remarked
(1817, II: 6), "sounds like a fable in the mouth of the degenerate Javan; and
it is only when it can be traced in monuments, which cannot be falsified,
that we are led to give credit to their traditions concerning it." Raffles
developed an elaborate theory to explain how the "Malays" (in the broad
sense) had declined through piracy, slavery, uncertain lines of succession,
arbitrary exactions and monopolies, and the lack of effective law—all of
which had been encouraged or tolerated by the Dutch but could be put right
by the beneficence of British rule (Raffles 1835, I: 90–100). At Angkor a
half-century later were uncovered "ruins of such grandeur . . . that, at first
view, one is filled with profound admiration, and cannot but ask what has
become of this powerful race, so civilized, so enlightened, the authors of these
gigantic works" (Mouhot 1864, 278–9).

It should be acknowledged that indigenous historiography often reinforced
this notion of decline. The more powerful kings of the past (Sejong,
Anawhrata, Boromatrailokanat, Le Thanh-tong, Iskandar Muda, Agung)
achieved legendary status as the founders of religion and the makers of the
law. In Korea and Vietnam the chronicles of the nineteenth century tended
to perceive political perfection in Tang Dynasty China, and to judge local
phenomena as deviations from this ancient model.

The intellectual climate in which colonial scholars constructed the first
modern national histories of the countries in question, therefore, determined
that the more remote past would attract most of the attention, and the
immediate pre-colonial past be seen in terms of failure and missed

opportunities. Japanese scholars such as Kawai (1916) and Itani (1928) saw the last Korean dynasty as marked by chaotic divisions and inability to cope with modern pressures. Coedès (1951) conceded that the Ecole Francaise d'Extrême-Orient preferred the intellectual challenge of reconstructing a lost history of ancient Cambodia to working on more recent periods where documentation was relatively rich—especially in the case of Vietnam. Those who did reconstruct the history of pre-colonial Vietnam (led by Luro 1878, Silvestre 1889, Schreiner 1900–2) took the view that "administration, justice, religion, literature, and science all came from the Middle Kingdom . . . and [after independence from China] the Annamites did not make any progress on Chinese civilization" (Schreiner 1900, I: 53–4). D.G.E. Hall's monumental *History* (1955), still the most influential general textbook for pre-colonial Southeast Asia, summed up well the scholarship of the colonial period. After 1635 Burma "surrendered to traditionalism and isolation, and its increasing intransigence and xenophobia made western trade with Burma . . . and even ordinary diplomatic relations, impossible" (378). The Emperor Tu-Duc in negotiating with the French "took his cue from China and was too simple-minded to realise . . . the consequences" (647). Aceh (here following Vlekke almost verbatim) and Brunei were nests of pirates, while the Balinese dynasty of Lombok exercised "cruel oppression" over the Sasaks (531–2, 577, 581). The major theme of the late eighteenth and nineteenth centuries is in fact the inexorable advance of European power.

Nationalist historiography might have been expected to reverse this pattern and turn the "last stand" into a heroic source of pride. But the nationalists were energetic modernizers who had learned their modernity in Western-style schools, through reading and reacting against colonial histories. The rulers who had compromised with or been humiliated by the colonial conquerors were sources of embarrassment rather than pride. They represented "feudal" hierarchies subsequently fossilized under the colonial umbrella into forms which the nationalists saw as an obstacle to progress. It was the shadowier ancient kingdoms of presumed great power which seized their imagination as it had that of the colonial scholars. Angkor became the central symbol of Cambodian nationalism, as Pagan, Sukhothai, the Melaka sultanate, Sri Vijaya and Majapahit did elsewhere. The Brunei sketched by the chronicler of Magellan's expedition has become the model for the newest of Southeast Asia's nationalisms. Sukarno's exhortation (1930, 118) may stand for many:

We have a glorious past . . . What Indonesian's national spirit will not live when hearing the greatness of the kingdoms of Melayu and Sriwijaya, the greatness of the first Mataram, the greatness of the time of Sindok and

Airlangga and Kediri and Singasari and Majapahit and Pajajaran—the greatness
too of Bintara, Banten, and Mataram under Sultan Agung.

Where they were not ignored altogether, the later kingdoms seemed
pathetic or reactionary. Nationalists preferred to focus on peasant or proto-
nationalist rebellion, of which the Tay Son in Vietnam and Diponegoro in
Java were particular exemplars.

The attractiveness of the Tay Son as a model "people's rebellion" was one
reason why the dynasty which crushed it was especially denigrated by
Vietnamese nationalist and Marxist histories. The stricture of the colonial
historians that the Nguyen regime was "pure monarchy, absolute, without
control, without effective constitution, without any other limit than powerful
custom become almost ritual and a code transmitted from time immemorial"
(Luro 1878, 100) was congenial enough to be quoted repeatedly by Marxist
nationalists (Tran 1958, 33; Phan 1961, III: 430). The dominant view in
Hanoi until recently was that the Nguyen dynasty "destroyed every
progressive policy of Quang Trung [the Tay Son ruler], and put a reactionary
'anti-commerce' policy into effect" (Phan 1961, III: 446). It represented a
"profound and irremediable crisis" of the feudal order (Nguyen 1987, 109).
In a similar way North Korean Marxists regarded the policy of the regent
Taewon'gun who dominated Korea after 1864 as "conservative,
anachronistic, and aimed at . . . revamping the feudal system" (Kang 1990,
9). Non-communist nationalists in both countries were almost as scathing
about the inadequacy of their last rulers (e.g. Le Thanh Khoi 1981, 345).

There are plenty of indications that these negative attitudes have begun to
change, among both historians and political decision-makers. Korean scholars
were probably the earliest and most determined revisionists, eager to overturn
the image, established by Japanese scholarship, of a stagnant and fossilized
late Choson Dynasty. Both in the north and south, Marxist categories
directed the early stages of this quest to a pursuit of "incipient capitalism".
The North Korean view had taken a clear if somewhat crude shape by the
1960s: "Weak capitalist relations gradually emerged in Korea in the
eighteenth century while feudal relations continued to be prevalent. The
newly emerged capitalist relations brought about a more naked and more
direct form of exploitation" (cited Kang 1990, 7). Southern historians were
also concerned to show that modern capitalism had begun independently
before it was forced upon Korea by the Japanese (Cho 1973), though there
was also greater readiness to question the Eurocentric Marxist progression
(Kang 1990, 7; Lee 1967, 226–63). The *Sirhak* (Practical Learning) school
of scholarship which became dominant in the eighteenth century has also
been celebrated in both North and South as an indigenous indication of

modernity and "part of the effort to recover the historical ego of the nation" (Kang 1990, 8).

The work on Konbaung Burma of Myo Myint (1987), Lieberman (1991, 1993) and Koenig (1990) has undermined the stagnant image by showing a process of almost constant reform. For Siam, Gesick (1976), Reynolds (1976) and Wyatt (1982) have suggested that Rama I, despite his claims to be recreating Ayudhya, "really intended something fundamentally new" (Wyatt 1982, 17). Nidhi Aeusrivongse (1978, 1984) has taken this further by pointing to the complete revolution in social and intellectual forms which underlay the changes from the top. Although Woodside (1971) still remains almost alone as a serious study in English of the Nguyen dynasty, the information available has been fundamentally transformed by the work on the local land registers by Nguyen Dinh Dau (1991), Nguyen Duc Nghinh (1974, 1980) and others in Vietnamese, and Yumio Sakurai (1976, 1987) in Japanese. Similar sources in Korea have recently been analyzed also in an empirical and careful spirit (Yi 1992). A revival of interest in the last dynasty has been marked by a 1989 conference in Ho Chi Minh City (Mac 1992), and by a number of publications about old Hue which seem motivated as much by nostalgia as by a desire to boost tourism.

James Warren's (1981) work on Sulu, van der Kraan's (1980, 1992) on Lombok, Trocki's (1979) on Riau-Johor and Shaharil Talib's (1990) on Trengganu have begun the revisionist task for some of the more dynamic Archipelago states, though almost everything remains to be done on the internal dynamics of states such as Aceh, Palembang, Bone and Wajo in this period. For the Javanese states after the Gianti Treaty (1755) the work of Ricklefs (1974), Kumar (1980) and Carey (1986) has begun to show the rich diversity and capacity for social and intellectual change even after the military disasters of the previous period.

A "CHINESE CENTURY"

The century 1740–1840 witnessed a remarkable growth of Chinese influence in the smaller Asian states, though this has been obscured in the Western literature by the opposite reaction of the European enclave ports, which sought to limit their earlier dependence on Chinese intermediaries. The massacre of about ten thousand Chinese in Batavia in 1740 was one tragic indication of the changing climate in these Europeans ports, but the Spanish exclusion of non-Catholic Chinese from the Philippines in 1755 (repeated in 1766) was of even greater long-term importance. A distinct overseas Chinese identity was for the following century much less attractive in the Dutch settlements and virtually impossible in the Spanish. Chinese in Java were more inclined to assimilate into the indigenous states, and in the Philippines to avoid Manila in favour of ports such as Sulu (Carey 1984; Wickberg 1965, 20–35).

China was meanwhile finally overcoming its disabling antipathy towards the overseas enterprise of its emigrant population. The last of the many imperial bans on private Chinese trade abroad was that of the Kanxi Emperor in 1717. Revocation in 1727 legitimated and encouraged an overseas junk trade already rapidly developing. Sojourning abroad, and especially serving a foreign government, continued to be condemned, but the immensely wealthy Batavia trader Chen Ilao may have been the last to be punished when he was sentenced to banishment on his return in 1749. In 1754 the Chinese authorities declared for the first time that any Chinese with valid reasons would be entitled to return home and have his property protected (Ng 1991). The effect of this relaxation was quickly evident in the outflow of traders, miners, planters and adventurers of all kinds.

This era saw the establishment of colonies of Chinese miners in northern Vietnam, western Borneo, Phuket, Kelantan and Bangka. Chinese planters established new export industries of pepper in Brunei, Cambodia and Chantaburi, and of gambier in Riau-Johor (Trocki 1979). In southeast Siam as well as Kedah and Java, sugar plantations were opened by Chinese immigrants. The Mekong delta area became a new frontier for Chinese agricultural and commercial enterprise. Whereas rulers in Burma and northern (Trinh) Vietnam reacted with fear and tight controls, the Nguyen rulers of Hue, like Taksin and Rama I in Siam and the Yamtuan Mudas in Riau, were eager to use Chinese colonists to increase not only their revenue but their control over frontier areas.

Most of these economic pioneers produced or traded for the China market. Hence a great expansion occurred in the junk trade to such ports as Ha Tien, Saigon, Trengganu, Riau, Brunei (where seven junks a year were said to be arriving in the 1770s) and Sulu. The greatest of all Chinese ports outside China, however, was Bangkok, which probably replaced Batavia at the end of the eighteenth century as the busiest port between Calcutta and Canton. According to Crawfurd (1828, 414–16) there were 280 junks and about 11,500 seamen, almost all ethnic Chinese, based in Bangkok in the second decade of the nineteenth century.

Despite its conservative Confucian ideology, the Chienlung Emperor's long reign was prosperous and relatively effective in dealing with its Asian neighbours. After abortive military interventions in Burma in 1766 and Vietnam in 1788, and a prickly conservatism towards the "usurper" Taksin, relations were quickly restored with all these states to a level of almost unprecedented warmth. Tribute missions visited the Chinese capital during the last ten years of the Chienlung reign (1785–95) at a rate of almost four a year—more than at any time since the sixteenth century. From Korea envoys continued to arrive about twice a year as late as 1874, while Vietnam sent missions almost every year and Siam was more zealous than it had been for four centuries—omitting to send tribute in only five years of the period 1784–1832. Even in the Archipelago, where no state had sent tribute to China since the early 1500s, Sulu recommended the practice in 1727 and sent seven formal missions between then and 1763 (Fairbank 1968, 11, 99–101, 265–6; Promboon 1971, 121–2; Majul 1973, 347–52).

There is as yet no historiography of this "Chinese century", at least in English. As a theme it is unlikely to appeal to nationalists, and few historians working on Southeast Asia handle the fragmentary Chinese records with ease. Nevertheless a comparative treatment of Southeast Asia in this period of wariness about the West must take account of the alternative economic and intellectual stimuli from China and Chinese.

CULTURAL INNOVATION AND THE PROBLEM OF MODERNITY

It is hardly an exaggeration to say that what we know of the so-called "traditional" literature and art of the countries in question was produced or reproduced in this "last stand" period. Earlier works have not survived well, and modern collections began to be formed in this period. Beyond that superficial point, however, it is also clear that the courts, the religious institutions and the new social classes called forth a vast quantity of creative work, which in each of the literary and artistic traditions represented changes so profound as to raise questions about the nature and the sources of modernity. These questions must be central to the agenda of the project we have embarked upon.

Nidhi's work (still primarily in Thai) has made the point most forcefully for early Bangkok literature (1788–1824), where he finds "a new and vigorous spirit of experimenting with new techniques, new motifs, new verse forms, and new ideas" which set Thai literature on a path which might have led to a modern sensibility even without the massive impact of Western models after 1855 (Nidhi's English summary of Aeusrivongse 1984). He notes a number of novel features both in genre (more prose, and more work intended to be read rather than recited; more "popular" forms being adopted into court literature; more drama; more fiction; less use of the Indic epics) and in content. There was a greater realism, with epic (and Indian) heroes giving way to kings, traders, foreigners and the people of everyday city life, as well as narrations of excursions into the countryside. There is a tendency to humanistic as well as realistic depictions. Ordinary people are often portrayed as comic, but the heroes have to learn exemplary behaviour through experience, unlike the god-like heroes of Ayudhya. There is therefore a more complex characterization. This trend towards realism in literature is parallelled by realism in painting, especially in the everyday urban scenes in the lower parts of temple murals.

Since some of the impetus for change was a greater emphasis on Buddhist morality rather than Hindu or animist cosmology, it is not surprising that parallel trends occurred in Burmese art and literature. Yet Korea and Vietnam appear to have experienced a somewhat similar evolution in a Confucian tradition. In Korea the "practical learning" (*sirhak*) school turned away from philosophical speculations and toward a thorough examination of contemporary affairs. Novels reached a wider audience (including women) and treated of Korean as well as Chinese themes, while painting became more naturalistic and included popular everyday scenes. The wider use of Korean as opposed to Chinese was parallelled by the flowering of a popular Vietnamese literature in *nom*, most successfully in the radical woman poet Ho Xuan Hong. The masterpiece of Vietnamese poetry, the Tale of Kieu, can still move modern readers even though it was written by a conventionally-educated Confucian scholar under the Emperor Gia Long (1802–20). In both countries neo-Confucian critiques of modern customs by some literati were accompanied by more popular and subversive forms.

In all these societies China may have been important less as a model than as a source of "otherness", of self-consciousness about individual and collective diversity. In the Malay World, Europeans and Arabs as well as Chinese provided that stimulus. The modernity of Munshi Abdullah's writing is sometimes dismissed as outside the Malay mainstream, but there were other authors of the period who were almost as radical in bringing an Islamic critique to bear on Malay society and history. The Buddhist ethic which Nidhi identifies as driving out animist, Hindu and royal-mythological mentalities may find parallels in the work of Islamic writers of the Palembang and Riau schools, such as Kemas Fakhruddin, Abdul-Samad al-Palimbani and Raja Ali Haji (Drewes 1977; Andaya and Matheson 1979). There is no doubt that the last-named wrote about foreigners and traders in a similar realistic spirit to that discerned by Nidhi, and not as if they were simply attributes of royal grandeur. On all these questions, however, and still more in relation to Bugis and Acehnese literatures, comparative work has barely begun.

In Java and Bali, despite the image of literary "decline" which colonial scholars picked up from indigenous informants, the eighteenth and nineteenth centuries are now more often seen as a period of cultural renaissance (Day 1983; Creese 1991, 414–15), when most of the existing corpus of literature was written. Despite the Dutch presence in Java, indigenous writers were almost as isolated from European literary norms as their Korean and Vietnamese counterparts. Nevertheless there were radically new types of writing (including the realistic court diary of a lady soldier); there was a new consciousness of Javanese as one people (*bangsa*) amongst a variety of others, to be criticized in the balance with other ethnic groups; and an Islamic ethic became much more influential (Kumar 1980, 1987). In Bali and Lombok new genres became popular, including new types of *kakawin* and Panji stories written not for the courts but for a variety of diverse patrons.

The colonial conquests of the nineteenth century in one sense mark the progressive retreat or extinction of one autonomous polity after another. Although these defeats have been seen as fundamental watersheds from both a colonial and a nationalist viewpoint, there may be deeper senses in which the high colonial era continued patterns of commercialization and intellectual innovation which had begun during the "Last Stand". This, I suggest, makes these innovations even more interesting. As the Japanese example forces us to reinterpret our understanding of modernity, these other Asian examples will be of increasing importance.

NOTES

1. This paper arises from a three-year project funded by the Toyota Foundation, to whom gratitude is first due. My collaborators in that project are the source of many of the ideas in this chapter—Nidhi Aeusrivongse, Martina Deuchler, Jeyamalar Kathirithamby-Wells, Alfons van der Kraan, Ann Kumar, Victor Lieberman, Yumio Sakurai and Carl Trocki. In addition I must thank Nola Cooke for much of the material on Vietnam, and the following for varied advice and assistance: Yang-hi Choe-Wall, Helen Creese, Lorraine Gesick, Patrick Jory, David Marr, Tessa Morris-Suzuki, Li Tana, Stewart Lone, Craig Reynolds and Tan Lay-cheng. A much fuller exposition of the period under discussion in Southeast Asia and Korea in now available in Reid (1997).

CHAPTER TWELVE

"HEAVEN'S WILL AND MAN'S FAULT": THE RISE OF THE WEST AS A SOUTHEAST ASIAN DILEMMA

In choosing this theme I do not mean to suggest that it is peculiar to Southeast Asia. The dilemma of a person or a people confronted with superior strength is universal and timeless. No people and no part of the world is especially prone to react to it in particular ways—with heroism, with pragmatism, with ingenuity, or with "oriental" fatalism. All of these possible reactions have of course been found in Southeast Asia, and in each of its major cultures, as they have elsewhere.

The reason I choose to bring together here some Southeast Asian responses to Western power and wealth is primarily because I want to emphasize how dominant an intellectual and psychological problem it has been, and continues to be, for that part of the world.

I do not wish to enter the important controversy about the point in time when European power became in reality the major problem for Southeast Asia. What is important in this context is that it has been so perceived by Southeast Asian leaders for about the past century. King Rama III of Siam prophesied on his deathbed in 1851:

> I personally think. . .that there will be no more wars with Vietnam and Burma. We will have them only with the West. Take care, and do not lose any opportunity to them (translated in Wyatt 1969, 30).

Within a generation of this remark the most intense period of European imperial conquest in Southeast Asia was under way, corresponding to the "great European peace" of 1870–1914. No Southeast Asian leader could escape the threat, which was at once military, economic, political and intellectual. Whether this *annus mirabilis,* 1975, has seen the end of Southeast

Asia's "wars with the west" remains to be seen.[1] The dilemma nevertheless loses none of its urgency, as the economic gulf between rich and poor nations grows ever wider. We may not succeed in seeing this problem from the other site of the fence, but let us at least begin to try.

The anonymous Vietnamese reaction to French conquest which I took as my text—"All these things came about because of Heaven's will but also because of man's fault"—expresses an important dichotomy. Many Southeast Asians must have understood their predicament in terms of "Heaven's will", as a product of circumstances beyond their control or comprehension. Yet not even among the most "traditional" or the most oppressed was there a lack of restless voices, demanding change, arguing that it was the remediable weaknesses in their own societies which had invited defeat. Neither in Southeast Asia nor anywhere else can we expect a society to accommodate itself passively to relative weakness and poverty.

PRE-NINETEENTH CENTURY

Prior to the nineteenth century the Western presence does not appear to have forced any Southeast Asian state to make a fundamental reassessment of its place in the world. European military skills were certainly appreciated. Portuguese mercenary soldiers were in great demand by the courts, while guns were for centuries the only European export of serious interest to Southeast Asians. Numerous examples could be cited of statesmen with a keen practical interest in European military and naval technology, like Karaeng Pattin-galloang, the Portuguese and Spanish-speaking prime minister of Makasar around 1650, with his fine library of European books (Boxer 1967, 4). Yet in technical matters the Europeans must have appeared so mediocre, if not barbarous, that they were not seen as a danger of an altogether new type.

During these centuries of gradual Western commercial penetration, only two important Southeast Asian states were defeated and destroyed in an overt contest with Europeans. Melaka was seized by the Portuguese in 1511, and Makasar by the Dutch in 1669. Since each of these disasters is treated in an important Malay work, it is worth pausing to see how they were perceived in the respective courts.

The *Sja'ir Perang Mengkasar* is a true battle epic written by the court writer of Makasar within a year or two of the events. It faces the fact that the Makasarese were beaten, but in a good fight which might have turned out differently had they not been "defeated by hunger" (Skinner 1963, 18, 217). The "Dutch devils" play no bigger part than their Indonesian allies, the "accursed Bugis", and both are denounced and ridiculed in a spirit similar to that which appears in reverse in contemporary Dutch writing (Skinner 1963, 10). The only suggestion that Dutch villainy might be of a different order to the usual kind comes in the line: "never make friends with the Dutch; they behave like devils and no country is safe with them" (Skinner 1963, 214).

The *Sejarah Melayu* or Malay annals is a much more elaborate court chronicle of the Melaka/Johor dynasty. One of the major reasons it was written, or as some would have it rewritten, in the early sixteenth century was the need to explain the cataclysmic loss of the dynasty's great capital to the Portuguese. The text of course mentions the Portuguese cannonballs "falling like rain" (Brown 1952, 167), but the real explanation for defeat was within, in Melaka's failure to heed the basic rules which governed its existence. At the founding of the Malay dynasty and in the dying testament of each of its great rulers, the contractual basis of the state is made plain: if the ruler humiliates his subjects unnecessarily they will not be bound by their oath of absolute loyalty (Brown 1952, 26, 44; Walls 1974).

The ruler who eventually loses Melaka, Sultan Mahmud, has been told by his dying father: "If you put them [your Malay subjects] to death when they have done no wrong, your kingdom will be brought to naught." The nemesis of Melaka follows relentlessly from Mahmud's crimes against the rules of kingship—in particular the murder of his loyal *Bendahara* (chief minister), Sri Maharaja. In terms of a distinction I want to make below, this was the analysis of a "revitalizer", who believed the kingdom could have been saved by a more faithful adherence to its own moral norms.

In other words, the perspective of these two Malay texts would have been the same if Melaka had fallen to the Siamese or Makasar to the Bugis alone. The worst the Europeans could do was still interpreted within the local context.

In the centuries that followed, the Western impact was still more muted in most of Southeast Asia. The Dutch and Spanish, who alone had substantial colonial footholds in the region, grew weaker while the European countries which first felt the industrial revolution were more interested in India and China. The Southeast Asian kingdoms themselves contributed to delaying a more intense confrontation with Europe by a more cautious attitude towards foreign commerce in general and Europeans in particular. From the late seventeenth to the early nineteenth century the agrarian countries for whom this was practicable—Burma, Siam, and to a lesser extent Vietnam—kept Europeans as much as possible at arm's length. I have not been able to find evidence which might show this isolation to have been a deliberate policy, rather than an involuntary consequence of the loss of profitable trade to foreigners. At a time when isolationism was becoming dangerously counter-productive, however, we have Vietnam's proud emperor Minh-Mang (1820–

41) insisting that it had saved his country from the fate China suffered in the
Opium Wars:

> The Ming [Chinese] people allowed [the barbarians] to live at random in
> various places. All the places that the barbarians came to, they sketched maps
> of. Of the strategic points of the entire sea coast of the Ming country there
> were none that the barbarians did not know . . . As to our court's relationship
> with Westerners, we do not resist their coming and do not chase them away . . .
> When transactions are finished, we immediately order them to sail away. We
> have never allowed them to live in residence ashore. Our people everywhere are
> not permitted to enter into private reciprocal trading relations with them
> (translated in Woodside 1971, 291–2).

On the other hand Mongkut, the king who ended this arm's-length
attitude to Westerners in Siam, was naturally very critical of it. In 1867 he
explained to the Siamese ambassador to France the superiority of his
European policy to that of Cambodia, which had quickly been seduced by
France, and that of the Vietnamese, who

> on the other hand, have been as deaf, dumb, and stubborn as the Siamese in
> previous reigns. Their stubbornness caused them to turn small incidents into
> serious ones, with the result that their country became a French colony in the
> end (translated in Pramoj and Pramoj 1958, 190).

Mongkut's more flexible policy should not, incidentally, be equated with
an affection for the West. His well-founded scepticism was expressed in the
same letter: "They seem to hold fast to the idea that all foreigners are animals,
and as such they deserve no pity when they are abused" (Pramoj and Pramoj
1958, 191, 187).

JAVA

In the many maritime states of Island Southeast Asia, trade was the basic state
resource and could not be simply turned off. These port-states remained
always open to Westerners, and the nearest parallel to the relative isolationism
of the agrarian states was a strong antipathy to allowing foreigners to build in
stone.[2] (Boxer 1967, 30–1; B. Andaya 1975, 30; Milburn 1825, 327; Wright
1961, 254). The Javanese provide a unique case. Like the mainland societies
they did turn away from trade and the sea in the seventeenth century, but
were not thereby able to avoid involvement with the Dutch in Batavia.
Most conflicts with the Dutch occurred in the coastal *pasisir* of Java, which

could be regarded as peripheral by the inland courts which now became the centres of Javanese life. The setback which was inescapable was the partition of the heart of Java between Jogjakarta and Surakarta, formalized by the Gianti Treaty of 1755. The existence of two kings in Java, recognizing each other's equality and legitimacy, and living in harmony, was to remain completely at odds with Javanese proprieties. The settlement was a product of Dutch minds, it was solemnized by strange Dutch rituals like quaffing a glass of beer together (Ricklefs 1974, 74), and it was ultimately only made possible by a Dutch force just strong enough to prevent either of the Javanese rivals getting the better of the other. Both Javanese courts saw the arrangement as artificial and temporary, yet gradually learned to live with it and rationalize it.

In a fascinating study, Merle Ricklefs has shown with reference to Jogjakarta how warfare was gradually abandoned as the means to reunite Java in favour of more esoteric devices. Dutch envoys were frequently entertained by fights staged between a *banteng* (buffalo), the symbol of Java, and a tiger, representing the foreigner. The *banteng* was always victorious in this symbolic duel, if not in the diplomatic bargaining (Ricklefs 1974, 274–5, 303). Similarly the most sacred court chronicles composed in the aftermath of the division appear to be devoted to overcoming it by magical or prophetic means. One written by the crown prince of Jogjakarta in 1774, corresponding to the end of a Javanese era (A.J. 1700), shows in an allegory how the Dutch ruler avoids certain destruction by the forces of a reunited Java when he miraculously receives illumination, converts to Islam, and thereafter enters a mystical dialogue with the ruler of Java (perhaps the author of the chronicle) (Ricklefs 1974, 188–218). Another *babad* from about the same period relates the extraordinary adventures of Baron Sakendar, who embodies within him elements of the Alexander the Great legend, the sixteenth century Spanish imperium, the Islamic conquest of Java, and the contemporary reality of the Dutch presence. The Dutch role in Batavia appears to be legitimated by a complex genealogy giving them sacral authority over the western (non-Javanese) portion of the island (Ricklefs 1974, 219; and see chapter 8).

Ricklefs' harsh judgement is that the Javanese courts "turned to traditional ideas to explain and to justify the irregular situation instead of attempting to correct it" (Ricklefs 1974, 219). Even though European power was still marginal, and its effects indirect, unplanned, and to a considerable extent unperceived, the responsibility for challenging it was already sidestepped by imputing cosmic power to Batavia. "Heaven's will" was indeed being preferred as an explanation to "man's fault". In terms of the *wayang* imagery beloved of Javanese, the gross, comical, unmannerly Europeans may have begun to be identified less with the giants and demons who huff and puff but are eventually defeated, and more with the *punakawan*—comical, misshapen and outrageously improper but at the same time possessing a supernatural wisdom and magic which is indispensable to the victorious Pendawas.[3]

The above chronicles were written in the late eighteenth century when the Dutch Company was physically weak and socially embedded in an Indonesian milieu. Some nineteenth century *babad* continued the desire to legitimate and domesticate European power, like the *Babad Inggris*, which gave Raffles half-Javanese ancestry (Kumar 1969, 500). The events of the nineteenth century, however, increasingly cast the Dutch in the role of both alien and master. The eighteenth century court chronicles were rewritten in terms of less harmonious relations between European and Javanese. Instead of accepting Islam and living in spiritual harmony with the Javanese courts, the Europeans are annihilated in a sea of blood (Ricklefs 1974, 210–11).[4] Whether the earlier texts were intended as prophecy or a magical reordering of reality is open to debate, but the growing colonial pressure seems to shift their character increasingly clearly in the direction of the prophetic and millenarian. As this becomes typical of late colonial responses elsewhere, I will return to it later.

THE "REVITALIZERS"

In the half-century which followed 1860, isolationism in any form proved useless, and all of Southeast Asia was humbled by the stark fact of European power. The choice between military defeat and political accommodation in practice meant only the difference between direct and indirect rule. The intellectual responses to this predicament were of course legion, and any categorization runs a grave risk of oversimplification. As a basis for analysis, however, I want to suggest a broad distinction between what I will call "revitalizers" and "borrowers". Both tendencies were reforming, seeking a way out of the powerlessness to which they had been reduced. The revitalizers however tended to see the problem as moral and religious, and the solution in a truer adherence to established norms; the borrowers to see the problem as primarily technical, and the solution in learning the tricks of the West.

Many of those who inspired their people most heroically to resist Western aggression were true revitalizers, sustained by a confidence that righteousness would prevail—on earth as in the cosmos. My examples are very different— the Confucian morality of Vietnam's scholar-mandarins on the one hand and the religious faith of Muslim *ulama* on the other. The Vietnamese patriot scholars drew their lessons from history, as in an anonymous 1864 appeal:

even in times of confusion, there remain books
that teach us how to overcome disorder.
Past generations can still be for us examples of right and wrong
                              (translated in Truong Buu Lam 1967, 76).

One anonymous appeal for resistance, written in southern Vietnam in
1864, cited Chinese history to show the triumph of (Chinese) righteousness
over barbarian invasion. As for the French, it went on:

Although they were very confident in their copper battleships surmounted by
chimneys; although they had a large quantity of steel rifles and lead bullets;
these things did not prevent the loss of some of their best generals in these last
years, when they attacked our frontier in hundreds of battles. The sun and
moon have always shown us the right way
                              (translated in Truong Buu Lam 1967, 77).

Twenty years later in northern Vietnam the royalist mandarin Phan Dinh
Phung presented a similar argument, but from Vietnamese rather than
Chinese righteousness:

I have concluded that if our country has survived these past thousand years
when its territory was not large, its army not strong, its wealth not great, it was
because the relationships between kings and subjects, fathers and children, have
always been regulated by the five moral obligations. In the past, the Han, the
Sung, the Yuan, the Ming, time and again dreamt of annexing our country and
of dividing it up into prefectures and districts within the Chinese administrative
system. But never were they able to realize their dream. Ah! if even China,
which shares a common border with our territory, and is a thousand times more
powerful than Vietnam, could not rely upon her strength to swallow us, it was
surely because the destiny of our country had been willed by Heaven itself.
Furthermore, the effectiveness of the Classics and of the Rites upon which we
base our behaviour was thereby demonstrated (translated in Truong Buu Lam
1967, 125).

A similar confident determination was being demonstrated at the same
time at the height of Aceh's guerrilla war against the Dutch in northern
Sumatra. At a time (1885) when the Dutch were in serious difficulty
retaining their position, the great Islamic leader of resistance, Teungku Cik
di Tiro, appealed to his weaker follow countrymen:

Do not let yourself be afraid of the strength of the *kafir* [infidels], their fine possessions, their equipment, and their good soldiers, in comparison with our strength, our property, our equipment and the Muslim people, for no-one is strong, no-one is rich, and no-one has fine armies but the great God . . . and no-one gives victory or defeat than God . . . the Lord of the Universe.

For we, his creatures, there is no movement, no peace, no life, no death, no honour, no humiliation, no victory and no defeat, except through the power of God . . . Thus these kafirs too can be overcome according to the promise of God (Zentgraaf 1938, 16–17).

Even the infidels themselves were not outside the scope of God's mercy. Teungku di Tiro appealed to the Dutch Resident in the same strong terms:

Verily, if you were all to accept Islam and follow the law of the prophet, that would be the best thing for you. You would thereby obtain security in this world; you would no longer have to run hither and thither in fear of being killed . . . while the greatest possible disgrace possibly now awaits you through the omnipotence of the Lord of the universe—namely that the [Dutch] *Kompeni* should be forced to leave Aceh altogether, that the soldiers and other servants of the *Kompeni* should be taken captive . . . and all at the hands of the Acehnese muslims, who are poor and weak.

The most serious thing of all that awaits you is however the punishment of the next world, in Hell, according to the law of Almighty God (Zentgraaf 1938, 18–19).[5]

In the event, even such sublime confidence eventually saw defeat staring it in the face. Some felt that the only way they could then keep faith with their convictions was a form of suicide, an implicit acknowledgment that the light by which they had lived and fought no longer corresponded with reality. Those for whom they had felt intellectually responsible would have to find their own new way. Phan Thanh Gian, a southern mandarin at the very centre of Vietnam's encounter with the West, expressed his choice this way:

The French have huge battleships, full of soldiers and armed with powerful cannons. Nobody can resist them . . . I, therefore, wrote to all the civilian and military officials to lay down their arms . . . But, if I have followed Heaven's will in averting calamities from the people's heads, I am a traitor to my King in surrendering without resistance the provinces that belong to him. I deserve death. You, officials and people, you may continue to live under the command of the French—who are ruthless only in battle—but their flag should not fly over a fortress where Phan Thanh Gian still lives

(translated in Truong Buu Lam 1967, 87–8).

Still more dramatic and effective as a release of followers from a heroic but tragically costly resistance was the *puputan* or ritual suicide of the Balinese ruling caste. After a defiant resistance to Dutch invasion the ruling families first of Lombok (1894), and later of South Bali (Badung and Klungkung, 1908), dressed in white and advanced on the Dutch guns to be slaughtered in hundreds—to the last child. The *puputan* was sanctioned by tradition as the honourable end for the defeated *ksatriya*. In this case, it also marked with dramatic suddenness the end of traditionally-inspired resistance to Western domination.

Islamic resistance seldom came to such a sudden and complete end, because moral responsibility for resistance lay squarely on the whole community rather than a military or intellectual elite. In practice, at least in the Malay world, the increasing hopelessness of the struggle caused a shift in the nature of revitalizer appeals from collective to individual salvation.[6] As the war turned against Aceh in the 1890s, the *ulama* who continued to resist abandoned their argument that the faithful would triumph in this world, in favour of depicting the superior advantages of the world to come.

> to die as a *shahid* [martyr] is nothing. It is like being tickled until we fall and
> roll over . . .
> Then comes a heavenly princess,
> Who cradles you in her lap and wipes away the blood,
> Her heart all yours . . .
> If the heavenly princesses were visible,
> everyone would go to fight the Dutch.[7]

This type of appeal from the verse epic, *Hikayat Perang Sabil*, inspired Acehnese attacks on the Dutch which became increasingly individual, desperate, and suicidal as the colonial regime became better established. As late as the Japanese occupation it was still a powerful stimulus to such attacks.

A similar, and roughly contemporary, experience was that of the Tausug and Balanguingui of the Sulu archipelago against first Spanish and then American occupation. In some of the early pitched battles there was heroic and total resistance, like the "scene of horror" described by the Spanish at Balanguingui in 1848, where "The Moros fight like wild beasts . . . piles of corpses, and dark flames devouring the huts. . . . More than 340 bodies are burned to forestall an epidemic" (cited in Costa 1965, 207–8).

One of the few survivors (Camarang) described the mood of sacrifice in the Muslim camp:

The chief Olangcaya therefore said: Let us all bear witness together by our deaths, for now is the appointed end of our faithful observance . . . And Binto replied: My father, there is nothing to hold us back; let us die fighting, and not part company ever again (Costa 1965, 208).

In the first decade of this century the Americans took fort after fort littered with the bodies of desperate Muslim defenders, just as Van Daalen's Dutch expedition did among the Gayo of North Sumatra at the same period and with the same gruesome photographic record (see figure 10). Once American rule was established, Tausug resistance tended to become individual and suicidal, inspired by the same type of salvation literature as the *Hikayat Perang Sabil* (Kiefer 1973, 108–23; Majul 1973, 353–60).

This kind of heroic preference for the next world over this one did not in itself answer the intellectual dilemma. Why was wrong prevailing over right; idolatry over faith? Some of the revitalizers caught in the inevitability of defeat could only conclude that the world was approaching its promised end.

The world is going to end,
The promise of God will be manifest,
The fate that is fore-ordained.

Fig. 10 Dutch documentation of the last stand of Aceh resistance at Benteng Kuto Reh, June 1904. A total of 561 Sumatrans fell in the defence of this fort. (KITLV, Leiden)

Already the heavens are in disorder,
Various signs are clear,
The Dajjal [Anti-Christ] is roaming about the world,
Going hither and thither . . .

Religion is in decline; there are no more blessings,
The world is approaching its end,
The ulama do nothing but think,
And pray over the dead to get a share in the inheritance . . .
Let them roast in Hell
                                   (Hasjmy 1971, 70, 235; my translation)

Thus again the Acehnese *Hikayat Perang Sabil*, which used the argument to urge martyrdom before it was too late. The same argument could however be used by those who abandoned the struggle, to emphasize the impossibility of victory. The Acehnese leaders who submitted to the Dutch in 1903 pointed out to the *ulama* still in the hills that Muslims everywhere were being defeated and humiliated "because the world is in its last phase":

There are many who, like us, all fought before against the Dutch *Kompeni*. But once all options were exhausted and we had no more strength to fight it was right for us to submit to the Kompeni . . .

It is certainly not we who began this practice; on the contrary it has occurred very often above the wind, for example the whole of India has submitted to the rule of the English Kompeni, the Maghrib has all submitted to French rule, and Egypt has allied its government with the English . . . and finally all of those beneath the wind submitted . . .

All of these submitted because they were weak and they feared they would be finished, their religion and their country destroyed. Once they had submitted they could each cultivate their religion, so that not everything was lost (Letter from Pangla Polem, Tuanku Mahmud and Tuanku Raja Keumala in Zentgraaf 1938, 35).

This particular eschatology was of course a Semitic one mediated through Islam, presupposing a linear view of history with a distinct beginning and an approaching end. An older and in some cultures stronger historical perception was cyclical, derived at least in part from the Hindu belief in a succession of periods from the good *Krta-Yuga* to the evil *Kali-Yuga* and back again. That the latter could be used in a similar way to the Islamic argument above, as an explanation of European domination, is demonstrated by the early twentieth century Balinese *Babad Buleleng*:

After some time, as if ordained by God Almighty, as the time of good fortune was complete, the dispensation of the one who regulates the unknown according to the division of the world into periods of years, gave rise to a time in which the world was agitated, when everyone acted in accordance with his own way of thinking and when there were many intrigues against the king. It was fitting that the Dutch ruler, who desired to protect the world, should take his own measures. Subsequently a way was found to punish and exile Ki Gusti Nrurah Ketut Jlantik . . . After that, the Dutch ruler continued as the supreme head of the land of Buleleng. There were no kings any more (translated in Worsley 1972, 205).

MILLENARIANISM

Much has been written on the influence of cyclical views of this type on the propensity for millenarian expectations exhibited by the Javanese in particular. The present evil and disturbed times seemed always about to be replaced by a golden age when

there will be no more conflicts, injustice and suffering; people will be freed from paying burdensome taxes, and performing compulsory services. There will be neither sickness nor theft; there will be abundance of food and clothes; everyone will possess a house; people will live in peace (cited in Kartodirdjo 1973, 8; see also Moertono 1968, 681–2; B. Anderson 1972, 19–22).

There is I think a distinction to be made, however, between the pre-nineteenth century versions of this expectation, which tended to focus on a new ruler or dynasty emerging to unify and strengthen Java; and the versions which followed the assertion of European control in the early nineteenth century. After the Diponegoro war (1825–30) the reality of alien domination could no longer be evaded. The humiliation this entailed could not be explained simply in terms of a changing cycle of Javanese dynasties. The courts which had made their profitable peace with the Dutch gradually ceased to provide a focus for popular expectations, which took on an increasingly millenarian character. No doubt the Islamic linear type of eschatology had an influence on this change of emphasis, but I believe colonialism itself was much more significant.[8]

Millenary hopes appear to have been most at home by the late nineteenth century in those areas which had been longest under European domination, so that the memory of any other state of things had faded to a remote and mysterious "golden age". Though differing in many other respects, Java and

Luzon both shared this predicament. What had to be explained was not
military defeat but a long period of weakness and humiliation. One Filipino
response to this dilemma was the Tagalog folk hero Bernardo Carpio,
imprisoned in a mountain, but ready to stir one day to free his oppressed
people (Ileto 1974, 130–1).[9] During the Philippine revolution Bonifacio's
Katipunan was able to reach Tagalog peasants because it understood and even
shared this popular longing for deliverance. The hope was beautifully put in
this allegory by Emilio Jacinto, which I cite from Rey Ileto's thesis. A
Philippine youth encounters a shadowy stranger, who is disappointed not to
be recognized:

> But I am not surprised, for it has been more than three hundred years since I
> visited your land. It is the will of your people to adore false gods of religion and
> men, your fellow-creatures, that is why my memory has been erased from your
> minds.
>
> . . . I am the origin of all things great, most beautiful and praiseworthy,
> precious and dignified, that is possible for humanity . . . For my cause men
> unite, each one forgetting his selfish interests; seeing nothing but the good of
> all; because of me slaves are rescued and lifted up from the mire of degradation
> and shame, the pride and malice of their cruel masters broken . . . My name is
> Liberty.
>
> In the early days, when the good customs of your ancestors were not sunk in
> cowardice and isolation or imprisonment, the Tagalog . . . people lived in the
> shade of my protection, and in my bosom she was happy and breathed the air
> that gave her life and strength.
>
> . . . But one day, which must be execrated and accursed, Slavery arrived
> saying that she was Virtue and Justice, and promised Glory to all who would
> believe in her . . .
>
> But now your sighs have reached me (translated in Ileto 1974, 112–14).

The Javanese predicament could be approached in similar ways. A text of
the 1870s, *Serat Dermagandul*, represents one type of response which cast
Islam in the invidious role occupied by Spanish Christianity in the quotation
above. As soon as the Majapahit King embraced Islam the Javanese had
ceased to be true men and begun to be ruled by foreigners. The guardian
spirits of Java "retired into concealment" after prophesying that they would
return after four centuries, when the Javanese again abandoned the alien
religion in favour of true knowledge (Drewes 1966, 359–62).[10]

More widespread in Java, however, at least from the late nineteenth
century, were the varied and elaborate prophecies attributed to King
Jayabaya. In one version which assumed written form in the early nineteenth

century, the reader/listener appears to be offered a choice between two prophetic expressions of the present time of darkness. In the first, foreigners come to Java to trade, but make war and divide the kingdom, inaugurating a time of increasing woe:

> The rulers are cruel to their people, who in turn are of an evil nature. Truth is in decline, only lies are spoken . . . The jurisdiction of the ruler is uncertain, wavering, and weak. The taxation he demands is erratic, but always increases . . . Gold and English coins are taken out of the country . . . Where the ruler lives is unclear. His commands bring ruin to the people. In short the government is worthless, it is as though devils ruled (*Serat Jayabaya* paraphrased by Wiselius 1872, 185–6).

This dark period is ended by the coming of the messianic ruler, Si Tanjung Putih, Ratu Adil, or Erucakra, who inaugurates a reign of righteousness, peace, and plenty.

There follows, however, as if offered by a later hand as an alternative scenario, a second period of more explicit foreign rule. The King of Peringgi (the Europeans) takes advantage of Javanese disunity to send a great army and conquer the island.

> This king rules Java tyrannically, and makes his power felt. Once a year he returns to Peringgi . . . This conquest and oppression finally comes to the ear of the exalted king, the bupati of Ngrum [Rum or Rome, identified with Turkey in the nineteenth century but also as the empire of antiquity from which Java was settled]. He is very angry and summons his minister. He says, "Minister, I hear that Java has been conquered by the men of Peringgi . . . Moreover their king has created chaos there, robbing the merchants and taking the inhabitants away to Peringgi as captives, each year 1000 men. Java however is my property (Wiselius 1872, 185–6; see also Brugmans 1960, 143–4; Mataram 1954).

Java is quickly liberated and the Peringgi annihilated by this foreign power, which withdraws after three years in favour of a restored king of Java.

Rural movements against the Dutch in Java were frequently inspired by Jayabaya prophecies, with many claiming to see the messianic *ratu adil* in their midst. In this century the foreign deliverer gained increasing popularity, with Japan gradually replacing Turkey as the major focus of hope.

Like the *Katipunan* leaders, Sukarno understood this popular longing and responded warmly to it:

What is the reason the people are forever believing in and awaiting the coming of the Ratu Adil? What is the reason the words of King Jayabaya still keep people's hopes alight? . . . Only that the heart of the people . . . never ceases to wait for the coming of help . . . Whoever understands the deeper basis for this popular belief . . . will also weep when he hears again and again the lament of the people: when, when will the Ratu Adil come (Sukarno 1956, 75)?

Like the *Katipunan* leaders too, he had enough of the same passion in his own veins to know how to use it for modern purposes. As he explained in 1930, the only way to make Indonesian nationalism a powerful force in the popular mind was to convey a three-stage view of Indonesian history: "the PNI arouses and revitalizes the people's consciousness that they have a 'glorious vanished past'; 'a time of darkness'; and 'the promise of a beckoning, glittering future'" (Sukarno 1956, 118).[11]

THE "BORROWERS"

Most of the above discussion has been limited to the perceptions of the men I have called revitalizers, seeking solutions within their own cultural and religious traditions. From the earliest contacts there have also been some, however, who put greater emphasis on the need to beat the West at its own game—my borrowers. The problem of course has always been what was the West's game? How much of the alien lifestyle had to be borrowed?

The technology of guns and steamships was the obvious outer sign of Western dominance, and was eagerly copied even by many of those who in other respects I would class as revitalizers. All the more significant Southeast Asian monarchs tried to obtain steamships as quickly as possible. Vietnam had them in the 1830s, Siam and Burma in the 1850s; while the subsequent attempts by Aceh and Lombok to purchase and deploy steamers were a source of conflict with the Dutch. The Vietnamese emperor Minh-Mang, mentioned above for keeping the Europeans firmly at arm's length, was foremost in attempting to reproduce the steam engines, building a special factory outside Hue in 1839 for the purpose (Woodside 1971, 283).

The secrets of the steamship proved intractable, and the next generation saw the need to go further. Throughout the nineteenth century, however, while there were still traditional monarchies to be saved, their elites were primarily concerned with a selective borrowing over a short term, to "catch up" with the technological knowledge in which Europe had got ahead. This was still the strategy behind an 1898 plan for sending Siamese students to Europe (Wyatt 1969, 202). As usual this option had already been clearly outlined by an early Vietnamese borrower, Nguyen Truong To, in 1866:

our best strategy now would consist in cutting off a portion of our territory on the frontier area and giving it to the French. They will then defend these frontier regions for us . . .

Then, while our population is enjoying its peace, we will send young students to foreign countries. They shall try to penetrate the secrets of their defenses and attacks, and they shall also study whatever the foreign countries have to teach them regarding technical civilisation . . . We will then accumulate our strength, waiting for the day when we shall go into action. Under these circumstances, we shall be completely sure of recovering in the evening what we lost in the morning (translated in Truong Buu Lam 1967, 90–1).

Greater experience with the West appeared to expose more and more aspects of the Western "secret" that might have to be borrowed. The debate between revitalizers and borrowers continued throughout the colonial period, but its ground shifted in favour of the latter. In the first decades of this century the borrowers were everywhere in full cry, and their opponents were frequently now themselves highly Westernized men trying to rediscover a lost heritage. Among the many specific borrowings which were demanded, two areas appear to demand at least a brief discussion—government reform and education.

REFORM OF GOVERNMENT

The ruling court circles which had either been defeated or co-opted by the Europeans were natural targets for blame by the reformers. A critical anti-monarchic tradition of this type began as early as the first half of the nineteenth century—though from the immunity of the colonial port-cities of Singapore and Batavia, rather than from the "inside". It was businesslike, cosmopolitan, Islamic, and almost as harsh on the "indolence" of Malays and Javanese, especially their rulers, as were the Europeans themselves. The successors of this tradition at the beginning of the twentieth century grouped around the reformist Muslim journal, *Al-Imam*, which Roff portrays indulging in "an orgy of self-vilification and self-condemnation" of Malay society (Roff 1967, 57). *Al-Imam* was particularly hard on the Malay rulers:

They are the seed of all evil and the cause of all distress. They are the great experts in throwing away money, and the kings of foolishness . . . All their wealth is obtained by squeezing blood out of the poor . . . Most of it runs straight back to the pockets of the Europeans.[12]

If the early Malay critics went on to make comparisons with European government, it was naturally with the relative efficiency or predictability of colonial autocracy, not with the inscrutable liberality of representative institutions. In his *Hikayat Mareskalk* written about 1815, Abdullah bin Mohammad al-Misri set out deliberately "to explain the ability and cunning of the white men in organizing their administration and drawing a profit for themselves, in other words stealing in an agreeable way (*merampas dengan manis*)" (Linden 1937, 128). The regime in question was that of Daendels and Janssens in Java, and what impressed Abdullah most about it was its thoroughness and attention to detail, and its ability to exploit everybody without actually driving them away (cited in Linden 1937, 129–33).

The most incisive borrower among Malay writers was however Munshi Abdullah, whose exceptional closeness to and fondness for British rule led him to make a more careful study of it. In his view the arbitrariness of the Malay rajas was the primary cause of the weakness and backwardness of their states. In closing his very critical report of his journey to the east coast of Malaya in 1837–8, he analysed the deficiencies of Malay rule in comparison to that of the British in Singapore as follows:

> Firstly, there is no security in the Malay states for property, person, or anything at all: whereas in English states there is security, in the form of protection from every danger.
>
> Secondly, peace: this exists in English states but not in Malay ones.
>
> Thirdly, in the Malay states the Raja's bondsmen can commit whatever offences they like to God's creatures, because if a Raja's bondsman is killed, seven men are executed in retaliation. Whereas in English states it is not so: if a son of the white ruler or even the ruler himself killed someone unlawfully, he would be sentenced to death.
>
> Further, in the Malay states there are too many people spending day and night in laziness and indolence . . . [The British] encourage hard workers: but in the Malay states the custom is quite different. When someone is seen to become rich, with much property and a good life, one accusation after another is manufactured against him, until he is ruined, his property exhausted, and perhaps his very life taken from him (Kassim Ahmad 1962, 124–5).[13]

Few Southeast Asians of the colonial era were privileged to see the workings of parliamentary democracy in Europe, and fewer still appear to have seen in it the key to European dominance. One group who did were the handful of Siamese aristocrats and princes educated in Europe who advised King Chulalongkorn in 1886 that Siam could only survive the European challenge on the basis of this type of constitutional change. Chulalongkorn, still in the happy position of being able to control the pace of change as an enlightened despot, revealed much of his pragmatic style in his careful reply:

> When I reached my majority I founded the Legislative Council (*Rata Montri*) wherein I became myself the Leader of the Opposition against my own ministers which was why the Council was at first so strong. As the work became more difficult to cope with, the old ministers began to fail; I had to take over more and more responsibility in the executive until I alone am the Government, and without my active support the Council was losing its influence and prestige . . .
>
> That we need in this country a reform of the whole system of government I entirely agree, but then members of an effective legislative council must be independent men. Where are we to find such men? . . . We must first of all see that we can get the right kind of people to be our future legislators, or we are better off without them (translated in Chakrabongse 1960, 262–3).

For Southeast Asians under European colonial rule, who had lost faith in the capacity to lead of the traditional ruling class, European constitutional models generally seemed remote from the real issues. Many nationalists were prepared to campaign for "Indonesia berparlemen", or ministerial responsibility in Burma, but as a short-term tactic rather than a real solution to the problem of foreign domination. More meaningful than these constitutional models was the revolutionary populism of Mazzini, Garibaldi or the Sinn Fein. Since the colonized peoples had no source of power except their numbers, an identification with the masses in some sense or another was inescapable. Populism was one of the meeting grounds of revitalizers and borrowers, and it could also be a transition stage from one to the other. Phan Boi Chau was in such a stage when he penned these lines in 1906:

> Why was our country lost? I submit the following: First the monarch knew nothing of popular affairs; Second the mandarins cared nothing for the people; . . . State matters to the King, other affairs to the mandarins, the people said. Hundreds of thousands, millions together worked To build the foundations of our country. The bodies, the resources are from the people; The people are in fact the country, the country is the people's (translated in Marr 1971, 129).

EDUCATION

The other great item on the agenda of the borrowers, the item most widely shared in the first decades of this century, was education. The earliest borrowers like Munshi Abdullah (1955, 157–9) had already insisted on the importance of education, but the colonial caste system of the twentieth century enormously increased its attractiveness. Those with European education immediately acquired status and a kind of modest power, while the "tutelage" argument of the colonizers could be answered by the growing number of Western-educated lawyers and doctors. Throughout Indonesia in particular it became a cliché for those who enjoyed secondary education that they were the harbingers of a new age, experiencing an unprecedented moment of progress, of "awakening from a long sleep", of "awareness". Those who did not share this confidence, like the Malays who sensed themselves dropping behind in the race, showed no less conviction that education was the answer: "There, and only there, can we find our salvation, there is no other way" (Za'ba 1928, 185).

The earliest enthusiasts for education were emphatically borrowers. As education became universally accepted as part of the solution, however, we begin to discern new lines of demarcation and debate between revitalizers and borrowers. A whole range of fascinating experiments in education began, whereby the "soul" of traditional values would be retained within the shell of modern learning. In Siam the balance was of course defined by the monarchy itself, and a relatively unified educational system was built on the basis of the Buddhist monastic schools. Wyatt professes to hear a "cry of relief" in Chulalongkorn's declaration after his visit to Europe in 1897 that there was a limit to the process of borrowing:

I have convinced myself in Europe of the great benefit which Asiatic nations may derive from the acquisition of European science, [but] I am convinced also that there exists no incompatibility between such acquisition and the maintenance of our individuality as an independent Asiatic nation (translated in Wyatt 1969, 232, 379).

Both Vietnamese Confucianism and Islam could look overseas, to the heartland of these two traditions in China and the Middle East, for legitimation in the borrowing process. After reading the Chinese reformers K'ang Yu-wei and Liang Ch'i-ch'ao, for example, the Vietnamese educational reformer Nguyen Quyen became immensely excited:

The more I read the more I became aware that the things we studied, our examination system, were wrong—indeed the real reasons for our having lost our country. From that point on I was determined to seize upon our country's literature and on modern learning to awaken our citizenry (translated in Marr 1971, 93).

Similarly the great reformist voices in Cairo—Muhammad Abduh and Rashid Rida—encouraged Southeast Asian Muslims to believe that the previous generation had got its "revitalism" wrong. As Hamka put it, the older *ulama* had responded to defeat by "cursing the world altogether, both what was good and what was bad in the world, all of it they looked at with eyes full of hatred" (Hamka 1961, 13). Islamic reformism was the primary example of saying that "revitalism" and "borrowing" were in fact the same thing—that true Islam demanded the most thorough and modern education; the most effective administration and technology.

How much original thought of their own Southeast Asian reformers added to these overseas models it is not my purpose to assess. They do however appear to have felt the dilemma of Western dominance more keenly and more widely than their mentors in Egypt or China. Perhaps the most explicit Islamic discussion of the theme of this essay, Shakieb Arsalan's "Why have the Muslims declined?", was prompted by a letter of enquiry sent to Rashid Rida by an Indonesian *ulama* in West Borneo in the 1920s. The question ran roughly as follows:

> What are the reasons the Muslims are weak and backward—especially the Muslims in Indonesia and Malaya—whether in worldly or religious matters? We Muslims have become the lowliest group, without wealth or strength, whereas God stated in the commands of His Holy Book "that glory will be for God, for His prophet, and for his faithful people" . . .
>
> What are the reasons for the progress of the Europeans, Americans, and Japanese, at such an astonishing rate? Is it possible for the Muslims to achieve the same progress, if the Muslims follow the same steps they have taken without transgressing the bounds of religion, or not? (Sjakieb Arsalan 1954, 6–7)

The answer of Arsalan, echoed by a growing army of reformers throughout Indonesia and Malaysia, was that the Muslims had declined because they had been untrue to their calling, and would rise again by devoting themselves unstintingly and sacrificially to building a revitalized Islamic society—especially through education and study.

Modernist Islam undoubtedly provided one structure within which a great deal of borrowing took place—the paradox of the most Islamic elements in Indonesia being also the most susceptible to western ideas has often been remarked. Others, including those Indonesians on whom Islam rested more lightly, experienced greater difficulty defining the inalienable national "soul" which would remain when the borrowing was done. One example of such an attempt by a Western-educated Javanese nationalist, writing in Dutch, was the following:

What is our [Javanese] national culture? A culture which aims at the intensification of *feeling* (*roso*) to achieve conscious life. What is its summit? To attain [inner] power—the *sabda pandita ratu*. What is the contrary western spirit? That in which *intellect* forms the basis of conscious life . . . What is its summit? Completely to master the skies and the seas through technology. (Soeriokoesoemo 1918, 3)

In the Indonesian intellectual debate of the 1920s and 1930s, this dichotomy became typified as a conflict between Arjuna, hero of the *Mahabharata* and embodiment of the Javanese virtues of calm inner control, and the Western Faust. The new Westernized revitalizers like Soeriokoesoemo tended to place heavy emphasis on this dichotomy, identifying materialism and individualism as the vices of Faust which could only lead Indonesia astray. At an intellectual level the pre-war debate was focused at the first Indonesian congress of education in 1937, which provided a platform for the many educationists who were calling for schooling with more moral, traditional, and "family" character than the Dutch model. Takdir Alisjabahna reacted with a counterblast which proved to be one of the pre-war landmarks of the borrower case:

The negative voice of the Educational Congress -Anti-intellectualism anti-individualism anti-egoism anti-materialism, must be changed into positive, enthusiastic, and fiery slogans:The Indonesian intellect must be sharpened until it resembles the western intellect! The individual must be brought to vigorous life! Consciousness of individual worth must be emphasized to the utmost! Indonesians must be exhorted to accumulate all the material wealth they can (Mihardja 1954, 41–2; see also Alisjabahna 1966, 126–32).

For Takdir no limits could be set to the borrowing; and although at the time nationalist reactions to his challenge were largely negative, it is fair to add that these have tended to weaken with the eclipse of colonialism.

UNITY

Most of the debates and prescriptions we have discussed thus far have been the concern of a fairly narrow elite—the elite which had lost a battle, a country, or a cultural heritage, and was painfully aware of the fact. How widely their feelings were shared by the masses, it is much more difficult to say. It seems reasonable to assume that most became aware of Western domination much more slowly—especially through the imposition by twentieth century colonial bureaucracies of taxes, regulations, and unwanted "welfare" measures, which were easy to connect causally with an experience of increasing poverty.

I have mentioned already government reform and education as two prominent items on the agenda of borrowers. A third popular key to unlock the chains of weakness was unity. The special significance of unity, I believe, was that it was not the property of the borrowers, nor even of the educated elite, but appeared to be a sentiment shared in some way by all sections of Southeast Asian societies. For the true borrowers unity was to be found in the organizational methods of the West, the political parties and modern associations. For the modern revitalizers it meant re-emphasizing a unity of thought or belief. Even modernist Muslims like Agus Salim, for example, were tireless in emphasizing that society would become whole if the Muslims would "hold fast together to the rope of God, without separating" (Salim 1954, 3–4; see also Siegel 1969). For nationalists who were both borrowers and revitalizers the populism mentioned above was a natural attempt to create a unity of the many against the colonial oppressors. Indeed the fact that the alien rulers were few, and the Asians poor but many, was not lost on any section of society.

Among the rural masses of Southeast Asia, however, unity was more than a political weapon. It appeared to be sought as a direct mystical experience of brotherhood, transcending and replacing the vertical allegiances undermined by the colonial process. There has been too little sympathetic attention to the beliefs of what the French called "secret societies" and magical movements in the Mekong delta, to the Saya San rebellion in Lower Burma, the "holy man's rebellion" in northern Siam, and many other manifestations of peasant enthusiasm. The externals do suggest, however, that we may find similar rituals of initiation, oaths of mutual solidarity, and readiness to face death in confidence of victory which we see in some movements of Island Southeast Asia—and indeed much more widely. In the Filipino Katipunan initiates were told to remember "that the way travelled by this Katipunan is the way of unity, mutual caring and mutual *damay* (compassion) that will not perish even unto death . . . the object of our journey is the purest and most immaculate existence that can ever be attained" (Ileto 1974, 127). In diverse areas of Indonesia the rural response to the first decade of Sarekat Islam (c.1912–22) demonstrated the same religious revival, high moral expectations from members and the community at large, and absolute loyalty to other members of the group, who represented both protection and social security to each other (Kartodirdjo 1973, 159). Journals and organizations sprang up with names like "Islam will become one" (*Islam menjadi satu*), "the union of the Indies" (*Hindia Sepakat*), "the equality of the Indies on the march" (*Same rata Hindia bergerak*) and so forth. No slogan was more popular than *sama rasa sama rata*, which could be inadequately rendered as "brotherhood and equality". One such exhortation to *Rasa sama merasa* ("feel as one") went as follows:

> promote a passion for togetherness (*sama-bersama*). Let the force of togetherness be seen. Implement the rationality of togetherness. Take on the thought of togetherness. Use the (secret) knowledge of togetherness. Face the future with togetherness.[14]

A Sarekat Islam political speech in rural Aceh made the point a little differently:

> Formerly we became *muslimin* [Muslims, but used in Aceh for the guerrillas who carried on the Muslim resistance] carrying a rifle, but now that is no longer necessary, now *sepakat* (accord, harmony) is enough. If we are in accord we are already numerous, and whatever we want to achieve will take place; and moreover what the Assistant Resident or Governor want will not take place, because they are simply individuals without numbers. From here as far as Java *sepakat* has been achieved among the descendants of Islam. Whoever does not join rejects brotherhood (*tidak bersaudara*).[15]

The leadership of Sarekat Islam, like elite politicians elsewhere, quickly recoiled from this sort of peasant longing, so prone to transform solidarity into action. It may be only the communist movements of the region that have continued to speak consistently to this popular need for brotherhood and regeneration.

MARXISM

This brings us to the newest and most systematic Southeast Asian explanation for the rise to power of the West—that provided by Marxism through Lenin's *Imperialism—the Last Stage of Capitalism*. The West rose through capitalism, and subordinated Asia to its economic interests through the requirements of that same capitalism. But capitalism was in its last phase, facing collapse from its own internal contradictions. The point I want to stress here is that this basic Marxist formula was influential among a far wider circle of Southeast Asians that members of communist parties, intellectuals with a serious interest in the nature of capitalism, or social revolutionaries. Its attraction lay in the fact that it could be used to provide an answer to the dilemma which is the subject of this lecture; and a promise that Western dominance could be overcome. In the words of Nguyen Khac Vien (n.d., 12):

> the Confucian scholar on the execution block repeated "I die, but I have fulfilled my duty". The militant communist, facing a firing squad, said, "I die, but you will be defeated", and thought, "When the contradictions come to a head, we will be there and we will win."

In their economic, political, and educational programmes the communist parties of Southeast Asia have been arch borrowers, international in spirit and impatient of outmoded values and practices. I do not wish to underrate that factor in their past and present strength in Southeast Asia. I do suggest, however, that wherever they have succeeded in obtaining enthusiastic peasant support in Southeast Asia they have ministered to three requirements discussed above, nearer in spirit to the emphases of the revitalizers, by: 1) their confidence that the problem of Western dominance *can* and *will* be overcome; 2) the intense moral regeneration they have demanded (Nguyen Khac Vien n.d., 15-52); 3) the sense of unity and brotherhood they have transmitted.

***

I hope that the examples of Southeast Asian thinking sketched here have demonstrated the centrality of "the problem of the West" over a considerable period. A few of the responses quoted have suggested resignation to "Heaven's will"—to events taken to be cosmically ordained and therefore inescapable. But the great majority of commentators were not prepared to leave the matter there; in all times and places during the last century the powerlessness of Southeast Asians was seen as an unacceptable aberration which demanded change of one sort or another if it was to be overcome. It was man's fault, and man could not rest until he had identified and corrected that fault.

As perhaps befits a cautious historian I have not continued my story beyond the second world war and the retreat of overt European colonialism from the region. I would not like you to think, however, that this issue is of purely esoteric interest, an historical problem in the psychology of colonized peoples. It is true that the direct racial humiliation which was a feature of colonialism has faded with independence; but independence has also dampened many hopes of quickly "catching up". The economic gap between the industrialized countries and Southeast Asia shows no sign of narrowing, even if the polarization is becoming North-South rather than East-West. Dependence on Western technology, industry, ideas and models grows more rather than less intense. Most serious of all, it grows ever more difficult for the nations of Southeast Asia to think their own thoughts and establish their own priorities, so pervasive are "international" consumption patterns and the international market of ideas. Some countries have sought to minimize these pressures by attempting once again to retreat into relative isolation. Others have allowed or encouraged their elites to join the "international superculture", transforming the gulf into an internal one between these elites and the rural mass. I think, however, we would be unwise to believe the problem has gone away.

NOTES

1. These words were written in the year when American involvement in Vietnam and Cambodia ended.

2. For this attitude in Makasar, see Boxer (1967, 30–1); for Perak, B. Andaya (1975, 30); for Aceh and the reasons for this ban more generally, Reid (1988, I:72–3).

3. Identification of *seberang* (overseas) characters with monsters and demons was natural in the *wayang* context, if only because they did not conform to Javanese norms of refined, restrained conduct. An example of this imagery for Dutchmen in an eighteenth century Javanese text is in Kumar (1969: 412, 550–1). The possibility of an analogy with the *punakawan* is discussed in Ricklefs (1974: 27–9).

4. See also the paraphrase in Praag (1947: 228–34) of a *Serat Achir-ing-jaman*, alternative endings of which have the kings of England, France, Holland and Bengal either perishing in defeat, or accepting the alternative of forced conversion.

5. Though the Dutch East India Company had been dissolved in 1800, the term *Kompeni* remained popular in the Archipelago to designate Dutch authority.

6. The usual doctrinal position is that holy war is *fard 'ala 'l kifaya*, obligatory on the whole community, and not *fardlu' ain*, obligatory for each individual muslim, *Shorter Encyclopedia of Islam*, 89.

7. This is the delightful translation of James Siegel (1969: 76) from a fragment of the *Hikayat Perang Sabil* captured by the Dutch in 1903 and published by Damsté in 1928. The *Hikayat* existed in many versions; the fullest published version to date is that of Hasjmy (1971).

8. Pigeaud (1967, 1: 97, 155–6) discusses this Islamic influence and also the possibility of more ancient messianic tendencies in Java. While Pigeaud seeks the origins of Jayabaya millenarianism (unconvincingly) in the turbulent centuries which preceded the blessings of the nineteenth century *pax Neerlandica*, he confirms that no prophecies of the Jayabaya type have been found in pre-eighteenth century sources. For the association of millenary movements with 'deprivation' and disaster see Thrupp (1970: esp. 26, 32–3, 44–7, 209-14) and Worsley (1970: esp. 233–9).

9. The fact that this particular Tagalog legend was derived from a Spanish model is a reminder that such themes are by no means limited to Southeast Asia. Compare also the sleeping Arthur of Welsh legend (Thrupp: 1970: 207).

10. See also Soeriokoesoemo (1919: 7) in the Java-nationalist *Wederopbouw*: "the beginning of this [foreign] domination was only made possible by the confusion which Islam introduced to the original conception of life of the Javanese people."

11. See Ileto (1974: 118) where an almost identical consciousness of these three stages was demanded of *Katipunan* initiates.

12. Sayyid Shaykh b. Ahmat Al-Hadi in *Al-Imam* II, 1 (July, 1907). I owe this source, in translation, to W. R. Roff.

13. In his autobiography (Hill 1955: esp. 235–40) Abdullah again compares Malay tyranny with British justice, concluding with the cry "God save Queen Victoria".

14. From the lengthy leading article entitled "Sama rasa," in *Hindia-Sepakat* (Sibolga), 2, 2 September 1920.

15. Speech of Abdoelmanap as reported in testimony of Nja'Gam, 23 April 1921, Mailr. 1259^X/21, Netherlands Colonial Archives. I owe this source to James Siegel.

ABBREVIATIONS

ASAA   Asian Studies Association of Australia
BEFEO   Bulletin de l'Ecole Française d'Extréme-orient
BKI   Bijdragen tot de Taal-, Land-, en Volkenkunde, published by the KITLV, Leiden
BSEI   Bulletin de la Société des Etudes Indochinoises
EFEO   Ecole Francaise de Extr?me-orient
EHESS   Ecole des Hautes Etudes en Sciences Sociales, Paris
IOL   India Office Library, London
ISEAS   Institute for Southeast Asian Studies, Singapore
JBRS   Journal of the Burma Research Society
JMBRAS Journal of the Malayan [Malaysian] Branch, Royal Asiatic Society
JRAS   Journal of the Royal Asiatic Society
JSEAH   Journal of Southeast Asian History
JSEAS   Journal of Southeast Asian Studies
KITLV   Koninklijk Instituut voor Taal-, Land-, en Volkenkunde, Leiden
MBRAS   Malaysian Branch, Royal Asiatic Society, Kuala Lumpur
PLPIIS   Pusat Latihan Penelitian Ilmu-ilmu Sosial, Ujung Pandang
RIMA   Review of Indonesian and Malaysian Affairs
TBG   Tijdschrift voor Indische Taal-, Land- en Volkenkunde, published by Koninklijk Bataviaasch Genootschap voor kunsten en Wetenschappen, Batavia.
VBG   Verhandelingen van het Bataviaasch Genootschap
VKI   Verhandelingen van het Koninklijk Instituut
VOC   Vereenigd Oost-Indische Compagnie

BIBLIOGRAPHY

Abdullah, Munshi. 1955. "The Hikayat Abdullah," trans. A. H. Hill. *JMBRAS* 28 (iii).

Abeyasekere, S. 1983. "Slaves in Batavia: Insights from a Slave Register," in Reid 1983a.

Abdurrazak daeng Patunru, 1969. *Sedjarah Goa*. Makassar: Jajasan Kebudajaan Sulawesi Selatan dan Tenggara.

Abendanon, Christian. 1918. *Voyages Géologiques et Géographiques à travers la Célèbes Centrale*. The Hague.

Actes du seminaire sur le Campa organisé à l'université de Copenhague, le 23 mai 1987. Paris: Travaux du centre d'histoire et civilisations de la Péninsule Indochinoise, 1988.

Adas, Michael 1989. *Machines as the Measure of Men. Science, Technology, and Ideologies of Western Dominance*. Ithaca: Cornell University Press.

Adatrechtbundels. 45 vols. The Hague: Nijhoff, 1910–55.

Aeusrivongse, Nidhi. 1978. *Prawatsat rattanakosin nai phraratchaphongsawadan Ayutthaya* [Bangkok history in Ayudhya chronicles]. Bangkok.

———. 1984. *Pak kai lae bai rua: ruam khwam riang wa duai wannakam lae prawatisat ton ratanakosin* [Pen and sail: collected essays on early Bangkok literature and history]. Bangkok.

Albuquerque, Braz de. 1557. *The Commentaries of the Great Afonso Dalboquerque*, trans. W. de Gray Birch. 3 vols. Reprint, London: Hakluyt Society, 1877–1880.

Alfian, T. Ibrahim. 1987. *Perang di Jalan Allah. Perang Aceh 1873–1912*. Jakarta: Sinar Harapan.

Alisjabahna, S. T. 1966. *Indonesia: Social and Cultural Revolution*. Kuala Lumpur: Oxford University Press.

Andaya, Barbara. 1975. "The Nature of the State in Eighteenth Century Perak," in Reid and Castles 1975.

————. 1993. *To Live as Brothers. Southeast Sumatra in the Seventeenth and Eighteenth Centuries.* Honolulu: University of Hawaii Press.

————. 1993a. "Cash-cropping and Upstream/Downstream Tensions: the Case of Jambi in the Seventeenth and Eighteenth Centuries," in Reid 1993c.

Andaya, B. and Virginia Matheson. 1979. "Islamic Thought and Malay Tradition: The Writing of Raja Ali Haji of Riau (ca.1809–ca.1870)," in Reid and Marr 1979.

Andaya, Leonard Y. 1975. "The Nature of Kingship in Bone," in Reid and Castles 1975.

————. 1981. *The Heritage of Arung Palakka. A History of South Sulawesi (Celebes) in the Seventeenth Century.* The Hague: Nijhoff for KITLV.

————. 1993. *The World of Maluku: Eastern Indonesia in the Early Modern Period.* Honolulu: University of Hawaii Press.

Anderson, B. 1972. "The Idea of Power in Javanese Culture," in *Culture and Politics in Indonesia,* ed. Claire Holt. Ithaca: Cornell University Press.

Anderson, John. 1826. *Mission to the East Coast of Sumatra in 1823.* Edinburgh and London: Blackwood. Reprint, Kuala Lumpur, 1971.

Anderson, John 1890. *English Intercourse with Siam in the Seventeenth Century.* London: Trubner. Reprint, Bangkok: Chalermnit, 1981.

Anderson, P. 1978. *Passages from Antiquity to Feudalism.* London: Verso Editions.

Argensola, L. de. 1708. *The Discovery and Conquest of the Molucco and Philippine Islands.* London. Reprint, Ann Arbor, University Microfilms, 1982.

Aung-Thwin, M. 1983. "*Athi, Kyun-Taw, Hpayà-Kyun*: Varieties of Commendation and Dependence in Pre-Colonial Burma," in Reid 1983a.

Aymonier, Etienne. 1891. *Les Tchames et leurs religions.* Paris: Ernest Leroux.

Aziz Ahmad. 1964. *Studies in Islamic Culture in the Indian Environment.* Oxford: Oxford University Press.

Babad Tanah Jawi. Babad Tanah Djawi: Javaanse Rijkskroniek. W. L. Olthof's vertaling van de prozaversie van J.J. Meinsma lopende tot het jaar 1721. Rev. ed. by J. J. Ras. Dordrecht: Foris for KITLV, 1987.

Bachtiar, Harsja. 1967. "Negeri Taram: A Minangkabau Village Community," in *Villages in Indonesia,* ed. Koentjaraningrat. Ithaca: Cornell University Press.

Barbosa, Duarte. 1518. *The Book of Duarte Barbosa. An Account of the Countries Bordering on the Indian Ocean and their Inhabitants,* trans. M. Longworth Dames. 2 vols. Reprint, London: Hakluyt Society, 1918.

Barros, João de. 1563. *Da Asia.* Four decades in 9 vols. Lisbon: Regia Officina, 1777;. Reprint, Lisbon, 1973.

Barrow, J. 1806. *A Voyage to Cochinchina in the Years 1792 and 1793.* London: Cadell and Davies. Reprint, Kuala Lumpur, 1975.

Bassett, D. K. 1958. "English Trade in Celebes, 1613–1667.é *JMBRAS* 31 (i): 1–39.

Beaulieu, Augustin de. 1666. "Memoires du voyage aux Indes Orientales du Général Beaulieu, dressés par luy-mesme," in *Relations de divers voyages curieux, vol II,* ed. Melchisedech Thévenot. Paris: Cramoisy.

Begin ende Voortgang van de Vereenigde Neederlandtsche Geoctroyeerde Oost-Indische

Compagnie, ed. Isaac Commelius. Amsterdam, 1646. Reprint, Amsterdam, 1974.

Bellwood, Peter. 1992. "Southeast Asia before History," in Tarling 1992, 1: 55–136.

Berg, C.C. 1927. "Kidung Sunda. Inleiding, tekst, vertaling en aantekeningen.é *BKI* 83: 1–161.

Berita Penelitian Arkeologi. 1980. "Laporan Penelitian Kepurbakalaan Kerajaan Gowa dan Tallo di Sulawesi Selatan." *BPA* 26, Jakarta: Departemen Pendidikan dan Kebudayaan.

Best, Thomas. 1614. *The Voyage of Thomas Best to the East Indies, 1612–1614,* ed. W. Foster. Reprint, London: Hakluyt Society, 1934.

Beyer, H. Otley. 1979. "The Philippines before Magellan," in *Readings in Philippine Prehistory,* ed. Mauro Garcia. Manila: Filipiniana Book Guild.

Bigalke, T. 1983. "Dynamics of the Torajan Slave Trade in South Sulawesi," in Reid 1983a.

Blair, E. H. and J. A. Robertson, eds. 1903–9. *The Philippine Islands, 1493–1898.* 55 vols. Cleveland: Arthur Clark.

Bloch, M. 1975. *Slavery and Serfdom in the Middle Ages. Selected Essays by Marc Bloch,* trans. W. R. Beer. Berkeley: University of California Press.

Blok, Roelof. 1759. "Beknopte Geschiedenis van het Makassaarsche Celebes en Onderhoorigheden." *Tijdschrift voor Nederlandsche Indie* X (i), 1848.

Blussé, L. 1982. "An Insane Administration and an Unsanitary Town: The Dutch East India Company and Batavia (1619–1799)," in *Colonial Cities,* eds. R. Ross and G. J. Telkamp. The Hague.

———. 1986. *Strange Company. Chinese Settlers, Mestizo Women and the Dutch in VOC Batavia.* Dordrecht: KITLV.

Blust, R. 1978. "Note on PAN *qa (R)(CtT)a, Outsiders, Alien People." *Oceanic Linguistics* XI (ii): 166–71.

Bochier, Francisco dal. 1518. "Referir de Francesco dal Bochier, quando ando in India," in Jean Aubin, "Francisco de Albuquerque: un juif castillan au service de l'Inde Portugaise (1510–1515)." *Arquivos do Centro Cultural Português* VII, 1973: 189-202.

Böeseken, A. J. 1977. *Slaves and Free Blacks at the Cape 1658–1700.* Cape Town: Tafelberg.

Bouchon, Geneviève. 1979. "Les premiers voyages portugais à Pegou (1515–1520)." *Archipel* 18: 127–58.

Bowrey, Thomas. 1680. *A Geographical Account of Countries round the Bay of Bengal,* ed. R. C. Temple. Cambridge: Hakluyt Society, 1905.

Boxer, C. R. 1965. *The Dutch Seaborne Empire 1600–1800.* London: Hutchinson.

———. 1967. *Francis Vieira de Figueiredo: A Portuguese Merchant-Adventurer in South East Asia, 1624–1667.* VKI 52. The Hague: Nijhoff.

Boxer, C. R. and B. P. Groslier. 1958. *Angkor et le Cambodge au XVIe siècle.* Paris: Presse Universitaire de France.

Braudel, Fernand 1972. *The Mediterranean and the Mediterranean World in the Age of Philip II,* trans. S. Reynolds. 2 vols. New York: Harper and Row.

Broecke, P. van den. 1634. *Pieter van den Broecke in Azie,* ed. W. Ph. Coolhaas. 2 vols. The Hague: Nijhoff for Linschoten-Vereniging, 1962–3.

Bronson, B. 1977. "Exchange at the Upstream and Downstream Ends: Notes toward a Functional Model of the Coastal State in Southeast Asia," in *Economic Exchange and Social Interaction in Southeast Asia,* ed. Karl Hutterer. Ann Arbor: Michigan Papers on South and Southeast Asia.

Brooke, J. 1848. *Narrative of Events in Borneo and Celebes down to the Occupation of Labuan,* ed. R. Mundy. London: John Murray.

Brown, C. C., ed. 1952. "Sejarah Melayu or 'Malay Annals': A Translation of Raffles MS 18." *JMBRAS* 25 (ii–iii).

Brugmans, I. J., ed. 1960. *Nederlandsch-Indiè onder Japanse Bezetting: Gegevens en Documenten over de Jaren 1942–1945.* Franeker: Wever.

Burger, D. H. 1956. *Structural Changes in Javanese Society,* trans. Leslie Palmier. Ithaca: Cornell Modern Indonesia Project.

————. 1962. *Sejarah Ekonomis Sosiologis Indonesia.* 3rd ed. Jakarta: Pradnjaparamita.

Calendar of State Papers, Colonial Series, East Indies, China and Japan, ed. W. N. Sainsbury. 5 vols. London: Longman, 1862–92.

Caplan, L. 1980. "Power and Status in South Asian Slavery," in Watson 1980.

Carey, Peter. 1984. "Changing Javanese Perceptions of the Chinese Communities in Central Java." *Indonesia* 37.

————. 1986. "Waiting for the 'Just King': the Agrarian World of South-Central Java from Giyanti (1755) to the Java War (1825–30)." *Modern Asian Studies* 20 (i): 59–138.

Cense, A. A. 1978. "Maleise invloeden in het Oostelijk Deel van de Indonesische Archipel." *BKI* 134 (4): 415–32.

Cense, A. A. and Abdoerrahim. 1979. *Makassaars-Nederlands Woordenboek.* The Hague: Nijhoff for KITLV.

Chabot, H. Th. 1950. *Verwantschap, Stand en Sexe in Zuid-Celebes.* Groningen and Jakarta: J. B. Wolters.

Chakrabongse, Chula. *Lords of Life: The Paternal Monarchy of Bangkok, 1782–1932.* New York: Taplinger.

Chaloemtiarana, Thak, ed. 1978. *Thai Politics: Extracts and Documents 1932–1957.* Vol I. Bangkok: Social Science Association of Thailand.

Chambert-Loir, H. 1987. "Notes sur les relations historiques et littéraires entre Campa et monde malais," in *Actes du seminaire* (see above), 95–106.

Chandra, Satish, ed. 1987. *The Indian Ocean: Explorations in History, Commerce and Politics.* New Delhi: Sage Publications.

Chang, Tsien-tsê. 1969. *Sino-Portuguese Trade, from 1514 to 1644.* Leiden: Brill.

Chaudhuri, K. N. 1985. *Trade and Civilisation in the Indian Ocean. An Economic History from the Rise of Islam to 1750.* Cambridge: Cambridge University Press.

Chaunu, Pierre. 1960. *Les Philippines et le Pacifique des Ibériques (XVIe, XVIIe, XVIIIe siècles): Introduction methodologique et indices d'activité.* Paris: SEVPEN.

Chen, Chingho A. 1974. *Historical Notes on Hôi-An (Faifo).* Carbondale: Southern Illinois University Centre for Vietnamese Studies.

Chirino, P. 1604. *Relacion de las Islas Filipinas,* trans. R. Echevarria. Manila: Historical Conservation Society, 1969.

Cho Ki-jun. 1973. *Han'guk chabonjuui songnip saron* [Discourses on the formative history of Korean capitalism]. Seoul.

Clercq, F. S. A. de. 1890. *Bijdragen tot de kennis der Residentie Ternate.* Leiden: Brill.

Clifford, H. 1897. *In Court and Kampong.* Reprint, London: Richard Press, 1929.

Coedès, Georges. 1951. "Etudes indochinoises." *BSEI* (ns) 26: 437–62.

———. 1968. *The Indianized States of Southeast Asia,* trans. Susan Brown Cowing. Honolulu: East-West Center Press.

Coen, J. P. 1919. *Jan Pieterszoon Coen: bescheiden omtrent zijn bedrijf in Indie. Vol. I,* ed. H. T. Colenbrander. The Hague: Nijhoff.

Cohen Stuart, A. B. 1850. *Geschiedenis van Baron Sakéndhèr.* Batavia.

Comte, M. 1976. "Rapports de classes et relations inter-ethniques dans le Cambodge precolonial." *Asie du Sud-est et Monde Insulindien* 7 (i): 55–90.

Coolhaas, W. Ph., ed. 1960-. *Generale Missiven van Gouverneurs-Generaal en Raden aan Heren XVII der Verenigde Oostindische Compagnie.* 7 vols. to date. The Hague: Nijhoff.

Cortesão, A. 1944. See Pires, 1515.

Costa, H. de la. 1965. *Readings in Philippine History.* Manila: Bookmark.

Coté, J. J. P. 1979. "The Colonization and Schooling of the To Pamona of Central Sulawesi, 1894 to 1924." M.Ed. thesis, Monash University.

Couto, Diego do. 1645. *Da Asia.* Nine decades. Lisbon: Regia Officina Typografica, 1778–88. Reprint, Lisbon, 1974.

Crawcour, E. S. 1961. "The Development of a Credit System in Seventeenth Century Japan." *Journal of Economic History* XXI: 342–60.

———. 1963. "Changes in Japanese Commerce in the Tokugawa Period." *Journal of Asian Studies* XXII.

Crawfurd, J. 1820. *History of the Indian Archipelago.* 3 vols. Edinburgh: Constable.

———. 1828. *Journal of an Embassy to the Courts of Siam and Cochin-China.* London.

———. 1856. *A Descriptive Dictionary of the Indian Islands and Adjacent Countries.* London. Reprint, Kuala Lumpur, 1971.

Creese, Helen. 1991. "Sri Surawiria, Dewa Agung of Klungkung (1722–1736)." *BKI* 147: 402–19.

Cruikshank, B. 1975. "Slavery in Nineteenth Century Siam." *Journal of the Siam Society* 63 (ii).

Cushman, J. W. and A. C. Milner. 1979. "Eighteenth and Nineteenth Century Chinese Accounts of the Malay Peninsula." *JMBRAS* 52 (i): 1–56.

Da San. 1699. *Hai Wai Ji Shi.* Vol. IV. Translated in *Southern Vietnam under the Nguyen,* ed. Li Tana and A. Reid. Singapore: ISEAS, 1993.

Dagh-Register gehouden in 't Casteel Batavia. 31 vols. Batavia and The Hague: Nijhoff, 1887–1931.

Dale, S. n.d. "Trade, Conversion, and the Growth of Islamic Communities." Unpublished paper.

Damais, L. C. 1954. "Etudes Javanaises 1. Les tombes musulmanes datées de Tralaya." *BEFEO* 48.

Dampier, William. 1697. *A New Voyage Round the World*, ed. Sir Albert Gray. London: Argonaut Press, 1927.

———. 1699. *Voyages and Discoveries*. London: Argonaut Press, 1931.

Das Gupta, Ashin and M. N. Pearson, eds. 1987. *India and the Indian Ocean*. Calcutta.

Davis, D. B. 1966. *The Problem of Slavery in Western Culture*. Ithaca: Cornell University Press.

Davis, John. 1905. "Voyage to the Easterne India." In *Hakluytus Posthumus, or Purchase His Pilgrimes*. Vol II. Glasgow: James Maclehose for Hakluyt Society.

Day, Anthony. 1983. "The Drama of Bangun Tapa's Exile in Ambon: The Poetry of Kingship in Surakarta 1830–58," in *Centres, Symbols and Hierarchies*, ed. Lorraine Gesick. New Haven.

Day, C. 1904. *The Policy and Administration of the Dutch in Java*. New York: Macmillan. Reprint, Kuala Lumpur, 1966.

De eerste schipvaart der Nederlanders naar Oost-Indië onder Cornelis de Houtman, ed G. P. Rouffaer and J. W. Ijzerman. 3 vols. The Hague: Linschoten-Vereniging, 1915-29.

"De Handelrelaties." See Noorduyn 1983.

De Hikajat Atjéh, ed Teuku Iskandar. The Hague: Nijhoff for KITLV, 1958.

De tweede schipvaart der Nederlanders naar Oost-Indië onder Jacob Cornelisz van Neck en Wybrant Warwijck, 1598–1600, ed. J. Keuning. The Hague: Nijhoff for Linschoten-Vereeniging, 1942.

Dias, Henrique. 1562. "Voyage and Shipwreck of the Great Ship São Paulo." trans. by C. R. Boxer, in *Further Selection from the Tragic History of the Sea 1559–1565*, C. R. Boxer. Cambridge: Hakluyt Society, 1968.

Diller, A. 1979. "Tension and Risk in Thai Self-Reference." Paper presented to the Conference of Australian Linguistics Society, Newcastle.

Djajadiningrat, Hoesein. 1913. *Critische Beschouwing van de Sadjarah Banten*. Ph.D. thesis, Leiden University. Haarlem: Joh. Enschede.

Donselaar, W. M. 1857. "Aanteekeningen over het eiland Saleijer." *Mededeelingen van wege het Nederlandsche Zendelinggenootschap* I: 277-328.

Douglas, Carstair. 1873. *Chinese-English Dictionary of the Vernacular or Spoken Language of Amoy*. London: Trubner.

Drakard, J. 1990. *A Malay Frontier: Unity and Duality in a Sumatran Kingdom*. Ithaca: Cornell University Southeast Asia Program.

———. 1993. "'A Kingdom of Words': Minangkabau Sovereignty in Sumatran History." Ph.D. thesis, Australian National University.

Drewes, G. W. J. 1966. "The Struggle between Javanism and Islam as Illustrated by the Serat Dermagandul." *BKI* 22 (3).

———. 1968. "New Light on the Coming of Islam to Indonesia." *BKI* 124.

———. 1969. *The Admonitions of Seh Bari*. The Hague: Nijhoff.

———. 1977. *Directions for Travellers on the Mystic Path*. The Hague: Nijhoff.

———. 1978. *An Early Javanese Code of Muslim Ethics*. The Hague: Nijhoff for KITLV.

Dumont, L. 1970. *Homo Hierarchicus: The Caste System and its Implications,* trans. M. Sainsbury. London: Weidenfeld and Nicolson.

Eaton, R. 1978. *Sufis of Bijapur 1300–1700. Social Roles of Sufis in Medieval India.* Princeton University Press.

Edwards, E. D., and C. O. Blagden. 1931. "A Chinese Vocabulary of Malacca Malay Words and Phrases collected between A.D. 1403 and 1511(?)." *Bulletin of the School of Oriental Studies* VI (3): 715–49.

Eerde, J. C. van. 1930. "Investituursteenen in Zuid-Celebes'." *Tijdschrift van het Aardrijkskundig Genootschap,* 813-25.

Emanuel, L. A. 1948. "Memorie van Overgave van den aftredenden Assistant Resident van Bone L.A. Emanuel, 1945–1948." Typescript in Algemene Rijksarchief, The Hague.

Empoli, Giovanni da. 1514. *Lettera de Giovanni da Empoli,* ed. A. Bausani. Rome: Istituto Italiano per il Medio ed Estremo Oriente, 1970, 107–61.

Encyclopaedie van Nederlandsch-Indië. 4 vols. The Hague: Nijhoff: 1895–1905.

Endicott, K. 1970. *An Analysis of Malay Magic.* Oxford: Clarendon.

———. 1983. "The Effects of Slave Raiding on the Aborigines of the Malay Peninsula." In Reid 1983a.

Erkelens, B. 1897. *Geschiedenis van het Rijk Gowa,* VBG 50. Batavia: Albrecht & Co.

Evelyn, John. 1955. *The Diary of John Evelyn. Vol. IV: 1673–1689,* ed. E. S. de Beer. Oxford: Clarendon.

Exemplar literarum ex Indiis. 1571. Rome.

Fairbank, John K., ed. 1968. *The Chinese World Order. Traditional China's Foreign Relations.* Cambridge, Mass.: Harvard University Press.

Farooqi, Naimur Rahman. 1986. "Mughal-Ottoman Relations: A Study of Political and Diplomatic Relations between Mughal India and the Ottoman Empire, 1556–1748." Ph.D. thesis, University of Wisconsin.

Fatimi, S. Q. 1963. *Islam Comes to Malaysia.* Singapore: Malaysian Sociological Research Institute.

Ferreira Flores, Maria da Conceição. 1989. "Mercenaires Portugais au Siam et au Cambodge pendant le XVIe siècle." Unpublished paper presented to Conference on Southeast Asia in the Fifteenth to Eighteenth Centuries, Social Science Research Council and Universitad Nova de Lisbôa, Lisbon.

Finley, M. I. 1968. "Slavery," in *International Encyclopedia of the Social Sciences,* vol. 14: 307–13. Crowell, Collier and Macmillan.

Fogel, R. W. and Engeman, S. L. 1974. *Time on the Cross: The Economics of American Slavery.* London: Woldwood House.

Forth, G. L. 1981. *Rindi: An Ethnographic Study of a Traditional Domain in Eastern Sumba.* The Hague: Nijhoff.

Fredericke, C. 1581. "The Voyage and Travell of Master Cesar Fredericke, Marchant of Venice, into the East India (1581)," in *Hakluyt's Voyages,* Everyman's Library edition, London: Dent, 1907.

Friedericy, M. J. 1929. "De Gowa-Federie." *Adatrechtbundels* 31: 364-401.

Fryke, C. 1692. "A Relation of a Voyage Made to the East Indies," in *Voyages to the*

East Indies, Christopher Fryke and Christopher Schweitzer, ed. C. E. Fayle. London: Casse and Company, 1929.

Fu, Lo-Shu. 1966. *A Documentary Chronicle of Sino-Western Relations.* Tucson: University of Arizona Press.

Galvão, Antonio. 1544. *A Treatise on the Moluccas (c.1544). Probably the Preliminary Version of Antonio Galvão's Lost História das Molucas,* trans. Hubert Jacobs. Rome: Jesuit Historical Institute, 1971.

Garnier, F. 1871. "Chronique Royale du Cambodge." *Journal Asiatique* 6e Serie, 18.

Gerbeau, H. 1979. "Quelques Réflections sur les moyens d'étudier les mouvements de population à travers l'Ocean Indien: Application aux Asiatiques amenés comme esclaves à la Réunion et à Maurice au XIX siècle." Paper presented to International Conference of Indian Ocean Studies.

Gerdin, I. 1981. "The Balinese Sidikara: Ancestors, Kinship, and Rank." *BKI* 137.

Gervaise, N. 1688. *Histoire naturelle et politique du royaume du Siam.* Paris.

———. 1701. *An Historical Description of the Kingdom of Macassar in the East Indies.* London: Tho. Leigh. Reprint, Farnborough, 1971.

Gesick, Lorraine. 1976. "Kingship and Political Integration in Traditional Siam, 1767–1827." Ph.D. thesis, Cornell University.

Goedhard, O. M. 1920a. "De Inlandsche rechtsgemeenschappen in de onderafdeling Takalar." *Adatrechtbundels* 31 (1929): 311–52.

———. 1920b, "De inlandsche rechtsgemeenschappen in de onderafdeling Bonthain'." *Adatrechtbundels* 36 (1933): 155–78.

Goens, Rijklof van. 1956. "De samenvattende geschriften." In *De vijf gezantschapsreizen van Rijklof van Goens naar het hof van Mataram, 1648–1654,* ed. H. J. de Graaf. The Hague: Nijhoff for Linschoten-Vereeniging.

Goudsward, A. 1854. "Brief van den zendeling A. Goudsward, Bonthain, 12 October, 1854." *Mededeelingen van wege het Nederlandsche Zendelinggenootschap* IV (1860): 345–66.

Graaf, H. J. de, ed. 1956, see Goens 1956.

Graaf, H. J. de and Th. G. Th. Pigeaud. 1974. *De eerste moslims vorstendommen op Java: studiën over de staatkundige geschiedenis van de 15de en 16de eeuw.* The Hague: Nijhoff for KITLV.

———. 1984. *Chinese Muslims in Java in the 15th and 16th centuries,* ed. M. C. Ricklefs. Melbourne: Monash University Southeast Asia Monographs.

Groeneveldt, W. P. 1880. *Historical Notes on Indonesia and Malaya, Compiled from Chinese Sources.* Batavia: VBG. Reprint, Jakarta: Bhratara, 1960.

Gubernatis, A. de. 1875. *Storia dei viaggiatori italiani nelle Indie Orientali.* Livorno.

Haan, E. de. 1922. *Oud Batavia.* 3 vols. Batavia: G. Kolff.

Hageman, J. 1859. "Aantekeningen nopens de Industrie, Handel en Nijverheid van Soerabaja." *Tijdschrift voor Nijverheid en Landbouw in Nederlandsch-Indiè,* v.

Hagen, S. van der. 1646. "Beschrijvinghe van de tweede Voyagie ghedaen met 12 Schepen naer d'Oost-Indien onder den Heer Admirael Steven van der Hagen," in *Begin ende Voortgang* (see above) III.

Haji ibn Ahmad, Raja Ali. 1982. *The Precious Gift: Tuhfat al-Nafis,* trans. Virginia Matheson and Barbara Andaya. Kuala Lumpur: Oxford University Press.

Hall, D. G. E. 1950. *Burma*. London: Hutchison.

———. 1955. *A History of Southeast Asia*. London: Macmillan.

Hall, K. R. 1976. "State and Statecraft in Early Sri Vijaya," in *Explorations in Early Southeast Asian History: The Origins of Southeast Asian Statecraft*, ed. K. R. Hall and J. K. Whitmore. Ann Arbor: University of Michigan Center for South and Southeast Asian Studies.

———. 1992. "Economic History of Early Southeast Asia," in Tarling 1992, I: 183–275.

Hamka. 1961. *Pengaruh Muhammad Abduh di Indonesia*. Jakarta: Tintamas.

Hanna, W. A. 1978. *Indonesian Banda: Colonialism and its Aftermath in the Nutmeg Islands*. Philadelphia: Institute for the Study of Human Issues.

Hardouin, E. and W. L. Ritter. 1855. *Java. Toneelen uit het leven*. The Hague: Fuhri.

Hasjmy, A. 1971. *Hikajat Prang Sabil mendjiwai Perang Atjeh lawan Belanda*. Banda Atjeh: Faraby.

Hatta, Mohammad. 1953. "Demokrasi Asli Indonesia den Kedaulatan Rakjat" [Original Indonesian democracy and the sovereignty of the people], in *Kumpulan Karangan* [Collected Works], vol. I. Jakarta: Balai Pustaka.

Hayami, Akira. 1989. "Introduction." In *Economic Development in Rice Producing Societies. Some Aspects of East Asian Economic History 1500–1900*, ed. Akira Hayami and Yoshihiro Tsubouchi. Tokyo.

Hertz, Solange, trans. and ed. 1966. *Rhodes of Vietnam: The Travels and Missions of Father Alexander de Rhodes in China and other Kingdoms of the Orient*. Westminster Md.: Newman Press.

"Hikayat Abdullah." See Abdullah, 1955.

Hikajat Bandjar. A Study in Malay Historiography, ed. J. J. Ras. The Hague: Nijhoff for KITLV, 1968.

Hikayat Hang Tuah, ed. Kassim Ahmad. Kuala Lumpur: Dewan Bahasa dan Pustaka, 1966.

Hikayat Patani: The Story of Patani, eds. A. Teeuw and D. K. Wyatt. 2 vols. The Hague: Nijhoff for KITLV, 1970.

"Hikayat Raja-Raja Pasai: A Revised Romanized Version of Raffles MS 67, together with an English Translation," ed. A. H. Hill. *JMBRAS* 33 (ii): 1961.

Hirth, F. and W. W. Rockhill. 1911. *Chau Ju-Kua: His Work on the Chinese and Arab Trade in the Twelfth and Thirteenth Centuries, entitled Chu-fan-chi*. St Petersburg: Imperial Academy of Sciences. Reprint, Taipei, 1970.

"History of Syriam," trans. J. S. Furnivall. *JBRS* 5 (ii), 1915.

Hoadley, Mason. 1983. "Slavery, Bondage and Dependence in Pre-colonial Java: the Cirebon-Priangan Region, 1700," in Reid 1983a.

———. 1988. "Javanese, Peranakan, and Chinese Elites in Cirebon: Changing Ethnic Boundaries." *Journal of Asian Studies* 47 (3):503–17.

Hooykaas, C. 1976. "Counsel and Advice to the Soul of the Dead." *RIMA* 10 (i).

Houben, V. J. H., H. M. J. Maier and W. van der Molen. 1992. *Looking in Odd Mirrors: The Java Sea*. Leiden: Vakgroep Talen en Culturen van Zuidoost-Azië en Oceanië.

Houtman, Frederick de. 1948. *De oudste reizen van de Zeeuwen naar Oost-Indie 1598–1604*, ed. W. S. Unger. The Hague: Linschoten-Vereniging.

Huntingdon, R., and P. Metcalf. 1979. *Celebrations of Death: The Anthropology of Mortuary Ritual.* Cambridge University Press.

Hutchinson, E. W. 1940. *Adventurers in Siam in the Seventeenth Century.* London: Royal Asiatic Society.

Ileto, R. C. 1974. "*Pasion* and the Interpretation of Change in Tagalog Society (ca. 1840–1912)." Ph.D. thesis, Cornell University.

———. 1979a. "Tagalog Poetry and Image of the Past during the War against Spain," in Reid and Marr 1979.

———. 1979b. *Pasyon and Revolution: Popular Movements in the Philippines, 1840–1900.* Manila: Ateneo de Manila Press.

Innes, R. L. 1980. "The Door Ajar. Japan's Foreign Trade in the Seventeenth Century", Ph.D. thesis, University of Michigan.

"Intercourse between Burma and Siam, as recorded in Hmannan Yazawindawgyi," ed. Phra Phraison, in *Selected Articles from the Siam Society Journal* 5. Bangkok: Siam Society, 1959.

Isa Sulaiman, M. 1979. *Dari Gecong hingga ke Rotary: Perkembangan Usaha Kerajinan Pandai Besi Massepe.* Ujung Pandang: Stencil PLPIIS.

Ishii, Yoneo. 1988. "Roles of Ryukyu in Southeast Asian Trade in the 15th and 16th Centuries." Paper presented at 11th IAHA Conference, Colombo.

———. 1993. "Religious Patterns and Economic Change in Siam in the Sixteenth and Seventeenth Centuries," in Reid 1993c.

———. Forthcoming. *The Junk Trade from Southeast Asia: Translations from the Tosen Fusetsu-gaki, 1674–1723.* Singapore: ISEAS.

Iskandar, T. 1958. See: *De Hikajat Atjeh.*

Itani Zen'ichi. 1928. *Chôsen keizai-shi* [An economic history of Korea]. Tokyo: Osumikaku.

Iwao, Sei'ichi. 1970. "Japanese Emigrants in Batavia during the 17th Century." *Acta Asiatica* 18: 1–25.

———. 1976. *Kaigai koshoshi no shiten* [Views on overseas contacts]. Vol. II. Tokyo, 1976.

Jacobs, H. 1979. "Un règlement de comptes entre Portugais et Javanais dans les mers de l'Indonésie en 1580." *Archipel* 18: 159–73.

Jarric, Pierre du. 1608–14. *Histoire des choses plus memorable advenues tant ez Indes Orientales, que autres pais de la descouverte des Portugais.* 3 vols. Bordeaux: Millanges.

Jessup, Helen. 1990. *Court Arts of Indonesia.* New York: Asia Society Galleries.

Johns, A. H. 1961. "Sufism in Indonesia." *JSEAH* 2 (ii): 10–23.

———. 1965. *The Gift Addressed to the Spirit of the Prophet.* Canberra: Australian National University

Johnston, D. B. 1975. "Rural Society and the Rice Economy in Thailand, 1880–1930." Ph.D. thesis, Yale University.

Jonge, J. K. J. de. 1862-88. *De Opkomst van het Nederlandsch Gezag in Oost-Indië.* Vol 2 of 13. The Hague: Nijhoff.

Jourdain, J. 1905. *The Journal of John Jourdain, 1608–1617*, ed. W. Foster. Cambridge: Hakluyt Society.

Kala, U. 1961. *Mahazawingyi* [Great chronicle], ed. Saya U Khin Soe. Vol III. Rangoon: Hanthawadi Pidakat Ponneik Taik

Kang Man-gil. 1990. "How History is Viewed in the North and in the South: Convergence and Divergence." *Korea Journal* 30 (ii): 4–19.

"Kapitein Malajoe te Makassar." 1920. In *Adatrechtbundels* 31: 110–12.

Kartodirdjo, Sartono. 1973. *Protest Movements in Rural Java.* Kuala Lumpur: Oxford University Press.

Kasetsiri, Charnvit. 1976. *The Rise of Ayudhya. A History of Siam in the Fourteenth and Fifteenth Centuries.* Kuala Lumpur: Oxford University Press.

Kassim Ahmad, ed. 1962. *Kisah Pelayaran Abdullah.* Kuala Lumpur: Oxford University Press.

Kathirithamby-Wells, J. 1969. "Early Singapore and the Inception of a British Administrative Tradition in the Straits Settlements (1819–1832)." *JMBRAS* 62 (ii): 48-73.

———. 1977. *The British West Sumatran Presidency (1760–85): Problems of Early Colonial Enterprise.* Kuala Lumpur: Penerbit Universiti Malaya.

——— and J. Villiers, eds. 1990. *The Southeast Asian Port and Polity: Rise and Demise.* Singapore: Singapore University Press.

Kaut, C. 1961. "*Utang na loob*: a System of Contractual Obligations among Tagalog." *Southwestern Journal of Anthropology* 17: 256–72.

Kawai Hirotami. 1916. "Chôsen ni okeru tôsô no gen'in to so tôji no jôkyô" [Cause of political factional strife in Choson dynasty and socio-political conditions of the period]. *Shigaku zasshi* 27.

Kelly, D, and A. Reid, eds. 1998. *Asian Freedoms: The Idea of Freedom in East and Southeast Asia.* Cambridge: Cambridge University Press.

Kennedy, R. 1953. *Field Notes on Indonesia: South Celebes 1949–1950.* New Haven: Human Relations Area Files.

Kern, R. A. 1939. *Catalogus van de Boegineesche, tot den I La Galigo behoorende handschriften der Leidsche Universiteitsbibliotheken.* Leiden, Universiteitsbibliotheek.

Kiefer, T. M. 1972. *The Tausug: Violence and Law in a Philippine Moslem Society.* New York: Holt, Rinehart and Winston.

———. 1973. "Parrang Sabbil: Ritual Suicide among the Tausug of Jolo." *BKI* 129 (1).

Kipp, R, and S. Rodgers, eds. 1987. *Indonesian Religions in Transition.* Tucson: University of Arizona Press.

Klein, Martin, ed. 1993. *Breaking the Chains: Slavery, Bondage and Emancipation in Modern Africa and Asia.* Madison: University of Wisconsin Press.

Kobata, Atsushi and Mitsugo Matsuda. 1969. *Ryukyuan Relations with Korea and South Sea Countries.* Kyoto: Atsushi Kobata.

Kock, V. de. 1971. *Those in Bondage. An Account of the Life of the Slave at the Cape in the Days of the Dutch East India Company.* 2nd ed. Port Washington, N.Y.: Kennikat.

Koenig, William. 1990. *The Burmese Polity, 1752–1819: Politics, Administration and Social Organization in the Early Konbaung Period.* Ann Arbor: University of Michigan South and Southeast Asian Studies.

Koentjaraningrat. 1974. *Kebudayaan, Mentaliteit, dan Pembangunan* [Culture, mentality, and development]. Jakarta: Gramedia.

Kooreman, P. J. 1883. "De feitelijke toestand in het gouvernementsgebied van Celebes en onderhoorigheden." *Indische Gids* V (1).

Koubi, J. 1975. "La première fête funeraire chez les Toraja Sa'dan." *Archipel* 10.

Kraan, Alfons van der. 1980. *Lombok: Conquest, Colonization and Underdevelopment, 1870–1940.* Singapore: Heinemann for ASAA.

———. 1983. "Bali: Slavery and Slave Trade," in Reid 1983a.

———. 1992. "Bali and Lombok in the World Economy." Paper presented at the Conference on Island Southeast Asia and the World Economy. ECHOSEA Project, Australian National University, November.

Krucq, K. C. 1941. "De geschiedenis van het heilig kanon van Makassar." *TBG* 81: 74–95.

Kruyt, A. C. 1911. "De Slavernij in Posso (Midden-Celebes)." *Onze Eeuw* 11: 61–97.

———. 1938. *De West Toradjas op Midden-Celebes.* 4 vols. Amsterdam: Koninklijk Nederlandsche Akademie van Wetenschap.

Kulke, Hermann. 1986. "The Early and Imperial Kingdom in Southeast Asian History," in Marr and Milner 1986.

Kumar, Anne. 1969. "Surapati: Portraits of a Hero in Javanese Babad Literature." Ph.D. thesis, Australian National University.

———. 1976. *Surapati: Man and Legend. A Study of Three Babad Traditions.* Leiden: Brill.

———. 1979. "Javanese Historiography in and of the 'Colonial Period': A Case Study," in Reid and Marr 1979.

———. 1980. "Javanese Court Society and Politics in the Late Eighteenth Century: the Record of a Lady Soldier." *Indonesia* 29: 1–46; 30: 67–111.

———. 1985. *The Diary of a Javanese Muslim. Religion, Politics and the Pesantren, 1883–1886.* Canberra: Australian National University, Faculty of Asian Studies.

———. 1997. "Java: A Self-Critical Examination of the Nation and its History." In Reid 1997.

Lafont, P.-B. 1987. "Aperçu sur les relations entre le Campa et l'Asie du Sud-Est," in *Actes du seminaire* (see above), 71–82.

La Loubère, Simon de. 1691. *A New Historical Relation of the Kingdom of Siam.* London: Tho. Horne. Reprint, Kuala Lumpur: Oxford University Press, 1969.

Lane, F. C. 1973. *Venice: A Maritime Republic.* Baltimore: John Hopkins University Press.

Lasker, B. 1950. *Human Bondage in Southeast Asia.* Chapel Hill: University of North Carolina Press.

Le Roux, C. C. F. M. 1935. "Boegineesche Zeekaarten van der Indische Archipel." *Tijdschrift van het Aardrijkskundige Genootschap*, 687–714.

Le Thanh Khoi. 1989. *Histoire du Vietnam des origines à 1858.* Paris: Sudestasie.

Leach, E. R. 1965. *Political Systems of Highland Burma. A Study of Kachin Social Structure.* Boston: Beacon Press.

Lee, Ki-baik. 1967. *A New History of Korea.* Revised 1967 edition, trans. Edward Wagner. Cambridge Mass: Harvard University Press, 1984.

Lennon, W. C. 1908. "Journal of an Expedition to the Molucca Islands under the Command of Admiral Rainier," ed. J. E. Heeres. *BKI* 60: 249–366.

Letters Received by the East India Company from its Servants in the East, 1896–1902, ed. F. C. Danvers. 6 vols. London: Sampson, Low Marston.

Lettres edifiantes et curieuses, écrites des missions etrangères. 1781. Paris: Merigot.

Leur, J. C. van. 1934. "On Early Asian Trade," trans. J. S. Holmes and A. van Marle, in van Leur 1955.

———. 1955. *Indonesian Trade and Society: Essays in Asian Social and Economic History.* The Hague: Van Hoeve.

Li Tana. 1992. "'The Inner Region': A Social and Economic History of Nguyen Vietnam in the Seventeenth and Eighteenth Centuries." Ph.D. thesis, Australian National University.

Liaw Yock Fang. 1976. *Undang-undang Melaka. The Laws of Melaka.* Bibliotheca Indonesica 13. The Hague: Nijhoff for KITLV.

Lieberman, Victor. 1980. "Europeans, Trade, and the Unification of Burma, c.1540–1620." *Oriens Extremus* 27 (ii).

———. 1986. "How Reliable is U Kala's Burmese Chronicle? Some New Comparisons." *JSEAS* 17 (ii).

———. 1990. "Wallerstein's System and the International Context of Early Modern Southeast Asian History." *Journal of Asian History* XXIV.

———. 1991. "Secular Trends in Burmese Economic History, c. 1350–1830." *Modern Asian Studies* 25 (i): 1–31.

———. 1993. "Was the Seventeenth Century a Watershed in Burmese History?" in Reid 1993c.

———. 1997. "Mainland-Archipelagic Parallels and Contrasts, c.1750–1850," in Reid 1997.

Ligtvoet, A. 1880. "Transcriptie van het dagboek der vorsten van Gowa en Tello, met vertaling en aanteekeningen." *BKI* 4:1–259.

Linden, A. L. V. L. van der. 1937. *De Europeaan in de Maleische Literatuur.* Meppel: Ten Brink.

Lodewycksz, Willem. 1598. "D'eerste Boeck: Historie van Indien vaer inne verhaelt is de avontueren die de Hollandtsche schepen bejeghent zijn," in *De eerste schipvaart* (see above).

Loeb, E. M. 1935. *Sumatra: Its History and People.* Vienna: Institut für Völkerkunde.

Loh Fook Seng, P. 1969. *The Malay States 1877–1896: Political Change and Social Policy.* Singapore: Oxford University Press.

Lombard, Denys. 1970. *Le "Spraeck ende Woord-Boeké de Frederick de Houtman. Première méthode de malais parlé (fin du XVIe s).* Paris: EFEO.

———. 1981. "Campa Dipandang dari Selatan." In *Kerajaan Campa,* ed. EFEO. Jakarta, Balai Pustaka, 285–95.

————. 1990. *Le carrefour javanais: essai d'histoire globale.* 3 vols. Paris: EHESS.

Lombard, D. and Jean Aubin, eds., 1988. *Marchands et hommes d'affaires asiatiques dans l'Océan Indien et la Mer de Chine 13e–20e siècles.* Paris: EHESS.

Luro, E. 1878. *Le Pays d'Annam: Etude sur l'organisation politique et sociale des Annamites.* 2nd ed. Paris, 1897.

Lyman, H. 1856. *The Martyr of Sumatra: A Memoir of Henry Lyman.* New York: Robert Carter and Brothers.

Ma Huan. 1433. "Ying-yai Sheng-lan [The overall survey of the ocean's shores]," in *Ying-yai Sheng-lan: "The Overall Survey of the Ocean's Shores,"* ed. J. V. G. Mills. Cambridge: Hakluyt Society, 1970.

Mabbett, Ian. 1986. "Buddhism in Champa," in Marr and Milner 1986.

Mac Duong, ed. 1992. *Chung van de van hoa xa hoi Thoi Nguyen* [Cultural and social issues of the Nguyen period]. Ho Chi Minh City.

Major, R. H., ed. 1857. *India in the Fifteenth Century.* London: Hakluyt Society.

Majul, C. A. 1973. *Muslims in the Philippines.* Quezon City: University of Philippines Press.

"Makassaarsche Historiën." 1855. *TBG* 4: 111–45.

Manguin, Pierre-Yves. 1979. "L'Introduction de l'Islam au Campa." *BEFEO* 66: 255–69.

————. 1980. "The Southeast Asian Ship: An Historical Approach." *JSEAS,* XI (2): 266–76.

————. 1983. "Manpower and Labor Categories in Early Sixteenth Century Malacca," in Reid 1983a.

————. 1984. "Relationship and Cross-influences between Southeast Asian and Chinese Shipbuilding Traditions." *Final Report, SPAFA Consultative Workshop on Maritime Shipping and Trade Networks in Southeast Asia.* Bangkok: Southeast Asian Ministers of Education Organization Special Project on Archeology and Fine Art.

————. 1985. "Late Mediaeval Asian Shipbuilding in the Indian Ocean: A Reappraisal." *Moyen Orient et Océan Indien* II (2): 1–30.

————. 1993. "The Vanishing *Jong:* Insular Southeast Asian Fleets in Trade and War (Fifteenth to Seventeenth Centuries)," in Reid 1993c.

Mantegazza, G. M. 1784. *La Birmanie.* Rome: Ed. A.S.

Manusama, Z. J. 1977. "Hikayat Tanah Hitu." M.A. thesis, University of Leiden.

Marr, D. 1971. *Vietnamese Anti-colonialism.* Berkeley: University of California Press.

Marr, D. and A. C. Milner, eds. 1986. *Southeast Asia in the 9th to 14th Centuries.* Singapore: ISEAS.

Marsden, William. 1811. *The History of Sumatra.* 3rd ed. London. Reprint, Kuala Lumpur: Oxford University Press, 1960.

————. 1812. *A Dictionary and Grammar of the Malayan Language.* 2 vols. London. Reprint, Singapore: Oxford University Press, 1984.

Maruzi, M. 1981. "Persamaan Hak dan Perimbangan Jasa: Studi Kasus tentang pola pewarisan tanah di kalangan masyarakat Bugis Desa Ompo, Kabupaten Dati II Soppeng." Ujung Pandang: Stencil PLPIIS.

Masselman, George. 1963. *The Cradle of Colonialism*. New Haven: Yale University Press.

Mataram, T. 1954. *Peranan Ramalan Djojobojo dalam revolusi kita*. Bandung: Masa Baru.

Matelief, Cornelis. 1608. "Historische verhael vande treffelijcke reyse, gedaen naer de Oost-Indien ende China," in *Begin ende Voortgang* (see above).

Matheson, V., and M. B. Hooker. 1983. "Slavery in the Malay Texts: Categories of Dependency and Compensation," in Reid 1983a.

Matthes, B. F. 1875. *Korte Verslag aangaande alle mij in Europa bekende Makassaarsche en Boeginesche Handschriften, vooral die van het Nederlandsch Bijbelgenootschap te Amsterdam*. Amsterdam: C. A. Spin.

――――. 1943. *Dr Benjamin Frederick Matthes: zijn leven en arbeid in dienst van het Nederlandsche Bijbelgenootschap*, ed. H. van den Brink. Amsterdam: Nederlandsche Bijbelgenootschap.

McDermott, J. P. 1981. "Bondservants in the T'ai-hu Basin During the Late Ming: A Case of Mistaken Identities." *Journal of Asian Studies* 40 (iv): 675–701.

Meersman, A. 1967. *The Franciscans in the Indonesien Archipelago, 1300–1775*. Louvain: Nauwelaerts.

Meilink-Roelofsz, M. A. P. 1969. *Asian Trade and European Influence in the Indonesian Archipelago between 1500 and about 1630*. The Hague: Nijhoff.

Metcalf, P. 1982. *A Borneo Journey into Death: Berawan Eschatology from its Rituals*. Philadelphia: University of Pennsylvania Press.

Meyer Ranneft, J. W. 1929. "The Economic Structure of Java," in *The Effect of Western Influence on Native Civilisations in the Malay Archipelago*, ed. B. Schrieke. Batavia: G. Kolff.

Miers, S. and I. Kopytoff, eds. 1977. *Slavery in Africa: Historical and Anthropological Perspectives*. Madison: University of Wisconsin Press.

Mihardja, Achdiat L., ed. 1954. *Polemik Kebudajaan*. Jakarta: Balai Pustaka.

Milburn, William. 1813. *Oriental Commerce, or the East India Traders Complete Guide*. 2 vols, London. Revised edition, London: Kingsbury, Parbury & Allen, 1825.

Miles, D. 1966. "Shamanism and the Conversion of the Ngadju Dayaks." *Oceania* 37 (i).

――――. 1972. "Yao Bride-Exchange, Matrifiliation and Adoption." *BKI* 128: 99–127.

――――. 1976. *Cutlass and Crescent Moon: A Case Study in Social and Political Change in Outer Indonesia*. Sydney: University of Sydney Centre of Asian Studies.

Mills, J. V. G. 1979. "Chinese Navigators in Insulinde about 1500 A.D." *Archipel* 18: 69–94.

――――. 1970. See Ma Huan 1433.

Mills, R. F. 1975. "The Reconstruction of Proto-South-Sulawesi." *Archipel* 10: 205–24.

Ming Shi Lu Chong Zhi Dong Nan Ya Shi Lao [Southeast Asia in Ming dynastic chronicles], ed. Zhao Ling Yang et al. 2 vols. Hong Kong: Hsuehtsin Press, 1968.

Moertono, Soemarsaid. 1968. *State and Statecraft in Old Java: A Study of the Later Mataram Period, Sixteenth to Nineteenth Century.* Ithaca: Cornell Modern Indonesia Project.

Montesquieu, Baron de. 1949. *The Spirit of the Laws,* trans. T. Nugent. New York: Hafner.

Morga, Antonio de. 1609. *Sucesos de las Islas Filipinas,* trans. J. S. Cummins. Cambridge: Hakluyt Society, 1971.

Morgan, E. S. 1975. *American Slavery—American Freedom: The Ordeal of Colonial Virginia.* New York: W. W. Norton.

Morris-Suzuki, Tessa. 1993. "Rewriting History: Civilization Theory in Contemporary Japan." *Positions: East Asian Cultures Critique* I (2): 526–49.

Motomitsu, U. 1978. "The Leaving of this Transient World: a Study of Iban Eschatology and Mortuary Practice." Ph.D. thesis, Australian National University.

Mouhot, Henri. 1864. *Travels in the Central Parts of Indo-China (Siam), Cambodia, and Laos, during the Years 1858, 1859, and 1860.* 2 vols. London: John Murray. RReprint, Bangkok: White Lotus, 1986.

Muller, H., ed. 1917. *De Ooost-Indische Compagnie in Cambodja en Laos. Verzameling van bescheiden van 1636 tot 1670.* The Hague: Nijhoff for Linschoten Vereeniging.

Myo Myint. 1987. "The Politics of Survival in Burma: Diplomacy and Statecraft in the Reign of King Mindon, 1853–1878." Ph.D. thesis, Cornell University.

Nagtegaal, Lucas. 1988. "Rijden op een Hollandse Tijger: De noordkust van Java en de V.O.C. 1680–1743." Ph. D. thesis, University of Utrecht.

Naguib al-Attas, Syed. 1970. *The Mysticism of Hamzah Fansuri.* Kuala Lumpur: University of Malaya Press.

Navarrete, D. 1962. *The Travels and Controversies of Friar Domingo Navarrete, 1618–1686,* ed. J. S. Cummins. 2 vols. Cambridge: Hakluyt Society.

Nederlandsch-Indisch Plakaatboek, 1602–1811, ed. J. A. van der Chijs (Batavia: Landsdrukkerij, 1885).

Netscher, E. and J. A. van der Chijs. 1864. *De munten van Nederlandsche-Indiè.* Batavia: Bataviaasch Genootschap.

Ng Chin Keong. 1991. "The Case of Ch'en I-lao: Maritime Trade and Overseas Chinese in Ch'ing Policies, 1717–1754," in Ptak and Rothermund 1991.

Nguyen Dinh Dau. 1991. "Remarques préliminaires sur les registres cadastraux (*dia ba*) des six provinces de la Cochinchine (Nam Ky Luc Tinh)." *BEFEO* 78.

Nguyen Duc Nghinh. 1974. "Tinh hinh phan phoi ruong dat o xa Mac Xa giua hai thoi diem (1789–1805)." *Nghien Cuu Lich Su* 161. Translated as "La préponderance des propriétaires moyens à Mac Xa entre 1789 et 1805," in *Propriété privée et propriété collective dans l'ancien Vietnam,* trans. G. Boudarel, Lydie Prin and Vu Can. Paris: Harmattan, 1987.

———. 1980. "Land Distribution in Tu Liem District according to the Land Registers." *Vietnamese Studies* (Hanoi) 61: 164-87.

Nguyen Khac Vien. n.d. [1974]. *Tradition and Revolution in Vietnam.* Berkeley: Indo-China Resource Center.

————. 1987. *Vietnam: une longue histoire.* Hanoi: Foreign Languages Publishing House.

Nieboer, H. J. 1910. *Slavery as an Industrial System. Ethnological Researches.* 2nd ed. The Hague: Nijhoff.

Nieuhoff, J. 1934. "Voyage to the East Indies," in *Seventeenth Century Visitors to the Malay Peninsula,* ed. J. J. Sheehan. *JMBRAS* 12 (ii): 71–107.

Nieuwenhuijze, C. A. O. van. 1945. "Samsu'l-din van Pasai." Ph.D. thesis, University of Leiden: Brill.

Nimmo, H. Arlo. 1972. *The Sea People of Sulu.* San Fransisco: Chandler.

Noorduyn, J. N. 1955. *Een achttiende-eenwse kroniek van Wadjo': Buginese historiografie.* The Hague: H. L. Smits.

————. 1956.   çDe Islamisering van Makasar." *BKI* 112: 247–66.

————. 1965. "Origins of South Celebes Historical Writing," in *An Introduction to Indonesian Historiography,* ed. Soedjatmoko et al. Ithaca: Cornell University Press.

————. 1972. "Arung Singkang (1700–1765): How the Victory of Wadjo' Began." *Indonesia* 13: 61–68.

————. 1978. "Majapahit in the Fourteenth Century." *BKI* 134: 207–74.

————. 1983. "De Handelsrelaties van het Makassaarse Rijk volgens de Notitie van Cornelis Speelman (1669)." *Nederlandse Historische Bronnen.* Vol. 3. The Hague: Nijhoff.

Nooy-Palm, Hetty. 1979. *The Sa'dan Toraja: A Study of their Social Life and Religion.* VKI 87. The Hague: Nijhoff.

Novena, A. 1982. "Tradition and Catholicism: Prayer and Prayer Groups among the Sikkanese of Flores." B.Lit. thesis, Australian National University.

Nowell, C. E., ed. 1962. *Magellan's Voyage around the World: Three Contemporary Accounts.* Evanston: Northwestern University Press.

Nuru'd-din ar-Raniri. See Raniri.

O'Kane, J., ed. 1972. *The Ship of Sulaiman.* London: Routledge and Kegan Paul.

Onghokham. 1976. "The Residency of Madiun. Priyayi and Peasant in the Nineteenth Century." Ph.D. thesis, Yale University.

Palleson, A. Kemp. 1978. "The Pepet in Sama-Bajaw." *Pacific Linguistics* C-45: 115–33.

Parker, Geoffrey. 1988. *The Military Revolution: Military Innovation and the Rise of the West, 1500–1800.* Cambridge: Cambridge University Press.

Parliamentary Papers, House of Commons. 1830. *First Report from the Select Committee on the Affairs of the East India Company (China Trade).*

Parmentier. 1883. *Le discours de la navigation de Jean et Raoul Parmentier de Dieppe.* Paris: Ernest Leroux.

Pastells, P., ed. 1925–33. *Catalogo de los documentor relativos a las Islas Filipinas, existentes en el Archivo de Indias de Sevilla,* by Pedro de Torres y Lanzas. 8 vols. Barcelona: Compania General de Tobacos de Filipinas.

Patterson, O. 1991. *Freedom in the Making of Western Culture.* New York: Basic Books.

Pelras, J. C. 1971. "Hiérarchie et pouvoir traditionnels en pays Wajo' (Celebes)." *Archipel* 1: 169–91; 2: 197–223.

———. 1972. "Notes sur quelques populations aquatiques de l'archipel nusantarien." *Archipel* 3: 133–68.

———. 1975. "Guide ùArchipelû II: la province de Célèbes-Sud." *Archipel* 10: 11–52.

———. 1977. "Les premières données occidentales concernant Célèbes-Sud." *BKI* 133: 227–60.

———. 1989. "Célèbes-Sud avant l'Islam, selon les premiers témoignages étrangers." *Archipel* 21: 153–84.

Pfister, J. 1972. "Compulsions to Engage in War . . . in an Early Modern Period of Mainland Southeast Asian History." Ph.D. thesis, University of Michigan.

Phan Huy Le et al. 1961. *Lich Su Che Do Phong Kien Viet-Nam* [History of the Vietnamese feudal system]. 3 vols. Hanoi.

Phelan, J. L. 1959. *The Hispanization of the Philippines: Spanish Aims and Filipino Responses, 1565–1700.* Madison: University of Wisconsin Press.

Pigafetta, Antonio. 1524. *First Voyage Round the World,* trans. J. A. Robertson. Manila: Filipiniana Book Guild, 1969.

———. 1972. *L'Indonesia nella relazione di viaggio di Antonio Pigafetta,* ed. A. Bausani. Roma: Istituto Italiano per il Medio ed Estreme Oriente.

Pigeaud, Th. G. Th. 1960–3. *Java in the Fourteenth Century. A Study in Cultural History.* 4 vols. The Hague: Nijhoff for KITLV.

———. 1967–8. *Literature of Java.* 3 vols. The Hague: Nijhoff for KITLV.

Pijper, G. F. 1934. *Fragmenta Islamica.* Leiden: Brill.

Pinto, Fernão Mendes. 1614. *The Voyages and Adventures of Ferdinand Mendes Pinto, the Portuguese, Done into English by H. Cogan.* London: H. Cogan, 1891.

———. 1578. *The Travels of Mendes Pinto,* trans. Rebecca Catz. Chicago: University of Chicago Press, 1989.

Pires, Tomé. 1515. *The Suma Oriental of Tomé Pires,* trans. A. Cortesão. 2 vols. London: Hakluyt Society, 1944.

Polo, Marco. 1298. *The Travels of Marco Polo,* trans. R. E. Latham. Harmondsworth: Penguin, 1958.

Pombejra, Dhiravat na. 1993. "Ayutthaya at the End of the Seventeenth Century: Was there a Shift to Isolation?é in Reid 1993c.

———. 1994. "Western Evidence Concerning the Role of Chinese at the Siamese Court, 1699–1734." Paper presented to the 13th IAHA Conference, Tokyo, September.

Ponchaud, F. 1990. *The Cathedral of the Rice Paddy: 450 Years of the Church in Cambodia.* Paris: Fayard.

Praag, S. van. 1947. *Onrust op Java.* Amsterdam: Nederlandsche Keurboekerij.

Pramoj, Seni, and Kukrit Pramoj, eds. 1958. *A King of Siam Speaks.* Bangkok: Asia Foundation.

Promboon, Suebsang. 1971. "Sino-Siamese Tributary Relations, 1282–1853." Ph.D. thesis, University of Michigan.

Ptak, Roderich and Dietmar Rothermund, eds. 1991. *Emporia, Commodities and Entrepreneurs in Asian Maritime Trade, c. 1400–1750*. Stuttgart: Franz Steiner Verlag.

Pyrard, Francis. 1619. *The Voyage of Francis Pyrard of Laval to the East Indies, the Maldives, the Moluccas, and Brazil*, trans. A. Gray. 2 vols. London: Hakluyt Society, 1887-89.

Raben, Remco. 1996. "Batavia and Colombo. The Ethnic and Spatial Order of Two Colonial Cities, 1600–1800." Ph.D. thesis, University of Leiden.

Rabibhadana, Akin. 1969. *The Organization of Thai Society in the Early Bangkok Period, 1792–1873*. Ithaca: Cornell University Southeast Asia Program.

Rafael, V. 1988. *Contracting Colonialism. Translation and Christian Conversion in Tagalog Society under early Spanish Rule*. Ithaca: Cornell University Press.

Raffles, T. S. 1817. *The History of Java*. 2 vols. London: Black, Parbury & Allen and John Murray. Reprint, Kuala Lumpur: Oxford University Press, 1965, 1978.

———. 1835. *Memoir of the Life and Public Services of Sir Thomas Stamford Raffles, by his Widow*. 2 vols. London: James Duncan.

Rahim, A. and S. Ridwan, eds. 1975. *Sedjarah Kerajaan Tallo' (Suatu Transkripsi Lontara')*. Ujung Pandang: Lembaga Sejarah den Anthropologi.

Raniri, Nuru'd-din ar-. c.1644. *Bustan as-Salatin, Bab II, Fasal 13*. ed. Teuku Iskandar. Kuala Lumpur: Dewan Bahasa dan Pustaka, 1966.

Records of the Relations between Siam and Foreign Countries in the 17th Century. 1915–16. 2 vols. Bangkok: Vajiranana National Library.

Reid, Anthony. 1969a. "Sixteenth Century Turkish Influence in Western Indonesia." *JSEAH* 10 (iii): 395–414.

———. 1969b. *The Contest for North Sumatra: Atjeh, the Netherlands, and Britain, 1858–1894*. Kuala Lumpur: Oxford University Press and University of Malaya Press.

———. 1973. "The French in Sumatra and the Malay World." *BKI* 129: 195-238.

———. 1979 "Trade and State Power in Sixteenth and Seventeenth Century Southeast Asia." *Proceedings Seventh IAHA Conference*, Bangkok 22-26 August 1977, I: 391–420.

———. 1980. "The Structure of Cities in Southeast Asia, Fifteenth to Seventeenth Centuries." *JSEAS* XI (2): 235–50.

———. 1982. *Europe and Southeast Asia: The Military Balance*. Townsville: James Cook University Southeast Asian Studies Committee.

———., ed. 1983a. *Slavery, Bondage and Dependency in Southeast Asia*. St Lucia: University of Queensland Press.

———. 1983b. "'Closed' and 'Open' Slave Systems in Pre-Colonial Southeast Asia," in Reid 1983a.

———. 1988. *Southeast Asia in the Age of Commerce 1450–1680. Vol. I: The Lands Below the Winds*. New Haven: Yale University Press.

———. 1990a. "An 'Age of Commerce' in Southeast Asian History?" *Modern Asian Studies* 24 (i): 1–30.

———. 1990b. "The Seventeenth Century Crisis in Southeast Asia." *Modern Asian Studies* 24 (iv).

————. 1993a. *Southeast Asia in the Age of Commerce, Vol. II: Expansion and Crisis.* New Haven: Yale University Press.

————. 1993b. "The Unthreatening Alternative: Chinese Shipping in Southeast Asia, 1567–1842." *Review of Indonesian and Malaysian Affairs* 27: 13–32.

————, ed. 1993c. *Southeast Asia in the Early Modern Era.* Ithaca: Cornell University Press.

————. 1996. "Flows and Seepages in the Long-term Chinese Interaction with Southeast Asia." In *Sojourners and Settlers: Histories of Southeast Asia and the Chinese.* Ed. Reid. Sydney: Allen & Unwin for ASAA.

————, ed. 1997. *The Last Stand of Asian Autonomies.* London: Macmillan.

———— and Lance Castles, eds. 1975. *Pre-colonial State Systems in Southeast Asia.* Kuala Lumpur: Malaysian Branch, Royal Asiatic Society, 1995.

———— and David Marr, eds. 1979. *Perceptions of the Past in Southeast Asia.* Singapore: Heinemann for ASAA.

Reynolds, Craig. 1976. "Buddhist Cosmography in Thai History, with Special Reference to Nineteenth Century Culture Change." *Journal of Asian Studies* 35 (2): 203–20.

Ribadeneira, M. de. 1601. *History of the Philippines and other Kingdoms,* trans. Pacita Fernandez. Manila: Historical Conservation Society, 1970.

Ricklefs, M. C. 1974. *Jogjakarta under Sultan Mangkubumi 1749–1792: A History of the Division of Java.* London: Oxford University Press.

————. 1978. *Modern Javanese Historical Tradition. A Study of an Original Kartasura Chronicle and Related Materials.* London: School of Oriental and African Studies.

————. 1992. "Unity and Disunity in Javanese Political and Religious Thought of the Eighteenth Century," in Houben et al. 1992.

Ricklefs, M. C., and P. Voorhoeve. 1977. *Indonesian Manuscripts in Great Britain: A Catalogue of Manuscripts in British Public Collections.* Oxford University Press.

Rizal, Jufrina. 1978. *Kehidupan Wanita Bira: Studi Sosiologis tentang Pola Perikelakuan Wanita Masyarakat Pelayar.* Ujung Pandang, Stencil PLPIIS.

Robson, Stuart O. 1981. "Java at the Crossroads." *BKI* 137.

Rockhill, W. W. 1915. "Notes on the Relations and Trade of China with the Eastern Archipelago and the Coasts of the Indian Ocean during the Fourteenth Century, Part II." *T'oung Pao* 16.

Rodinson, M. 1977. *Islam and Capitalism.* Harmondsworth: Penguin.

Roff, W. R. 1967. *The Origins of Malay Nationalism.* New Haven: Yale University Press.

Rouffaer, G. P. 1904. *De voornaamste industrieèn der inlandsche bevolking van Java en Madoera.* The Hague: Nijhoff.

Sá, A. B. de, ed. 1954. *Documentacão para a historia das missões do padroado Portugues do Oriente: Insulindia.* Vol I. Lisboa: Agencia Geral do Ultramar.

Saffet Bey 1912. "Bir Osmanli Filosofunun Sumatra Seferi." *Tarihi Osmani Encumeni Mecmuasi* 10.

Sakurai, Yumio 1976. "A Study of Landownership in Some Early Nineteenth Century Vietnamese Villages." *Southeast Asia, History and Culture* 6.

————. 1987. *Beronamu Sonraku no Keisei* [Formation of the Vietnamese village]. Tokyo: Soubunsha.

Salim, Agus. 1954. *Djedjak Langkah Hadji A. Salim. Pilihan karangan, utjapan den pendapat beliau dari dulu sampai sekarang.* Jakarta: Tintamas.

San Antonio, Gabriel Quiroga de. 1604. *Brève et véridique relation des événements du Cambodge,* ed. Antoine Cabaton. Paris: Ernest Leroux, 1914

Sande, F. de. 1903–9. "Relation of the Filipinas Islands 7 June 1576," in Blair and Robertson 1903–9, IV: 21–97.

Sarasin, P. and F. Sarasin. 1905. *Reisen in Celebes.* 2 vols. Wiesbaden: C. W. Kreidel.

Sargent, R. L. 1925. *The Size of the Slave Population at Athens during the Fifth and Fourth Centuries before Christ.* Urbana: University of Illinois; Reprint, Rome, 1971.

Saya Lun. 1920. "Life of Bayinnaung," trans. Maung Ba Kya. *JBRS* 10 (iii).

Schadee, W. H. M. 1918. *Geschiedenis van Sumatra's Oostkust.* 2 vols. Amsterdam: Oostkust van Sumatra Instituut.

Schärer, H. 1963. *Ngaju Religion: The Conception of God among a South Borneo People,* trans. R. Needham. The Hague: Nijhoff.

Schmidt, S. W., J. C. Scott, C. Lande, and L. Guasti, eds. 1977. *Friends, Followers, and Factions. A Reader in Political Clientism.* Berkeley: University of California Press.

Schreiner, A. 1900–2. *Les Institutions annamites en Basse-Cochinchine avant la conquête française.* Saigon.

Schrieke, B. J. O. 1955–7. *Indonesian Sociological Studies.* 2 vols. The Hague: Van Hoeve.

Schulte Nordholt, H. 1980. "Macht, mensen en middelen: patronen van dynamiek in de Balische politiek." M.A. thesis, Vrije Universiteit.

————. 1993. "Leadership and the Limits of Political Control. A Balinese 'Response' to Clifford Geertz." *Social Anthropology* 3: 291–307.

Schumacher, J. N. 1979. "'The Propagandists' Reconstruction of the Philippine Past," in Reid and Marr 1979.

Schurhammer, Georg 1977. *Francis Xavier: His Life, His Times.* Vol II, trans. Joseph Costelloe. Rome: Jesuit Historical Institute.

Scott, E. 1606. "An Exact Discourse of the Subtilties, Fashions, Policies, Religion, and Ceremonies of the East Indians, as well Chyneses as Javans, there Abyding and Dweling, 1606," in *The Voyage of Sir Henry Middleton to the Moluccas 1604–1606,* ed. William Foster. London: Hakluyt Society, 1943.

Scott, William Henry. 1983. "*Oripun* and *Alipin* in the Sixteenth Century Philippines," in Reid 1983a.

————. 1984. *Prehispanic Source Materials for the Study of Philippine History.* Rev. ed. Quezon City: New Day.

Sedjarah Goa. n.d. Romanised text with Indonesian translation, eds. G. J. Wolhoff and Abdurrahim. Makassar: Jajasan Kebudajaan Sulawesi Selatan and Tenggara.

Sedjarah Kerajaan Tallo'. See Rahim and Ridwan 1975.

Sejarah Melayu, ed. W. G. Shellabear. 10th ed. Singapore: Malaya Publishing House, 1961

Sejarah Melayu. See Winstedt 1938; Brown 1952.

Serjeant, R. B. 1988. "Yemeni Merchants and Trade in Yemen, 13th-16th Centuries," in Lombard and Aubin 1988.

Shaharil Talib. 1990. "The Port and Polity of Terengganu during the Eighteenth and Nineteenth Centuries," in Kathirithamby-Wells and Villiers 1990.

Shorter Encyclopedia of Islam, ed. H. A. R. Gibb and J. H. Kramers. Leiden: Brill, 1961.

Siegel, J. 1969. *The Rope of God.* Berkeley: University of California Press.

———. 1979. *Shadow and Sound, The Historical Thought of a Sumatran People.* Chicago: University of Chicago Press.

Silva, C. R. de. 1994. "Beyond the Cape: The Portuguese Encounter with the Peoples of South Asia," in *Implicit Understandings,* ed. Stuart Schwartz. Cambridge: Cambridge University Press.

Silvestre, J. 1889. *L'Empire d'Annam et le peuple annamite.* Paris.

Simon, G. 1912. *The Progress and Arrest of Islam in Sumatra.* London: Marshall Brothers.

Sjakieb Arsalan. 1954. *Mengapa Kaum Muslimin Mundur, dan mengapa kaum selain mereka madju?* Indonesian translation by Moenawar Chalil. Jakarta: Bulan Bintang.

Skeat, W. W. 1900. *Malay Magic: Being an Introduction to the Folklore and Popular Religion of the Malay Peninsula.* London: Macmillan. Reprint, New York: Dover Publications, 1967.

Skinner, C., ed. 1963. *Sja'ir Perang Mengkasar (The Rhymed Chronicle of the Macassar War) by Entji Amin.* VKI 40. The Hague: Nijhoff.

"Slapat Rajawan Datow Smin Ron: A History of Kings," trans. R. Halliday. *JBRS* 13 (i), 1923.

Smith, George Vinal. 1974. "The Dutch East India Company in the Kingdom of Ayutthaya, 1604–1694." Ph.D. thesis, Northern Illinois University.

Smith, Thomas. 1988. *Native Sources of Japanese Industrialization 1750–1920.* Berkeley: University of California Press.

Snouck Hurgronje, Christiaan. 1906. *The Achehnese,* trans. A. W. S. O'Sullivan. Leiden: Brill.

Soeriokoesoemo. 1918. "Het Javaansche vraagstuk." *Wederopbouw* 1: 2–6.

———. 1919. "Een beschouwing over de vormen der overheersching." *Wederopbouw* 2.

Soesangobeng, Herman. 1977. "Perkampungan Bajo di Bajoe." Ujung Pandang: Stencil PLPIIS.

Sopher, David E. 1965. *The Sea Nomads. A Study of the Maritime Boat People of Southeast Asia.* Singapore, National Museum.

Speelman, Cornelis. 1670. "Notitie dienende voor eeneen Korten Tijd en tot nader last van de Hooge Regeering op Batavia voor den onderkoopman Jan van Oppijnen." 3 vols. Typescript copy held at KITLV, Leiden.

Stapel, F. W. 1922. *Het Bongaais Verdrag*. Published thesis, University of Leiden.

Stavorinus, J. S. 1798. *Voyages to the East Indies, by the late John Splinter Stavorinus*, trans. S. H. Wilcocke. 3 vols. London: G. G. and J. Robinson. Reprint, London: Dawsons, 1969.

Steinberg, D. J. et al. 1971. *In Search of Southeast Asia*. Praeger, 1971.

Stöhr, W., and P. Zoetmulder. 1968. *Les religions d'Indonesie*. Paris: Payot.

Sukarno. 1930. *Indonesia Menggugat. Pidato pembelaan Bung Karno dimuka hakim kolonial.* Jakarta: Seno, 1956.

Sutherland, Heather. 1983. "Slavery and the Slave Trade in South Sulawesi, 1660s-1800," in Reid 1983a.

Swearer, D. K., and Sommai Premchit. 1978. "The Relations between the Religious and Political Orders in Northern Thailand (14th-16th Centuries)," in *Religion and Legitimation of Power in Thailand, Laos, and Burma*, ed. Bardwell L. Smith. Chambersburg, PA: Anima.

Tarling, Nicholas, ed. 1992. *The Cambridge History of Southeast Asia*. 2 vols. Cambridge University Press.

Taylor, K. 1993. "Nguyen Hoang and the Beginning of Vietnam's Southward Expansion," in Reid 1993c.

Terwiel, B. 1983. "Bondage and Slavery in Early Nineteenth Century Siam," in Reid 1983a.

Than Tun, ed. 1983, 1985. *The Royal Orders of Burma, A.D. 1593–1885*. 2 vols. Kyoto: Kyoto University Centre for Southeast Asian Studies.

Thomaz, Luis Filipe. 1966. *De Malaca a Pegu. Viagens de um feitor Português (1512–1515)*. Lisboa: Instituto de Alta Cultura.

————. 1979. "Les portugais dans les mers de l'Archipel au XVIe siècle." *Archipel* 18: 105-25.

Thrupp, S., ed. 1970. *Millenial Dreams in Action. Studies in Revolutionary Religious Movements*. New York: Schocken.

Tideman, J. 1908. "De Toe Badjeng en de Legenda omtrent hun oorsprong." *BKI* 60: 448–500.

————. 1938. *Djambi*. Amsterdam: de Bussy.

Tiele, P. A. and J. E. Heeres, eds. 1886-95. *Bouwstoffen voor de geschiedenis der Nederlanders in den Maleische Archipel: Tweede Reeks (Buitenbezittingen)—De opkomst van het Nederlandsch gezag in Oost-Indië.* 3 vols. The Hague.

T'ien Ju-kang. 1981. "Chêng Ho's Voyages and the Distribution of Pepper in China." *JRAS* 2: 186-97.

Tran Van Giau. 1958. *Su Khong hoang cua che do phong kien nha truoc 1858* [The crisis of the Vietnamese feudal system before 1958]. Hanoi.

Tres-saincte Trinité, Philippe de la. 1652. *Voyage d'orient*. Lyon.

Trimingham, J. S. 1971. *The Sufi Orders in Islam*. Oxford: Clarendon.

Trocki, Carl. 1979. *Prince of Pirates: the Temenggongs and the Development of Johor and Singapore, 1784–1885*. Singapore: Oxford University Press.

Truong Buu Lam. 1967. *Patterns of Vietnamese Response to Foreign Intervention: 1858–1900*. New Haven: Yale Southeast Asian Studies.

Turpin, M. 1908. *History of the Kingdom of Siam*, trans. B. O. Cartwright. Bangkok: Vajiranana National Library.

Uhlenbeck, E. M. 1978. *Studies in Javanese Morphology.* The Hague: Nijhoff.

Ulaen, Alex J. 1979. *Onto di Bantaeng.* Ujung Pandang: Stencil PLPIIS.

Valentijn, François. 1724. *Oud en Nieuw Oost-Indiën.* 2nd ed. Vol. II. Dordrecht

Varthema, Ludovico di. 1510. *The Travels of Ludovico di Varthema in Egypt, Syria, Arabia Deserta and Arabia Felix, in Persia, Egypt and Ethiopia, A.D. 1503 to 1508,* trans. J. W. Jones. London: Hakluyt Society, 1863.

"Verhaal van eenige oorlogen in Indië." 1622. In *Kroniek van het Historisch Genootschap te Utrecht.* 1871, 497–658.

Viraphol, Sarasin. 1977. *Tribute and Profit: Sino-Siamese Trade, 1652–1853.* Cambridge, Mass.: Harvard University Press.

Vlekke, B. H. M. 1959. *Nusantara. A History of Indonesia.* The Hague: Van Hoeve.

Vliet, Jeremias van. 1636. "Description of the Kingdom of Siam," trans. L. F. van Ravenswaay. *Journal of the Siam Society* 7 (i), 1910: 1–105.

Volkman, T. 1979. "The Riches of the Undertaker." *Indonesia* 28.

Wade, Geoffrey. 1991. "The 'Ming Shi-lu' as a Source for Southeast Asian History— 14th to 17th Centuries." Paper presented at the Twelfth Conference of the International Association of Historians of Asia, Hong Kong.

———. 1993. "On the Possible Cham Origin of Philippine Scripts," *JSEAS* 24 (1): 44-87.

Wallace, A. R. 1869. *The Malay Archipelago.* 2 vols. London: Macmillan. Reprint, New York: Dover Publications, 1962.

Wallerstein, I. 1980. *The Modern World-System II: Mercantilism and the Consolidation of the Modern World-Economy, 1600–1750.* New York: Academic Press.

Walls, C. 1974. "Legacy of the Fathers: Testamentary Admonitions, and Thematic Structure of the Sejarah Melayu." Ph.D. thesis, Yale University.

Wang Gungwu. 1981. *Community and Nation: Essays on Southeast Asia and the Chinese.* Singapore: Heinemann for ASAA.

Warren, J. F. 1981. *The Sulu Zone 1768–1898: The Dynamics of External Trade, Slavery, and Ethnicity in the Transformation of a Southeast Asian Maritime State.* Singapore: Singapore University Press.

Watson, J. L., ed. 1980. *Asian and African Systems of Slavery.* Berkeley: University of California Press.

Werner, R. 1974. *Mah-Meri of Malaysia: Art and Culture.* Kuala Lumpur: Penerbit Universiti Malaya.

Wessels, C. 1925. "Wat staat geschiedkundige vast over de Oude Missie in Zuid Celebes 1525–1669." *Studien* 193: 403–41.

Westermann, W. L. 1955. *The Slave Systems of Greek and Roman Antiquity.* Philadelphia: American Philosophical Society.

Whitmore, John K. 1985. *Vietnam, Hô Quy Ly, and the Ming (1371–1421).* New Haven: Yale Southeast Asia Studies.

Wickberg, Edgar. 1965. *The Chinese in Philippine Life 1850–1898.* New Haven, Yale University Press.

Wilken, G. A. 1888. "Het Pandrecht bij de volken van den Indischen Archipel." *BKI* 37: 555–609.

Wills, John E. 1974. *Pepper, Guns and Parleys: The Dutch East India Company and China, 1622–87*. Cambridge, Mass.: Harvard University Press.

Winstedt, R. O., ed. 1938. "The Malay Annals; or Sejarah Melayu. The Earliest Recension from Ms No. 18 of the Raffles Collection in the Library of the Royal Asiatic Society, London." *JMBRAS* 16 (iii).

———, ed. 1956. "Undang-undang Laut," in "The Maritime Laws of Malacca." *JMBRAS* 29 (iii): 22–59.

Wiselius, J. A. B. 1872. "Djaja Baja, zijn leven en profetieèn." *BKI* 19.

Wisseman, Jan. 1977. "Markets and Trade in pre-Majapahit Java." In *Economic Exchange and Social Interaction in Southeast Asia*, ed. K. L. Hutterer. Michigan Papers on South and Southeast Asia.

———. 1986. "Negara, Mandala, and Despotic State: Images of Early Java," in Marr and Milner 1986.

Wolhoff, G. I. and Abdurrahim. See *Sedjarah Goa*.

Wolters, O. W. 1970. *The Fall of Srivijaya in Malay History*. London: Lund Humphries.

———. 1982. *History, Culture and Region in Southeast Asian Perspectives*. Singapore: ISEAS.

Woodside, Alexander. 1971. *Vietnam and the Chinese Model: A Comparative Study of Nyugen and Ch'ing Civil Government in the First Half of the Nineteenth Century*. Cambridge, Mass.: Harvard University Press.

Worcester, D. C. 1913. *Slavery and Peonage in the Philippine Islands*. Manila: Department of the Interior.

Worsley, P. J. 1972. *Babad Buleleng: A Balinese Dynastic Genealogy*. The Hague: KITLV.

Worsley, P. M. 1970. *The Trumpet Shall Sound. A Study of Cargo Cults in Melanesia*. London: Paladin.

Wouden, F. A. E. van. 1968. *Types of Social Structure in Eastern Indonesia*, trans. R. Needham. The Hague: Nijhoff.

Wusthoff, Gerrit. 1642. "Journael van de reyse naer de Lauwen-Landt door Gerrit Wuysthoff, 20 Juli 1641 tot 24 October 1642," in *De Oost-Indische Compagnie in Cambodia en Laos: verzameling van bescheiden van 1636 tot 1670*, ed. Hendrik Muller. The Hague: Linschoten-Vereniging, 1917.

Wyatt, D. K. 1969. *The Politics of Reform in Thailand: Education in the Reign of King Chulalongkorn*. New Haven: Yale.

———. 1982. "The 'Subtle Revolution' of King Rama I of Siam," in *Moral Order and the Question of Change: Essays on Southeast Asian Thought*, eds. David Wyatt and Alexander Woodside. New Haven: Yale University Southeast Asian Studies.

———. 1982a. *Thailand: A Short History*. New Haven: Yale University Press.

Wybrandt van Waerwijck. 1646. "Historische Verhael, van de Reyse, gedaen inde Oost-Indien, met 15 Schepen voor Reeckeninhe vande vereenichde Cheocttroyeerde Oost-Indische Compagnie: onder het beleydt van den

Vroomen ende Manhaften Wybrandt van Waerwijck als Admirael," in *Begin ende Voortgang* (see above) II.

Yi T'ae-jin. 1992. "Choson hugi yangban sahoe ui pyonhwa" [Transformation of *yangban* society in late Choson], in *Han'guk sahoe palchon saron* [Discourse on the development of Korean society]. Seoul.

Yule, Henry and A. C. Burnell. 1903. *Hobson-Jobson. A Glossary of Colloquial Anglo-Indian Words and Phrase.* New edition, ed. William Crooke, Reprint, New Delhi: Manoharlal, 1979.

Za'ba. 1928. "Jalan keselamatan bagi orang-orang Melayu," in *Pendita Za'ba dalam kenangan,* eds. Abdullah Hussain and Khalit Hussain. Kuala Lumpur: Dewan Bahasa dan Pustaka, 1974.

Zentgraaf, H. C. 1938. *Atjeh.* Batavia: De Unie.

Zerner, Charles. 1981. "Signs of the Spirits, Signature of the Smith: Iron Forging in Tana Toraja." *Indonesia* 31: 89–112.

Zhang Xie. 1618. *Dong xi yang kao* [A study of the eastern and western oceans]. New edition. Beijing, 1981.